VALUABLE AND VULNERABLE

Program in Judaic Studies
Brown University
Box 1826
Providence, RI 02912

BROWN JUDAIC STUDIES

Edited by

David C. Jacobson
Ross S. Kraemer
Maud Mandel
Saul M. Olyan
Michael L. Satlow
Adam Teller

Number 355
VALUABLE AND VULNERABLE
Children in the Hebrew Bible,
Especially the Elisha Cycle

by
Julie Faith Parker

# VALUABLE AND VULNERABLE

## CHILDREN IN THE HEBREW BIBLE, ESPECIALLY THE ELISHA CYCLE

Julie Faith Parker

Brown Judaic Studies
Providence, Rhode Island

© 2013 Brown University. All rights reserved.

No part of this work may be reproduced or transmitted in any form or by any means, electronic or mechanical, including photocopying and recording, or by means of any information storage or retrieval system, except as may be expressly permitted by the 1976 Copyright Act or in writing from the publisher. Requests for permission should be addressed in writing to the Rights and Permissions Office, Program in Judaic Studies, Brown University, Box 1826, Providence, RI 02912, USA.

Library of Congress Catalog Number: 2013019847

ISBN: 978-1-930675-85-8

Printed in the United States of America
on acid-free paper

*to Bill*

זֶה דוֹדִי וְזֶה רֵעִי
*Song of Songs 5:16bα*

# Contents

Acknowledgments . . . . . . . . . . . . . . . . . . . . . . . . . . . . . xi

Abbreviations . . . . . . . . . . . . . . . . . . . . . . . . . . . . . . . xiii

Introduction . . . . . . . . . . . . . . . . . . . . . . . . . . . . . . . . . 1
   *Theoretical Concerns, Methodological Considerations,*
      *and Ensuing Approach* . . . . . . . . . . . . . . . . . . . . . 11
   *Childist Interpretation* . . . . . . . . . . . . . . . . . . . . . . . . 16

### I. Frameworks for Understanding

1 • Concepts of Children and Childhood:
   A Theoretical and Historical Framework . . . . . . . . . . . . . . . 21
   *Understanding Childhood* . . . . . . . . . . . . . . . . . . . . . . 21
   *Contemporary Western Assumptions about Childhood* . . . . . . . . . 24
   *The Formal Study of Children and Childhood* . . . . . . . . . . . . . 28
      *Enlightenment Thinkers and Their Legacy* . . . . . . . . . . . . . 28
      *Philippe Ariès and* Centuries of Childhood . . . . . . . . . . . 31
      *Arguments after Ariès* . . . . . . . . . . . . . . . . . . . . . . 34
   *Continuing Changes in Childhood* . . . . . . . . . . . . . . . . . . 37

2 • Learning about Children and Youth in the Hebrew Bible
   through Language: A Contextual and Linguistic Framework . . 41
   *The Presence and Value of Children* . . . . . . . . . . . . . . . . . 41
   *Vocabulary and Understanding* . . . . . . . . . . . . . . . . . . . 44
   *Words That Designate Children and Youth* . . . . . . . . . . . . . 46
      *Children in Families* . . . . . . . . . . . . . . . . . . . . . . . 46
         בן and בת . . . . . . . . . . . . . . . . . . . . . . . . . 46
         אח and אחות . . . . . . . . . . . . . . . . . . . . . . . 49
         בכור and בכירה . . . . . . . . . . . . . . . . . . . . . 50
         קטן, צעיר, and שנית, שלישית, רביעית, חמישית, etc. . . . . . . . . . 52
      *Children without Families* . . . . . . . . . . . . . . . . . . . . 53
         יתום . . . . . . . . . . . . . . . . . . . . . . . . . . . . . 53
      *Youth* . . . . . . . . . . . . . . . . . . . . . . . . . . . . . . . 55
         עלם and עלמה . . . . . . . . . . . . . . . . . . . . . . 56

Contents

    בתולה and בחור . . . . . . . . . . . . . . . . . . . . . . . . 57
    נער and נערה . . . . . . . . . . . . . . . . . . . . . . . . . 60
  Children . . . . . . . . . . . . . . . . . . . . . . . . . . . . . . 64
    ילד and ילדה . . . . . . . . . . . . . . . . . . . . . . . . . 64
    טף . . . . . . . . . . . . . . . . . . . . . . . . . . . . . . . 66
    Young Children and Babies . . . . . . . . . . . . . . . . . . . 67
      גמל / גמול . . . . . . . . . . . . . . . . . . . . . . . . . 69
      יונק . . . . . . . . . . . . . . . . . . . . . . . . . . . . 69
      עולל . . . . . . . . . . . . . . . . . . . . . . . . . . . . 71
      עול / עויל . . . . . . . . . . . . . . . . . . . . . . . . . 71
  Abstract Words for Childhood and Youth . . . . . . . . . . . . . 73
  Concepts of Children and Childhood in the Hebrew Bible . . . . . . . 74

3 • Approaching the Elisha Cycle:
    A Literary and Methodological Framework . . . . . . . . . . . . 77
  The Elisha Cycle: Literary Context and Genre . . . . . . . . . . . 77
  Credibility, Child Characters, and the World of the Text . . . . . . . . 83
  Methodology for Childist Interpretation . . . . . . . . . . . . . 86

## II. Analyses of Stories—Children and Elisha

4 • The Mockers of Bethel (2 Kings 2:23–25) . . . . . . . . . . . 91
  Setting: Bethel . . . . . . . . . . . . . . . . . . . . . . . . . .91
  Characters . . . . . . . . . . . . . . . . . . . . . . . . . . . . 92
    נערים קטנים and ילדים . . . . . . . . . . . . . . . . . . . 92
    Elisha . . . . . . . . . . . . . . . . . . . . . . . . . . . . . 94
  Re-viewing the Plot from a Childist Perspective . . . . . . . . . . . 94
  Childist Interpretation: Children as Agents and Victims . . . . . . . . 96
  Insights about Children and Power . . . . . . . . . . . . . . . . 98
  Children and Textual Connections . . . . . . . . . . . . . . . . 99

5 • The Moabite Prince (2 Kings 3:26–27) . . . . . . . . . . . . . 103
  Setting: The Battle at Moab . . . . . . . . . . . . . . . . . . . 103
  Characters . . . . . . . . . . . . . . . . . . . . . . . . . . . . 104
    The Many . . . . . . . . . . . . . . . . . . . . . . . . . . 104
    Elisha . . . . . . . . . . . . . . . . . . . . . . . . . . . . . 105
    The Child Soldiers . . . . . . . . . . . . . . . . . . . . . . 106
    The Prince and His Father . . . . . . . . . . . . . . . . . . 107
  Re-viewing the Plot from a Childist Perspective . . . . . . . . . . . 109
  Childist Interpretation: Wrath from Child Sacrifice . . . . . . . . . . 111
  Insights about Children, War, and Sacrifice . . . . . . . . . . . . . 114
  Children and Textual Connections . . . . . . . . . . . . . . . . . 116

## Contents    ix

6 • The Debt-Collateral Children (2 Kings 4:1–7) . . . . . . . . . . . . 119
    Setting: Situation, Not Site . . . . . . . . . . . . . . . . . . . . . 119
    Characters . . . . . . . . . . . . . . . . . . . . . . . . . . . . . . 120
        The Mother . . . . . . . . . . . . . . . . . . . . . . . . . . . 120
        Elisha . . . . . . . . . . . . . . . . . . . . . . . . . . . . . . 122
        The Dead Husband and the Encroaching Creditor . . . . . . . . . . 123
        The Two Children . . . . . . . . . . . . . . . . . . . . . . . . 124
    Re-viewing the Plot from a Childist Perspective . . . . . . . . . . . . 124
    Childist Interpretation: One Miracle and Two Questions . . . . . . . 126
    Insights about Children and Debt Slavery . . . . . . . . . . . . . . 128
    Children and Textual Connections . . . . . . . . . . . . . . . . . . 133

7 • The Shunammite's Son (2 Kings 4:8–37) . . . . . . . . . . . . . . 137
    Settings: Town, Home, Field, Road, Mountain, and Room . . . . . . . 137
    Characters . . . . . . . . . . . . . . . . . . . . . . . . . . . . . . 139
        The Shunammite . . . . . . . . . . . . . . . . . . . . . . . . 139
        The Shunammite's Husband . . . . . . . . . . . . . . . . . . 140
        Elisha . . . . . . . . . . . . . . . . . . . . . . . . . . . . . . 141
        Gehazi . . . . . . . . . . . . . . . . . . . . . . . . . . . . . . 142
        Two Anonymous Servants . . . . . . . . . . . . . . . . . . . 144
        The Son . . . . . . . . . . . . . . . . . . . . . . . . . . . . . 144
    Re-viewing the Plot from a Childist Perspective . . . . . . . . . . . . 146
    Childist Interpretation: Paradigms Combined and Subverted . . . . . 149
    Insights about Children and Their Worth . . . . . . . . . . . . . . 152
    Children and Textual Connections . . . . . . . . . . . . . . . . . . 153

8 • The Israelite Slave Girl (2 Kings 5:1–14) . . . . . . . . . . . . . . 157
    Settings: Houses, Palaces, and Rivers . . . . . . . . . . . . . . . . . 157
    Characters . . . . . . . . . . . . . . . . . . . . . . . . . . . . . . 159
        Naaman . . . . . . . . . . . . . . . . . . . . . . . . . . . . . 159
        Raiding Bands . . . . . . . . . . . . . . . . . . . . . . . . . . 160
        The Israelite Slave Girl . . . . . . . . . . . . . . . . . . . . . 160
        Naaman's Wife . . . . . . . . . . . . . . . . . . . . . . . . . 161
        The Kings of Aram and Israel . . . . . . . . . . . . . . . . . . 162
        Elisha and His Messenger . . . . . . . . . . . . . . . . . . . 163
        Naaman's Servants . . . . . . . . . . . . . . . . . . . . . . . 164
    Re-viewing the Plot from a Childist Perspective . . . . . . . . . . . . 164
    Childist Interpretation: Insight and Irony . . . . . . . . . . . . . . . 167
    Insights about Children and Captivity . . . . . . . . . . . . . . . . 170
    Children and Textual Connections . . . . . . . . . . . . . . . . . . 172

9 • The Sons of the Starving Mothers (2 Kings 6:24–31) . . . . . . . . 175
    *Setting: Samaria under Siege* . . . . . . . . . . . . . . . . . . . . . . . 175
    *Characters* . . . . . . . . . . . . . . . . . . . . . . . . . . . . . . . . . . . 176
        *Two Kings* . . . . . . . . . . . . . . . . . . . . . . . . . . . . . . . . 176
        *Two Mothers* . . . . . . . . . . . . . . . . . . . . . . . . . . . . . . 177
        *Two Sons* . . . . . . . . . . . . . . . . . . . . . . . . . . . . . . . . 178
        *People of Samaria* . . . . . . . . . . . . . . . . . . . . . . . . . . 179
        *Elisha* . . . . . . . . . . . . . . . . . . . . . . . . . . . . . . . . . . 179
    *Re-viewing the Plot from a Childist Perspective* . . . . . . . . . . . 180
    *Childist Interpretation: Motherhood Deconstructed*
       *and Childhood Destroyed* . . . . . . . . . . . . . . . . . . . . . 183
    *Insights about Children: Defenseless unto Death* . . . . . . . . . . 185
    *Children and Textual Connections* . . . . . . . . . . . . . . . . . . 187

10 • Epilogue: The Boy Restored to Life (2 Kings 8:1–6) . . . . . . 191
    *The Boy Restored to the Text* . . . . . . . . . . . . . . . . . . . . . . 191
    *From Destruction to Deliverance (2 Kings 2:23–25)* . . . . . . . . 192
    *The Power of One Child (2 Kings 3:26–27)* . . . . . . . . . . . . . 193
    *Advocating Mothers – Rescued Sons (2 Kings 4:1–7)* . . . . . . . 193
    *New Incarnations and Relations (2 Kings 4:8–37)* . . . . . . . . 194
    *Living Testimonies to Prophetic Power (2 Kings 5:1–14)* . . . . . 195
    *Starvation and Salvation (2 Kings 6:24–31)* . . . . . . . . . . . . 196
    *Insights about Children and Elisha* . . . . . . . . . . . . . . . . . 197

Conclusions . . . . . . . . . . . . . . . . . . . . . . . . . . . . . . . . . . . 199

Bibliography . . . . . . . . . . . . . . . . . . . . . . . . . . . . . . . . . . 203

Index . . . . . . . . . . . . . . . . . . . . . . . . . . . . . . . . . . . . . . . 233

# Acknowledgments

Writing a book is a journey, and, like any journey, it is profoundly influenced by the company you keep. I am blessed to have gone down this road surrounded by caring and smart colleagues, friends, and family members. While many more people deserve thanks beyond these brief acknowledgments, I am compelled to mention these few by name.

This book is a revision of my Yale dissertation. I began serious research in 2005 and completed the dissertation in 2009. The format and the bulk of the content are original to the dissertation, although I have incorporated subsequent scholarship into the book. Gratitude to my advisor, Robert Wilson, transcends words. Any contribution I may make to this field that we love and share will always be, in some measure, in his debt. Further professors also guided me through the doctoral program with insight and encouragement that many Ph.D. students would envy. John Collins combined rigorous training with kindness and humor. Carolyn Sharp mentored me with intelligence and compassion. Christl Maier and Ivan Marcus also expanded my thinking and encouraged this project. Fellow students in the doctoral program provided essential support and thoughtful companionship. I would especially like to thank Kyong-Jin Lee, Ryan Stokes, and Alison Gruseke for their cherished friendship.

I am also grateful to many people outside of New Haven who have contributed to this work. Former colleagues at Colby College, Rob Weisbrot and David Freidenreich, generously read the dissertation and offered excellent suggestions for transforming it into a book. My former student at Colby, Spencer Kasko, helped greatly with manuscript revisions. The two anonymous readers and Saul Olyan of the Brown Judaic Studies series provided invaluable feedback. Friends at the Larchmont Temple (New York), especially Rabbi Jeffrey Sirkman, Ze'ev Aviezer, and Marcelline Fischoff, shared precious space in which to write uninterrupted. All these considerate individuals, and more not here named, improved this book; any faults, of course, are my own.

Finally, I would like to thank my family. My mother, Merolyn Graham Parker, died during the course of this writing, but her love and support are deeply engrained in this work. My father, David Parker, and my sisters, Kate Parker-Burgard and Valerie Parker, have unwaveringly encouraged me. My brother-in-law, Don Parker-Burgard, deserves special mention for his gracious help with editing questions. Deepest gratitude goes to those closest to home. Our children, Graham and Mari, have grown along with this project, constantly offering perspective and filling my life with joy. My husband, Bill Crawford, believes in my ability in ways that astound me. I cannot imagine a more supportive and loving spouse than the one I am blessed to have, and I dedicate this book to him.

# Abbreviations

| | |
|---|---|
| AB | Anchor Bible |
| ABG | Arbeiten zur Bibel und ihrer Geschichte |
| *AJET* | *Africa Journal of Evangelical Theology* |
| *ANET* | *Ancient Near Eastern Texts Relating to the Old Testament.* Edited by J. B. Pritchard. Princeton: Princeton University Press, 1958 |
| AOTC | Abingdon Old Testament Commentaries |
| ASV | American Standard Version (1901) |
| ATD | Das Alte Testament Deutsch |
| ATSAT | Arbeiten zu Text und Sprache im Alten Testament |
| *BAR* | *Biblical Archaeology Review* |
| *BASOR* | *Bulletin of the American Schools of Oriental Research* |
| BBET | Beiträge zur biblischen Exegese und Theologie |
| *BBR* | *Bulletin for Biblical Research* |
| BDB | Francis Brown, S. R. Driver, and Charles A. Briggs. *The Brown-Driver-Briggs Hebrew and English Lexicon*. Peabody, MA: Hendrickson, 1999; repr., Boston: Houghton, Mifflin, 1906 |
| Berit | Berit Olam: Studies in Hebrew Narrative and Poetry |
| *BHS* | *Biblia Hebraica Stuttgartensia* |
| *Bib* | *Biblica* |
| BJS | Brown Judaic Studies |
| *BN* | *Biblische Notizen* |
| BZAW | Beihefte zur Zeitschrift für die alttestamentliche Wissenschaft |
| CahRB | Cahiers de la Revue biblique |
| CBC | Cambridge Bible Commentary |
| *CBQ* | *Catholic Biblical Quarterly* |
| *CBR* | *Currents in Biblical Research* |
| CC | Continental Commentaries |
| CDA | *A Concise Dictionary of Akkadian*. Edited by Jeremy Black, Andrew George, Nicholas Postgate. Weisbaden: Harrassowitz, 2000 |
| ConBOT | Coniectanea biblica: Old Testament Series |
| *COS* | *The Context of Scripture*. Edited by William W. Hallo. 3 vols. Leiden: E. J. Brill, 1997–2002 |

| | |
|---|---|
| DCH | *Dictionary of Classical Hebrew*. Edited by David J. A. Clines. 8 vols. Sheffield: Sheffield Academic Press, 1993–2011 |
| DLU | *Diccionairo de la lengua ugarítica*. G. del Olmo Lete and J. Sanmartín. Barcelona: Editorial AUSA. Vol. 1, 1996. Vol. 2, 2000 |
| DSS | Dead Sea Scrolls |
| EHAT | Exegetisches Handbuch zum Alten Testament |
| ESV | English Standard Version (2001) |
| FAT | Forschungen zum Alten Testament |
| FCB | Feminist Companion to the Bible |
| FOTL | Forms of the Old Testament Literature |
| FRLANT | Forschungen zur Religion und Literatur des Alten und Neuen Testaments |
| GKC | *Gesenius' Hebrew Grammar*. Edited by E. Kautzsch. Translated by A. E. Cowley. Second edition. Oxford: Oxford University Press, 1910 |
| GNV | Geneva Bible (1599) |
| HALOT | Ludwig Koehler and Walter Baumgartner. *The Hebrew and Aramaic Lexicon of the Old Testament, Study Edition*. Rev. Walter Baumgartner and Johann J. Stamm. Translated and edited under the supervision of M. E. J. Richardson. 2 vols. Leiden: Brill, 2001 |
| HBS | Herders Biblische Studien |
| HO | Handbuch der Orientalistik |
| HR | *History of Religions* |
| HSM | Harvard Semitic Monographs |
| IBC | Interpretation: A Bible Commentary for Teaching and Preaching |
| ICC | International Critical Commentary |
| Int | *Interpretation* |
| JANES | *Journal of the Ancient Near Eastern Society* |
| JAOS | *Journal of the American Oriental Society* |
| JBL | *Journal of Biblical Literature* |
| JBLMS | Journal of Biblical Literature Monograph Series |
| JBTh | *Jahrbuch für Biblische Theologie* |
| JFSR | *Journal of Feminist Studies in Religion* |
| JHCY | *Journal of the History of Childhood and Youth* |
| JHS | *Journal of Hebrew Scriptures* |
| JLA | *Jewish Law Annual* |
| JNES | *Journal of Near Eastern Studies* |
| JPS | Jewish Publication Society Tanakh (1917) |
| JR | *Journal of Religion* |
| JSJ | *Journal for the Study of Judaism in the Persian, Hellenistic, and Roman Periods* |

| | |
|---|---|
| JSOT | *Journal for the Study of the Old Testament* |
| JSOTSup | Journal for the Study of the Old Testament: Supplement Series |
| JTS | *Journal of Theological Studies* |
| KJV | King James Version (1611) |
| KTU | *Die keilalphabetischen Texte aus Ugarit*. Edited by M. Dietrich, O. Loretz, and J. Sanmartín. Neukirchen-Vluyn, 1976. Second enlarged edition of *KTU: The Cuneiform Alphabetic Texts from Ugarit, Ras Ibn Hani, and Other Places*. Edited by M. Dietrich, O. Loretz, and J. Sanmartín. Münster, 1995 |
| KUSATU | *Kleine Untersuchungen zur Sprache des Alten Testaments und seiner Umwelt* |
| LHBOTS | Library of Hebrew Bible/Old Testament Studies |
| LXE | Brenton's English Translation of the Septuagint (1851) |
| LXX | Septuagint |
| MT | Masoretic Text |
| NAB | New American Bible (1970) |
| NAS | New American Standard Bible (1977) |
| NCB | New Century Bible |
| NIBCOT | New International Biblical Commentary on the Old Testament |
| NIDOTTE | *The New International Dictionary of Old Testament Theology and Exegesis*. Edited by Willem VanGemeren. 5 vols. Grand Rapids: Zondervon, 1997 |
| NIV | New International Version (1984) |
| NJB | New Jerusalem Bible (1985) |
| NJPS | *Tanakh: The Holy Scriptures: The New JPS Translation according to the Traditional Hebrew Text* (1985) |
| NKJV | New King James Version (1982) |
| NRSV | New Revised Standard Version (1989) |
| OBO | Orbis biblicus et orientalis |
| OBT | Overtures to Biblical Theology |
| OTL | Old Testament Library |
| OtSt | *Oudtestamentische Studiën* |
| RBL | *Review of Biblical Literature* |
| RevExp | *Review and Expositor* |
| RSV | Revised Standard Version (1952) |
| SANT | Studien zum Alten und Neuen Testaments |
| SBLABS | Society of Biblical Literature Archaeology and Biblical Studies |
| SBLBSNA | Society of Biblical Literature Biblical Scholarship in North America |
| SBLDS | Society of Biblical Literature Dissertation Series |

| | |
|---|---|
| SBLSBS | Society of Biblical Literature Sources for Biblical Study |
| *SBLSP* | *Society of Biblical Literature Seminar Papers* |
| SBLSymS | Society of Biblical Literature Symposium Series |
| SBLWAW | Society of Biblical Literature Writings from the Ancient World |
| SBTS | Sources for Biblical and Theological Study |
| SemeiaSt | Semeia Studies |
| SHR | Studies in the History of Religions (supplement to *Numen*) |
| *SPhilo* | *Studia philonica* |
| STAR | Studies in Theology and Religion |
| *TAPA* | *Transactions of the American Philological Association* |
| *TDOT* | *Theological Dictionary of the Old Testament*. Edited by G. Johannes Botterweck and Helmer Ringgren. Translated by J. T. Willis, G. W. Bromiley, and D. E. Green. 15 vols. Grand Rapids, MI: Eerdmans, 1974–2006 |
| *TynBul* | *Tyndale Bulletin* |
| *UF* | *Ugarit-Forschungen* |
| *VT* | *Vetus Testamentum* |
| VTSup | Vetus Testamentum Supplements |
| WBC | Word Biblical Commentary |
| WEB | Webster Bible (1833) |
| YLT | Young's Literal Translation (1868) |
| *ZABR* | *Zeitschrift für altorientalische und biblische Rechtsgeschichte* |
| *ZAW* | *Zeitschrift für die alttestamentliche Wissenschaft* |
| * | hypothetical form |

# Introduction

Children are integral to the literature of the Hebrew Bible and the world that gave rise to its stories, yet they have been largely overlooked in biblical scholarship. One pioneering contribution was *The Jewish Family in Antiquity*, edited by Shaye Cohen and published in the Brown Judaic Studies series in 1993. In the introduction, Cohen noted that the evidence for studying the Jewish family in antiquity was abundant, but the research was slim. He rightly observed that this was due to "lack of interest" and added, "the purpose of this volume is to stimulate interest in this underexplored field."[1] Twenty years later, this book seeks to build on Cohen's seminal volume by offering a scholarly treatment of children in the Hebrew Bible.

Research in this area is still sparse. The field of childhood studies has expanded greatly over the past few decades with new academic departments and journals emerging.[2] However, childhood studies in the biblical

---

1. Shaye J. D. Cohen, *The Jewish Family in Antiquity* (BJS 289; Atlanta: Scholars Press, 1993), 2.
2. For introductions to childhood studies, see Dominic Wyse, ed., *Childhood Studies: An Introduction* (Malden, MA: Blackwell, 2004); Mary Jane Kehily, ed., *An Introduction to Childhood Studies* (2nd ed.; Maidenhead, NY: Open University Press, 2009); and Jens Qvortrup, William A. Corsaro, and Michael-Sebastian Honig, eds., *The Palgrave Handbook of Childhood Studies* (New York: Palgrave Macmillan, 2009). Many related topics appear in the *Encyclopedia of Children and Childhood: In History and Society* (ed. Paula S. Fass; 3 vols.; New York: Macmillan, 2004). Academic journals include *The Journal of Childhood and Religion* (published by Sopher Press and established in 2010), *The Journal of the History of Childhood and Youth* (in association with the Society for the History of Children and Youth, published by Johns Hopkins University Press, and established in 2008), *Childhoods Today* (www.childhoodstoday.org, in association with the University of Sheffield and established in 2007), and *Childhood* (published by Sage and established in 1993). Allison James points out that children have long been a focus of academic research in a variety of disciplines, including literature, science, psychology, sociology, etc. However, scholars have only recently started engaging children themselves and combining interdisciplinary approaches to create the emerging field of childhood studies. See Allison James, "Understanding Childhood from an Interdisciplinary Perspective: Problems and Potentials," in *Rethinking Childhood* (ed. Peter B. Pufall and Richard P. Unsworth; New Brunswick, NJ: Rutgers University Press, 2004), 26. Colleges and universities in the United States with interdisciplinary childhood studies programs include Antioch University Los Angeles, Brooklyn College, Bucknell University, Case Western Reserve University, Charter Oak State College, Christopher Newport University, Eastern Washington University, Farleigh Dickinson University, George Mason University, Hampshire College, King's University College at the University of Western

2  *Valuable and Vulnerable*

field lag far behind those of other disciplines.³ Within biblical and wider antiquity studies, scholarship on children in the New Testament and the Greco-Roman context far outpaces that on children in the Hebrew Bible.⁴ For example, a review of over nine hundred titles of articles published in

---

Ontario, Lesley University, Missouri Western State University, Montclair State University, Post University, Rutgers University-Camden, University of North Carolina at Charlotte, Vanderbilt University, Washington University in St. Louis, Wilfrid Laurier University, and York University. (I am indebted to Professors John Wall and Dan Cook of the Center for Children and Childhood Studies at Rutgers University for this list of institutions.)

3. Much of the recent scholarship about children in the Bible has surfaced in other fields of religious studies. For a collection of essays from various faith traditions, see Marcia J. Bunge, ed., *Children, Adults, and Shared Responsibilities: Jewish, Christian, and Muslim Perspectives* (Cambridge: Cambridge University Press, 2012). For discussions of children, ethics, theology, and religious traditions, which often engage biblical texts, see John Wall, *Ethics in Light of Childhood* (Washington, DC: Georgetown University Press, 2010); Don S. Browning and Marcia J. Bunge, eds., *Children and Childhood in World Religions: Primary Sources and Texts* (New Brunswick, NJ: Rutgers University Press, 2009); Don S. Browning and Bonnie J. Miller-McLemore, eds., *Children and Childhood in American Religions* (New Brunswick, NJ: Rutgers University Press, 2009); Annette Esser, Andrea Günter, Rajah Scheepers, eds., *Kinder haben, Kind sein, Geboren sein: Philosophische und theologische Beiträge zu Kindheit und Geburt* (Königstein/Taunus: Ulrike Helmer, 2008); Patrick McKinley Brennan, ed., *The Vocation of the Child* (Grand Rapids, MI: Eerdmans, 2008); Douglas McConnell, Jennifer Orona, and Paul Stockley, eds., *Understanding God's Heart for Children: Toward a Biblical Framework* (Colorado Springs: Authentic, 2007); Martin Marty, *The Mystery of the Child* (Grand Rapids, MI: Eerdmans, 2007); Marcia J. Bunge, "The Child, Religion, and the Academy: Developing Robust Theological and Religious Understandings of Children and Childhood," *JR* 86.4 (2006): 549–79; John Wall, "Childhood Studies, Hermeneutics, and Theological Ethics," *JR* 86.4 (2006): 523–48; Kristin Herzog, *Children and Our Global Future: Theological and Social Challenges* (Cleveland: Pilgrim, 2005), 21–50; David H. Jensen, *Graced Vulnerability: A Theology of Childhood* (Cleveland: Pilgrim, 2005), 13–33; among others.

4. For discussion of Jewish children in Greco-Roman society, see three articles in Cohen, *Jewish Family in Antiquity*: Adele Reinhartz, "Parents and Children: A Philonic Perspective," 61–88; Ross S. Kraemer, "Jewish Mothers and Daughters in the Greco-Roman World," 89–112; and Dale B. Martin, "Slavery and the Ancient Jewish Family," 113–129. For bibliographies, see Marcia J. Bunge, ed., *The Child in the Bible* (Grand Rapids, MI: Eerdmans, 2008), 423–34, and Reidar Aasgaard, "Children in Antiquity and Early Christianity: Research History and Central Issues," *Familia* 33 (2006): 37–46. New Testament studies are too numerous to be listed here, but for a helpful introduction, see Judith M. Gundry-Volf, "The Least and the Greatest: Children in the New Testament," in *The Child in Christian Thought* (ed. Marcia J. Bunge; Grand Rapids, MI: Eerdmans, 2001), 29–60. For a (Christian) theological discussion of children in the Old and New Testaments, see John T. Carroll, "Children in the Bible," *Int* 55.2 (2001): 121–34. For a more detailed overview of daily life at the beginning of the Common Era (although less explicit with respect to children), see Carolyn Osiek and David L. Balch, eds., *Families in the New Testament World: Households and House Churches* (Louisville, KY: Westminster John Knox, 1997). O. M. Bakke's monograph, *When Children Became People: The Birth of Childhood in Early Christianity* (trans. Brian McNeil; Minneapolis: Augsburg Fortress, 2005) focuses primarily on the differences between children in Christian communities versus the surrounding Greco-Roman pagan culture. However, his title may lead readers to erroneously infer that children were not considered people prior to the Common Era, or that childhood did not exist before early Christianity.

the *Journal of Biblical Literature* since the year 2000 yields no articles with children in the Hebrew Bible as the explicit focus.[5] Beyond Bible dictionary entries, information about children in the Hebrew Bible generally must be ferreted out from works dealing with wider topics.

Books on ancient Israelite society usually give little if any attention to children, with some exceptions. An early contribution comes from Carl Heinrich Cornill's *The Culture of Ancient Israel*.[6] One-fifth of this book focuses on children in an overview of passages pertaining to both boys and girls. Roland de Vaux gathers and surveys texts related to birth, naming, circumcision, and education in *Ancient Israel: Its Life and Institutions*.[7] In *Life in Biblical Israel*, Philip King and Lawrence Stager address a similar range of topics related to children, based on textual and archaeological evidence.[8] Oded Borowski's *Daily Life in Biblical Times* offers additional archaeological treatment that discusses the household and includes children, largely by inference.[9] Karel van der Toorn's reporting of an imagined sojourn with an ancient Israelite family, "Nine Months among the

---

5. A few articles reference children, but only tangentially. Michael Carasik, "Why Did Hannah Ask for 'Seed of Men'?" (*JBL* 129.3 [2010]: 433–36) discusses Hannah's request for a child, but concentrates on the phrase זרע אנשים, and not children per se. Child sacrifice surfaces as part of larger discussions in Alice Logan, "Rehabilitating Jephthah," *JBL* 128.4 (2009): 665–85; and John S. Rundin, "Pozo Moro, Child Sacrifice, and the Greek Legendary Tradition," *JBL* 123.3 (2004): 425–47. Only one article arguably looks at a child character in the Hebrew Bible (Jonathan Grossman, "'Gleaning among the Ears'—'Gathering among the Sheaves': Characterizing the Image of the Supervising Boy [Ruth 2]," *JBL* 126.4 [2007]: 703–16, although this article focuses more on the interpretation of Ruth 2:7. Two articles appear on children and youth in the New Testament (Reidar Aasgaard, "Paul as a Child: Children and Childhood in the Letters of the Apostle," *JBL* 126.1 [2007]: 129–59; and Ross Kraemer, "Implicating Herodias and Her Daughter in the Death of John the Baptizer: A [Christian] Theological Strategy?" *JBL* 125.2 [2006]: 321–49). Scholarship on children in the Hebrew Bible is slowly emerging, and the Society of Biblical Literature approved a new section on Children in the Biblical World in 2008 to foster this research.

6. See the chapter on "The Education of Children in Ancient Israel" in Carl Heinrich Cornill, *The Culture of Ancient Israel* (trans. W. H. Carruth; Chicago: Open Court, 1914), 68–100.

7. Roland de Vaux, *Ancient Israel: Its Life and Institutions* (trans. John McHugh; New York: McGraw-Hill, 1961), 41–52. De Vaux combines biblical passages about children with anthropological comparisons to surmise what life would have been like for children in ancient Israel; however, his interpretation can border on romantic. See, for example, his observations on children's play on pp. 48–49.

8. Philip J. King and Lawrence E. Stager, *Life in Biblical Israel* (Louisville, KY: Westminster John Knox, 2001), 40–49. Due to the organization of this material (reflecting concerns of the text), King, Stager, and de Vaux focus primarily on boys. For explicit attention to girls, see the work of Carol Meyers, Hennie Marsman, and Jennie Ebeling (citations below).

9. Oded Borowski, *Daily Life in Biblical Times* (SBLABS 5; Atlanta: Society of Biblical Literature, 2003). Borowski discusses children briefly under "family" (p. 22); the chapters on "The Household and Life Cycles" (pp. 63–85) and "A Day in the Life of the Ahuzam Family" (pp. 109–26) also pertain to children.

4    *Valuable and Vulnerable*

Peasants in the Palestinian Highlands," draws on anthropological comparisons to portray daily routines and religious practices of the home.[10] These works include children as part of the household and society.

Scholarship with a primary interest in women often includes children through attention to issues such as marriage, pregnancy, childbirth, domestic labor, and child rearing. Tikva Frymer-Kensky's essay in *Religion, Feminism, and the Family* examines relationships within the hierarchies of the family and the state.[11] Noted works combining feminist and social-scientific approaches with textual evidence include *Discovering Eve: Ancient Israelite Women in Context* by Carol Meyers, *From Her Cradle to Her Grave: The Role of Religion in the Life of the Israelite and Babylonian Woman* by Karel van der Toorn, *Women in Ugarit and Israel: Their Social and Religious Position in the Context of the Ancient Near East* by Hennie Marsman, and *Women's Lives in Biblical Times* by Jennie R. Ebeling.[12] As with other

---

10. Karel van der Toorn, "Nine Months among the Peasants in the Palestinian Highlands: An Anthropological Perspective on Local Religion in the Early Iron Age," in *Symbiosis, Symbolism, and the Power of the Past: Canaan, Ancient Israel, and Their Neighbors from the Late Bronze Age through Roman Palaestina* (ed. William G. Dever and Seymour Gitin; Winona Lake, IN: Eisenbrauns, 2003), 393–410. In *Family Religion in Babylonia, Syria, and Israel: Continuity and Change in the Forms of Religious Life* (Leiden: E. J. Brill, 1996), van der Toorn mentions children explicitly only once (p. 130), although children are implicitly part of the household structure he describes. *Household and Family Religion in Antiquity* (ed. John Bodel and Saul M. Olyan; Oxford: Blackwell, 2008) also discusses quotidian life in ancient Israel, with an emphasis on family religion. See the essays in that volume by Rainer Albertz ("Family Religion in Ancient Israel and Its Surroundings," pp. 89–112); Saul M. Olyan ("Family Religion in Israel and the Wider Levant of the First Millennium BCE" pp. 113–26); and Susan Ackerman ("Household Religion, Family Religion, and Women's Religion in Ancient Israel," pp. 127–209). (These articles have little direct discussion about the role of children in the ancient Israelite household.)

11. Tikva Frymer-Kensky, "The Family in the Hebrew Bible," in *Religion, Feminism, and the Family* (ed. Anne Carr and Mary Stewart van Leeuwen; Louisville, KY: Westminster John Knox, 1996), 55–73. Frymer-Kensky offers a succinct overview of family relations drawing on specific texts (notably Genesis and Judges).

12. Carol Meyers, *Discovering Eve: Ancient Israelite Women in Context* (New York: Oxford University Press, 1988). Meyers explains the levels of technological skill required of girls and women to make products essential for a family's survival (pp. 139–49). For discussion of parents, children, and education, see pp. 149–54 and Meyers's general overview in "Everyday Life: Women in the Period of the Hebrew Bible," in *The Women's Bible Commentary* (ed. Carol A. Newsom and Sharon H. Ringe; Louisville, KY: Westminster John Knox, 1998), 251–59. See also Karel van der Toorn, *From Her Cradle to Her Grave: The Role of Religion in the Life of the Israelite and Babylonian Woman* (trans. Sara J. Denning-Bolle; Sheffield: JSOT Press, 1994); and Phyllis A. Bird, *Missing Persons and Mistaken Identities: Women and Gender in Ancient Israel* (Minneapolis: Fortress, 1997), esp. pp. 52–66. For extensive discussion, see Hennie J. Marsman, *Women in Ugarit and Israel: Their Social and Religious Position in the Context of the Ancient Near East* (OtSt 49; Leiden: Brill, 2003). Topics especially relevant to children include mothers and childbirth (pp. 222–43), sibling relationships (pp. 247–52), daughters (pp. 274–91), and orphans (pp. 323–24). Finally, see Jennie R. Ebeling, *Women's Lives in Biblical Times*

books on ancient Israelite society, children are not the primary focus but are incorporated into wider discussions.

Works that more directly address the topic of children can be found under the rubric of the family. Daniel Block's essay in *Marriage and Family in the Biblical World* surveys language pertaining to children in the Hebrew Bible and discusses children's integral role in society.[13] Focusing on the postexilic period and selected texts, Friedrich Fechter explores the changing role of the family in *Die Familie in der Nachexilszeit: Untersuchungen zur Bedeutung der Verwandtschaft in ausgewählten Texten des Alten Testaments*.[14] *Families in Ancient Israel*, with contributions by Leo Perdue, Joseph Blenkinsopp, John J. Collins, and Carol Meyers, provides overviews of the family in the different periods of the Hebrew Bible, designated as "Early Israel" (Meyers), "First Temple Israel" (Blenkinsopp), and "Second Temple Judaism" (Collins). These essays are followed by synthesis and reflection from Perdue, who offers overarching conclusions about relationships in ancient Israelite and early Jewish households.[15] Patricia Dutcher-Walls contributes

---

(London: T&T Clark, 2010). Ebeling's book includes direct discussion of girls in ancient Israel as she portrays the life of a fictious female character from birth through death.

13. Daniel I. Block, "Marriage and Family in Ancient Israel," in *Marriage and Family in the Biblical World* (ed. Ken M. Campbell; Downers Grove, IL: InterVarsity, 2003), 33–102. For theological discussion of the family, see J. Andrew Dearman, "The Family in the Old Testament," *Int* 52.2 (1998): 117–29; as well as John Rogerson, "The Family and Structures of Grace in the Old Testament," in *The Family in Theological Perspective* (ed. Stephen C. Barton; Edinburgh: T&T Clark, 1996), 25–42.

14. Basing his discussion on Josh 7, Lev 18, Ruth, and Mic 7:1–7, Fechter posits that the family grew stronger as the monarchy grew weaker. He suggests that paternal bonds gained increased importance in structuring society during the post-exilic period. See Friedrich Fechter, *Die Familie in der Nachexilszeit: Untersuchungen zur Bedeutung der Verwandtschaft in ausgewählten Texten des Alten Testaments* (BZAW 264; Berlin: de Gruyter, 1998). For Fechter's review of scholarship related to the family, see pp. 12–31. For discussion of the kinship structure as pervasive and stable throughout the monarchy, see Shunya Bendor, *The Social Structure of Ancient Israel: The Institution of the Family (beit 'ab) from the Settlement to the End of the Monarchy* (Jerusalem: Simor, 1996).

15. Leo G. Perdue, Joseph Blenkinsopp, John J. Collins, and Carol Meyers, *Families in Ancient Israel* (Louisville, KY: Westminster John Knox, 1997). Most scholarship on the Jewish family in the ancient world focuses on Greco-Roman or rabbinic contexts. In addition to *The Jewish Family in Antiquity* (BJS 289), mentioned above, see Amram Tropper, "Children and Childhood in Light of the Demographics of the Jewish Family in Late Antiquity," *JSJ* 37.3 (2006): 299–343; Margaret Williams, "The Jewish Family in Judaea from Pompey to Hadrian — the Limits of Romanization," in *The Roman Family in the Empire: Rome, Italy, and Beyond* (ed. Michele George; Oxford: Oxford University Press, 2005), 159–82; *Families and Family Relations as Represented in Early Judaisms and Early Christianities: Texts and Fictions* (ed. Jan Willem van Henten and Athalya Brenner; STAR 2; Leiden: Deo, 2000); John M. G. Barclay, "The Family as the Bearer of Religion in Judaism and Early Christianity," in *Constructing Early Christian Families: Family as Social Reality and Metaphor* (ed. Halvor Moxnes; London: Routledge, 1997), 66–80; and David Kraemer, "Images of Childhood and Adolescence in Talmudic Literature," in *The Jewish Family: Metaphor and Memory* (New York: Oxford, 1989), 65–80.

a helpful overview of sociological and anthropological research related to the family in *Family in Life and in Death: The Family in Ancient Israel: Sociological and Archaeological Perspectives*.[16] The above works help to sketch life for children in ancient Israel, as they explore issues around labor, education, marriage, war, religion, domestic architecture, individual roles, family relations, burial, and societal structure.

Only very recently have children grown to merit a place as primary subjects of scholarship on the Hebrew Bible. One of the first efforts is Roy Zuck's *Precious in His Sight: Childhood and Children in the Bible*, which looks at both the Hebrew Bible and the New Testament. This book supplies a helpful compilation of biblical material related to children, yet is heavily laden with conservative Christian social ethics on topics such as abortion and corporal punishment.[17] Danna Nolan Fewell offers an innovative contribution with *The Children of Israel: Reading the Bible for the Sake of Our Children*, inviting readers to engage biblical stories and creatively explore possibilities for children in the text.[18] In the first chapter of *The Child in Jewish History*, John Cooper combines textual, archaeological, and anthropological evidence to provide an overview of children in the Hebrew Bible.[19] Kristine Garroway uses archaeological and textual data from the ancient Near East to determine a child's status in biblical Israel.[20] A landmark col-

---

16. Patricia Dutcher-Walls, "The Clarity of Double-Vision: Seeing the Family in Sociological and Archaeological Perspective," in *Family in Life and in Death: The Family in Ancient Israel: Sociological and Archaeological Perspectives* (ed. Patricia Dutcher-Walls; Edinburgh: T&T Clark, 2009), 1–15.

17. Roy B. Zuck, *Precious in His Sight: Childhood and Children in the Bible* (Grand Rapids, MI: Baker, 1996). For Zuck's discussion of abortion, "'You Shall Not Murder': America's National Crime against the Unborn," see pp. 71–81. Zuck interprets Proverbs as encouraging modern parents to use the rod judiciously as a sign of their love (pp. 121–24).

18. Danna Nolan Fewell, *The Children of Israel: Reading the Bible for the Sake of Our Children* (Nashville, TN: Abingdon, 2003). Fewell's treatment of children in the text is both scholarly and popularly accessible, offering exegetical discussion with ethical implications regarding children today. For discussion of her methodology, see pp. 22–25, 36–40. For a much earlier (but not academic) re-telling of stories of the Bible's children, see Eveleen Harrison, *Little-Known Young People of the Bible* (New York: Round Table, 1937). Harrison elaborates on the stories of eleven youngsters in the Hebrew Bible; in the second part of this book, I discuss three of Harrison's subjects ("The Little Captive Maid" and "Brothers: The Story of a Wonder Jar"). For a reflective engagement on Samuel as a youngster, see Margaret Anne Doody, "Infant Piety and the Infant Samuel," in *Out of the Garden: Women Writers on the Bible* (ed. Christina Büchmann and Celina Spiegel; New York: Fawcett Columbine, 1994), 103–22.

19. John Cooper, *The Child in Jewish History* (Northvale, NJ: Jason Aronson: 1996), 7–33.

20. Kristine Sue Henriksen Garroway, "The Construction of 'Child' in the Ancient Near East: Towards an Understanding of the Legal and Social Status of Children in Biblical Israel and Surrounding Cultures" (Ph.D. diss., Hebrew Union College, 2009). Garroway's work focuses largely on evidence from burial remains of children during the Bronze and Iron ages in Canaan and the environs. For archaeological discussion of children and games in ancient Palestine (with illustrations from archaeological evidence on pp. 218–29), see Ulrich Hübner, *Spiele und Spielzeug im antiken Palästina* (OBO 121; Göttingen: Vandenhoeck & Ruprecht,

lection, *The Child in the Bible*, edited by Marcia Bunge, assembles essays on topics and texts related to children, giving child characters overdue recognition in biblical scholarship.[21] Laurel Koepf's dissertation marks another significant contribution to the field with her perspicacious analysis highlighting the essential role of children as agents of familial and cultural survival.[22]

Much of the emerging scholarship is in German and modern Hebrew. Joseph Fleischmann's *Parent and Child in Ancient Near East and the Bible* (in Hebrew) looks at the legal status of children in biblical law, Mesopotamian law, and the Talmud.[23] *"Du hast mich aus meiner Mutter Leib gezogen": Beiträge zur Geburt im Alten Testament*, edited by Detlef Dieckmann and Dorothea Erbele-Küster, offers a series of textually based essays focused on birth, as does *Geburt—ein Übergang: Rituelle Vollzüge, Rollenträger und Geschlechterverhältnisse* by Kathrin Gies.[24] Andreas Michel's monograph, *Gott und Gewalt gegen Kinder im Alten Testament*, catalogs various forms of violence against children, pervasive throughout the Hebrew Bible, and discusses the problematic portrayal of an abusive God.[25] "Schaffe Mir

---

1992). For essays exploring the relationship between the family in ancient Israel and archaeology, including questions of burial, domestic architecture, and familial relationships, see Dutcher-Walls, ed., *Family in Life and Death*. For a broader discussion of archaeological approaches to studying children and childhood, see Jane Eva Baxter, *The Archaeology of Childhood: Children, Gender, and Material Culture* (Walnut Creek, CA: AltaMira, 2005); Kathryn A. Kamp, "Where Have All the Children Gone?: The Archaeology of Childhood," *Journal of Archaeological Method and Theory* 8.1 (2001): 1–34; Joanna Sofaer Derevenski, ed., *Children and Material Culture* (London: Routledge, 2000); and Jenny Moore and Eleanor Scott, eds., *Invisible People and Processes: Writing Gender and Childhood into European Archaeology* (London: Leicester University Press, 1997).

21. Bunge, *Child in the Bible*, 2008.

22. Laurel W. Koepf, "Give Me Children or I Shall Die: Children and Communal Survival in Biblical Literature," Ph.D. diss., Union Theological Seminary, 2012.

23. Joseph Fleishman, *Parent and Child in Ancient Near East and the Bible* (Jerusalem: Magnes, 1999). Also by Fleishman, see "The Age of Legal Maturity in Biblical Law," *JANES* 21 (1992): 35–48; "Does the Law of Exodus 21:7–11 Permit a Father to Sell His Daughter to Be a Slave?" *JLA* 13 (2000): 47–64; "A Daughter's Demand and a Father's Compliance: The Legal Background to Achsah's Claim and Caleb's Agreement," *ZAW* 118 (2006): 354–73; *Father-Daughter Relations in Biblical Law* (Bethesda, MD: CDL Press, 2011).

24. Dieckmann and Erbele-Küster discuss Gen 3:16, Jer 30:6, Ps 22, and Song of Solomon, among others. See Detlef Dieckmann and Dorothea Erbele-Küster, eds., *"Du hast mich aus meiner Mutter Leib gezogen": Beiträge zur Geburt im Alten Testament* (Neukirchen-Vluyn: Neukirchener, 2006). Gies focuses largely on Gen 18:1–16; 21:1–8; Lev 12; Jer 20:14–18; Ezek 16:1–14. See Kathrin Gies, *Geburt—ein Übergang: rituelle Vollzüge, Rollenträger und Geschlechterverhältnisse* (ATSAT 88; St. Ottilien: Erzabtei St. Ottilien: 2009).

25. Andreas Michel, *Gott und Gewalt gegen Kinder im Alten Testament* (FAT 37; Tübingen: Mohr Siebeck, 2003). Michel discusses vocabulary used to designate children and youth in the Hebrew Bible (pp. 21–27) and reviews the nearly two hundred violent acts perpetrated against children, who are victimized by war, gods, their parents, and society. Michel notes that portrayals of children as joyful are rare. He also shows how the Septuagint's translation

8   *Valuable and Vulnerable*

*Kinder . . .": Beiträge zur Kindheit im alten Israel und in seinen Nachbarkulturen*, edited by Andreas Kunz-Lübcke and Rüdiger Lux, places discussions of adolescence, violence against children, children in prophetic texts, and children's upbringing within the context of the broader ancient Near East.[26] Andreas Kunz-Lübcke also offers an important comparative study with *Das Kind in den antiken Kulturen des Mittelmeers: Israel, Ägypten, Griechenland*, which explores topics such as birth, adoption, work, play, and violence, among others.[27] Irmtraud Fischer's article "Über Lust und Last, Kinder zu haben: Soziale, genealogische und theologische Aspekte in der Literatur Alt-Israels" examines the sociological and genealogical role of children in the Hebrew Bible.[28] However, at the time of this writing, I know of no other monographic study that brings a theoretical and historical discussion of children to studies in the Hebrew Bible and combines this with detailed analysis of one set of stories.

My goals with this book are fourfold: First, to help fill a void in Hebrew Bible scholarship, especially in English. Second, I will show that children were recognized as different from adults in the minds of the biblical writers. The Hebrew Bible contains awareness, and therefore concepts, of childhood. Third, this book offers and demonstrates an inter-

---

mitigates YHWH's culpability in theologically troubling passages. While Michel's important contribution calls attention to the prevalence and plight of children in the Hebrew Bible, his discussion focuses on children as objects, not agents.

26. Andreas Kunz-Lübcke and Rüdiger Lux, eds., *"Schaffe Mir Kinder . . .": Beiträge zur Kindheit im alten Israel und in seinen Nachbarkulturen* (ABG 21; Leipzig: Evangelische Verlagsanstalt, 2006). This collected volume explores issues related to children in antiquity. Articles on the ancient Near East address the following issues: evidence for childhood research in antiquity (Dieter Hoof, "Das Evidenzproblem in der althistorischen Kindheitsforschung," pp. 19–43); the sale and deportation of children in Babylonia and Assyria (Konrad Volk, "Von Findel-, Waisen-, verkauften und deportierten Kindern. Notizen aus Babylonien und Assyrien," pp. 47–87); education and labor among Egyptian children (Erica Feucht, "Kinderarbeit und Erziehung im Alten Ägypten," pp. 89–117); and childhood in Greco-Roman antiquity (Josef N. Neumann, "Kindheit in der griechisch-römischen Antike. Entwicklung—Erziehung—Erwartung," pp. 119–33). The second part of the book focuses on ancient Israel. Andreas Michel surveys violence against children then focuses on child sacrifice, especially associated with *mlk* offerings ("Gewalt gegen Kinder im alten Israel. Eine sozialgeschichtliche Perspektive," pp. 137–63). Andreas Kunz-Lübcke discusses adolescent biblical characters, particularly as they emerge from crisis situations ("Wahrnehmung von Adoleszenz in der Hebräischen Bibel und in den Nachbarkulturen Israels," pp. 167–95). Rüdiger Lux reviews passages with vulnerable children in prophetic literature ("Die Kinder auf der Gasse. Ein Kindheitsmotiv in der prophetischen Gerichts- und Heilsverkündigung," pp. 197–221). Otto Kaiser looks at children's education in Ben Sira ("Erziehung und Bildung in der Weisheit des Jesus Sirach," pp. 223–51).

27. See Andreas Kunz-Lübcke, *Das Kind in den antiken Kulturen des Mittelmeers: Israel, Ägypten, Griechenland* (Neukirchen-Vluyn: Neukirchener, 2007).

28. Irmtraud Fischer, "Über Lust und Last, Kinder zu haben: Soziale, genealogische und theologische Aspekte in der Literatur Alt-Israels," *JBTh* 17 (2002): 56–82. This volume of *Jahrbuch für biblische Theologie*, entitled *Gottes Kinder*, is devoted to the topic of children.

pretive approach and methodology by which scholars might examine biblical stories with child characters, especially those who appear in the text briefly and are easy to bypass. Fourth, I seek to convince readers that appreciating these young characters greatly enriches our understanding of the Hebrew Bible. My hope is that more biblical scholars will notice child characters and will be prompted to explore their fascinating stories.

The children of the Hebrew Bible merit this attention for multiple reasons. Most significantly, many people in the ancient world did not survive to adulthood. Incorporating excavation evidence from a tomb in Palestine, with remains dated between the first century BCE and the fourth century CE, John Cooper reports that nearly half of this population did not live to age eighteen.[29] Milton Eng points out that the *life expectancy*, or average age of a person at death, differs from the *life span*, which is the age one could expect to reach without interference from war, disease, death in childbirth, etc. He estimates that the life expectancy in ancient Israel was probably in the mid-thirties, whereas the typical life span (barring calamities) would be between forty and fifty.[30] In societies with short life expectancies approximately one-third of the total population consists of children.[31] For scholars to ignore this significant demographic while discussing ancient Israel (as many do) is to miss much of the culture that they try to understand.

Analyzing the children in the Hebrew Bible leads scholars to reassess characters, narratives, and the issues they raise. Topics such as adop-

---

29. Cooper, *Jewish Childhood*, 11.
30. See Milton Eng, *The Days of Our Years: A Lexical Semantic Study of the Life Cycle in Biblical Hebrew* (LHBOTS 464; New York: T&T Clark, 2011), 35–44.
31. Andrew Chamberlain, "Minor Concerns: A Demographic Perspective on Children in Past Societies," in *Children and Material Culture* (ed. Joanna Sofaer Derevenski; London: Routledge, 2000), 207. Chamberlain further observes that scholars who ignore children bypass "the predominant group of individuals in most past societies." Andrew T. Chamberlain, "Commentary: Missing Stage of Life—Towards the Perception of Children in Archaeology," in Jenny Moore and Eleanor Scott, eds., *Invisible People and Processes: Writing Gender and Childhood into European Archaeology* (London: Leicester University Press, 1997), 250. Anthropological studies suggest that in societies without developed medical care and lacking clean water supplies, 20 percent (or more) of babies do not survive to reach one year old, and another 25 percent do not reach age two. See Robert A. LeVine, "Child Rearing as Cultural Adaptation," in *Culture and Infancy: Variations in the Human Experience* (ed. P. Herbert Leiderman, Steven R. Tulkin, Anne Rosenfeld; New York: Academic Press, 1977), 24. N. Ray Hiner and Joseph Hawes note that children comprised a substantial demographic in past populations and played essential roles in economies. They were also crucial in the transmission of culture, even though historians have given them relatively little attention until recently. See Joseph M. Hawes and N. Ray Hiner, eds., *Children in Historical and Comparative Perspective: An International Handbook and Research Guide* (Westport, CT: Greenwood, 1991), 2. In his study on the highlands of Israel during Iron I, Lawrence Stager estimates that approximately two of six children would live to become adults. Lawrence Stager, "The Archaeology of the Family in Ancient Israel," *BASOR* 260 (1985): 18.

tion, birth order, sibling rivalry, inheritance, education, labor, discipline, continuance of the covenant, family rituals, sexuality, child sacrifice, warfare, prostitution, captivity, slavery, abandonment, and incest, to name a few, are seen differently when focusing on the children. Also, children help to shape the stories of the text, even when they play minor roles. Beyond the dramatic characters, those acting in subtle ways frequently mirror important human activity.[32]

Episodes from the childhood or youth of a character merit attention since they can help us to fully appreciate his or her adult manifestation. A person's early years help to shape the rest of his/her life. Stories of a character's youth then add dimension to the overall persona, adding complexity to our reading.[33]

Children also have an essential theological role in Jewish tradition. James M. M. Francis points out that "Israel as God's child and thereby God as Israel's Father, constitutes a particularly important and predominant motif (Deut. 1.31, 32.1–13; Jer. 3.4; 31.20; Is. 63.16, 64.8–9)."[34] The people of Israel describe themselves as children in relation to YHWH and Israel (בני ישראל), and children are part of Israel's restoration (Isa 49:22). Jewish customs and rituals are celebrated in the home and passed down through children. Parents and children have vital obligations to each other, as discussed in the Talmud and other early Jewish literature.[35] The Israelite covenant continues through children, who are integral to families, tribes, and nations.

Perhaps paramount, children permeate the Hebrew Bible. Their presence is tied to questions of legacy, survival, family strength, and honor. Many individual children, from slaves to princes, offer overlooked but riveting stories. Similarly, women in the Bible were neglected throughout most of the history of biblical interpretation. Just forty years ago, there were almost no academic books about biblical women. Today there are

---

32. Childhood historian Paula Fass explains that children's behavior is highly significant, even when focused on self-preservation. She notes, "Some of the most important kinds of human activities are defensive, preservative, un-self-consciously conservative." See Paula S. Fass, "Social History and the History of Childhood" in the *Society for the History of Children and Youth Newsletter* 13 (Winter 2009): 16.

33. For example, Ishmael (Gen 21:9–20), Isaac (Gen 22:1–19), Rebekah (Gen 24:10–67), Joseph (Genesis 37), Moses (Exod 2:1–10), Miriam (Exod 2:1–10), Samuel (1 Sam 3:1–18), David (1 Sam 17), and Jeremiah (Jer 1:4–10), all have pivotal incidents from their childhood or youth portrayed in the text. For discussion of biblical characters and the role of youth in shaping characterization, see Jon L. Berquist, "Childhood and Age in the Bible," *Pastoral Psychology* 58 (2009): 521–30. For discussion of David's development, see Kunz-Lübcke,"Wahrnehmung von Adoleszenz," 179–86.

34. James M. M. Francis, *Adults as Children: Images of Childhood in the Ancient World and the New Testament* (Oxford: Peter Lang, 2006), 67–68.

35. See O. Larry Yarbrough, "Parents and Children in the Jewish Family of Antiquity," in *Jewish Family in Antiquity*, 41–53. See also Cooper, *Child in Jewish History*, 35–110.

hundreds, if not thousands. Yet children in the Hebrew Bible still languish in textual obscurity.

## Theoretical Concerns, Methodological Considerations, and Ensuing Approach

Before embarking on our study of children in the Hebrew Bible, we need a theoretical foundation. Ideas about children and childhood are social constructs that are culturally bound. Our conceptions of children stem from social and economic conditions, as well as contemporary Western intellectual legacies. The biblical field has barely addressed these wider issues in childhood studies.

Modern theories of childhood have been shaped by the seminal work of Philippe Ariès. In 1960, this French historian published *L'enfant et la vie familiale sous l'ancien régime* (English title: *Centuries of Childhood*), which suggests that childhood was essentially not recognized as a separate period of life until after the Middle Ages.[36] His thesis sparked formidable controversy and has been widely disputed. However, prominent biblical scholars have adopted Ariès's conclusion that children were seen as "miniature adults" until the modern era. In his essay "The Family in First Temple Israel," Joseph Blenkinsopp highlights Ariès's study and gleans an understanding of childhood from Hebrew terms for children, although he finds the biblical conception of childhood "rather vague and ill-focused."[37] He concurs with Ariès that childhood was not known as a distinct phase of life and adds, "in fact, no biblical source alludes to childhood or youth in the abstract before Koheleth, who speaks of the days of youth (*yaldût*, Eccl. 11:9–10)."[38] Building on Blenkinsopp's study, Philip King and Lawrence Stager also cite Ariès and observe, "The issue as to whether the Israelites treated their children as children or as 'small-scale adults' remains unresolved."[39] However, to ask whether the Hebrew Bible understands children as "miniature adults" or "children" is to impose a

---

36. Philippe Ariès, *L'enfant et la vie familiale sous l'ancien régime* (Paris: Plon, 1960), and translated by Robert Baldick as *Centuries of Childhood: A Social History of Family Life* (New York: Vintage, 1962).

37. Blenkinsopp, "The Family in First Temple Israel," in Leo G. Perdue, Joseph Blenkinsopp, John J. Collins, and Carol Meyers, *Families in Ancient Israel* (Louisville, KY: Westminster John Knox, 1997), 67. While not explicitly mentioning Ariès, Andrew Dearman also adopts his thesis. He sees children in the Hebrew Bible as "'little adults' as they grow toward maturity in their family identity" ("Family in the Old Testament," 125).

38. Blenkinsopp, "The Family in First Temple Israel," 67. Blenkinsopp overlooks other words that indicate youth, such as נעורים (46 attestations), נער (Job 33:25; 36:14; Ps 88:16; Prov 29:21), *נערות (Jer 32:30), עלומים (Job 20:11; 33:25; Ps 89:46; Isa 54:4), צעירה (Gen 43:33), *בחורות (Eccl 11:9; 12:1) and *בחורים (Num 11:28). Further discussion follows.

39. King and Stager, *Life in Biblical Israel*, 41.

distinction that the text itself has no means to express.[40] There remains a need for a discussion of *Centuries of Childhood* that serves the biblical field and exposes Ariès's methodological flaws.[41]

Some scholars question whether an academic conversation about childhood in the Bible is even appropriate. Andreas Michel maintains that to look for childhood in the Hebrew Bible may be largely irrelevant since children and adults led deeply integrated lives. He argues that applying current ideas of childhood to the Bible is anachronistic and has "cultural-colonist features."[42] Like Michel, Andreas Kunz-Lübcke and Rüdiger Lux assert that Ariès's work may be irrelevant for Hebrew Bible studies, hence the dearth of attention to childhood.[43] These scholars are right to suggest that childhood is not cordoned off from adulthood in biblical understanding, nor does it resemble modern ideas of childhood. Yet this is not the same as saying that there is no concept of childhood in the Hebrew Bible. Understandings of childhood must not be limited to current Western presumptions. The question is not whether "the Israelites treated children as children," as King and Stager ask (above), because that assumes *our* understanding of childhood, carrying expecations that children should be coddled, cared for, educated, and cherished. Rather, we should ask, How did they treat their children? What can we infer about adults' attitudes toward children and children's attitudes toward adults? Was there any recognition of children's separate status? How can we discover what the ancient writers of the Hebrew Bible thought about children and childhood?

I offer two strategies: linguistic and literary. With the majority of biblical scholars, I think that the Hebrew Bible is grounded in the lives of real people in the region of Palestine during the millennium before the Common Era. Exactly who the Bible writers were and precisely how much the Hebrew Bible reflects historical reality are ultimately unanswerable questions.[44] This project then focuses on the world portrayed in the Hebrew

---

40. Biblical Hebrew does not have a gender-neutral word specifying that a person has reached maturity (i.e., "adult"). The closest equivalents, "man" (איש) and "woman" (אשה), carry a broad range of connotations, including, but certainly not limited to, adulthood. See *HALOT* 1:43–44, 93.

41. Naomi Steinberg's introduction to Ariès's work for biblical scholarship is helpful but very brief. See Naomi Steinberg, "Sociological Approaches: Toward a Sociology of Childhood in the Hebrew Bible," in *Method Matters: Essays on the Interpretation of the Hebrew Bible in Honor of David L. Petersen* (ed. Joel M. LeMon and Kent Harold Richards; Atlanta: Society of Biblical Literature, 2009), 260.

42. Andreas Michel, "Sexual Violence against Children in the Bible," in *The Structural Betrayal of Trust* (ed. Regina Ammicht-Quinn, Hille Haker, and Maureen Junker-Kenny; London: SCM Press, 2004), 52.

43. Kunz-Lübcke and Lux, "*Schaffe Mir Kinder,*" 12.

44. For a succinct overview of the Minimalist-Maximalist debate, see Ziony Zevit, "Three Debates about Bible and Archaeology," *Bib* 83 (2002): 1–27.

Bible, that is, biblical Israel. I understand that the writers of these texts were primarily privileged men who came from the upper echelons of society.[45] Presumably, their writings and the environment they portray must have borne some resemblance to people's lives to be not only relevant but compelling. Still, the extent to which the literary and historical worlds mirror each other is not my concern. This level of correspondence remains the reader's interpretive choice, while I focus on how the Hebrew Bible portrays its children, through both vocabulary and narratives.

This book is divided into two sections: Part I offers theoretical, historical, contextual, linguistic, literary, and metholodogical frameworks to recognize and appreciate children in biblical texts, and Part II analyzes stories with children in the Elisha cycle. Tales about Elisha begin in 1 Kgs 19:15–21, when Elijah chooses Elisha as his successor, and end with Elisha's death in 2 Kgs 13:14–21. Highlighting Elisha's role as a wonderworker among common people, the bulk of these narratives appear in 2 Kings 2–8. Taken together, these seven chapters contain forty-nine child characters, which is a strikingly high number. These child characters have received little attention from biblical scholars, further contributing to my decision to focus on them. Finally, by concentrating on one literary collection, I can offer more cohesive conclusions.

In Part I, Chapter 1 ("Concepts of Children and Childhood: A Theoretical and Historical Framework") discusses issues in the wider field of childhood studies to bring this knowledge to the biblical field. This chapter also reviews the history of current Western understandings about children and childhood to increase awareness of our own biases. By acknowledging our assumptions about what it means to be a child, we can keep these presumptions at bay and replace them with knowledge revealed in the text.

Chapter 2 ("Learning about Children and Youth in the Hebrew Bible through Language: A Contextual and Linguistic Framework") operates from the premise that language derives from experience and vocabulary

---

45. Ancient societies functioned with little reliance on the written word. Those with education and access to expensive writing materials were likely among the elite. However, writers of texts may have been semi-literate functionaries producing tangible items to sell. Susan Niditch, citing the work of Denise Troll, cautions against idealizing about the motivation and dedication of medieval scribes. See Susan Niditch, *Oral World and Written Word* (Louisville, KY: Westminster John Knox, 1996), 131–34. David Carr notes that the rarity of the written word in antiquity imbued writing with power. See David McLain Carr, *Writing on the Tablet of the Heart: Origins of Scripture and Literature* (New York: Oxford University Press, 2005), 10. For detailed discussion about the writers of the Hebrew Bible, see Karel van der Toorn, *Scribal Culture and the Making of the Hebrew Bible* (Cambridge, MA: Harvard University Press, 2007). Van der Toorn posits that the Hebrew Bible was produced by an elite cadre of scribes associated with the Jerusalem Temple.

14   *Valuable and Vulnerable*

is an index of a culture's ideas.[46] After noting the prevalence of children in the Hebrew Bible and briefly touching upon linguistic theory, I examine Hebrew terms that designate children and young people, approximately up to the age of marriage.[47] Previous works have also reviewed these terms, along with others for children and youth, though usually in less detail.[48] The analysis here focuses primarily on textual usage and the insights gained from these terms to develop an understanding of childhood in the Hebrew Bible. I group these words by family association, gender, and stages of growth since they lend themselves to these categorizations.

Chapter 3 ("Approaching the Elisha Cycle: A Literary and Methodological Framework") offers contextual discussions for understanding the Elisha cycle then proposes a methodology for childist interpretation (explained below). This chapter looks at the genre of these narratives, as well as their theological role within the Deuteronomistic History. I explain why minor characters, such as children whom biblical commentators frequently fail to notice, are nonetheless highly significant. I then propose a methodology that gives attention to the setting, characters, and plot of the story, followed by an interpretation that leads to insights about children. The final step of analysis connects the passage at hand with other references to children in the Hebrew Bible to show wider implications for understanding biblical concepts of childhood. In sum, the discussion of each narrative consists of six sections entitled *Setting, Characters, Reviewing the Plot from a Childist Perspective, Childist Interpretation, Insights about Children,* and *Children and Textual Connections.*

Part II consists of textual analyses that follow the prescribed six-step

---

46. Ferdinand de Saussure, often cited as the father of modern linguistics, observes, "The value of a word is mainly or primarily thought of in terms of its capacity for representing a certain idea." See Ferdinand de Saussure, *Course in General Linguistics* (ed. Charles Bally and Albert Sechehaye; trans. Roy Harris; London: Duckworth, 1983), 112. Edward Sapir asserts that language colors all our thinking and functions as a "guide to 'social reality.'" See Edward Sapir, *Selected Writings in Language, Culture, and Personality* (ed. David G. Mandelbaum; Berkeley: University of California Press, 1985), 162.

47. Scholars suggest that girls would be considered marriageable at the onset of puberty (i.e., early teenage years) and young men would be at least ten years older. See Blenkinsopp, "The Family in First Temple Israel," 77; King and Stager, *Life in Biblical Israel,* 54. To use marriage as the cutoff point between childhood and adulthood provides practical limits for examining vocabulary that designates children and youth. However, this boundary between youth and adulthood remains flexible since the vocabulary does not offer separate words for married and unmarried youth. For example, an עלמה (generally translated as "young woman" [BDB, 761] or "a marriageable girl" [*HALOT* 1:836]) could be single (see Exod 2:8) or married (see Isa 7:14). (In Isa 7:14, עלמה is frequently translated as "virgin"; see p. 58 n. 58.)

48. See Blenkinsopp, "The Family in First Temple Israel," 67–68; Block, "Marriage and Family in Ancient Israel," 78–85; Fischer, "Über Lust und Last," 56–57; Michel, *Gott und Gewalt,* 21–27; Zuck, *Precious in His Sight,* 149–53. Milton Eng offers extensive discussions of three terms for young people: נער, ילד, and טף (Eng, *Days of Our Years,* 58–94).

methodology.⁴⁹ The title of each discussion centers on the children in the selected passage of the Elisha cycle. These are the Mockers of Bethel (2 Kgs 2:23–25), the Moabite Prince (2 Kgs 3:26–27), the Debt-Collateral Children (2 Kgs 4:1–7), the Shunammite's Son (2 Kgs 4:8–37), the Israelite Slave Girl (2 Kgs 5:1–14), the Sons of the Starving Mothers (2 Kgs 6:24–31), and the Boy Restored to Life (2 Kgs 8:1–6).⁵⁰ Unlike better-known children in the Hebrew Bible,⁵¹ the children in the Elisha cycle do not grow up to assume larger roles in the text and acquire biblical fame. They are not named nor do they reappear, save a brief return by a boy who is brought back to life (2 Kgs 4:8–37; 8:1–6). Since the spotlight is *not* on the young characters in the Elisha cycle, they offer a textual "back window" through which readers might peer in to get an honest glimpse at life for children in the periods that produced and preserved these texts.⁵²

A few further notes on this book's approach: I work primarily from the Masoretic text (MT) of the *Biblia Hebraica Stuttgartensia* (*BHS*), including English translations for comparison when relevant. Versification corresponds to that of the MT, with English chapter and verse noted in parentheses when different. Translations not attributed to another source are my own. The term "text" simply refers to the Hebrew Bible or portions thereof.⁵³ The interdisciplinary discussions draw upon narrative criticism, while incorporating insights from historical criticism and social-scientific disciplines, notably archaeology and anthropology.

---

49. The discussion of the final text analyzed here (2 Kgs 8:1–6) diverges from this pattern since this passage re-introduces a child character who has already been discussed.

50. The small children briefly mentioned in 2 Kgs 8:12 (עלליהם) are part of a literary trope and do not appear in a scene, so I do not analyze this passage.

51. E.g., Isaac being sacrificed (Gen 22:1–13), Joseph with his coat (Genesis 37), Moses and Miriam at the bulrushes (Exod 2:1–9), or Samuel in the temple (1 Sam 2:18–21; 3:1–19).

52. Reidar Aasgaard observes that the writers' disinterest in children can lead to less polished and more forthright portrayals. He notes that the lack of "rhetorical or ideological adaptation" offers readers an opportunity to learn about the lives of children or attitudes toward them ("Children in Antiquity," 25).

53. In linguistic studies, "text" refers to "a unit of language in use . . . [i.e.,] a meaning unit which is structured so that it coheres and functions as a unity with respect to its environment," be it written or oral. See Janet Jones, Sandra Gollin, Helen Drury, and Dorothy Economou, "Systemic-Functional Linguistics and Its Application to the TESOL Curriculum," in *Language Development: Learning Language, Learning Culture. Meaning and Choice in Language: Studies for Michael Halliday* (ed. Raqaiya Hasan and J. R. Martin; Norwood, NJ: Ablex, 1989), 316. For consistency, I use the word "text" (here as elsewhere) as generally applied in biblical studies, referring to the writings of the Bible. For a brief theoretical introduction to the role of text and interpretation, see Anne Cluysenaar, "Text," in *The Routledge Dictionary of Literary Terms* (ed. Peter Childs and Roger Fowler; London: Routledge, 2006), 237–38.

## Childist Interpretation

Since the academic study of children is new within the biblical guild, corresponding language is still developing. Reidar Aasgaard, in his well-reasoned appeal for more antiquity scholarship focused on children, argues for a "childish" reading that stems from children's interests and perspectives.[54] Aasgaard's use of "childish" is innovative, but this term (like many words associated with children) carries a subtle derogatory connotation.[55] Kristine Garroway uses "not-yet-adult" (abbreviated NYA) to describe a child or youth.[56] This term conveniently covers a wide range of young people, however it defines them by what they are not. In *The Child in the Bible*, Marcia Bunge explains that the contributors "re-examine selected biblical texts through the 'lens' or category of 'the child.'"[57] While my project takes a similar tack, I prefer not to refer to "*the* child" (emphasis added). Analogously, to speak of "the adult" is simply too broad.[58] We want to avoid the ideological fallacy that there is a presumed archetypical child any more than there is a standard adult. More compelling is the phrase "child-centered biblical interpretation" adopted by Laurel Koepf.[59] This language is helpful and workable, yet for reasons explained below I find "childist" more compelling.

Recent scholarship introduces the terms "childist" and "childism," while disagreeing as to what these words mean. Ethicist John Wall speaks of a "childist" paradigm that incorporates the concerns and experiences of children into theological ethics. Wall sees a need for this term as a self-critique of a society that neglects and impoverishes its children without

---

54. Aasgaard, "Children in Antiquity," 37.
55. Similar pejorative adjectives related to youth include "infantile," "puerile," "jejune," "callow," "immature," and "juvenile." Conversely, the terms "young" and "youthful" generally carry neutral or positive connotations in English, but to speak of a "young" or "youthful" reading of texts is confusing.
56. Garroway, "Construction of 'Child'," 2.
57. Bunge, *Child in the Bible*, xviii.
58. Sociologists Allison James and Adrian James note that to speak of "the child" erases children's individuality in an abstract sense. While people rarely speak of "the adult," "the child" metonymically stands for all children. James and James see childhood as a "structural site" common to children as a collective, within which an individual child exercises her or his own agency. See Allison James and Adrian L. James, *Constructing Childhood: Theory, Policy and Social Practice* (New York: Palgrave Macmillan: 2004), 14–15. See also Jens Qvortrup, "Childhood Matters: An Introduction," in *Childhood Matters: Social Theory, Practice and Politics* (ed. Jens Qvortrup, Marjatta Bardy, Giovanni Sgritta, Helmut Wintersberger; Aldershot, England: Avebury, 1994), 5–7. Qvortrup et al. view childhood as a structural concept to be compared with other categories in a given society, and children are the 'incumbents' of this structural category (p. 6).
59. Koepf, "Give Me Children or I Shall Die." Similarly, the term "child-centered exploration of texts" was introduced in the dissertation form of this book.

awareness of its anti-child prejudices. He asserts that "childist" theological ethics reframes questions of human responsibility toward all people, including those who are young.[60] For Wall, "childism" joins movements appreciating the full personhood of every individual, akin to feminism, womanism, or humanism.[61] Psychoanalyst Elisabeth Young-Bruehl agrees that an underlying bias against children is pervasive and disregarded in North American society. Both Wall and Young-Bruehl maintain that a focus on "childism" will help to identify and counter anti-child discrimination. However, for Young-Bruehl "childism" names a harmful prejudice, like racism, sexism, classism, ageism, or anti-Semitism. She cites publications in psychology and psychiatry dating from the late 1960s that introduced the term "childism" as decidedly negative.[62] (Working in a different field, Wall makes no reference to these early studies.)

This poses a quandary. On one hand, the negative term "childism," reflecting demeaning and harmful attitudes, has already been established and used by academics for decades. On the other hand, to use the term "childism" positively can offer a fresh and galvanizing lens through which to view not only ethics but texts. Since "childism" has not yet reached popular parlance as a term that reflects a bias either for or against children, the jury is still out. Therefore, this book should weigh in to influence if and how the term might be used in biblical studies.

I encourage biblical scholars to adopt Wall's understanding of the term "childism." Using this word positively emphasizes children's active role in shaping culture, instead of seeing them as largely passive or victimized. Many adults view children as living according to adults' rules and decisions, with little power of their own. While this is true in many respects, adults often fail to notice how children strategize and act to accomplish goals, exert control, maintain relationships, and organize their lives. Even babies and toddlers have tremendous ability to restructure adult lives. Just as we often do not acknowledge children's influence in families and societies, we have largely ignored their roles in the text. "Childism," as an affirming term, helps us recognize children as agents in culture and in literature.

To speak of a childist interpretation seems appropriate for this book that explores stories of the Bible's children much as feminist biblical scholars have focused on women. The approach here also reassesses previously neglected characters. Like feminist biblical interpretation, childist biblical interpretation becomes part of a larger movement that questions engrained patterns of thought that minimize the contributions of certain kinds of people. Certainly, to use the word "childist" carries risks. This

---

60. Wall, "Childhood Studies, Hermeneutics, and Theological Ethics," 524.
61. Wall, *Ethics in Light of Childhood*, 3.
62. Elisabeth Young-Bruehl, *Childism: Confronting Prejudice against Children* (New Haven: Yale University Press, 2012), 299–300.

term is still relatively obscure, and many scholars will find such language awkward. Others might hear something similar to "racist" or "sexist." However, I trust that the following discussion will be clear in its childist goal: to identify and appreciate the influence and importance of promising, compelling young biblical characters.

# I

# Frameworks for Understanding

# 1

# Concepts of Children and Childhood
*A Theoretical and Historical Framework*

## Understanding Childhood

This chapter seeks to lay the groundwork for determining how the writers of the Hebrew Bible thought about children by first acknowledging our own ideas about what it means to be a child. Who is a child? Where does childhood begin? Where does it end? Are children defined by their physical development, social immaturity, intellectual knowledge, sexual inexperience, legal status, financial dependence, rational abilities, familial roles, cultural expectations—or some combination of the above? How do the identifying markers of children change over time and in different cultural contexts?[1] Various factors that many of us take to be incisive indicators of being a child, such as age or biology, are actually social constructs created around our self-understanding.[2] To determine who is a child is to create another social construct that informs the way people of

---

1. For detailed discussion, see Hugh Cunningham, *The Invention of Childhood* (London: BBC Books, 2006).
2. Relating the body and theory, social constructionists suggest that "the body is a receptor, rather than a generator, of social meanings." See Chris Shilling, *The Body and Social Theory* (London: Sage, 1993), 70. For fuller discussion of the body as a social construct, including an assessment and comparison of the works of Mary Douglas, Michel Foucault, and Erving Goffman, see pp. 70–99. Sociologist Ann Oakley asserts, "Children *are* biologically different from adults, but biology is socially constructed." See Ann Oakley, "Women and Children First and Last: Parallels and Differences between Children's and Women's Studies," in *Children's Childhoods: Observed and Experienced* (ed. Berry Mayall; London: Falmer, 1994), 25. Oakley discusses the similarities and differences between studies of women and studies of children, especially their shared lack of status and rights in patriarchal culture. Similarly, archaeologist Mary Baker discusses the marginalization of children and women in traditional archaeology who "exist as the negative, non-public, non-authoritative, weak, subordinate, unknown. They are absent as active, knowledgeable agents in their own history." See Mary Baker, "Invisibility as a Symptom of Gender Categories," in Moore and Scott, *Invisible People and Processes*, 187.

all ages think about children, behave toward them, teach them, learn from them, and order societies.

Conceptions of children and childhood inform and shape culture. At the same time, they may mislead adults into thinking that they understand children. Studies prove that events in the life of a child are perceived differently by children and adults, yet adults usually have the power and resources to gather, interpret, qualify, categorize, and disseminate knowledge of the experience.[3] Within a specific context, such as North America in the twenty-first century, people of different geographical regions, economic classes, ethnic communities, religious backgrounds, racial heritages, sexual orientations, and political beliefs, may have strikingly different ideas about children and approaches to raising them. These attitudes can also change quickly. For example, opinions about corporal punishment have altered dramatically in the United States over the past few generations. The parent's spank or the teacher's smack with a ruler, once commonly considered appropriate discipline, is now deemed by many to be child abuse. While parents remain convinced that their way of rearing children is most enlightened, history shows that their grandchildren may well choose other practices and feel equally justified. If such changes take place over a couple of decades, how much more might the customs of ancient Israelite culture vary from today's "normative" attitudes?

Theories of childhood recognize qualities that distinguish children as a group from adults. However, to discern these characteristics can become a circular process, as a particular culture encourages desired behaviors in its children. These preferences, in turn, serve a culture's understanding about who is a child and how a child behaves, influencing its concept of childhood. Social historian Catherine Burke explains that the concepts of childhood derive from a combination of ideas and technology within a specific social, economic, and political environment.[4] Historian Steven Mintz points out that studying the history of childhood helps scholars realize that present ideas are as exotic as those of any age.[5] Concepts of childhood emerge

---

3. Scholars frequently presume to understand children's worlds and perspectives without consulting children themselves. For discussion of methodologies in researching children, see Emily Cahan, Jay Mechling, Brian Sutton-Smith, and Sheldon H. White, "The Elusive Historical Child: Ways of Knowing the Child of History and Psychology," in *Children in Time and Place: Developmental and Historical Insights* (ed. Glen H. Elder, Jr., John Modell, and Ross D. Parke; Cambridge: Cambridge University Press, 1993), 192. See also Doris Bühler-Niederberger, "Introduction: Childhood Sociology—Defining the State of the Art and Ensuring Reflection," *Current Sociology* 58 (2010): 155–64.

4. Catherine Burke, "Theories of Childhood," in Fass, *Encyclopedia of Children and Childhood*, 3:818.

5. Steven Mintz, "Why the History of Childhood Matters," *JHCY* 5.1 (2012): 23. This comes from Mintz's presidential address to the Society for the History of Children and Youth (pp. 17–28) in which he argues that the study of the history of childhood has been unfairly marginalized.

from the realities of a given time and culture combined with theory, even when these beliefs about children remain largely unarticulated.

Philosopher David Archard notes that it is quite possible to have a general sense of children as different from adults without having a clear conception of childhood. He draws a distinction between the *concept* of childhood (recognizing children as different from adults) and the *conception* of childhood (in which those differences are specified and articulated). Archard maintains that there are "good reasons for thinking that all societies at all times have had the concept of childhood."[6] To discern how a culture views its children, Archard looks at the boundaries, divisions, and dimensions of childhood. Boundaries mark where childhood begins and ends, and offer insight about a culture's priorities. These liminal transitions may be manifest through rites of passage, independence from parents, legal definitions, or marital status. Divisions categorize the different phases within childhood and are marked by various terms (e.g., "infant," "toddler," "child," "adolescent," and "teenager").[7] Phases of childhood and youth are measured by levels of ability, responsibility, judgment, knowledge, and political power.

Yet even with an awareness of the varying boundaries, divisions, and dimensions of childhood, the distinctions between children and adults are not always tidy.[8] A teenager might be considered a child legally, but an adult sexually.[9] A person who is neurologically impaired may have the body of an adult and the mind of a child. Conversely, someone with a

---

6. David Archard, *Children: Rights and Childhood* (London: Routledge, 1993), 23.

7. These terms change with social and economic realities. For example, the word "tween" appears in the *Random House Webster's Unabridged Dictionary* as "a youngster between ages 10 and 12 years of age, considered too old to be a child and too young to be a teenager." See "tween" in *Random House Webster's Unabridged Dictionary* (New York: Random House: 2001), 2041. This relatively recent coinage coincides with the increased buying power of this age group. See David Siegel, Timothy Coffey, and Gregory Livingston, *The Great Tween Buying Machine: Capturing Your Share of the Multi-Billion-Dollar Tween Market* (Chicago: Dearborn Trade, 2004). Dating from an earlier period, the KJV uses the term "suckling" to refer to a nursing child (e.g., Deut 32:25; 1 Sam 15:3; 22:19; Ps 8:2; Jer 44:7; Lam 2:11; Matt 21:16). This translation dates from 1611 when babies were commonly entrusted to paid wet nurses and filled an economic niche.

8. When is childhood over (high school graduation? college? first job? marriage? parenthood?)? Celebrated rites of passage, such as Bar or Bat Mitzvahs, confirmation, *quinceañeras*, and debutante balls, do not generally alter a youth's daily life. The practical significance of communal commemorations of life transitions varies widely according to time and culture. For a helpful history of Jewish rituals that mark successive stages of life, see Ivan G. Marcus, *The Jewish Life Cycle: Rites of Passage from Biblical to Modern Times* (Seattle: University of Washington Press, 2004), esp. pp. 82–123.

9. Just as the line between childhood and adulthood is blurry, distinctions between male and female, once thought to be simple questions of biology or physiology, are now recognized as social constructs developed around common (but not universal) physical characteristics. For a brief but enlightening fantasy on the constraints of traditional gender

condition that limits physical growth may have the body of a child but the mind of an adult. A young teenager with her own baby may act like a child herself or may be the head of a household, depending on economic and cultural circumstances. While turning twenty-one becomes a legal milestone, a young adult may be financially dependent (perhaps as a college student) or married with children and supporting a household. Indeed, the same young person might be considered more of a child or an adult depending on a given situation or setting. How a society understands children says more about what is important to adults in a particular culture than it does about children themselves.

## Contemporary Western Assumptions about Childhood[10]

Our society has many assumptions about children, often defining them by what they are not, that is, adults.[11] Laws treat children and adults differently through adjusted rights and responsibilities; a "minor" is less than a full person in the eyes of the law. Children and adults often spend much of their days in separate spheres. What children do is called "play," which can be dismissed as "child's play," and what adults do is called "work," which bears the weight of importance. Yet, as social anthropologist Judith Ennew explains, "child energy is not frittered away in idle play or innocent enjoyment. Children work."[12] Children spend their time acquiring necessary skills and navigating a wide array of social networks. Their days are structured in school and other activities that carry expectations and demands, perhaps including sports, lessons, homework, chores, or paid employment. Ennew suggests that children's time is regulated to keep their schedules in accordance with those of adults. Childhood and youth are often understood as periods of training for adulthood.

---

theory, see Laurel Walum Richardson, *The Dynamics of Sex and Gender: A Sociological Perspective* (Boston: Houghton Mifflin, 1981), 3.

10. I use the term "Western" to refer to European and North American contexts. I recognize the ethnocentricity of the term, but find other alternatives verbose or confusing.

11. Ideas of limitations and inferiority often accompany conceptions of children. See Diana Gittins, "The Historical Construction of Childhood," in Kehily, *Introduction to Childhood Studies*, 26–28. Child rights advocate Joachim Theis notes that generally "Children are seen as immature, irrational, incompetent, passive, vulnerable, and helpless, as compared to adults who are perceived as mature, social, and autonomous." See Joachim Theis, "Participatory Research with Children in Vietnam," in *Children and Anthropology: Perspectives for the 21st Century* (ed. Helen B. Schwartzman; Westport, CT: Bergin & Garvey, 2001), 100. See also Archard, *Children: Rights and Childhood*, 29–41.

12. Judith Ennew, "Time for Children or Time for Adults?" in Qvortrup et al., *Childhood Matters*, 143.

Nonetheless, modern Western culture generally holds that children should be dependent, innocent, and carefree. Such universal characteristics are not foisted on adults. Children are viewed as entitled to happiness, but not privacy or autonomy. From about the age of five through their teenage years, young people are required to go to school to learn a wide range of academic subjects (regardless of their interests or aptitudes) and absorb many untaught rules about acceptable behavior. In exchange for protection, provision, and information, adults commonly expect courtesy and subordination from children.

Children's bodies are of utmost concern in Western culture.[13] Children are expected to grow and mature in accordance with their chronological peers; this physical development is charted by pediatricians and measured by parents. Parents are led to believe their children should be "normal," although definitions of "normal" are subjective.[14] People frequently ask how old a child is, whereas to directly ask the age of an adult is considered rude. Indeed, a child's age is presumed to be laden with information about this young person. Age is usually the determining factor for children's placement in school or organized group activities. Yet ages are also social constructs, not universal keys to unlock understanding about children.[15]

Adults are expected to earn their living, but children get an unquestioned free ride, now often well past teenage years. Parents who have their children contribute to work within the home often assign tasks to help instill a conscientious work ethic.[16] For a child to have a job and contribute to family income, as many children do in the developing world, is considered unfortunate.[17]

---

13. On the role of the body in understandings of childhood, see Allison James, Chris Jenks, and Alan Prout, *Theorizing Childhood* (Cambridge: Polity, 1998), 146–68.

14. Children with abilities and challenges beyond the typical population are frequently marginalized. See Jane Baker, "Disabled Children," in Wyse, *Childhood Studies*, 244–48.

15. For discussion of the history and development of age categorization in Western culture, see Howard P. Chudacoff, *How Old Are You? Age Consciousness in American Culture* (Princeton: Princeton University Press, 1989), 29–48. Grouping people by age finds some precedent in the biblical text (e.g., Lev 27:1–7); however, ages in the Bible are often rounded numbers (e.g., Gen 17:17; 21:5; 25:20; 26:34; 2 Sam 2:10; 5:4). This is typical of tribal societies in which lineage and generational rank are more important than chronological age. See Meyer Fortes, "Age, Generation, and Social Structure," in *Age and Anthropological Theory* (ed. David I. Kertzer and Jennie Keith; Ithaca, NY: Cornell University Press, 1984), 113–14.

16. A sociological study of 1,800 Nebraskan families found that most parents who assigned chores to children stressed the benefits to the child's work ethic. Relatively few parents cited a need for help. See Lynn K. White and David B. Brinkerhoff, "Children's Work in the Family: Its Significance and Meaning," *Sociological Review* 43 (November 1981): 792–93.

17. According to the International Labor Organization, over 300 million children labor to help provide for their families or to survive themselves, whether or not they receive wages. http://www.ilo.org/ipecinfo/product/viewProduct.do?productId=13313 (accessed January 2013). Many children work on farms or in domestic and factory work. Impoverished children

Given these expectations, children become powerful markers of an ideal society. Societies that view childhood as a golden age (read: romanticized years of no worries) induce nostalgia for bygone days.[18] If a child is denied a halcyon youth, adults feel that he or she has been "robbed" of childhood. Children come to epitomize what is right or wrong with a particular society. For example, a picture in the newspaper of a soldier carrying a machine gun may have little emotional impact. But if that soldier looks to be about seven years old, the image is shocking and sad. The same holds for photos of child war victims or prostitutes.

The emotional value of children can stem from cultural symbolism, personal attachment, or economic conditions. Sociologist Viviana Zelizer suggests that when children ceased to be common wage-earners in Western industrial society they became "economically 'worthless' but emotionally 'priceless.'"[19] However, these opposing values assigned to children need not be mutually exclusive. Farming families often depend on children as integral to the work of planting and harvesting crops, as well as tending to animals. Many children around the world also work in industries to help feed their families. The death of a child would be deeply mourned if the loss of wages threatens the family's survival. As socialist historian E. P. Thompson notes, "Feelings may be *more*, rather than less, tender or intense *because* relations are 'economic' and critical to mutual survival."[20] Children's emotional value can be inextricably intertwined with economic expectations.

While ideas of children as precious and pure appear to protect them, these lofty sentiments can be dangerous. Beliefs that children should be innocent can perpetuate ignorance, as adults withhold information that children might need for self-protection. More alarmingly, keeping chil-

---

may be forced to work as beggars or prostitutes. For further discussion of children and work, see James et al., *Theorizing Childhood*, 101–23; see also Hugh Cunningham, "Work," in Fass, *Encyclopedia of Children and Childhood*, 3:892; and Nicholas Medforth, "Children Working," in Wyse, *Childhood Studies*, 262–68.

18. For discussion of this idealization, see Judith Ennew, *The Sexual Exploitation of Children* (Cambridge: Polity, 1986), 18. On the development of nostalgia for childhood, see John R. Gillis, "Life Course and Transitions to Adulthood," in Fass, *Encyclopedia of Children and Childhood*, 2:547–52.

19. Viviana Zelizer, *Pricing the Priceless Child: The Changing Social Value of Children* (New York: Basic, 1985), 3. Zelizer documents how children changed from an economic asset to an economic liability around the turn of the twentieth century. At the same time, children increased in social value, and their lives became increasingly commercialized. For discussion of Zelizer's work, see Koepf, "Give Me Children," 28–31. See also the retrospective on *Pricing the Priceless Child* in *JHCY* 5.3 (2012): 445–484, especially the articles by Viviana A. Zelizer, "The Priceless Child Turns Twenty-seven" (pp. 449–56); and Paula A. Fass, "Viviana Zelizer: Giving Meaning to the History of Childhood," (pp. 457–61).

20. E. P. Thompson, "Happy Families," review of Lawrence Stone, *The Family, Sex and Marriage in England, 1500–1800*, *New Society* 41 (1977): 501.

dren naive can render them vulnerable to sexual predators. Molesters who would be titillated by violating those who are undefiled then turn to children for sexual stimulation. Communications scholar Jenny Kitzinger notes that media articles and programs against child sexual abuse portray such treatment as the ruination of childhood, implicitly assuming that childhood is usually untroubled. She observes that the image of childhood as a peaceful, asexual time of idealized play is "both ethnocentric and unrealistic."[21] Documentation intended to oppose child sexual abuse can inadvertently promulgate innocence as a sexual commodity. Once a child has been violated (or adulterated), he or she is often deemed as less deserving of protection.

Pedagogical theorist Henry Giroux observes that associations between innocence and childhood are explicitly linked to white children and are not automatically equated with children of color. Issues of class, frequently tied to race, play a huge role in determining children's futures.[22] Children are unable to vote, making it easy for politicians to overlook their struggles. White young people who are guilty of crimes have their behavior excused more frequently than African-American and Latino youth, who are incarcerated more often.[23] Giroux suggests that the language of innocence ignores gritty realities for poor children. He observes, "Historically poor kids and children of color have been considered to be beyond the boundaries of both childhood and innocence; they have been associated with cultures of crime, rampant sexuality, and drug use."[24] While Giroux's generalizations are broad, he highlights key questions of race and class that discussions about children often omit.[25]

---

21. Jenny Kitzinger, "Defending Innocence: Ideologies of Childhood," *Feminist Review* 28 (January 1988): 78.

22. Henry A. Giroux, *Stealing Innocence: Youth, Corporate Power, and the Politics of Culture* (New York: St. Martin's Press, 2000). See also Annette Lareau, *Unequal Childhoods: Class, Race, and Family Life* (2nd ed.; Berkeley, CA: University of California Press, 2003); and Robin Bernstein, *Racial Innocence: Performing American Childhood from Slavery to Civil Rights* (New York: New York University Press, 2011). By reviewing children's play things and other markers of culture, Bernstein argues that concepts of "childhood innocence" are central to racial identity and excluded black children and ignored other children of color until the Civil Rights Movement.

23. Giroux reviews the judicial language used to describe Eric Harris and Dylan Klebold, the teenagers who killed twelve peers and themselves at Columbine High School in 1999. Both had been in trouble with the law prior to this massacre but were sentenced to counseling and community service. This relatively lenient punishment, Giroux observes, is more often meted to white offenders (*Stealing Innocence*, 6–9). The U.S. Department of Justice reports that African-American males are 6.5 times more likely to be imprisoned than white males. Hispanic males are incarcerated over white males at a rate of 2.5 to 1. See Heather C. West and William J. Sabol, "Prisoners in 2007," *Bureau of Justice Statistics Bulletin* (Dec 2008): 4.

24. Giroux, *Stealing Innocence*, 9.

25. For discussion of race and childhood studies, see Russell Jones, "Ethnicity and

Recognizing common assumptions about children and childhood challenges presumptions about what is normative. To grasp a particular concept of childhood, anthropologists compile information about a culture's attitudes and practices toward children, as well as noticing the speech, strategies, and actions of children themselves. In addition, researchers stay attentive to unspoken manifestations of how children fare in a given culture. As in all societies, concepts of childhood commonly held by people today in Western society have their own history. More specifically, they are a legacy of the Enlightenment period.

## The Formal Study of Children and Childhood

### Enlightenment Thinkers and Their Legacy

The emergence of formal observations about children in modern Western culture dates to the seventeenth century.[26] Johann Amos Comenius (1592–1670) wrote concerning the education and treatment of children, and John Locke (1632–1704) observed children and commented on their nature, offering advice for their care. These works noted the distinct needs of children and offered counsel regarding their upbringing and education. They paved the way for later philosophers, notably Jean-Jacques Rousseau, who promulgated views that have greatly influenced how we understand children today.

Comenius endured difficult early years, which likely fostered his empathy for children.[27] His own harsh and turbulent experience in schools prompted him to try to reform education,[28] and he wrote *Didactica magna* in Czech in 1628–32, which was later translated into Latin. This progres-

---

Race," in Wyse, *Childhood Studies*, 239–43.

26. Burke, "Theories of Childhood," in Fass, *Encyclopedia of Children and Childhood*, 3:818. See also John Cleverley and D. C. Phillips, *From Locke to Spock: Influential Models of the Child in Modern Western Thought* (Carlton, Australia: Melbourne University Press, 1976), 11–21; and Neil Postman, *The Disappearance of Childhood* (New York: Delacorte, 1982), 56–62.

27. By the time Comenius was twelve, his parents and two older sisters were dead. His guardians robbed him of his small inheritance, and Comenius had to fend for himself. He was a Protestant born in Moravia (modern Czech Republic) and moved frequently throughout Europe during the course of his life due to the Thirty Years War and the violent, relentless religious disputes that ensued. For brief autobiographical sketches of Comenius's life, see John E. Sadler, *Comenius* (London: Collier-Macmillan, 1969), 5–16. See also M. W. Keatinge, trans., *The Great Didactic of John Amos Comenius* (London: Adam & Charles Black, 1896; repr., New York: Russell & Russell, 1967), 1–101.

28. Comenius reflects on his own harrowing years as a student in his allegorical pilgrim's tale, *Labyrinth of the World*. He relays that "fist, canes, sticks, birch-rods struck them [the students] on their cheeks, heads, backs and posteriors till blood streamed forth, and they were almost entirely covered with stripes, scars, spots and weals." See John Amos Komensky

sive treatise on education advocated mandatory, free schools for all children, including girls, with attention to children's care and development. Comenius suggested that education be organized on four levels following children's increasing abilities and progressing from parental instruction to elementary school, high school, and college. Children should learn various academic subjects, as well as personal skills for their own development.[29] Comenius's pedagogical innovations became so renowned that he was invited to become the first president of Harvard College. (He did not accept.)

Like Comenius, John Locke, the physician and philosopher, encouraged education for both girls and boys that took children's needs into account. In 1693 John Locke published *Some Thoughts Concerning Education*, a compilation of letters he had written to a friend offering advice for bringing up children.[30] Locke viewed the mind of a baby as a *tabula rasa*; a child eventually grew in his or her ability to reason. While parents did not own their children, they were entrusted with their care and usually had the children's best interests at heart. Locke urged adults to notice the characteristics of individual children. Having witnessed their cruelty, Locke did not believe that children were inherently innocent or kind. Still he felt that parents and teachers should help children develop judgment, virtue, and self-control without resorting to forced coercion or beating. These child-rearing strategies affirmed parents while respecting children. However, Locke was convinced that his approach seriously contradicted those of his contemporaries, and he was reluctant to make this collection of correspondence available to a wider audience. When he eventually did so (at the urging of colleagues), Locke published *Some Thoughts Concerning Education* anonymously. Before Locke died in 1702, this immensely popular book had appeared in four editions.[31]

Jean-Jacques Rousseau promulgated his Enlightenment philosophy about children in his novel *Émile* or *On Education*.[32] Ironically, Rousseau

---

(Comenius), *Labyrinth of the World and the Paradise of the Heart* (trans. Count Lützow; New York: E. P. Dutton, 1901), 116–17.

29. On Comenius's pedagogical program, see Matthew Spinka, *John Amos Comenius: That Incomparable Moravian* (Chicago: University of Chicago Press, 1943), 46–49. Jean Piaget relates Comenius's stages of child development to psychology in "Jean Amos Comenius," *Prospects* 23, no. 1/2 (1993): 173–96.

30. For further discussion of Locke's life and educational treatises, see James L. Axtell, *The Educational Writings of John Locke* (Cambridge: Cambridge University Press, 1968).

31. Locke's anonymity did not last long, and by the third edition (1695) Locke included a signed dedication. Over the course of the eighteenth century, *Some Thoughts Concerning Education* was reprinted over twenty times and translated into Dutch, French, German, Italian and Swedish (and later was translated into Spanish, Polish and Romanian).

32. Jean-Jacques Rousseau, *Émile ou De l'éducation* (Francfort [i.e. London?]): 1762. For discussion of the philosophical intentions of Rousseau's novels (*Émile* and *Julie*), see Tom Furniss, "Rousseau: Enlightened Critic of the Enlightenment?" in *The Enlightenment*

did not raise his own children, borne by his lover Thérèse Lavasseur. Instead he brought the infants to a Paris foundling home (a contradiction noted by his critics, including Voltaire).[33] Nonetheless, Rousseau dispensed advice for schools and parents. *Émile* was a philosophical argument, couched as a novel, urging consideration for young people in their natural state. Eschewing the Bible, a common tool for teaching literacy at the time, the character of the tutor (not so coincidentally named Jean-Jacques) entrusts the young protagonist, Émile, with a copy of *Robinson Crusoe*. Rousseau looked to reclaim human attachment to what is natural, which he found in children. In the preface to *Émile* he observes, "Childhood is unknown."[34] He then explains that adults presume to know what children should learn and how they should learn it, without paying much attention to children themselves. Rousseau urged readers to recognize the natural state of a child as a human being who is morally innocent, but still possesses knowledge that needs to be appreciated.

Rousseau's influence was profound. *Émile* encouraged the belief that "[c]hildhood has its ways of seeing, thinking, and feeling which are proper to it."[35] Romantic writers embraced this notion, extolling the innocent virtue of children.[36] Yet during the eighteenth and nineteenth centuries, many poor children worked under abysmal conditions in factories and mines with little societal regard for their needs. Eventually, the idea of childhood that had been maintained in the upper classes filtered down to less-moneyed people, and laws were passed in Europe and the United

---

*World* (ed. Martin Fitzpatrick, Peter Jones, Christa Knellwolf, and Iain McCalman; London: Routledge, 2004), 604–7.

33. In his defense, Rousseau claimed that the children would receive better care at this institution, which seems unlikely (at best). Given the miserable conditions in eighteenth-century orphanages, it is quite possible that his children perished at a young age. (John Boswell notes that the mortality rate could be as high as 90 percent in foundling homes. See John Boswell, *The Kindness of Strangers: The Abandonment of Children in Western Europe from Late Antiquity to the Renaissance* [New York: Pantheon, 1988], 432.) At first Rousseau expressed stunningly little remorse for abandoning his children, but he later came to regret this choice. In *Émile*, Rousseau warns, "I predict to whoever has vitals and neglects such holy duties [of raising his children] that he will long shed bitter tears for his offense and will never find consolation for it." See Jean-Jacques Rousseau, *Émile* or *On Education* (trans. Allan Bloom; New York: Basic, 1979), 49. For a more colorful (and perhaps apologetic) view of Rousseau's personal and paternal history, see Jaromír Janata, *Masochism: The Mystery of Jean-Jacques Rousseau* (Danbury, CT: Rutledge, 2001), 83–101.

34. Rousseau, *Émile*, 33.

35. Rousseau, *Émile*, 90.

36. See, for example, William Blake's "Songs of Innocence and Experience" or William Wordsworth's "Ode: Imitations of Immortality." Charles Dickens also portrayed his young heroes as naturally moral, as in *Oliver Twist* or *David Copperfield*. For discussion about children in Wordsworth, Blake, and Dickens (among others), see Peter Coveney, *The Image of Childhood* (Baltimore: Penguin, 1967). See also Judith Plotz, *Romanticism and the Vocation of Childhood* (New York: Palgrave, 2001), esp. pp. 1–85.

States intended to protect children.[37] The understanding of children as unique and distinct from adults, still prevalent today, first gained a cultural foothold with the publication of *Émile* and was further perpetuated in Romantic literature.[38]

The thinkers and writers of the Enlightenment and Romantic eras encouraged earnest consideration of children's lives. The influence of their works on modern views is evident, but can also bolster the seductive belief that our attitude toward children is on an ineluctable trajectory of "enlightenment" that increasingly benefits children. This alluring idea attracted Philippe Ariès, an intellectual child of Enlightenment thinkers. He is also often touted as the father of childhood studies.

## *Philippe Ariès and* Centuries of Childhood

Philippe Ariès (1914–1984), the French demographer and cultural historian, pioneered the modern academic study of childhood. In 1960, he published *L'enfant et la vie familiale sous l'ancien régime*, which soon appeared in an English translation entitled *Centuries of Childhood: A Social History of Family Life* (translated by Robert Baldick in 1962). In this landmark study, Ariès suggests that the concept of childhood as a distinct phase of life did not emerge until the end of the Middle Ages. Drawing largely on iconography (such as portraits, engravings, sculptures, tombs, and stained-glass windows), as well as some diaries and correspondence, Ariès attempts to show the four-century evolution of the concept of a child as distinguished from a miniature adult.

Ariès begins his study with a discussion of language in the Middle Ages, when, he suggests, "the *concept* of the family was unknown"[39] (emphasis added). He notes the absence or ambiguous usage of French terms for various phases of young life, such as "baby," "child," and "adolescent," and maintains that this lack of specific language about children reflected a dearth of understanding about them.[40] Ariès also argues that children were not really valued by their parents, or anyone else, until they were old enough to stand a strong chance of surviving. He observes that people at this time did not retain keepsakes from children who died young and infers that babies and toddlers were considered to be of little importance.[41] This was not due to parental callousness, Ariès adds, but

---

37. For further discussion, see Postman, *Disappearance of Childhood*, 52–56.
38. See Alan Richardson, *Literature, Education, and Romanticism: Reading as Social Practice, 1780–1832* (Cambridge: Cambridge University Press, 1994), 8–9.
39. Ariès, *Centuries of Childhood*, 353. See also pp. 405–7.
40. Ariès, *Centuries of Childhood*, 25–32.
41. Ariès, *Centuries of Childhood*, 38–39.

rather was a means of emotional self-defense since childhood death was relatively common. People in the Middle Ages were not advocating for the neglect or abandonment of children;[42] rather, they lacked awareness of children as having their own particular nature, according to Ariès. Once a child had reached the age of seven, he or she simply joined the world of adults.[43]

Ariès sees a progression from no concept of childhood (prior to the fifteenth century) to a period of coddling (fifteenth and sixteenth centuries) to an emphasis on discipline (seventeenth century). He explores aspects of children's culture, noting the rise of distinct dress, games, pastimes, literature, festivals and celebrations that gave children their own roles and social spaces. Ariès traces how the development of schooling as an institution for children contributed to the concept of childhood, as education became a prerequisite for assuming many adult responsibilities. Schools began to group students by age, and academic standards started to emerge in the seventeenth century. Earlier attention on the nurturing of children was replaced by a focus on training and chastisement. The newly perceived distance between children and adults resulted in increased corporal punishment for children and adolescents.[44] This harsh treatment began to wane in the eighteenth century (in France, before England, Ariès observes).

According to Ariès, the idea of childhood was fully developed by the seventeenth century. Scenes of families increased markedly in paintings, engravings, and calendars, distinguishing different stages of life through the family members. Previously much of the art had portrayed crowds and communities, which Ariès attributes to a lack of awareness about children and families. He observes the variations among classes and nationalities (all European), but highlights the evolving emphasis on private family life. Superseding individualism or communal activity, Ariès concludes, the family had triumphed.

Ariès's exploration of the history of childhood was overlooked at first; it did not fit with existing disciplines and so got few reviews.[45] Once noticed, however, the book caused quite a stir. Medievalists decried what seemed a callous disregard for the Middle Ages, as Ariès depicts people

---

42. Ariès, *Centuries of Childhood*, 128.
43. Ariès claims that the idea of childhood sexual innocence is a modern invention, since previously children had not been sheltered or cordoned off from adult sexual innuendos or activity. For example, Ariès argues that touching and fondling children's genitals, as repeatedly described in the diary that chronicled the childhood of Louis XIII, was not understood as sexual since children were thought to be indifferent to such activity. This diary belonged to Héroard, the doctor of Henri IV (*Centuries of Childhood*, 100–106).
44. Ariès, *Centuries of Childhood*, 262.
45. See Richard T. Vann, "The Youth of *Centuries of Childhood*," *History and Theory* 2 (1982): 279–97.

of this period as unfeeling toward their own children.[46] These scholars noted that Ariès ignores most of the medieval literary evidence, such as legal documents, church records, and medical writings, many of which acknowledge a separate nature of children. They charged that Ariès's documentation is often skewed or misleading. For example, he draws substantial evidence from the diary that describes Louis XIII's childhood, yet this could hardly be taken as representative of the early seventeenth century, since this boy was raised in a palace and destined to become king. Also, Ariès's chronology is far from precise, tracing the rise of childhood in various centuries as a particular piece of evidence indicated. Ariès proposes that a growing concern for children corresponds to a decrease in infant mortality, but this is not necessarily a cause-and-effect correlation. Ariès expresses "surprise in the earliness of the idea of childhood, seeing that conditions were still so unfavorable to it,"[47] but does not re-examine his underlying theory. He was also criticized for taking a literalist approach to painting, when styles in art simply change over time. The appearance of children in formal clothes looking like miniature adults in medieval paintings did not necessarily mean that children were understood as small-scale adults.[48] Ariès suggests that a lack of child-specific terms mirrors a disregard for children, yet an abundance of terms could reflect fluidity, nuance, confusion, or a lack of regard for their meanings.[49] Perhaps most

---

46. For a helpful overview of critiques of Ariès, see Albrecht Classen, "Philippe Ariès and the Consequences: History of Childhood, Family Relations, and Personal Emotions: Where do we stand today?" in *Childhood in the Middle Ages and the Renaissance: The Results of a Paradigm Shift in the History of Mentality* (ed. Albrecht Classen; Berlin: de Gruyter, 2005), 1–65. See also P. J. P. Goldberg, Felicity Riddy, and Mike Taylor, "Introduction: After Ariès," in *Youth in the Middle Ages* (ed. P. J. P. Goldberg and Felicity Riddy; York: York Medieval Press, 2004), 1–10. Other works that dispute many of Ariès's claims include Linda A. Pollock, *Forgotten Children: Parent-Child Relations from 1500 to 1900* (Cambridge: Cambridge University Press, 1983); Shulamith Shahar, *Childhood in the Middle Ages* (London: Routledge, 1990); Hugh Cunningham, *Children and Childhood in Western Society since 1500* (London: Longman, 1995); Ivan G. Marcus, *Rituals of Childhood: Jewish Acculturation in Medieval Europe* (New Haven: Yale University Press, 1996); and Danièle Alexandre-Bidon and Didier Lett, *Children in the Middle Ages: Fifth–Fifteenth Centuries* (trans. Jody Gladding; Notre Dame, IN: University of Notre Dame Press, 1999).

47. Ariès, *Centuries of Childhood*, 39.

48. Analogously, Valerie French notes that ancient Egyptians did understand people as having one eye, even though this is how human figures appear in Egyptian art. Valerie French, "Children in Antiquity" in Hawes and Hiner, *Children in Historical and Comparative Perspective*, 24 n. 2.

49. On the ambiguity of the many terms for children used in ancient Greece, see Mark Golden, "Childhood in Ancient Greece," in *Coming of Age in Ancient Greece: Images of Childhood from the Classical Past* (ed. Jenifer Neils and John H. Oakley; New Haven: Yale University Press, 2003), 16. For similar discussion related to medieval times, see David Nicholas, "Childhood in Medieval Europe," in Hawes and Hiner, *Children in Historical and Comparative Perspective*, 33–34.

important, Ariès was criticized for his pervasive "presentism," or his tendency to interpret the past through current concerns and attitudes. Ariès suggests that people in the Middle Ages had *no* concept of childhood, when what they lacked was *his* concept of childhood, shared by many in the modern world.[50]

Ironically, the strongest condemnation of this work highlights its greatest contribution. Ariès forced this realization: *Concepts of childhood that are different from our own are still concepts of childhood.* By chronicling some of the ways that children's lives have changed over time, Ariès points out the widening gulf between children and adults, at least in his European context. This separation should not be assumed for all cultures. Ariès also offered the first comprehensive study of the history of children and childhood that had extensive impact. By the 1970s, *Centuries of Childhood* was widely renowned, and Ariès's innovative suggestion that childhood had altered over the course of history proved to be hugely influential.[51] Yet, Ariès did not seem to recognize that his own view of childhood was subject to change or scrutiny as much as any other. The English title of his study might more palpably be translated as *Centuries of Childhoods*, for childhood changes.

## *Arguments after Ariès*

Ariès's views on the history of childhood are mixed. On the one hand, he seems to lament the divisions between the realms of children and adults that developed during the modern period. On the other, he understands history as progressing in its attentiveness to children's needs and vulnerabilities. At points Ariès sees the Middle Ages as the Dark Ages, making it hard for him to notice the bright spots in children's lives during this period. If this is a trap into which Philippe Ariès falls, it is the pit in which Lloyd deMause wallows.

In response to Ariès, deMause provided what he felt was a fuller representation of childhood history.[52] DeMause edited *The History of Child-*

---

50. See John Clarke, "Histories of Childhood," in Wyse, *Childhood Studies*, 3–12. Clarke essentially concurs with Ariès's thesis that "childhood didn't exist before the seventeenth century" (p. 3). However, only the *modern* concept of childhood had not yet come into existence.

51. Patrick Hutton suggests that *Centuries of Childhood* was so successful in part because it helped parents of the 1960s and 1970s place their own changing roles in historical perspective. See Patrick H. Hutton, *Philippe Ariès and the Politics of French Cultural History* (Amherst: University of Massachusetts Press, 2004), 109–10.

52. DeMause offered a psycho-historical approach to the study of children and founded the *History of Childhood Quarterly*. His work developed the theory of George Payne's *The Child in Human Progress* (New York: Putnam, 1916), which suggests that concern for protecting

*hood*, which begins, "The history of childhood is a nightmare from which we have only recently begun to awaken."[53] The tenor of the book descends from there, as essays document various forms of cruelty endured by children throughout the ages, beginning with classical antiquity.[54] Sensing that Ariès dismisses child abuse, deMause compensates by focusing on the mistreatment of children. DeMause criticizes Ariès's approach, but nonetheless supports his central theory by concluding that Western cultures largely disregarded (at best) any specific needs of children prior to modern times.[55]

Not surprisingly, deMause also elicited negative reactions from classical and medieval scholars who felt their eras had been rendered unfairly.[56] Harmful practices that deMause resoundingly denounces may have stemmed from benevolent intentions. For example, John Boswell argues that placing children in orphanages, which deMause largely ascribes to parental indifference, could be attributed to many factors, including the hope that a child might be adopted into a better life.[57] Louis Haas notes that sending infants to the country to be raised by wet nurses, also condemned by deMause, was often thought to be in the best interest of the child since the country was considered a healthier environment.[58] Linda

---

children only emerged in the mid-nineteenth century. Payne's book is clearly dated (and, to current sensibilities, blatantly racist at points [e.g., p. 11]), yet maintains that treatment toward children has become increasingly humane throughout history.

53. Lloyd deMause, ed., *The History of Childhood* (Northvale, NJ: Jason Aronson, 1974), 1.

54. DeMause suggests that parents in antiquity "routinely resolved their anxieties about taking care of children by killing them," and there was "widespread sodomizing of the child" (*History of Childhood*, 51).

55. For a succinct overview of the treatment of children in Western culture, see Benjamin B. Roberts, "History of Childhood: Europe" and N. Ray Hiner and Joseph M. Hawes, "History of Childhood: The United States," in Fass, *Encyclopedia of Children and Childhood*, 2:422–30.

56. E.g., David Nicholas describes *The History of Childhood* as a "hysterical lament." See Nicholas, "Childhood in Medieval Europe," in Hawes and Hiner, *Children in Historical and Comparative Perspective*, 31.

57. Boswell, *Kindness of Strangers*, 428–34. Boswell traces the history of child abandonment from its classical roots to the Renaissance. However, the archetypical story of the abandoned child goes back much further, as seen in the tale of Moses (Exod 2:1–10) and the eighth century BCE text recounting the exposure of Sargon of Akkad (ca. 2334–2379 BCE). See "The Birth Legend of Sargon of Akkad" (trans. Benjamin R. Foster; *COS* 1.133:461).

58. For discussion of the business of wet nursing, see Louis Haas, *The Renaissance Man and His Children: Childbirth and Early Childhood in Florence 1300–1600* (New York: St. Martin's Press, 1998), 89–132. Haas suggests that parents and agencies both took precautions to find suitable women who would care for the nursing infants. This contrasts with portrayals by other scholars. Elisabeth Badinter notes that approximately 21,000 babies were born in Paris in 1780 and all but a thousand or so were sent to wet nurses. These young women were often poor and lived in hovels; many infants died before the age of two. See Elisabeth Badinter, *Mother Love: Myth and Reality; Motherhood in Modern History* (New York: Macmillan, 1981), xix, 91–99. Badinter suggests that "the wet-nurse system was 'objectively' a disguised form

Pollock reviews nearly five hundred diaries from the sixteenth through the twentieth century and finds strong evidence of parental devotion and concern for children.[59] Shulamith Shahar examines childhood in the Middle Ages, and similarly concludes that care for an offspring's well-being was constant at this time.[60] Shahar underscores that practices that might seem harsh to modern sensibilities, such as sending a young child away from home to become an apprentice, could help a child to learn a trade.[61] These scholars raise well-researched and incisive critiques of Ariès and deMause, yet they risk romanticizing about childhood in history.

As these historians document, changes in the larger society fostered shifting family structures and altered children's roles. Lawrence Stone charts the evolution during the fifteenth through nineteenth centuries from the extended family to the single-family household, noting the rise of industrialized society and resulting demographic factors that helped to create close nuclear families. His class-based analysis observes that lower-class children were exploited and treated brutally, while upper-class children suffered from neglect and physical punishment. Stone concludes, "The only steady linear change over the last four hundred years seems to have been a growing concern for children, although the actual treatment has oscillated cyclically between the permissive and the repressive."[62] Edward Shorter explores the role of romantic love in the formation of family life and its implications for raising children.[63] Like Stone and deMause, Shorter views the eighteenth century as a turning point in child-rearing history. Many historians reasoned that the decline in infant mortality rates at this time spurred increased affection for children, since parents in earlier periods had tried not to get too attached to babies and small children who might easily die. Further studies, however, show that the parental response to a child's death centered on whether or not the

---

of infanticide" that, in effect, substituted for abortion. Badinter, *Mother Love*, 112. For further evidence of casual attitudes toward abandoning children, see Edward Shorter, *The Making of the Modern Family* (New York: Basic, 1977), 171–75. For a counter-argument, see Pollock, *Forgotten Children*, 51–52.

59. Pollock, *Forgotten Children*, 124–42.

60. Shahar directly contradicts Ariès and finds medieval parents highly invested in their children. She further asserts that in the Middle Ages "childhood was in fact perceived as a distinct stage in the life cycle, that there was a conception of childhood, and that educational theories and norms existed" (*Childhood in the Middle Ages*, 3).

61. See Shahar, *Childhood in the Middle Ages*, 223–41, esp. p. 237.

62. Lawrence Stone, *The Family, Sex and Marriage in England 1500–1800* (New York: Harper & Row, 1977), 683.

63. Shorter observes a dramatic difference between modern societies, in which mothers "place the welfare of their small children above all else," and traditional societies, in which "mothers viewed the development and happiness of infants younger than two with indifference" (*Modern Family*, 168).

child had been desired.⁶⁴ Accordingly, the rise in birth control led to more babies whose birth was planned. This fostered improved treatment for children, since parents wanted these offspring and felt better equipped to provide for them. Changing social, economic, personal, medical, technological, and demographic factors all exerted profound influence on children and families, redefining responsibilities and expectations.⁶⁵

## Continuing Changes in Childhood

Roles of children and understandings of childhood persistently change, perhaps now with unprecedented speed due to the rate of technological developments. In 1982 media critic Neil Postman suggested that childhood is quickly fading from our modern culture. Like deMause's *The History of Childhood*, Postman's *The Disappearance of Childhood* is largely a lament. Postman notes that sartorial distinctions between children and adults have blurred, and other aspects of children's culture, such as games, have become largely organized and controlled by adults.⁶⁶ He describes between 1850 and 1950 as "the high watermark of childhood." Although this was not an idyllic time for children, childhood came to be viewed as a distinct period of life to which every person was entitled.⁶⁷ However, Postman argues, television and print media have eroded childhood by bombarding children (and adults) with information that they are ill-equipped to handle. Further, he suggests that rapid-fire stories and images prevent audiences from understanding the implications of this input. Postman believes that the knowledge children gain via media has "expelled [them] from the garden of childhood."⁶⁸

---

64. For further discussion, see Mark Golden, *Children and Childhood in Classical Athens* (Baltimore: Johns Hopkins University Press, 1990), 82–91.

65. Badinter outlines the growing separation between women's and men's roles, which became accentuated during the Industrial Revolution. She suggests that the increased dependence upon women as children's caretakers led to the development of maternal love, which was an acquired social value, not a natural instinct (*Mother Love*, 168–201).

66. Postman, *Disappearance of Childhood*, 3–4. Psychologist David Elkind and education writer Kay Hymowitz also suggest that childhood has suffered in recent decades, although for different reasons. Elkind blames society and overworked parents who, in turn, demand too much of their children. See David Elkind, *The Hurried Child: Growing Up Too Fast Too Soon* (Reading, MA: Addison-Wesley, 1981). Hymowitz faults professionals in child-related fields who urge so much respect for children that adults largely relinquish their supervisory and instructive roles. See Kay S. Hymowitz, *Ready or Not: Why Treating Children as Small Adults Endangers Their Future—and Ours* (New York: Free Press, 1999). For further resources on the endangerment of childhood, see Sharon Stephens, ed., *Children and the Politics of Culture* (Princeton: Princeton University Press, 1995), 8–9.

67. Postman, *Disappearance of Childhood*, 67.

68. Postman, *Disappearance of Childhood*, 97. For a critique of Postman, see David

While Postman first sounded this alarm about the disappearance of childhood in the early 1980s, subsequent advances in technology make his concerns seem almost quaint. What does it mean for the nature of childhood when Internet access fills the air and children can instantly get information about every imaginable topic, regardless of how lurid or violent it might be? Can children be sexually innocent when they see commercials for Victoria's Secret that broadcast soft porn during prime time? What is children's relationship with the media as they share videos and create profiles that can be viewed by millions on YouTube and Facebook? When young people text and tweet each other, how much influence can parents have in monitoring their children's social lives? How does childhood change when children's ability to work with the latest technology routinely exceeds that of their parents? Do we understand children differently when our tech-savvy youth earn incomes that surpass those of many adults? If traditionally children are those who receive knowledge and care, and adults are their teachers and providers, how is childhood redefined when roles can be so easily reversed?[69] Even from our own lived experience, we recognize that childhood is constantly being reshaped. Childhood is not gone, as Postman suggests, but it changes along with society.

This historical and theoretical overview offers points to keep in mind as we turn our attention to the study of children in the Hebrew Bible. As mentioned previously, we need to be receptive to how the text presents children. To do this, we recognize our own ideas about children and the tendency to push the evidence toward them, so we can resist this urge. However, there may be features of childhood that have persisted in strikingly similar forms. When another culture shares a tendency of our own we tend to disregard it, presuming it to be normative and therefore not noteworthy. Yet any mutual similarities between childhood in the text and today are also significant observations, and not just assumptions of what automatically comprises childhood. Professed ideals or written laws about children frequently do not mirror children's lived experiences. Society's treatment of children is not inexorably improving for children's increased benefit.[70] Attitudes that may be foreign to us are not necessar-

---

Buckingham, "Television and the Definition of Childhood," in Mayall, *Children's Childhoods*, 80–81.

69. David Buckingham points out that children's access to technology can be viewed as a source of liberation or corruption, depending on how one understands childhood. See David Buckingham, "New Media, New Childhoods? Children's Changing Cultural Environment in the Age of Digital Technology," in Kehily, *Childhood Studies*, 115.

70. For example, child abuse kills three to five children daily, and homicide is among the top five causes of child mortality in the United States. See the Center for Disease Control report for 2010 http://www.cdc.gov/injury/wisqars/pdf/10LCID_All_Deaths_By_Age_Group_2010–a.pdf (accessed January 2013). See also Jill E. Korbin, "'Good Mothers,'

ily inferior. The material available for understanding children in history is skewed, since surviving attestations about the lives of children rarely come from children themselves. Nonetheless, children influence society, as they have throughout the ages. They are active participants in perpetuating cultures and significant agents in forming history, not just those who are acted upon.

We now turn to study the biblical text with a focus on children, but the text we study does not share our focus of interest. The stories of the Hebrew Bible are certainly not *by* children, nor explicitly *for* children, and only rarely *about* children. Rather, this literature simply *includes* children. As we search the text for the child characters and scrutinize their lives through thick lenses of time, language, and cultural differences, we cannot help but see dimly. Yet, it is still worthwhile to look.

---

'Babykillers,' and Fatal Child Maltreatment," in *Small Wars: The Cultural Politics of Childhood* (ed. Nancy Scheper-Hughes and Carolyn Sargent; Berkeley: University of California Press, 1998), 254–55; and Fewell, *Children of Israel*, 19–22.

## 2

# Learning about Children and Youth in the Hebrew Bible through Language:
*A Contextual and Linguistic Framework*

Since the Hebrew Bible does not directly divulge the ancient writers' views on children or childhood, we need to develop strategies to gain these insights. One helpful approach is to focus attention on words that designate young people. This chapter first asserts that children play an essential role in the Hebrew Bible since they are integral to its world and pervade the text. A brief discussion of linguistic theory then establishes that the vocabulary of a given culture reflects its realities. Next, this chapter examines terms for children and youth to increase awareness of their presence in the text and discover how these words convey the writers' ideas. I categorize these terms by family identity, gender, and stages of growth, and explore their context and usage. This overview helps build a foundation for the literary analyses in the second part of this book.

### The Presence and Value of Children

Children play a far greater role in the Hebrew Bible than most readers realize. The covenant established with Abraham is perpetuated through circumcision of infant boys (Gen 17:9–27; 21:4; Lev 12:3).[1] Without proselytization, ancient Israelites needed children to bequeath traditions to successive generations. Women and children are essential for this people to continue into eternity (see Gen 13:14–15; 1 Chr 28:8). Bearing children then becomes an obligation, envisioned as a vital part of creation (Gen 1:27–28) and integral to YHWH's covenant with the Israelites (Gen 9:7; 35:11–12). In the ancestral narratives, YHWH promises children as a sign of blessing

---

1. For an overview of circumcision in the ancient Near East, see King and Stager, *Life in Biblical Israel*, 43–45. While adult males are also circumcised (Gen 17:23–27; 34:14–24, Exod 12:43–48), circumcising children is central to Israelite identity (Josh 5:2–8).

(Gen 12:2–3; 15:5;[2] 16:10; 17:4–8; 22:17–18;[3] 26:3–4; 28:13–14). YHWH takes on dimensions of a fertility god (Lev 26:9), promising that none shall miscarry or be barren (Exod 23:26; Deut 7:14).[4] Yet what YHWH has the power to give, he can also withhold (Lev 20:20–21; 2 Sam 6:23 [?]; Hos 9:11–16; Isa 14:22). The Psalms celebrate children as a source of joy (Pss 113:9; 127:3–5; 128:3–4), and they are openly desired.

Women are vocal about wanting children, which is not surprising given children's integral role in the economic structure and societal pressure to bear sons.[5] Not only were sons considered necessary to continue the father's name and retain the family's inheritance, but grown sons and their wives would also care for the son's parents when they were older, whereas grown daughters would relocate to their husband's household. Childless wives struggle with their barrenness (Gen 16:1–2; 29:31–30:24; Judg 13; 1 Sam 1:1–20), or their husbands seek divine assistance (Gen 25:21). Inability to bear children is perceived as the woman's fault. However, not all childless women are desperate to become a mother (see 2 Kgs 4:13–16). Women also risk death in bringing forth life.[6] Both Rachel (Gen 35:16–19) and Phinehas's wife (1 Sam 4:19–20) die in childbirth, but female characters do not voice this fear.[7]

The text offers a few insights about the arrival of a child. Ezekiel 16:4 suggests that a newborn baby is first washed, then rubbed with salt and wrapped in swaddling cloths. Jeremiah 20:15 indicates that the birth of a child was announced with joy. The mother, father, or deity names the child, with women bestowing names on children in over half of the instances where naming occurs.[8] The weaning of a child is celebrated in

---

2. Upon closer examination, however, the promise here may be compromised. In Gen 15:5, YHWH takes Abram outside and instructs, "'Look toward heaven and count the stars, if you can count them.' Then he said to him, 'So shall your descendants be.'" Yet not until v. 12 does the sun set.

3. Cf. Rebekah's blessing in Gen 24:60.

4. Responsibility for the procreation of children accrues to YHWH as other deities are eclipsed. See Tikva Frymer-Kensky, *In the Wake of the Goddesses: Women, Culture, and the Biblical Transformation of Pagan Myth* (New York: Free Press, 1992), 85.

5. In most biblical narratives (save Gen 25:21), the barren mother (admittedly an oxymoron) seeks to have children, in contrast to other ancient Near Eastern literature in which procuring sons is the man's responsibility. For comparison of ancient Israelite and other ancient Near Eastern views on childlessness, see Mary Callaway, *Sing O Barren One: A Study in Comparative Midrash* (SBLDS 91; Atlanta: Scholars Press, 1986), 13–18. See also Marsman, *Women in Ugarit and Israel*, 241–42.

6. The World Health Organization estimates that 287,000 women died in childbirth in 2010. See http://www.who.int/mediacentre/factsheets/fs348/en/index.html (accessed January 2013).

7. Ironically, Rachel implores, "Give me children or I shall die!" (Gen 30:1), but in having children, she does die (Gen 35:18).

8. See Clarence Vos, *Woman in Old Testament Worship* (Amsterdam: Delft, Judels, and Brinkman, 1968), 161 n. 83.

Gen 21:8, but more often the birth of a child does not occasion a formal ritual or celebration.⁹ However, this is not to imply parental disregard for children among cultures with high infant mortality rates (*contra* Ariès). The text explicitly describes a father loving his child (e.g., Gen 44:20), seeing a child as a delight (metaphorically for Israel in Jer 31:20), and understanding children as a gift from God (e.g., Gen 33:5; Ps 127:3–5).

While children are not excessively doted upon, we do see great concern for children's lives and affectionate expressions of care and concern, especially from parents. Hagar fears for the life of Ishmael and weeps while her child suffers (Gen 21:16). Jacob notes the challenge of his children's ability to undertake a long journey because of their relative fragility, observing that their pace is different from that of adults (Gen 33:13–14). Moses' mother (named Jochebed in Exod 6:20 and Num 26:59) devises a plan to save her child's life (Exod 2:3, 6–9). Ruth bears a son and the women of Bethlehem celebrate, blessing and naming the child as he is held in his grandmother's embrace (Ruth 4:16). David, during his powerful reign as king, mourns and fasts as he pleads with YHWH for the life of his newborn child (2 Sam 12:15, 18–22). The prostitute who comes before King Solomon is willing to give up a child to save his life (1 Kgs 3:27); this devotion proves (or creates?) her claim on the baby. The wife of Jeroboam seeks a prophet's help for her sick child; when he dies, all Israel mourns his loss (1 Kgs 14:12). The widow of Zarephath beseeches the prophet Elijah when her son is dead (1 Kgs 17:17–24), and the widow of one of the sons of the prophets seeks Elisha's help to keep her children from becoming debt slaves (2 Kgs 4:1–7). The Shunammite woman refuses lackey assistance when she needs prophetic intervention to revive her dead child (2 Kgs 4:17–35), then bows to Elisha when her son's life is restored (vv. 36–37). These parents simply seem to care for their children whom they love.¹⁰

Beyond individual families, children and youth are key components in the general population. To acknowledge their role in society, readers should envision children as part of larger groups conveyed through common words such as עם, גוי, and לאום, as well as names of nearby peoples (e.g., פרזי, כנעני, אמרי, יבוסי, חוי, etc.) or foreigners (בני נכר נכרים). References to the people of Israel (בני ישראל) or tribes (designated with expanding terms: שבט/מטה, משפחה, בית אב)¹¹ include children. Even very young

---

9. E.g., Gen 25:23–26; 29:32–35; 30:1–24; 38:1–5; 41:50–52; Exod 2:2, 22; Judg 8:31; 13:24; 1 Sam 1:20; 2 Kgs 4:17; Isa 8:3; Hos 1:2–9.

10. For more detailed discussion of mothers and children, see Leila Leah Bronner, *Stories of Biblical Mothers: Maternal Power in the Hebrew Bible* (Dallas: University Press of America, 2004), 1–58. For essays that explore biblical mothers from a wide range of perspectives, see Cheryl A. Kirk-Duggan and Tina Pippin, eds., *Mother Goose, Mother Jones, Mommie Dearest: Biblical Mothers & Their Children* (SemeiaSt 61; Atlanta: Society of Biblical Literature, 2009).

11. On the fluidity of kinship terms, see Robert B. Coote, "Tribalism: Social Organization

children are part of the Israelite assembly (Deut 29:9–12; 31:11–13; Num 14:31; Joel 2:16; Ezra 10:1; Neh 12:43; 2 Chr 31:18), and viewed as the community's own remnant (Num 14:28–31).[12] Genealogies (תולדות) that focus on descendants suggest children obliquely. Other words that connote offspring (זרע, פרי, פרי בטן, נכד, נין, *צאצאים) or descendants (דור, מולדת) emphasize the need for children to perpetuate the covenant.

Children and youth are omnipresent in the text, although they are often overlooked. They are necessary for individual families, the covenant community, and the wider society to continue. We can become more aware of children's pervasive presence and critical role in this literature by attention to its language.

## Vocabulary and Understanding

Literature reflects a continuum of thought, word, and language creating a world that comes to life as ideas and images are transmitted from writer to reader. Vocabulary is essential for this transfer of information.[13] Anthropologist and linguist Edward Sapir asserts that a complete thesaurus of any particular society would provide a thorough index of its culture, occupations, and setting. He observes that "it is the vocabulary of a language that most clearly reflects the physical and social environment of its speakers."[14] Since words are bound to their cultural milieu, vocabulary conveys patterns of living.

Further considerations bear mention. A word's "meaning potential" encapsulates a range of interpretation. One word can be used in various ways, even by the same speaker or writer. The meaning of the same word can also change over time. A certain term can carry clear or subtle implications or be used in a nonliteral way. The writer may seek to bring out an ironic or metaphorical meaning in a particular context. Definition and context simultaneously shade the sense of a given passage.

In the quest for understanding, context trumps definition. Linguists

---

in the Biblical Israels," in *Ancient Israel: The Old Testament in Its Social Context* (ed. Philip F. Esler; Minneapolis: Fortress, 2006), 41.

12. Referring to children as implicitly included in the קהל varies. In Josh 8:35, Joshua reads Moses' commandments before כל־קהל ישראל והנשים והטף והגר, suggesting that the women, dependents (including children), and sojourner are in addition to the קהל.

13. Christopher Beedham maintains that language is "our vehicle of thought." See Christopher Beedham, *Language and Meaning: The Structural Creation of Reality* (Amsterdam: John Benjamins, 2005), 1. Anna Wierzbicka affirms that studying vocabulary "more deeply, more rigorously, and in a broader theoretical perspective" leads to a fuller understanding of a particular culture. See Anna Wierzbicka, *Understanding Cultures through Their Key Words: English, Russian, Polish, German, and Japanese* (New York: Oxford University Press, 1997), 31.

14. Sapir, *Selected Writings*, 90.

Michael Barlow and Suzanne Kemmer note, "Language does not hold or 'convey' meaning per se, but simply provides *cues* for meaning construction in context."[15] However, word choices also contribute to forming context.[16] The variety of words clustered around one concept clarifies nuances of definition. Therefore, an existing translation for a word may need to be re-examined due to its context. As Milton Eng points out, "words do not have meanings, meanings have words."[17]

Words grant access to another world, yet they also impede it. Since our culture is unlike that of the Bible, the terms we use in translation may carry different nuances. Sapir notes that "distinctions which seem inevitable to us may be utterly ignored in languages which reflect an entirely different type of culture, while these in turn insist on distinctions which are all but unintelligible to us."[18] Expanding our knowledge about children and youth requires close attention to a word's connotations, which may be different from its meaning in translation. We also may need to resist facile translations for convenience.

The writers of the Hebrew Bible convey their ideas about young people through the choice and placement of vocabulary to describe them. However, the forthcoming review of terms refrains from etymological discussion since most speakers and writers use words with little to no idea of their history.[19] When examining a culture so foreign to our own, conclusions must remain tentative. Still, through a study of vocabulary we can gain vital insights as to how the writers of the Hebrew Bible thought about children.

---

15. Suzanne Kemmer and Michael Barlow, "Introduction: A Usage-Based Conception of Language," in *Usage-Based Models of Language* (ed. Michael Barlow and Suzanne Kemmer; Stanford, CA: Center for the Study of Language and Information, 2000), xxi. While Michael Halliday notes that "text affects context even as choices determined by context are realized in text," linguists generally agree that context is the overriding factor in producing meaning. See Raqaiya Hasan and J. R. Martin, eds., *Language Development: Learning Language, Learning Culture. Meaning and Choice in Language: Studies for Michael Halliday* (Advances in Discourse Processes 50; Norwood, NJ: Ablex, 1989), 8.

16. Geoff Thompson explains that word choices are influenced by the relationship between speakers. He adds that "the influence is not one-way: while speakers show their understanding of what the context is by their choices, those language choices simultaneously create the context." See Geoff Thompson, "M. A. K. Halliday," in *Key Thinkers in Linguistics and the Philosophy of Language* (ed. Siobhan Chapman and Christopher Routledge; Oxford: Oxford University Press, 2005), 117–18.

17. Eng, *Days of Our Years*, 23. For detailed linguistic discussion, see his chapter on "The Quest for the Meaning of Words," 1–32.

18. Sapir, *Selected Writings*, 27.

19. James Barr explains that understanding should not be based on etymologies, which relate to a word's history, not its usage. See James Barr, *The Semantics of Biblical Language* (Oxford: Oxford University Press, 1961), 109.

46 *Valuable and Vulnerable*

## Words That Designate Children and Youth[20]

### Children in Families

בן and בת

The most prevalent common noun in the Hebrew Bible is בן (occurring approximately 4,850 times), indicating the centrality of the father-son relationship in this society based on kinship. Translated as "son" or (occasionally) "grandson" (e.g., Gen 11:31; 2 Sam 9:9–10; 19:24; 2 Chr 22:9), בן exhibits a broad semantic range. It can denote a member of a profession or association (e.g., בני־הנביאים: 2 Kgs 4:1; בן־חכמים: Isa 19:11; בני־הכהנים: Ezra 2:61); people belonging to a tribe or nation (e.g., בני־ישראל; בני־לוי: Exod 6:16; בני־בבל: Ezek 23:15); a certain type of person (e.g., בני־בליעל: Deut 13:14 [Eng. 13:13]; בני־חיל: 2 Kgs 2:16); a kind of animal, perhaps as offspring (e.g., בן־יונה: Lev 12:6; בני־צאן: Ps 114:4; בני־ערב: Ps 147:9); or an individual's younger follower or student (e.g., בני: 2 Sam 18:22; Prov 2:1; Eccl 12:12). The word בן may also be modified to suggest specific ages (e.g., בן־שמנת ימים: Gen 17:12; בן־שנה: Exod 12:5),[21] and frequently portrays a child. The plural בנים can also serve as a generic term for children. Like ילדים (or the Spanish word *niños*), בנים can incorporate girls (e.g., Gen 3:16; Exod 21:5; Ps 128:3), since females are often included in linguistically masculine terms.[22]

References to daughters are far less prevalent than the mention of sons (בת appears about 585 times). Along with expressing family relationship, the meanings of בת can extend to a people (e.g., בת־עמי: Isa 22:4; Jer 4:11) or nation (e.g., בת־בבל: Ps 137:8; בת־תרשיש: Isa 23:10; בת־ציון: Lam 1:6; בת־אדום: Lam 4:21). Characters designated as a בת can be babies (e.g., Gen 30:21; Exod 1:16; 1 Sam 2:21), girls (e.g., 2 Kgs 23:10), adolescents or young women (e.g., Gen 24:23; 29:6, 23; 38:2; Exod 2:7–10; Num 26:33; Judg 11:40;

---

20. For further attention to cognate terms, see standard lexica and theological dictionaries, e.g., F. Brown, S. R. Driver, and C. A. Briggs, *The Brown-Driver-Briggs Hebrew and English Lexicon* (repr., Peabody, MA: Hendrickson, 1999; Boston: Houghton, Mifflin, 1906); Ludwig Koehler and Walter Baumgartner, *The Hebrew and Aramaic Lexicon of the Old Testament* (rev. W. Baumgartner and J. J. Stamm; trans. M. E. J. Richardson; 2 vols.; Leiden: Brill, 2001); David J. A. Clines, ed., *The Dictionary of Classical Hebrew* (8 vols.; Sheffield: Sheffield Academic Press, 1993–2011); G. Johannes Botterweck and Helmer Ringgren, eds., *Theological Dictionary of the Old Testament* (trans. J. T. Willis, G. W. Bromiley, and D. E. Green.; 15 vols.; Grand Rapids, MI: Eerdmans, 1974–2006). For a more extensive list of lexical resources, see Eng, *Days of Our Years*, 157–58.

21. For hundreds more examples, see *TDOT* 2:145–59; *HALOT* 1:137–38.

22. This is explicit in Deut 12:12 as the masculine plural injunction שמחתם includes women, revealed by the parallel enumeration of אתם ובניכם ובנתיכם ועבדיכם ואמהתיכם.

21:7, 21), and women who are married (e.g., 1 Kgs 4:11, 15; 16:31; 2 Kgs 8:18, 26) or widowed (Ruth 1:11) (to cite a few of many examples).[23]

Often it is difficult to tell whether the terms "son" and "daughter" indicate a child or an adult, because the relationship or lineage is the focus rather than the age of the person so designated (as in genealogies, e.g., Gen 5; 11:10–32). Indeed, questions of age are irrelevant in some contexts. In other passages, the reference to a son or a daughter seems to portray a child, or certainly include that possibility. The mention of sons and daughters along with wives suggests dependent children who live with their parents (e.g., Exod 32:2; 1 Sam 30:3; 2 Sam 5:13; 19:6 [Eng. 19:5]; 2 Chr 29:9, 31:18; Neh 4:8 [Eng. 4:14]; 10:29 [Eng. 10:28]).

Sons and daughters often appear together. When these references are in the context of the household or clan of the father, בת indicates girls because grown (and thus married) daughters would be associated with the household of their husbands. For example, in Gen 46:7 Jacob moves his family: "His sons, and his sons' sons with him, his daughters, and his sons' daughters, and all his offspring he brought with him to Egypt." Jacob's sons and their children continue with the family tribe, including the unmarried (i.e., pre-pubescent) daughters. There is no reference to the daughters' children, presumably because adult daughters with offspring would no longer be counted in the clan of Jacob. Therefore, the mentioned daughters are probably girls who are not yet sexually mature.

While boys were circumcised and had privileges reserved for males (e.g., Num 3:15; 18:9–10; 2 Chr 31:16), daughters are also explicitly included in the covenant community (e.g., Exod 10:9; Lev 10:14; Num 18:11, 19; Neh 10:29 [Eng. 10:28]; 2 Chr 31:18). Children are needed to receive the family inheritance (נחלה), especially firstborn sons. This property can go to daughters in the absence of sons (Num 27:1–11), with the proviso that they marry within the tribe (Num 36:1–12). Daughters are not disparaged as inherently inferior offspring. Both sons and daughters are part of the prophets' visions of restoration and promise (Isa 56:5; 60:4; Joel 3:1 [Eng. 2:28]). The text shows parents who provide for them (e.g., 1 Sam 1:4), advocate for them (e.g., 2 Kgs 4:1), and fight for them (e.g., Neh 4:8 [Eng. 4:14]).

Andreas Michel points to a pattern when בן and בת are linked. Of the 120 instances where these terms appear together, 50 (or over 40 percent) involve violence with sons and daughters as the victims.[24] Michel observes that this number hinges on how one defines "violence," yet clearly sons and daughters may share grim fates. They fall prey to cannibalism (Lev

---

23. For further citations, see *TDOT* 2:332–38; *HALOT* 1:165–66.
24. Michel, *Gott und Gewalt*, 26.

26:29; Deut 28:53; Jer 5:17;[25] 19:9) and die violent and untimely deaths (Amos 7:17; Jer 16:3–4; Ezek 23:47; 24:21). They are taken captive (Num 21:29; Deut 28:32, 41; 1 Sam 30:3; Jer 48:46; Joel 4:8 [Eng. 3:8]; 2 Chr 28:8) and sold into slavery (Neh 5:5; cf. 2 Kgs 4:1–7).[26]

Sons and daughters also are sacrificial victims. Three separate narratives portray fathers driven to sacrifice children as a burnt offering (עולה): Isaac (Gen 22:1–14), Jephthah's daughter (Judg 11:29–40), and the Moabite king's son (2 Kgs 3:26–27). (Of the three, only Isaac survives.) Children can be slaughtered (שחט: Ezek 16:21; cf. Gen 22:10), taken away (לקח: Ezek 16:20; 23:25), sacrificed (זבח: Ezek 16:20; Ps 106:37–38), offered up as food for "idols" (אכל: Ezek 16:20; 23:37), burned (שרף: Deut 12:31; 2 Kgs 17:31; Jer 7:31; 19:5; בער באש: 2 Chr 28:3), and made to pass through the fire (העביר באש: Deut 18:10; 2 Kgs 17:17; 23:10). Some scholars understand העביר באש to portray child sacrifice, although this is debated.[27] Yet even the potential for sacrifice introduces another extreme calamity for children.

---

25. Jeremiah 5:17a portrays a gruesome scene of enemy vengeance, with the threat of children being eaten: ואכל קצירך ולחמך יאכלו בניך ובנותיך יאכל צאנך ובקרך יאכל גפנך ותאנתך. While sons and daughters are listed as two among eight comestibles (along with harvest, food, sheep, cattle, vines, and fig trees), translators try to mitigate this violent image. The KJV (similarly the ASV) translates as follows: "And they shall eat up thine harvest, and thy bread, *which* thy sons and thy daughters should eat . . . ," erasing (or at least obfuscating) the portrayal of child cannibalism.

26. Nehemiah 5:5 further indicates that daughters were sold before sons. Exodus 21:7–11 legislates the selling of a daughter as a servant (אמה), but the wider passage omits any regulation regarding the sale of sons. If girls were sold before boys, as these texts suggest, this could be because girls were valued more highly as workers, concubines, or potential mothers, and were therefore more saleable. Young women are also needed to continue patriarchal lines of inheritance. See Carolyn Pressler, "Wives and Daughters, Bond and Free: Views of Women in the Slave Laws of Exodus 21.2–11," in *Gender and Law in the Hebrew Bible and the Ancient Near East* (ed. Victor H. Matthews, Bernard M. Levinson, and Tikva Frymer-Kensky; JSOTSup 262; Sheffield: Sheffield Academic Press, 1998), 155. Joseph Fleishman, however, suggests that this legislation permits a father only to sell his daughter as a concubine, not a slave ("Law of Exodus 21:7–11"). Phyllis Bird reasons that girls were valued less than boys and so were surrendered first. See Phyllis Bird, "Poor Man or Poor Woman? Gendering the Poor in Prophetic Texts," in *On Reading Prophetic Texts: Gender-Specific and Related Studies in Memory of Fokkelien van Dijk-Hemmes* (ed. Bob Becking and Meindert Dijkstra; Biblical Interpretation Series 18; Leiden: E. J. Brill, 1996), 45–46. Either explanation as to why girls were sold before boys is plausible; both render girls more vulnerable. For further discussion of debt slavery in ancient Israel and its environs, see Gregory C. Chirichigno, *Debt-Slavery in Israel and the Ancient Near East* (JSOTSup 141; Sheffield: Sheffield Academic Press, 1993). Chirichigno notes that small landowners were pushed into debt by increasing social stratification (especially during the eighth century BCE) and were forced to sell their dependents, including children (p. 141).

27. For example, Rainer Albertz, following Moshe Weinfeld, denies that these texts refer to child sacrifice. He instead suggests that the expression of making sons and daughters "pass through the fire" describes a purification rite as a means of religious dedication. See Rainer Albertz, *A History of Israelite Religion in the Old Testament Period. Volume I: From the Beginnings to the End of the Monarchy* (trans. John Bowden; OTL; Louisville: Westminster/John

When they are paired together, "sons and daughters" appear to portray children. Not surprisingly, this phrase usually occurs with possessive pronouns, further underscoring relationships. The precious value of children is epitomized in Ezek 24:25b, where YHWH recognizes them as cherished: את־מחמד עיניהם ואת־משא נפשם בניהם ובנותיהם ("the desire of their eyes and the treasure of their lives—their sons and daughters"). When children become victims, the text presumes that their parents suffer, and perhaps the wider society. Sons and daughters become a powerful vehicle for showing what can be wrong or right with the people and their relationship with YHWH.

## אח and אחות

Like the terms בן and בת, אח and אחות signify kinship, although in a lateral instead of linear relationship. Both words designate full siblings and half siblings, without semantic distinction (e.g., 2 Sam 13:4–20). Some relations within the family have distinct terms (e.g., כלה "daughter-in-law," חתן "son-in-law," דוד "uncle," דודה* "aunt"), but relations are frequently inferred by context (e.g., אח meaning "nephew" in Gen 14:16; 29:15) or suggested by combined words (e.g., "cousin" בן־דוד: Jer 32:8, 9; בת־דוד: Esth 2:7).[28] Beyond family relations, the terms אח and אחות can describe peoples (e.g., Jer 3:8; Obad 10, 12; Mic 5:2 [Eng. 5:3]; Mal 1:2), function as forms of address (e.g., Gen 19:7; 29:4; Judg 19:23; 1 Kgs 9:13), suggest bonds of familiarity (e.g., Deut 18:15; 23:7; Neh 5:8), or serve as terms of endearment (e.g., 2 Sam 1:26; Song 4:9–12).

When אח and אחות indicate young people, themes of protection and rivalry emerge. Stories of youthful brothers, such Ishmael and Isaac (Gen 21:8–11) and Joseph and his brothers (Gen 37:1–27), show competition that runs from tense to fatal. Yet caring fraternal bonds also surface with little brother Benjamin in the Joseph novella.[29] The overwhelming emotion Joseph feels for Benjamin (Gen 43:30) illustrates ardent tenderness

---

Knox, 1994), 192–93. This interpretation seems unlikely since references to "making sons and daughters pass through the fire" appear in polemical lists of reviled practices. It seems more plausible that some forms of child sacrifice surfaced in popular worship. For views counter to Albertz, see Susan Ackerman, *Under Every Green Tree: Popular Religion in Sixth-Century Judah* (HSM 46; Atlanta: Scholars Press, 1992). Ackerman suggests that child sacrifice existed in Yahwistic circles despite Deuteronomistic teachings. See also Francesca Stavrakopoulou, *King Manasseh and Child Sacrifice: Biblical Distortions of Historical Realities* (BZAW 338; Berlin: de Gruyter, 2004).

28. For further discussion of family relations, see E. J. Revell, *The Designation of the Individual: Expressive Usage in Biblical Narrative* (Kampen: Kok Pharos, 1996), 29–40.

29. The prevalence of terms emphasizing Benjamin's youth suggest that he is a boy: אחיכם הקטן :42:13; הקטן את־אבינו :44:2, 12, 20, 23; קטן (with or without a definite article): 42:32; הצעיר :and ,34 ,[2x] 33 ,32 ,31 ,30 ,44:22 ;43:8: הנער ;[2x] 44:26: אחינו הקטן ;43:29 ;34 ,20 ,42:15: 43:33.

between brothers.³⁰ Unmarried sisters, young teenagers by modern standards, are desirable (e.g., Gen 24:60; 34:13–31; 2 Sam 13:1–20; Song 8:8). In the stories of Dinah (Genesis 34) and Tamar (2 Sam 13:1–29), brothers avenge raped sisters, who are probably in adolescence. Moses' sister watches over her baby brother in the bulrushes, seeking his safety (Exod 2:1–10).³¹ The family functions as a protective association, especially when children are involved.³²

Two scenes of interaction among brothers show a youthful lack of maturity. In Gen 37:1–11, seventeen-year-old Joseph gets in trouble with his brothers. First, he tattles on the sons of Zilpah and Bilhah (v. 2) with no reported motivation. He then receives a robe from his father, which brings into relief his preferential position among the brothers (v. 3) and escalates their hatred (v. 4). Showing little common sense, Joseph reports not one (vv. 6–7) but two dreams (v. 9) that symbolize his superiority over his brothers. In a powerful pun, the text reports twice (vv. 5b, 8b): ויוספו עוד שנא אתו—lit.: they [the brothers] increased (ויוספו) in hating him (i.e., יוסף). In 1 Sam 17:12–29, David's older brother, Eliab, is angry at David for coming to see the battle with the Philistines. His questions seem typical of an annoyed older brother who thinks his pesky younger sibling should be doing something else (v. 28), and they elicit David's defensive response (v. 29). These fraternal encounters show teenagers as callow, defensive, and hot-headed. The youthfulness of Joseph and David makes these portrayals more convincing, perhaps reflecting awareness that maturity and judgment come with age.

## בכירה and בכור

The term בכור indicates the firstborn of human and animal offspring. Generally the firstborn male is entitled to the birthright of primogeniture (בכורה), including extra status, power, and property over the other sons (2 Chr 21:3),³³ even when not most favored (Deut 21:15–17). Yet this picture of unquestioned inheritance is challenged in the ancestral narratives of Genesis as younger siblings repeatedly gain the place of primacy.³⁴ It

---

30. Just as Joseph feels his insides grow warm with feeling for his brother in Gen 43:30 (כי־נכמרו רחמיו אל־אחיו), the prostitute in 1 Kgs 3:26 also has stirring compassion for her infant son (כי־נכמרו רחמיה על־בנה). Both passages reveal visceral concern for a young and vulnerable child.

31. Readers presume this is Miriam (see Num 26:59), but nowhere in the passage is this sister named.

32. For analyses of selected texts that focus on sibling relationships (Cain and Abel; Leah and Rachel; Jacob and Esau; Joseph and his brothers; and Tamar, Amnon, and Absalom), see Anne-Laure Zwilling, *Frères et sœurs das la Bible: Les relations fraternelles dans L'Ancien et le Nouveau Testament* (Paris: Éditions du Cerf, 2010), 7–134.

33. See King and Stager, *Life in Biblical Israel*, 47–48.

34. For example, Ishmael, Esau, Reuben, and Manasseh are all firstborn sons without

should not be surprising that the Israelites, a relatively small and poor people in comparison with those of the great Mesopotamian and Egyptian empires, would want to tell stories about the supremacy of an unexpected winner. Yet the changing place of the בכור calls the role and status of the "firstborn," as well as the translation of בכור, into question.

The female בכירה probably suggests the older of two sisters. This term only appears in the stories of Lot's daughters (Gen 19:31, 33, 34, 37), Leah and Rachel (Gen 29:26), and Merab and Michal (1 Sam 14:49). In all cases, the בכירה contrasts a younger sibling who is designated as either צעירה (Gen 19:31, 34, 38; 29:26) or קטנה (1 Sam 14:49). Leah and Merab, the בכירה daughters of Laban and Saul respectively, are to be married before their younger siblings, recognizing that birth order matters among girls (Gen 29:26; 1 Sam 18:17–21). In the story of Lot's daughters, the בכירה shows initiative, planning the incestuous encounter with their father (Gen 19:31–32) and instructing her younger sister (Gen 19:34). Lot's younger daughter remains silent, suggesting the older daughter is a leader. Usage of בכירה shows that the writers took notice of girls and their relationships within the family, as well as the appropriate order for marriage. However, the בכירה does not bear the same responsibilities as the בכור.

To be the בכור is a weighty position. This son is marked for sacrifice, although some texts arrange for substitution, either by animals (Exod 13:11–15; 34:20; Num 18:15; cf. Gen 22:13 [although Isaac is not Abraham's firstborn]), the consecration of the Levites (Num 3:12–13, 39–45; 8:15–18), or monetary compensation (Num 3:46–51). In other passages, YHWH's ownership of the בכור stands unmitigated (Exod 22:28 [Eng. 22:29]; Neh 10:36–38 [Eng. 10:35–37]). The killing of the Egyptian firstborn is anticipated (Exod 4:23; 11:5; 12:12), described (Exod 12:29; Num 3:13; 8:17), and celebrated (Pss 78:51; 105:36; 135:8; 136:10).

The prophet Micah recounts appropriate sacrifices, including the firstborn (Mic 6:6–7). The list appears to crescendo with increasing opulence. After burnt offerings, year-old calves, thousands of rams, and tens of thousands of rivers of oil comes the most prized offering: the firstborn. The poet emphasizes the visceral connection to the giver for this gift is "the fruit of my body" (פרי בטני, v. 7b).[35] The firstborn appears honored above other children, and therefore designated for YHWH. However, passages describing the sacrifice of the firstborn do not necessarily mean

---

according privilege. For detailed discussion of this pattern in Genesis, see Roger Syrén, *The Forsaken First-Born: A Study of a Recurrent Motif in the Patriarchal Narratives* (JSOTSup 133; Sheffield: Sheffield Academic Press, 1993). Syrén views these stories as an effort of the postexilic community to rebuild its identity as those who are chosen, but also reconciled with neighboring peoples (pp. 142–45).

35. The term בטן can refer specifically to the "womb" (see Num 5:22; Isa 49:15; Prov 31:2; Job 3:10), as well as to the body or belly more generally.

that such customs were carried out, much less widespread. These texts offer good examples of writings that probably do not reflect ancient life. As Frederick Greenspahn observes, "Requiring the death of all firstborns would be tantamount to societal suicide."[36]

Nonetheless YHWH has vested interest in the בכור. In Exod 4:22, YHWH instructs Moses to tell Pharaoh בני בכרי ישראל: "Israel is my firstborn son," conveying their fierce and intimate bond. YHWH not only cares for Israel, but will advocate for his people, as one would do for a firstborn child. This arrangement carries both symmetry and irony. YHWH loves Israel as a בכור; unless the Egyptian king allows this בכור to live in freedom, the בכור of the Egyptians must die (Exod 4:23). YHWH speaks of the Israelites' status as firstborn to affirm his relationship with the people. Yet ironically, the Israelites are to relinquish their firstborn to YHWH for sacrifice, not safety. At the core of either exchange is the value of the firstborn, and how painful and meaningful it would be to part with this child.

References to the בכור carry nuances about relationship and can be used to express a special bond instead of a literal emphasis on primogeniture (see Deut 21:16). Greenspahn suggests that the meaning of בכור is tied to concepts of youth.[37] This term recognizes the first male offspring in a family and can also signify favored children and youth. This exalted position may be due to birth order, and translated as "firstborn," but is not limited to this meaning.

### חמישית, רביעית, שלישית, שנית, and צעיר, קטן, etc.

Other siblings are designated by adjectives suggesting their younger status, or by ordinal numbers indicating their place in the line of offspring (1 Sam 17:13; 2 Sam 3:2–5; 1 Chr 2:13–15; 3:1–3, 15; 8:1–2; 12:10–14 [Eng. 12:9–13]). The terms צעיר and קטן can indicate the youngest child in the family or comparative smallness. The abstract of צעיר indicates youth (*צעירה: Gen 43:33). The words צעיר and בכור are often contrasted (e.g., Gen 19:31–38; 29:26; 43:33; 48:14; Josh 6:26; 1 Kgs 16:34); similarly קטן is frequently juxtaposed with גדול (e.g., Jer 6:13; 16:6; 31:34; Jonah 3:5; Ps 115:13; Esth 1:5, 20; 2 Chr 31:15; 34:30). These pairs appear as lexical associates, and often function as merisms.[38] As a qualifying adjective, קטן can suggest a child by modifying age-ambiguous nouns, such as בן (e.g., 2 Sam 9:12), נער (e.g., 1 Kgs 11:17; 2 Kgs 2:23; 5:2), or ילד (e.g., Gen 44:20). To be קטן can

---

36. Frederick E. Greenspahn, *When Brothers Dwell Together: The Preeminence of Younger Siblings in the Hebrew Bible* (New York: Oxford University Press, 1994), 35. For further discussion, see pp. 30–36.

37. Greenspahn, *When Brothers Dwell Together*, 69.

38. The lexical pair גדל/קטן exists in English (little/big), but בכור/צעיר has no easy English equivalent, perhaps because our culture does not emphasize the role of the firstborn. When paired with צעיר, בכור may simply indicate being older.

also have a derogatory connotation as "insignificant," or "weak," as in English (e.g., to be of "little" importance).

Passages in Jeremiah show the צעירים facing challenges. In Jer 14:3 they try (unsuccessfully) to seek water; these could be "little ones" (ASV, KJV), "lads" (JPS), or "servants" (NIV, NJPS, NRSV). In context any of these translations is plausible, showing the connection between children and service, seen also with the word נער. If we understand these water-gatherers to be children, this passage portrays young people exhibiting strong emotion as they cover their heads in shame and humiliation (v. 3bβ: בשו והכלמו וחפו ראשם). This would also show the value of children's labor in tasks necessary for survival, along with their painful recognition of failure. In Jer 48:4, צעירים is consistently translated as "little ones" (e.g., ASV, JPS, KJV, NIV, NRSV [NJPS: "young ones"]), as the children of Moab cry out amidst destruction. Along with Jer 14:3, Jer 48:4 shows צעירים suffering. The distress of the צעירים heightens the anguish in both passages as pervasive drought and destruction affect children. No one is spared, increasing the tension of the prophecy. These images may reflect empathy for suffering children and reveal an implicit sense of responsibility to protect them.

## Children without Families

יתום

In a society organized around families, perhaps no character is as powerless as the orphan. The word יתום has cognates in Syriac, Ugaritic, Phoenician, Aramaic, Arabic, and Ethiopic,[39] reflecting widespread awareness of the social reality of children without parents. Verbs that refer to the יתום as their object include "afflict" (ענה [piel]: Exod 22:21–22 [Eng. 22:22–23]), "snatch" (גזל: Job 24:9), "abandon" (עזב: Jer 49:11), "not have compassion" (לא רחם [piel]: Isa 9:16), "plunder" (בזז: Isa 10:2), "oppress" (עשק: Jer 7:6; Zech 7:10; ינה [hifil]: Ezek 22:7), and "murder" (רצח [piel]: Ps 94:6).[40] These actions suggest a range of sad fates for orphans.

Along with the widow and sojourner, the orphan is frequently characterized by defenselessness and destitution.[41] Protection of the orphan, widow, and sojourner has a long and documented history in the ancient

---

39. *HALOT* 1:451.
40. For further examples, see "יתום" *DCH* 4: 342.
41. Not all widows were ipso facto impoverished. On this point, see Karel van der Toorn, "Torn between Vice and Virtue: Stereotypes of the Widow in Israel and Mesopotamia," in *Female Stereotypes in Religious Traditions* (ed. Ria Kloppenborg and Wouter J. Hanegraaff; SHR 66; Leiden: E. J. Brill, 1995), 5.

Near East.[42] However, scholars question the reliability of this legislation. As Mark Sneed notes, laws regarding care for the poor in the Covenant and Holiness Codes (Exod 23:1–11; Lev 25:1–7, 35–37) and Deuteronomic injunctions (Deut 24:17–21) are apodictic, lacking penalty for those who fail to comply. Sneed maintains that these rules actually served the elite, allowing them to express moral sensitivity but not forcing them to act accordingly.[43] Prophetic admonishments suggest that the widow, orphan, and sojourner continue to suffer, despite legislation.[44]

English translations frequently render יתום as "fatherless."[45] This makes sense in Exod 22:23 (Eng. 22:24), Ps 109:9, and Lam 5:3, but should not hold for the entire Hebrew Bible. The frequent pairing of אלמנה with יתום may lead translators to assume that the orphans are the widow's children, and therefore have their mother. Of the forty-two instances where יתום appears in the Hebrew Bible, fifteen pair the widow (אלמנה) with the orphan, and eighteen include the sojourner (גר) in a triad of oppression. No one suggests a blood connection between the sojourner and the orphan, although interpreters often presume the orphan belongs to the widow. As J. Renkema points out, the widow in 2 Kgs 4:1 does not refer to her offspring as "orphans"; rather they are "my children" (ילדי).[46] It seems very likely that a יתום can be an orphan without both parents or a child without a father. To translate יתום only as "fatherless" excludes the possibility of children without any parents and minimizes the vulnerability of such a child's life.

Abandoned children might also have been considered orphans. Naomi Steinberg describes Ishmael's fate as "double abandonment"—first by Abraham (Gen 21:14) and then by Hagar (Gen 21:15). Although Ishmael is never called an "orphan," and indeed has his mother into adulthood (Gen

---

42. See F. Charles Fensham, "Widow, Orphan, and the Poor in Ancient Near Eastern Legal and Wisdom Literature," *JNES* 21 (1962): 129–39.

43. Mark Sneed, "Israelite Concern for the Alien, Orphan, and Widow: Altrusim or Ideology?" *ZAW* 111 (1999): 498–507, see esp. p. 504. For further discussion on these laws, see Donald E. Gowan, "Wealth and Poverty in the Old Testament: The Case of the Widow, the Orphan, and the Sojourner," *Int* 41 (1987): 341–53.

44. See Isa 1:17, 23; 9:16 (Eng. 9:17); 10:2; Jer 5:28; 7:6; 22:3; 49:11; Ezek 22:7; Zech 7:10; and Mal 3:5. For discussion of YHWH as an advocate for the orphan, see Walter Brueggemann, "Vulnerable Children, Divine Passion, and Human Obligation," in Bunge, *Child in the Bible*, 411–20.

45. The ASV, KJV, JPS, NIV, and RSV translate יתום as "fatherless" in nearly every occurrence.

46. See J. Renkema, "Does Hebrew *ytwm* Really Mean 'Fatherless'?" *VT* 45 (1995): 121. Renkema also notes that the יתום of Job 24:9 who is snatched from the breast may or may not be the woman's child (p. 120). Harold Bennett discusses Deuteronomy 12–26 and concludes if the יתום had a father, this paternal figure either did not or could not help his child. See Harold V. Bennett, *Injustice Made Legal: Deuteronomic Law and the Plight of Widows, Strangers, and Orphans in Ancient Israel* (Grand Rapids, MI: Eerdmans, 2002), 48–56.

21:21), Steinberg argues that focusing solely on the term יתום causes scholars to miss other marginalized and disenfranchised children. Stories with the verbs עזב ("abandon"), נתש ("uproot"), and the *hifil* of שלך ("throw" "cast") may point to additional children who fall outside the accepted and expected protection of a family.[47]

## Youth

The distinctions between youth and adulthood are blurry since the text does not offer accounts of crossover rituals or indicate clear delineation between one life phase and the next. It is tempting to make the divider between these phases hinge on marriage, but this is a demarcation for our own convenience that the text does not consistently uphold. Vocabulary for older youth does not distinguish between those who are married and those who are not. As Andreas Kunz-Lübcke notes, Joel 1:8 and Mal 2:14 both portray people married in their youth (נעורים). Kunz-Lübcke further states, "Verheiratung und Jugendlichkeit schließen sich für Mann und Frau nicht gegenseitig aus—im Gegenteil, sie bedingen einander." ("Marriage and youth are not mutually exclusive for man and woman—on the contrary, they require each other.")[48] At the same time, there is a point at which terms for youth no longer apply to a full-grown person.

While marriage is not a firm dividing line between youth and adulthood, it does provide one benchmark to note the progression between stages of life. The difference between life before and after marriage might have been noticed more in the lives of young women than young men. A girl would be expected to marry shortly after the onset of menstruation and move to the household of her husband, altering her life significantly.[49] Men would be past teenage years upon marriage (see Gen 25:20; 26:34; 41:45–46), presumably at least ten years older than young women (really, adolescents) (see Gen 17:17).[50] This gap in marriageable ages allowed men to prove their development through competence in military, economic, or social spheres.[51] Young men had to gain enough social standing to progress beyond dependency, showing that they could bear more responsi-

---

47. Steinberg, "Toward a Sociology of Childhood in the Hebrew Bible," 163–64. For examples of שלך in violent contexts, see Michel, *Gott und Gewalt*, 92.

48. Andreas Kunz-Lübcke, "Wahrnehmung von Adoleszenz in der Hebräischen Bibel und in den Nachbarkulturen Israels," in *"Schaffe Mir Kinder,"* 188. My translation.

49. Kunz-Lübcke suggests that girls were viewed as most beautiful and desirable at this age (see Ezek 16:7–8) ("Wahrnehmung von Adoleszenz," 186–87).

50. For comparison with other ancient Near Eastern cultures, see Eng, *Days of Our Years*, 54.

51. See Kunz-Lübcke, "Wahrnehmung von Adoleszenz," 167–68.

bility. Words for youth reflect this liminal stage for both young men and young women.

## עלמה and עלם

The masculine noun עלם connotes youth with attested feminine and abstract forms. The abstract *עלומים occurs four times in the Hebrew Bible (Isa 54:4; Ps 89:46 [Eng. 89:45]; Job 20:11; 33:25). In Job 33:25, עלומים is juxtaposed with נער, suggesting parallel connotations of youth. This verse notes a young person's fresh flesh, observing a physical distinction between children and adults (see also 2 Kgs 5:14).

The only references to עלם appear in near textual proximity (1 Sam 17:56; 20:22), perhaps suggesting that this word was known or favored by a particular author or during a specific time period.[52] In both citations עלם is so closely associated with נער that nuances or distinctions in meaning are difficult to determine. In 1 Sam 17:55, Saul seeks information about the youth who has killed the giant Philistine and inquires, בן־מי־זה הנער ("whose son is this lad?"). When Abner is unable to answer, Saul asks again, honing his question, בן־מי־זה העלם ("whose son is this boy?" v. 56). Perhaps Saul is being more specific, since נער has a wide range of meaning (discussed below) and עלם appears to suggest a boy. Still uninformed, Saul asks David the same question directly, but switches back to נער: בן־מי אתה הנער ("whose son are you, lad?" v. 58). Interestingly, David is the only character referred to as an עלם until he uses the word himself. In 1 Sam 20:21b, David explains to Jonathan אם־אמר אמר לנער הנה החצים ממך ("If I say to the lad, 'Look, the arrows are on this side of you'") and in v. 22 reiterates the instructions, substituting כה for אמר and עלם for נער: אם־כה אמר לעלם הנה החצים ממך ("If I say thus to the boy, 'Look, the arrows are on this side of you'"). When the character who will fetch the arrows appears (1 Sam 20:35), he is a נער קטן. Once this boy has been described as a נער קטן, the text simply refers to him as a נער (vv. 36 [2x], 37 [2x], 38 [2x], 39, 40). The initial qualification of קטן implies that עלם connotes a youthful נער. Eng suggests that נער קטן designates a boy who is beyond the toddler stage but before puberty.[53] As in 1 Sam 17:56, the term עלם in 1 Sam 20:22 seems to portray a boy, sharpening the focus of the polysemous נער, which is not necessarily age-specific. Like נער, עלם appears to link youth and service.

The female עלמה suggests a girl or teenager. Some occurrences presume sexual maturity (Isa 7:14; Prov 30:19; Song 1:3; 6:8), whereas others could cover a broad spectrum of ages (Gen 24:43; Exod 2:8; Ps 68:26

---

52. *HALOT* 1:835 gives a third possible reference, also clustered near these two other citations, in 1 Sam 16:12 (admittedly conjectural), substituting עלם for עם. BDB, 761, suggests the same emendation might also belong in 1 Sam 17:42. These readings are logical, although they lack textual support.

53. Eng, *Days of Our Lives*, 76.

[Eng. 68:25]). The image of girls as celebrating musicians in Ps 68:26 may be further supported by Pss 9:1, 46:1, and 1 Chr 15:20 in which על־עלמות may mean [singing] "in the style of young girls."[54] These passages show a range of roles for girls or young women who bear children, tend to their care, work as part of the family economic unit, and join in celebrations.

Perhaps the most comprehensive portrait of an עלמה is that of Rebekah. In Genesis 24, Abraham's respected servant (עבדו זקן) has gone seeking a wife for Isaac (אשה: vv. 3, 4, 5, 7, 8, 39, 40, 44, 51, 67). He prays that YHWH will send a נערה who will water the camels, thus revealing herself as the future bride (v. 14). On cue, Rebekah emerges with her water jar, as the text underscores her proper patrilineal connections (v. 15). Her suitability for marriage is made clear through her family ties (בת: vv. 23, 24, 47, 48; אחות: vv. 30, 59, 60), youth (and capacity to work?) (נערה: vv. 14, 16, 28, 55, 57), and nubility (בתולה: v. 16; עלמה: v. 43). She is טבת מראה מאד (very pretty), a בתולה (the right age for marrying), and איש לא ידעה (a virgin) (v. 16). The servant later tells Laban that he had asked YHWH to send an עלמה (v. 43), not a נערה as in his initial petition (v. 14). Perhaps Abraham's servant wants to remove any servile connotation when he speaks of Rebekah to her family. As with the masculine עלם and נער, עלמה appears to focus on one aspect of נערה, indicating a young person before adulthood.

This scene in Genesis 24 offers insight into the role and responsibilities of an עלמה. Rebekah's future husband is a generation older than she is; Isaac is the son of Abraham, while Rebekah is his great niece (v. 15). She is an industrious worker (vv. 16–20) who is able to invite guests to the family home (vv. 23–25). The servant has come with expensive gifts (vv. 22 [even noting the cash value], 53), showing her worth as a bride. However, Rebekah is not chattel; her brother and mother consult with her before she decides to go with the servant (vv. 54–58). She leaves her family with her nurse (מנקתה, v. 59), her maids (נערתיה, v. 61), and a blessing (v. 60). Indeed, the text underscores Rebekah's importance as this blessing (v. 60) harkens back to Abraham (see Gen 22:17). Like Abraham (see Gen 18:1–8), Rebekah is articulate, industrious, hospitable, and energetic. A young woman is bound to her family of origin and then the family of her husband, yet she can have authority, respect, and some autonomy.

## בתולה and בחור

Both בתולה and בחור refer to teenagers or young adults, yet merit brief discussion as the ending echelons of youth. While not semantically related, these words appear as male and female counterparts since they are frequently paired together (Deut 32:25; Isa 23:4; 62:5; Jer 51:22; Ezek 9:6; Amos 8:13; Zech 9:17; Pss 78:63; 148:12; Lam 1:18; 2:21; 2 Chr 36:17).

---

54. See *HALOT* 1:836 and BDB, 761. BDB reads על־עלמות for על־מות and adds Ps 48:15 (Eng. 48:14) as portraying soprano singing.

A בחור may be married (Isa 62:5) and have children (Jer 11:22). The בחורים appear in scenes of battle and are often made to suffer (Isa 31:8; Jer 48:15; 49:26; 51:3). They are felled by the sword (2 Kgs 8:12; Jer 11:22; 18:21; Amos 4:10; Lam 2:21), shattered (Jer 51:22), taken into captivity (Lam 1:18), slain (Ps 78:31), crushed (Lam 1:15), and put to forced labor (Isa 31:8; Lam 5:13). They stumble (Isa 40:30), fall [publicly] in the squares (Jer 9:20 [Eng. 9:21]; 49:26), and are denied pity (Isa 9:16 [Eng. 9:17]; Jer 51:3).[55] Other passages suggest the בחור is promising (Amos 2:11), handsome (1 Sam 9:2), socially adept (Judg 14:10), and desirable (Ruth 3:10). During this period spanning late puberty to young adulthood, the בחור has desired traits of strength and stamina. Lexica underscore that a בחור is "fully-grown," "vigorous" and "choice, in the prime of manhood," while בתולה is simply defined as "virgin."[56]

This definition has come under dispute in recent decades, but still persists. G. J. Wenham argues, "Akkadian and Ugaritic cognates suggest that Hebrew *bᵉtûlāh* should be translated 'girl of marriageable age' rather than 'virgin,'" noting that only in later Christian understanding does בתולה take on implications of someone who has not yet had sex.[57] The sexual emphasis of the translation "virgin" is not always warranted in context (as when paired with the בחורים above), or indeed can run counter to the sense of the passage (Joel 1:8; Isa 7:14).[58] Peggy Day points out that a בתולה may have had sex since the explanatory qualifier "did not know a man" accompanies the designation of בתולה in Gen 24:16 and Judg 21:12 (see also Gen 19:8; Judg 11:39). Day further posits that a בתולה has reached puberty but has yet to become a mother.[59]

The translation of "virgin" has adhered to בתולה largely based on Deut

---

55. E.g., See Michel, *Gott und Gewalt*, 25 n. 33.
56. *HALOT* 1:118, 167; BDB, 104, 143.
57. Gordon J. Wenham, "*Bᴱ TÛLĀH* 'A Girl of Marriageable Age,'" *VT* 22 (1972): 347. For discussion of the epithet *btlt* used of Anat in Ugaritic narrative poetry, see Peggy L. Day, "Anat," in *Dictionary of Deities and Demons in the Bible* (ed. Karel van der Toorn, Bob Becking, and Pieter W. van der Horst; Leiden: E. J. Brill: 1999), 36–43. See also Neal H. Walls, *The Goddess Anat in Ugaritic Myth*, (SBLDS 135; Atlanta: Scholars Press, 1992), 78–79.

58. Rendering עלמה as "virgin" in Isa 7:14 stems from the LXX translation of עלמה as παρθένος. As M. Tsevat notes, even if a virgin does conceive in this passage (as frequently maintained in Christian tradition), the text says nothing about the young woman remaining a virgin once she is pregnant (*TDOT* 2:343). Nonetheless, changes from "virgin" in English translations of Isa 7:14 have provoked dramatic responses. Perhaps this was exemplified best in 1952 by the public burnings of the page of the RSV that contained Isa 7:14 with עלמה translated as "young woman." See Peter J. Thuesen, *In Discordance with the Scriptures: American Protestant Battles over Translating the Bible* (New York: Oxford, 1999), sixth page of photos.

59. Peggy L. Day, "From the Child Is Born the Woman: The Story of Jephthah's Daughter," in *Gender and Difference in Ancient Israel* (ed. Peggy L. Day; Minneapolis: Augsburg Fortress, 1989). See also Tikva Frymer-Kensky, "Virginity in the Bible," in Matthews et al., *Gender and Law*, 79.

22:13–21. In this passage, parents must present a cloth as proof of their daughter's virginity to her unsatisfied husband. This cloth, commonly presumed to be bloody, is evidence of the daughter's בתולים (vv. 14, 17 [2x], 20).[60] Wenham argues that the stained cloth is a 'token of adolescence,' containing menstrual blood indicating that the נערה (vv. 15 [2x], 16, 19, 20, 21) or בתולה (v. 19) was old enough to marry.[61] Day similarly suggests that בתולה "refers to a particular stage in the female life cycle and, like the word 'adolescence,' is best understood as a social recognition of puberty."[62] However, Tikva Frymer-Kensky draws on anthropological data to argue that blood-stained cloths are evidence for virginity, not puberty.[63] She maintains that בתולים *does* indicate celibacy, but a בתולה is simply a young woman or older girl of marriageable age. Use of this term in contexts of sexual violence and vulnerability further enforces the idea that a בתולה is not necessarily chaste (Exod 22:15 [Eng. 22:16]; Deut 22:23, 28; Judg 21:12; 2 Sam 13:2; 1 Kgs 1:2; Lam 5:11; Esth 2:3).[64] The abstract בתולים then appears to focus on one aspect of being a בתולה (i.e., sexual status), much as the abstract נעורים conveys one aspect of being a נער (i.e., youth).[65]

The בחור and בתולה are near or have completed physical maturation and are considered desirable. Due to different cultural expectations for men and women, the בחור is probably older than the בתולה. A בחור can be married or unmarried, chaste or sexually active. While we have only a few attestations of עלם and עלמה from which to draw conclusions, comparing these words with בחור and בתולה can add nuance to our understanding of these terms. The word עלם seems to indicate a boy, while בחור suggests a male in later teenage years and early adulthood. Both of the terms בתולה and עלמה convey adolescent girls or young women, although עלמה could portray pre-pubescent girls as well. The בחור has more social standing than the עלם. The value of the בתולה is further underscored by metaphors using this image for peoples and places (e.g., 2 Kgs 19:21 [Isa 37:22]; Isa 23:12, 47:1; Jer 14:17; 18:13; 31:4, 21; 46:11; Amos 5:2; Lam 1:5; 2:23).[66] Young men, needed as warriors, and young women, esteemed as

---

60. For further discussion of this passage and the function of virginity in maintaining family honor, see Joseph Fleishman, "The Delinquent Daughter and Legal Innovation in Deuteronomy xxii 20–21," *VT* 58 (2008), 196–97. Fleishman suggests that the girl's punishment of stoning is so severe because she has, in effect, cursed her parents with her illicit sexual behavior (see Exod 21:17).
61. Wenham, "B^ETÛLĀH," 331.
62. Day, "From the Child Is Born the Woman," 59.
63. For relevant discussion of virginity in cross-cultural studies, see Frymer-Kensky, "Virginity in the Bible," 79–85.
64. For more detailed discussion, see Michel, "Sexual Violence against Children," 54–56.
65. Analogously, "babyish" suggests immaturity, focusing on one aspect of being a baby (as opposed to being defenseless, cute, inarticulate, incontinent, etc.).
66. For insightful analysis of female metaphors related to sacred spaces, see Christl M.

brides and future mothers, have noted significance. Yet this phase of life carries dangers, notably due to war (e.g., 2 Kgs 8:12; Isa 31:8; Jer 18:21; 51:3), abduction (Judg 21:12–23), and rape (e.g., Judg 19:24; 2 Sam 13:2). Nonetheless, we can read these terms for youth on a continuum of status, paralleling growth and development.

## נער and נערה

The terms נער and נערה are also found in Ugaritic, although they are lacking in other Northwest Semitic languages.[67] Several studies isolate or emphasize one aspect of these multivalent words.[68] Hans-Peter Stähli wrote the first monograph on נער, arguing that this term suggests a dependent, frequently referring to either a young man in a service role or to someone unmarried under the authority of his *pater familias*. When a servant is married but not living in the house of his father (e.g., Ziba in 2 Samuel 9, who has fifteen sons and twenty servants [v. 10]), Stähli notes the character's clear place as an underling (here as a trusted servant of Saul).[69] A נערה can be a concubine (e.g., Judg 19:3–8), a married woman (e.g., Deut 22:13–21), or a widow (e.g., Ruth 2:6). Stähli maintains that a נערה is a dependent female either before or after marriage since women maintained their reliance on men.[70] Indeed, dependency is the hallmark of being a נער or נערה in Stähli's understanding, although this is not a hard claim to sustain in a society where most everyone (save the few who were wealthy and royalty) struggled to survive through mutual dependency.

Refining Stähli's study, subsequent scholarship often associates the נער with a particular role. While John MacDonald criticizes Stähli for his myopic understanding of נער,[71] MacDonald's own interpretation is also narrow. MacDonald argues that נער signifies a young man born to a family with means, and ultimately urges that נער be translated as "squire," with נערה as "lady-in-waiting."[72] He interprets merisms that pertain to age as laden with connotations of class (see נער and זקן in Gen 19:4; Exod 10:9;

---

Maier, *Daughter Zion, Mother Zion: Gender, Space, and the Sacred in Ancient Israel* (Minneapolis: Fortress, 2008).

67. Ugaritic cognates (n‛r, n‛rt; see *DLU*, 315–16) carry similar meanings. For discussion, see B. Cutler and J. MacDonald, "Identification of the Na'ar in the Ugaritic Texts," *UF* 8 (1976): 27–35.

68. For further review of this scholarship, see Eng, *Days of Our Years*, 59–63.

69. Hans-Peter Stähli, *Knabe-Jüngling-Knecht: Untersuchungen zum Begriff* נער *im Alten Testament* (BBET 7; Frankfurt am Main: Peter Lang, 1978), 180–81.

70. For his discussion of נערה see Stähli, *Knabe-Jüngling-Knecht*, 218–33. To presume female dependency on males ignores economic interdependence among family members. On the essential role of women as workers, see Meyers, *Discovering Eve*, 142–49.

71. John MacDonald, "*Untersuchungen zum Begriff* נער *im Alten Testament*," review of Hans-Peter Stähli, *Knabe-Jüngling-Knecht*, *JBL* 99.4 (1980): 594–95.

72. John MacDonald, "The Status and Role of the Na'ar in Israelite Society," *JNES* 35.3 (1976): 170. MacDonald asserts, "Na'ar stands out, let it be repeated, as descriptive of high-

Deut 28:50; Josh 6:21; Isa 3:5, 20:4; Jer 51:22; Ps 148:12; Lam 2:21; Esth 3:13). While "squire" is an appropriate (albeit archaic) translation in certain passages (e.g., 2 Sam 9:9; 2 Kgs 19:6; Esth 2:2; 6:3), to limit נער to this meaning runs counter to its apparent sense in too many cases to be uniformly (or even primarily) adopted (e.g., Gen 21:12; Exod 2:6; Judg 13:5, 7, 8, 12; 1 Sam 1:22, 24; 4:21; 2 Kgs 2:23; Isa 8:4).

Lawrence Stager, influenced by both Stähli and MacDonald, understands נערים as males who were struggling to find their economic niche and so found work (careers?) associated with warfare, government, or cultic service.[73] Stager views these occupations as options for those who did not have their own households. Yet, again, only the barest modicum of information is supplied regarding so many נערים that the reasoning seems circular.[74] Scholars decide that נער suggests a character's dependency, status, or vocation, then inject this idea into each instance where נער appears.

Brent Strawn sees נער as related to status, yet signifying lowliness, not prestige.[75] He reads Jeremiah's self-description as a נער in Jer 1:6 as the prophet's prayerful profession of ineptitude, seeking YHWH's sympathy and support. Strawn does not provide a succinct translation for נער, but instead summarizes,

> The use of נער in Jer. i 6 is best understood, not as a precise indicator delineating Jeremiah's chronological age, but as a rhetorical device in which a pray-er appeals to their weak or insignificant status in order to summon the Deity's compassion.[76]

However, to translate נער as connoting youth in Jer 1:6 might elicit a similar response from YHWH or the reader. Still, Strawn's interpretation remains tenable largely because he interprets נער in this specific context, and does not attempt to project his definition on the overall use of this word.

Carolyn Leeb, like Stähli, has contributed a monograph to this conversation that suggests that נער and נערה convey information about a person's station in life.[77] More specifically, she suggests that a נער or נערה

---

born male young" (p. 150). However, in many instances נערים act as servants with no relevant information provided regarding their class or birth.

73. Stager, "Archaeology of the Family," 25–28.

74. E.g., Gen 14:24; 18:7; 22:3, 5; Num 11:27; 22:22; Josh 6:23; Judg 8:14; 16:26; 19:3ff.; 1 Sam 9:3–10; 10:14; 14:1, 6; 20:21, 35, 36; 26:22; 2 Sam 20:11; 1 Kgs 18:43; 19:3; 2 Kgs 2:23; Ruth 2:5–6; Neh 4:16 (Eng. 4:22); 5:15.

75. Brent A. Strawn, "Jeremiah's In/Effective Plea: Another Look at נער in Jeremiah I 6," VT 55.3 (2005): 366–77.

76. Strawn, "Jeremiah's In/Effective Plea," 377.

77. Carolyn S. Leeb, *Away from the Father's House: The Social Location of na'ar and na'arah*

is one who is socially located "away from the father's house." Leeb disagrees that being a נער primarily hinges on dependency (Stähli), high status (MacDonald), or vocation (Stager). Instead, Leeb maintains that a נער or נערה has been separated from his or her בית אב of origin and has had to re-associate with another household through a position of service. She offers "servant," "fledgling," "outcast," "apprentice," "fosterling," and "client" (in an anthropological sense), as useful translations.[78]

While Leeb helpfully catalogs the various capacities in which נערים and נערות often function, her study falters because it is built on two debatable assumptions. First, she concludes that נערים and נערות live away from home, but (as noted above) there is simply not enough information about most of these characters to determine their life particulars, such as possible relocation from their original בית אב. Indeed, in many instances the נער or נערה appears to be *within* the realm of his or her household of origin.[79] Second, Leeb states categorically, "Since both Hebrew and Ugaritic have other perfectly functional ways to express the concept 'young,' I will reject at the outset the notion that the 'root' meaning of נער is 'young.'"[80] However, "young" remains a key meaning of נער, which Leeb explains away when this meaning seems apparent.[81] Also, Leeb cites two other words that indicate youth in the text: קטן and צעיר.[82] Why not have three (or more), including נער? As one word indicates a certain concept, other words can convey similar ideas, as Leeb's own examples of קטן and צעיר illustrate.[83]

Milton Eng proposes two central meanings for נער. The first focuses on youth ("boy, youth, young man"), and the second conveys service ("servant, attendant") and carries overtones of personal attachment.[84] Citing

---

*in Ancient Israel* (JSOTSup 301; Sheffield: Sheffield Academic Press, 2000).

78. Leeb, *Away from the Father's House*, 192.

79. E.g., Gen 24:14–61; 25:27; 34:19; 37:2; 44:22–34; Deut 22:15–29; Judg 13:5–24; 19:3–9; 1 Sam 1:22; 16:11; 1 Kgs 3:7; 14:1–3; 2 Kgs 4:29–35; Job 29:5.

80. Leeb, *Away from the Father's House*, 188.

81. For example, Leeb maintains that Abishag, described as a נערה in 1 Kgs 1:2–4, is not necessarily young but rather is "evidently fatherless and husbandless. . . . Perhaps she was a captive (or orphan) of war" (Leeb, *Away from the Father's House*, 130). Although Rebekah (another נערה, Gen 24:16, 28, 55, 57) has her father present and speaking (Gen 24:50–51), Leeb reasons, "Perhaps her father has died, or has been incapacitated, either physically or mentally" because he is not more vocal (pp. 135–36). The נער in Isa 7:16 who does not "know how to refuse the evil and choose the good" is not a young child, Leeb maintains, but נער "may reflect the fact that only his mother is mentioned or that the siege represents danger from which even his father cannot protect him" (p. 159). More examples appear in the chapter on "Other Uses of נער" (Leeb, *Away from the Father's House*, 151–65).

82. Leeb, *Away from the Father's House*, 188 n. 74.

83. Examples (from this current study) of words that have overlapping connotations are בתולה, עלמה, and נערה; עלם, and ילד; גמל, יונק, and עולל.

84. Eng, *Days of Our Years*, 81–82. See also the table in the appendix analyzing attestations of נער, pp. 137–47.

Dennis Pardee's review of Stähli's monograph, Eng points out that "boy" may be the best English translation because of its range of potential meaning. "Boy" has been used to indicate gender ("It's a boy"), size ("still a boy"), relationship ("our boy"), soldiers ("boys overseas"), servant ("do this boy"), or men ("boys at the office").[85] Eng maintains that the qualifier קטן is used to specify younger boys, underscoring that נער refers to a youthful period.[86] While Eng sees נער as a life-cycle term, this word can also indicate humility, as Strawn suggests regarding Jer 1:6 (above). In 1 Kgs 3:7, Solomon also refers to himself as a נער קטן, surely a self-effacing expression, when he is a grown and powerful man. Eng's discussion nonetheless brings thorough and impressive research to our understanding of נער.

Words for youth can be intertwined with ideas about status, as seen with various forms and uses of נער. The word נער is repeatedly paired with זקן as a merism indicating all ages.[87] The abstract נערים designates youth as a period of life prior to adulthood.[88] A נער is frequently associated with work, as many נערים and נערות enter a scene just to do someone's bidding.[89] This suggests a close relationship between youth and service, including work outside of one's own home (regardless of permanent social relocation). In many places where a נער or נערה appears, the text focuses not on age but on role. Sometimes the youthfulness of a נער or נערה is made explicit by stating his or her age (e.g., Gen 37:2) or by an adjectival modification (e.g., 2 Kgs 5:2; 1 Sam 20:35). In other passages it is implied by context (e.g., Gen 21:12, 17–19; 24:14, 16, 28, 55, 57; Exod 2:6; Judg 13:12; Esth 2:4, 7). We therefore correctly envision the נערים and נערות as characters who are often young and/or appear in subordinate positions.

Several English words need to be culled to provide an equivalent for נער or נערה due to its polysemous nature. Within different contexts, workable translations include "lad," "lass," "damsel" (although somewhat antiquated), "boy," "girl," "youth," "adolescent," "young man," "young woman," "fellow," "maid," "servant," "serving-girl," or "attendant." Yet one translation better avoided is "child" (contra the ASV, JPS, KJV, and ESV). As E. J. Revell points out, "It [the word נער] is used over the same age range as 'child' (ילד), but differs from that term in that it does not view

---

85. Eng, *Days of Our Years*, 80.
86. Eng, *Days of Our Years*, 80.
87. As noted earlier, see Gen 19:4; Exod 10:9; Deut 28:50; Josh 6:21; Isa 3:5; 20:4; Jer 51:22; Ps 148:12; Lam 2:21; Esth 3:13.
88. E.g., Gen 46:34; 1 Sam 12:2; 17:33; 2 Sam 19:8 (Eng. 19:7); 1 Kgs 18:12; Isa 47:12, 15; Jer 3:24–25; 22:21; 31:19; 32:30; Ezek 4:14; Zech 13:5; Pss 71:5, 17; 103:5, 129:1; Job 31:18.
89. Citing Victor Hamilton (*NIDOTTE* "נער"), Eng notes that the female נערות, when appearing with a pronominal suffix, always suggests "servants" (Eng, *Days of Our Years*, 79). However, often there is very little information given about the נערות (e.g., Job 40:29 [Eng. 41:5]).

the person designated in the context of his family."⁹⁰ When parents refer to their own children as נערים, there seems to be an intentional distancing on the part of the speaker since the child is to be separated from the parents by dedication (e.g., Judg 13:5–7; 1 Sam 1:22) or perhaps death (e.g., 1 Sam 4:21; 2 Kgs 4:29–35).⁹¹ Revell distinguishes a בן [or בת] as related to one or both parents, a ילד as a family member, and a נער as an individual without regard to familial relation.⁹² The word נער is not inherently a term of kinship.

## Children

### ילד and ילדה

The root ילד connoting "to bring forth, bear, beget" takes various forms and frequently signals the arrival of children. As a verb, ילד appears nearly five hundred times in the Hebrew Bible (often in genealogies), noting the importance of mothers and offspring. Overt references to female children are few; ילדה occurs a mere three times (Gen 34:4; Joel 4:3 [Eng. 3:3]; and plural in Zech 8:5), compared to the eighty-nine references to ילד or ילדים. However, context reveals that ילדים can include girls (e.g., Gen 30:21 and 33:2; 1 Sam 1:2–4; Hos 1:2–6). More frequently, the presence of girls is signaled by use of the term בת within familial settings, as discussed above.

As with נער, the ages of characters described as a ילד vary significantly.⁹³ A ילד can be as young as a fetus (Exod 21:22), but more often suggests a newborn child (e.g., Gen 21:8; Exod 2:3–10; 2 Sam 12:15; 1 Kgs 3:25; Isa 9:5 [Eng. 9:6]; Ruth 4:16). Young boys and girls appear designated by ילד and ילדה in Joel 4:3 (Eng. 3:3) and Zech 8:5. Noticeably older are the accomplished young men (ילדים) brought from Israel to Babylon (Dan 1:4). After the seventeen-year-old Joseph (Gen 37:2) has been sold into slavery, Reuben describes him a ילד(Gen 37:30), and uses the same term later when referring to this incident (Gen 42:22). Perhaps surprisingly, the advisors to Rehoboam are called ילדים in 1 Kgs 12:8–14 (2 Chr 10:8–14), even though they are grown men in positions of power. This usage, however, may be an intentionally ironic choice by the author to disparage the poor advice that these "men" provide to the king.

While ילד frequently indicates someone who is young, it can also suggest a kinship relationship. This usage differs from בן, since בן might

---

90. Revell, *Designation of the Individual*, 31.
91. For further examples, see Revell, *Designation of the Individual*, 31.
92. Revell, *Designation of the Individual*, 31–32.
93. As the book of Ruth demonstrates, the same story can use ילד to refer to different life stages, as it describes the husbands Mahlon and Chilion (Ruth 1:5), as well as the infant Obed (Ruth 4:16).

indicate a grandson, who is not immediate offspring.[94] Eng notes that the majority of attestations of ילד convey a baby or very young child. He recommends "infant" as an "initial understanding" and places a ילד at the first stage on a continuum of life phases.[95] However, given the various contexts in which ילד appears (which Eng also discusses), this definition is too age-specific for a term that primarily suggests kinship. Other words (discussed below) seem to be better equivalents for "infant" because they appear consistently in contexts that portray newborns or very small children. Rather, ילד often refers to babies and children who are pre-pubescent, as well as signifying relationship.

Attestations of ילד show the perils and rare privileges of being a child.[96] Andreas Michel notes that threats, death, and violence surface in 60 percent of the instances in which ילד designates a child.[97] Passages that depict children as joyful or carefree are few and far between. Uplifting images of boys and girls appear in Zech 8:5 (ילדים וילדות) and Neh 12:43 (ילדים).[98] Yet Zech 8:5 remains an unrealized vision, not a description of a situation that the prophet has witnessed. Andreas Kunz-Lübcke points out that the emphasis here is not on children playing, but rather their safe existence, since they have not perished in the streets.[99] Nehemiah's portrayal of exuberant children, as they join in the celebration of Jerusalem's rebuilt wall (Neh 12:43), is likewise exceptional. Job 21:7–13 also describes children who appear lighthearted and unencumbered, although they belong to the wicked (ילדיהם in v. 11b). The writer understands that for a parent to have thriving children is a source of happiness, albeit one that the evildoers do not deserve. Use of the term ילד illustrates the paradox of being a child in ancient Israelite understanding, as the writers recognize children's value and vulnerability, then use these ideas to rouse reaction from the reader.

---

94. See Eng, *Days of Our Years*, 84–88.
95. Eng, *Days of Our Years*, 88.
96. For example, political decrees order the slaughter of male children (Exod 1:16). YHWH smites a child with a fatal illness for the sins of his father (2 Sam 12:15, 18–22). Children can be used to pay debts (2 Kgs 4:1). The prophet Joel describes a boy sold as a prostitute and a girl sold for drink (Joel 4:3 [Eng. 3:3]). Wild animals rip children apart (2 Kgs 2:24). Mothers eat their own children (2 Kgs 6:28–29; Lam 2:20; 4:10). Children weep in the rain, along with their families, anticipating their expulsion (Ezra 10:1). Children are slain in valleys as a practice of worship (Isa 57:5).
97. See Michel, *Gott und Gewalt*, 21–22.
98. Michel suggests these are the only two images of carefree children in the entire Hebrew Bible (Michel, *Gott und Gewalt*, 21–22).
99. Kunz-Lübcke, *Das Kind in den antiken Kulturen*, 221. See also Rüdiger Lux, "Die Kinder auf der Gasse: Ein Kindheitsmotiv in der prophetischen Gerichts- und Heilsverkündigung," in *"Schaffe Mir Kinder,"* 197–221.

## טף

Traditional scholarship suggests that טף may be derived from *טפף, akin to the Arabic for "trip, take quick little steps," indicating those who have trouble walking, that is, the very young and the very old.[100] Referring to the Ethiopic *ṭaff* (infant), BDB defines טף primarily as a collective indicating children.[101] *HALOT* gives "little children" as its first definition, then "those of a nomadic tribe who are not (or only to a small extent) able to march," as the meaning with more attestations.[102] *TDOT* suggests טף is a very general word to fill in semantic gaps, with a basic meaning of "hangers-on" who have minor significance.[103] More recent studies by Eng and Michel agree that טף has a complementary function whose specific meaning is determined in context.[104]

The term טף suggests dependents, or a particular group of dependents.[105] In Num 16:27, טף are listed in addition to the בנים and נשים (as the family of Korah is about to perish), suggesting that they are another group besides the offspring (בנים). In Ezek 9:6, the roster of those to be slain includes זקן בחור ובתולה וטף ונשים, pairing women and children together.[106] Yet in Num 31:17–18, טף may not be young. Every male among the טף is to be killed, giving little clue as to age (v. 17). However, in v. 18 Moses commands the death of Midianite טף בנשים who have lain with men, suggesting these are women. Even in cases where it can imply a broader group (e.g., Gen 43:8; 47:12, 24; Exod 12:37; Deut 2:34; 3:6; 31:12), טף frequently includes children.

The treatment of טף can be clustered into categories. Overall, טף are vulnerable, especially when this word portrays children.[107] They are taken captive (Gen 34:29; Num 31:9; Deut 20:14; Jer 41:16), go into exile (Jer 43:6–7), or barely avoid this fate (Jer 40:7). In addition to facing threats (Esth 8:11), the טף are put to the sword (Judg 21:10), slain (Num 31:17; Ezek 9:6), exterminated (Deut 2:34; 3:6), and made to perish (Num 16:27–33; Esth 3:13). Yet their welfare also matters. Characters express concern about their safety (Gen 43:8; Num 14:3, 31; Deut 3:19; Ezra 8:21) and ability to

---

100. BDB, 381; see also *HALOT* 1:379.
101. BDB, 381–82.
102. *HALOT* 1:378.
103. *TDOT* 5:348.
104. Michel, *Gott und Gewalt*, 17; Eng, *Days of Our Lives*, 89–94.
105. Exodus 10:9–10 provides an instructive example. In v. 9 Moses negotiates with Pharaoh as to who shall be allowed to leave Egypt as a result of the eighth plague. Moses enumerates those who must be released: נערינו, זקנינו, בנינו, בנותנו, צאננו, בקרנו. In v. 10, Pharaoh responds by summarizing regarding אתכם ואת־טפכם "you and your dependents," apparently lacking the patience to reiterate Moses' list.
106. The ASV, KJV, NRSV, and RSV translate טף as "little children" in this verse, highlighting their dependency.
107. See Michel, *Gott und Gewalt*, 27.

travel (Gen 45:19; 46:5; 50:8; Judg 18:21; Ezra 8:21). They need provisions (Gen 47:12, 24; 50:21[108]) and protection in times of battle (Num 32:16, 17, 24, 26; Josh 1:14). They are to be released from slavery in Egypt (Exod 10:10, 24) and journey with the rest of the congregation (2 Sam 15:22). The טף are also integral to the Israelite covenant community (Deut 29:9–12 [Eng. 29:10–13]; 31:12; 2 Chr 31:18).

Deuteronomy 1:39 shows special attention to the טף as children. Here YHWH upbraids the Israelites for rebellion, but preserves the טף. "Moreover, your little ones (טפכם), who you thought would become plunder, your children (בניכם), who today do not know good from bad, they shall go in there; I will give it to them, and they shall inherit it." YHWH explicitly addresses the presumed fate of the טף as booty (see also Num 14:31).[109] The text further notes that youth do not yet have the ability to reason (ובניכם אשר לא־ידעו היום טוב ורע; cf. Isa 7:16) and promises them land. YHWH appears to give this possession to the טף because of their blamelessness. This verse shows טף as easy prey with different abilities from adults, both in reasoning and self-protection. Yet they are part of the community and merit attention from YHWH, who spares them wrath and gives them land. This seems a reward for their innocence, and this author appears to recognize naiveté as a trait of children.

## Young Children and Babies

Small children in Israelite society are recognized by words with ties to weaning (גמל) or nursing (ינק). A third term for young children, עולל, may carry an inherently violent connotation (discussed below). Used in a general sense, these words offer insight about the perception and rearing of small children.

Scholars assert with surprising confidence and consistency that women in ancient Israel breastfed their children for about three years.[110] This conclusion seems derived from 2 Macc 7:27 and possibly Hannah's offering of a three-year-old bull at the dedication of Samuel after he has

---

108. When used alone, טף may suggest "household" (*TDOT* 5: 348).

109. The LXX of Deut 1:39 omits any reference to a threatened future: καὶ πᾶν παιδίον νέον ὅστις οὐκ οἶδεν σήμερον ἀγαθὸν ἢ κακὸν οὗτοι εἰσελεύσονται ἐκεῖ καὶ τούτοις δώσω αὐτὴν καὶ αὐτοὶ κληρονομήσουσιν αὐτήν ("and every young child who today does not know good from evil, they will enter that place and I will give it to them and they shall possess it"). This reflects a typical pattern for the Septuagint translation, which minimizes or excises references to violence against children. See Michel, *Gott und Gewalt*, pp. 129–34.

110. See *TDOT* 3:26; Block, "Marriage and Family in Ancient Israel," 88; King and Stager, *Life in Biblical Israel*, 41; Terence Fretheim, "God Was with the Boy," in Bunge, *Child in the Bible*, 8 n. 9; Blenkinsopp, "The Family in First Temple Israel," 68; Marsman, *Women in Ugarit and Israel*, 202; Meyers, *Discovering Eve*, 151. Meyers also cites 2 Chr 31:16 as possible evidence for a three-year-long weaning period, but admits that this is tenuous (p. 206 n. 30).

been weaned (1 Sam 1:24).[111] Yet anthropological studies show a wide age range of breastfeeding practices and caution against too much certainty regarding ages of nursing children.[112] However, we can infer that breastfeeding was the standard practice in ancient society as a practical necessity (see Gen 21:7; 1 Sam 1:23; 1 Kgs 3:21). Rich women, however, might employ a wet nurse. In Exod 2:7–9, Pharaoh's daughter offers to pay wages for a wet nurse. As Mayer Gruber notes, this proposal and its instant acceptance presume a context in which such contracts were arranged.[113] Genesis 24:59; 35:8; and 2 Kgs 11:2 (2 Chr 22:11) similarly portray women as professional nurses, although only within relatively affluent or royal households.[114]

Gruber suggests that widespread breastfeeding kept down population growth. Feeding a baby exclusively by breast delays the return of menses and ovulation (a biological process called "lactational amenorrhea"), thereby functioning as birth control. Gruber cites Hos 1:8, in which Gomer conceives a son after weaning her daughter,[115] and contrasts such a scenario with the Old Babylonian context. The practice of hiring wet nurses is well attested in Babylonian texts, as is the problem of an overabundant population.[116] A smaller family size in ancient Israel accords with biblical portrayals of families with two or three children, as well as archaeological estimations.[117]

---

111. This reading of בפר משלש is *contra* the MT, but supported by the LXX, Peshitta, and 4QSam$^a$. See Mayer I. Gruber, "Breast-Feeding Practices in Biblical Israel and in Old Babylonian Mesopotamia," *JANES* 19 (1989): 66 n. 21.

112. Among the Kalahari Desert San (southern Africa), for example, the length of time a child breastfeeds depends on birth order; the last child is weaned later, sometimes not until eight years old. See Melvin Konner, "Infancy among the Kalahari Desert San," in *Culture and Infancy: Variations in Human Experience* (ed. P. Herbert Leiderman, Steven R. Tulkin, Anne Rosenfeld; New York: Academic Press, 1977), 292. The Tairan people from an Okinawan village (southernmost Japan) would wean their children between the ages of eighteen months to two years. See Thomas and Hatsumi Maretzki, "Taira: An Okinawan Village," in *Six Cultures: Studies of Child Rearing* (ed. Beatrice B. Whiting; New York: John Wiley and Sons, 1963), 477. Among the Tarong people (in the Philippines), the age of weaning is predicated on the mother's next pregnancy and takes place between the ages of one and four years old. See William F. Nydegger and Corinne Nydegger, "Tarong: An Ilocos Barrio in the Philippines," in Whiting, *Six Cultures*, 828.

113. Gruber, "Breast-Feeding Practices," 81.

114. The role of Rebekah's nurse (מנקת: Gen 24:59; מינקת: Gen 35:8) may suggest that the young Rebekah's wet nurse has become a family servant still tending to Rebekah (analogous to Juliet's nurse in *Romeo and Juliet*). For further examples of the nurse in literature, see Gruber, "Breast-Feeding Practices," 82 n. 133.

115. Gruber, "Breast-Feeding Practices," 68.

116. Gruber, "Breast-Feeding Practices," 69–71.

117. See Gen 25:23–26; 38:27–30; Exod 18:2–4; Num 26:59; 2 Kgs 4:1; Ruth 1:1. Lawrence Stager suggests that families in the highland villages were usually nuclear units of about four people (4.1 to 4.3) during the Iron I period (Stager, "Archaeology of the Family," 18). Families with many children usually require multiple wives (see Gen 46:5–7; 2 Chr 11:18–21; 13:21).

## גמול/גמל

The verb גמל means "to wean" and "to complete."[118] Applied in the nominal form to a small child, this word may suggest the completion of one's nursing or the most perilous period of childhood, that is, early infancy (although this is difficult to prove). The same verb also means "to ripen"[119] (Num 17:23 [Eng. 17:8]; Isa 18:5) and may indicate an awareness of developing stages as children grow.

The terms גמול and גמל occur infrequently with reference to children (Gen 21:8 [2x]; 1 Sam 1:22–24 [4x]; 1 Kgs 11:20; Isa 11:8; 28:9; Hos 1:8; Ps 131:2 [2x]), partially because small children are rarely the text's concern. Also, גמל can suggest the period of being recently weaned, which is a temporary state through which a child would pass relatively quickly. Children who are said to be weaned are also identified as נער (1 Sam 1:23–24), ילד (Gen 21:8), or בן (1 Kgs 11:20). The most detailed picture the text offers of weaning is with Hannah and young Samuel (1 Sam 1:22–24). This mother advocates to keep her son until he is done nursing; the father acknowledges and accedes to her request. In nursing her child, Hannah recognizes his needs and perhaps her own. The positive image in Ps 131:2 portrays closeness between mother and גמל to convey a calm and quieted soul.

None of the (albeit few) passages that use גמל or גמול of young children portrays a child who is harmed. The only threatening situation appears in Isa 11:8b as the גמול puts his hand over the den of the poisonous snake. While there is tension in this image, the small child remains safe in the foretold blissful kingdom, despite potential danger. As Andreas Kunz-Lübcke observes, the author draws on expectations that young children are curious and need to be educated about potential threats.[120] A גמול resides peaceably in the text, while small children designated by other words are more likely to suffer destructive fates.

## יונק

The verb ינק "to suck" describes the lactation of both animals (Lam 4:3) and humans (Exod 2:9; 1 Sam 1:23; 1 Kgs 3:21). Usually related to mothers (e.g., Job 3:12; and metaphorically in Isa 66:11, 12[?][121]), sucking also refers to snake poison (said of the wicked in Job 20:16), or the abundance of the seas (Deut 33:19). Sucking the milk of nations and the breast of kings (Isa

---

118. *HALOT* 1:197.
119. BDB, 168.
120. Kunz-Lübcke, *Kind in den antiken Kulturen*, 223.
121. Here יונקת can be read either as a noun or a verb. Most translators read as a *waw* conversive *qal* perfect 2nd masc. pl. verb, "then you will suck." *HALOT* 1:416–17, following text critical notes and the LXX (τὰ παιδία αὐτῶν), persuasively suggests this word be read as a collective noun meaning "offspring, descendants."

60:16) suggests a physical connection with wealth and royalty (Isa 49:23).[122] The image of the nursing mother and the infant also evokes feelings of comfort, abundance, delight, and maternal tenderness (Isa 66:11–12).

As a participle suggesting a baby or young child, יונק is found in Num 11:12; Deut 32:25; 1 Sam 15:3; 22:19; Isa 11:8;[123] Jer 44:7; Joel 2:16; Ps 8:3 [Eng. 8:2]; Song 8:1[124]; and Lam 2:11; 4:4. Whereas small children indicated by גמל can be named (e.g., Genubath in 1 Kgs 11:20) or become developed as adult characters (as with Isaac in Gen 21:8 and Samuel in 1 Sam 1:23–24), the term יונק never specifies a child who is otherwise known as an adult or independently existing character. This lack of identity may heighten the vulnerability of the יונק, as this word usually appears in contexts of ruin. Often the term is part of a merism and the object of destructive verbs. The יונק is cut down by the sword (Deut 32:25; 1 Sam 22:19), struck down and destroyed (1 Sam 15:3), and cut off from Judah (Jer 44:7). The noun יונק only functions as the subject (along with עולל) in Lam 2:11 with the verb עטף ("to faint"[125]). In Lam 2:12, these children plead with their mothers, "Where is grain and wine?" suggesting that they are old enough to speak coherently, instead of simply wailing from hunger.[126] *Contra* the NRSV translation here for עולל ויונק as "infants and babes," the image of children able to articulate their needs suggests that a יונק was not always a baby. Perhaps children were nursed for a few years and still considered a יונק, or the term indicates a baby, toddler, or small child in general. Isaiah 11:8 provides an idealized image of children (יונק and גמול) playing near the home of a venomous snake, combining images of defenselessness and danger. The יונק is old enough to engage in play (שעשע—lit., "to take delight in"), at least on a rudimentary level. While גמול may indicate a slightly older child, the parallelism of the poetry suggests this writer may have viewed the two terms as roughly synonymous in terms of age. However a גמול may show more promise, or at least be safer, than the יונק.

---

122. *KTU* 1.15 ii 26–28 suggests parallels to Isa 49:23; 60:16, in which nursing suggests a close association between the two involved parties. See Day, "Anat," 37 and W. G. E. Watson, "The PN *yṣb* in the Keret Legend," *UF* 11 (1979): 807–9. Walls similarly discusses Anat's role as "divine nutrix." See Walls, *Goddess Anat*, 152–54.

123. This masc. participle found in Isa 53:2 (יונק) is commonly rendered by translations as "tender plant" (KJV, WEB, ASV), "young plant" (NRSV, ESV), or "sapling" (JPS, NAB, NJB), parallel to שרש ("root"). Only the LXX (παιδίον) and its English translation (LXE: "child") interpret יונק in human terms here.

124. Here the participle is not necessarily functioning substantively.

125. This verb in the *hitpael* (here in the infinitive construct) means "to feel weak" (*HALOT* 1:815) or "faint, faint away" (BDB, 742). Other meanings of עטף ("to turn" or "to envelope oneself") appear in the *qal*. See BDB, 742; *HALOT* 1:814.

126. The request of the swooning children for דגן ויין ("grain and wine") suggests either "wine" as a general term for "drink" or portrays precocious children (more likely, the former). In Lam 4:4 the יונק is silenced by a tongue that cleaves to his palate, while the עוללים ask for bread.

## עולל

The עולל is repeatedly paired with the יונק, suggesting a literary trope.[127] In 1 Sam 15:3 and 22:19, the prepositions מן and עד flank יונק and עולל, forming an inclusive binary. When the terms appear in a pair, the age range of the עולל appears to extend to that of a child, who may not be small. In 1 Sam 15:3 מעלל ועד־יונק appears in a list of pairs with the larger creature first: from man to woman, מעלל ועד־יונק, from ox to sheep, and from camel to donkey. Since there is no other word to convey children who may be older in this list, it seems that the עולל may suggest a dependent child who is not necessarily very young. The same phrase appears in 1 Sam 22:19, again portraying an עולל as larger than a יונק, suggesting a child.[128] However, images of the עולל dashed into pieces (Isa 13:16; Hos 14:1, Nah 3:10; Ps 137:9) conjure visions of babies.[129] Like יונק, עולל seems to include infants, but is not strictly limited to this sense.

Given the threatening situations in which עולל occurs, Andreas Michel suggests this word has inherently violent connotations.[130] The עוללים are struck down (נכה: 1 Sam 22:19) and utterly destroyed (מות, חרם: 1 Sam 15:3), dashed to pieces (רטש: 2 Kgs 8:12; Isa 13:16; Hos 14:1 [Eng. 13:16]; Nah 3:10), shattered (נפץ: Ps 137:9), cut off (כרת: Jer 9:20 [Eng 9:21], 44:7), sent into captivity (הלך שבי: Lam 1:5), fainting in the streets (עטף: Lam 2:11, 19), and begging for bread (שאל לחם: Lam 4:4). They are the objects of YHWH's wrath (שפך . . . חמת יהוה: Jer 6:11) and risk being eaten by their mothers (אכל: Lam 2:20). The only instance in which an עולל could be viewed positively is in Ps 8:3, although this is a very enigmatic verse.[131] The term עולל then appears to suggest a small child, including but not limited to babies, in a situation of danger. This word also associates small children with misery and terror.

## עול/עויל

The root letters עול are widely attested in Semitic languages as related to sucking.[132] As Soebø notes, the explicit emphasis on sucking seems to

---

127. See 1 Sam 15:3; 22:19; Jer 44:7; Lam 2:11; Joel 2:16; Ps 8:3 (Eng. 8:2).
128. Accordingly, Eng simply defines עולל as "child" (*Days of Our Lives*, 58).
129. The NJPS translates עולל in these passages as "babies" (Ps 137:9), "infants" (Hos 14:1), or "babes" (Isa 13:16; Nah 3:10).
130. Michel, *Gott und Gewalt*, 24.
131. Comparing Ps 8:3 with *KTU* 1.23:59, 61, Helmer Ringgren suggests that Ps 8:3 portrays boys (not babies) who are devouring demons, consuming all between heaven and earth. See Helmer Ringgren, "Some Observations on the Text of the Psalms," *Maarav* 5–6 (Spring 1990): 307–9. See also Andreas Kunz-Lübcke, "Gotteslob aus Kindermund: Zu einer Theologie der Kinder in Psalm 8," in *Mensch und König: Studien zur Anthropologie des Alten Testaments Rüdiger Lux zum 60. Geburtstag* (ed. Angelika Berlejung and Raik Heckl; HBS 53; Freiburg: Herder, 2008), 84–106.
132. *TDOT* 11:518.

fade in nouns that convey a baby or small child more generally.¹³³ Forms of this root suggesting children or animals can be found in Arabic, Aramaic, Ethiopic, Punic, Syriac and Ugaritic, while only a few attestations appear in the Hebrew Bible.¹³⁴

עויל. This word occurs just twice (Job 19:18; 21:11).¹³⁵ In Job 19:18 the עוילים are the subject of their clause, capable of independent action, even as strong as rejecting, scorning, or despising Job: גם־עוילים מאסו בי אקומה וידברו־בי "Even small children reject me; I get up, and they speak against me." The emphatic particle גם exacerbates the insult and perhaps lessens the children's status or size. If children are mocking Job, this offense is even greater when the children are low in stature. In Job 21:11, עויליהם is parallel to ילדיהם, describing the delights (unfairly) enjoyed by the wicked. These include children in their presence (Job 21:8), suggesting that progeny are a blessing. Yet Job 21:19 threatens punishment for the evildoer's children.

עול. This noun appears only three times. While the attestations in Isa 49:15 and 65:20 are undisputed, the citation in Job 24:9 requires revocalization of the MT עַל to עוּל (BHS). This reading seems logical, rendering עול parallel to יתום and eliminating the otherwise enigmatic preposition על.¹³⁶ This attestation (if accepted) puts יגזלו משד יתום ("they tear away an orphan from the breast") parallel to ועל־עני יחבלו ("and the על of the afflicted they take as pledge"), suggesting the עול is a nursing baby. In Isa 65:20, עול is in construct with ימים, portraying a baby who is a few days old. However, the construct chain creates this impression of young infancy, and not the word עול per se. In context it seems the poet suggests the עול only *lives* a few days.¹³⁷ Likewise in Isa 49:15, the phase עולה ("her baby") corresponds to בן־בטנה ("son of her womb"). The reference to the womb conjures images of a newborn, although to be from the womb could refer to someone of any age. While the references to עול are few, its attestations suggest infants.¹³⁸

---

133. *TDOT* 11:518.
134. Similar forms in Semitic languages include the words for "girl" (Middle Hebrew); "suckling" (Jewish Aramaic, Syriac, Punic); "young, suckling animal" (Ugaritic); "young animal" (Syriac and Ethiopic); "to feed," "small child," and "to suckle" (Arabic) or "family" (Old South Arabian). In the DSS (11QPs) עלה is attested meaning "wet nurse" (*HALOT* 1:797–98).
135. See *HALOT* 1:797. The third possible attestation of this word suggesting a child (Job 16:11) should be rejected. In context this word is more logically read as a variant of עול, meaning "unjust one" (BDB, 732).
136. This reading has been adopted by the NIV, NJB, NRSV, RSV, and NJPS.
137. This verb is supplied in multiple translations, including the NIV, NJB, RSV, and NRSV.
138. The word עול is translated as "infant" in Isa 65:20 by the ASV, ESV, JPS, KJV, NAB, NAS, NIV, NJB, NKJV, NRSV, RSV, NJPS, and WEB; and in Job 24:9 by the NIV, NRSV, and RSV. In Isa 49:15 עול is translated as "infant" (NAB),"sucking child" (ASV, KJV, RSV),

As with עולל, עול appears to carry connotations of helplessness. A mother forgets her עול (Isa 49:15), and the poor person's עול is taken as a pledge (Job 24:9). Andreas Michel reads Isa 65:20 as one of the few instances where an עולל or עול is in a positive situation.[139] The prophet describes the new creation in which the young will live out their lives: לא־יהיה משם עוד עול ימים "from then on there shall no longer be an infant of a few days old." Yet while the context affirms the desire for a baby to live, it also assumes that babies die young. Overtones of vulnerability then surface with each attestation of this word.

## Abstract Words for Childhood and Youth

In addition to the words discussed above, the Hebrew Bible has abstract terms for childhood, showing that the writers conceptualized and compartmentalized earlier periods of life. Along with the general ילדות (Eccl 11:9–10, Ps 110:3), other terms break down childhood and youth into various stages. Genesis 43:33 tells of the Joseph's brothers seated at the vizier's table: הבכר כבכרתו והצעיר כצערתו, lit., "the first according to his state of being older and the young one according to his youth." Since Benjamin seems to be a boy, as evidenced by repeated emphasis on his youth (see n. 29 above), צעירה may indicate young childhood. The abstract *עלומים (Isa 54:4; Ps 89:46 [Eng. 89:45]; Job 20:11; 33:25) is parallel to נער in Job 33:25, perhaps implying older youth. As with the nominal forms of עלם and נער, the abstract terms seem closely related in meaning. The terms *בחורות (Eccl 11:9; 12:1) and *בחורים (Num 11:28), generally defined as "youthful condition" or "youth,"[140] seem to suggest the period near adulthood. These words can be laid in progression בחורים/בחורות, עלומים, צעירה, as designating successive stages of development.

The most common word for "youth" or "childhood" is נעורים, occurring forty-six times (also נעורות in Jer 32:30 and נער in Ps 88:15; Prov 29:21; Job 33:25; 36:14). These attestations offer insights about perceptions of this young phase of life. During נעורים, children are workers (Gen 46:34; Isa 47:12; Zech 13:5). Childhood is when a girl lives in her father's home (Lev 22:13; Num 30:4 [Eng. 30:3], 17 [Eng. 30:16]). Further occurences of נעורים suggest that children and youth gain belief (1 Kgs 18:12; Ps 71:17), form lasting bonds (Jer 3:4), commit transgressions (Ps 25:7; Job 13:26), and retain memories (Job 31:18) during this time. The writers recognize childhood as a period of learning and formation.

---

"nursing child" (ESV, NKJV, NRSV), "baby at the breast" (NIV, NJB), and "suckling" (YLT), all suggesting a small baby.

139. Michel, *Gott und Gewalt*, 24 n. 28.
140. *HALOT* 1:118; BDB, 104, respectively.

## Concepts of Children and Childhood in the Hebrew Bible

Before drawing conclusions about children and childhood in the Hebrew Bible, we need to recall that the cohesion of this literary corpus is our own projection. The writings of the Hebrew Bible span about a thousand years, pulling together a broad range of theological perspectives and historical circumstances. General observations about children (and most other topics) therefore should be made cautiously. For example, to say that the Bible understands children to lack sense (Prov 7:7), disgrace their mothers (Prov 29:15), and require beatings (Prov 22:15)[141] gives a perspective found in Proverbs (itself a varied collection) that is not in other books. We can more reliably grasp how different writers thought about children or how select collections portray them, as we will see in our subsequent discussion of the Elisha cycle. However, we cannot find a homogenous picture of children that spans the entire Hebrew Bible. With these caveats in mind, we can notice various ways that these ancient writers thought of children.

While the Hebrew Bible lacks *conceptions* of childhood that specifically articulate a set of cultural expectations, it has *concepts* of childhood that generally reflect awareness that children are different from adults. Writers share passing observations of children's physical attributes: they have healthy skin (2 Kgs 5:14; Job 33:25) and trouble traveling (Gen 33:13–14). More significantly, the writers recognize successive stages of children's growth and development. These can be generally categorized as babies (עול, יונק), babies or small children (עולל), very small children (גמול), (generally) pre-pubescent children (ילד, ילדה, and עולל when paired with יונק), older children and adolescents (עלם, עלמה), older adolescents/teenagers/young men or women (בחור, בתולה), and young men (בחור). Some words have few attestations, making it hard to get a full sense of their meaning, and these divisions certainly do not apply to every occurrence of words that appear often.

The boundaries between terms may be fluid, yet nonetheless reveal cultural distinctions that English does not similarly convey. Attention to gender grows in the language as youth develop sex characteristics, whereas in English "adolescent" and "teenager" remain gender-neutral. Hebrew nouns have masculine and feminine gender more frequently than in English; however, terms that appear in masculine and feminine forms can convey differences in meaning in addition to gender. For example, ילד can mean "offspring," "baby," "boy," or "child," but the three attestations of ילדה mean "girl" (Gen 34:4; Joel 4:3 [Eng. 3:3]; pl. Zech 8:5). Also

---

141. See Eng, *Days of Our Years*, 81.

the divisions of different phases of childhood do not correspond neatly to English words such as "infant" or "teenager." Instead of "baby" or "toddler," we find terms for very small children that evoke nursing (יונק) or weaning (גמול), with nuances not easily captured in modern English, beyond the antiquated "suckling." Other words for small children (עולל, עול) carry overtones of danger. One word, נער, bears multivalent connotations of status, lack of kinship, and/or youth. These nuances challenge us to keep in mind a word's complexities when reading or translating a text.

The Hebrew Bible conceptualizes children on the basis of kinship. The terms בן and בת suggest close relationship, even when not describing one's own offspring. When designating family members, בן and בת signify a linear relationship into successive generations. As noted above, אח and אחות show kinship through lateral connection. The term בכור functions both linearly, related to parents, and laterally, related to siblings. The female בכירה shows relations between sisters. A firstborn child, if a girl, would not have the status of the firstborn male child, so the relational claim of בכירה functions only laterally in the text. Terms for older girls and younger women show liminal status in age and kinship affiliation, as the בתולה (and often the עלמה) is at the cusp of adulthood and transfers to another household. The טף is defined through relationship to the family as a dependent, and not a specific stage of life. The term ילד conveys familial relationship, although not necessarily as close as a בן. Even though נער can be used in kinship situations, the term itself does not designate familial relation.[142] Without context to suggest otherwise, נער indicates someone outside the family. To be missing family relations, sometimes entirely, is the defining feature of the יתום. Terms for children and youth convey proximity, direction, or lack of relationships with family members.

Words for children and especially youth can also convey social standing. Whether a young man is a בחור or נער hinges on role and prestige, not age. Ideas of service and youth are closely intertwined, and indeed נער frequently combines the two concepts, as does עלם. Terms for older girls and young women (עלמה and בתולה) appear to carry overtones of sexual maturity, also a form of status. Concerns for status are less evident with small children.

Instead, questions of safety surface. Words for children frequently appear in violent contexts, although this is also true with older youth. Interestingly, a נער is much less likely to be a victim than a ילד.[143] Since references to a נער (regardless of age) generally suggest someone who is not kin, the characters (and readers) are not as invested in the well-being of the נער as in that of the ילד. Images of ילדים being burned, slain, or passed

---

142. Analogously, to say "She has a boy" implies kinship in context, although "boy" does not overtly convey kinship, as "son" or "child" would.

143. Michel, *Gott und Gewalt*, 22.

through the fire function to elicit outrage, or at least strong reactions from readers. As discussed above, when the terms בנים and בנות are paired, these children are frequently victims. This also inadvertently testifies to children's importance since their destiny merits concern. Select terms also hint at a child's fate, perhaps alerting the reader for full effect. Various forms of גמל appear to indicate a small child who is free from harm. A יונק may or may not be safe, whereas the עולל or עול is a small child in danger. This vocabulary reflects awareness that dangerous threats were frequent, and small children were especially susceptible.

Concepts of children and childhood are not only present in the Hebrew Bible, but layered and complex. While the categorization here groups terms for children and youth by relationship, gender, and phases of progression, distinctions which matter to the writers gravitate not only around kinship, growth, and gender but also around status and safety. The writers notice children's stages in life and the relationships they have within and outside of family and the wider society. Children and youth are an integral and indispensable part of the layered nexus of relationships that comprises the biblical world.

# 3

# Approaching the Elisha Cycle:
## *A Literary and Methodological Framework*

This book now progresses from a linguistic to a literary approach as the focus turns to the Elisha cycle (2 Kings 2–8). Knowledge of terms for children and youth brings nuanced understanding to our reading. By examining not only words but their context and usage, we see how the child characters emerge and shape their stories, even when they appear briefly. Through sustained reflection on one set of stories, we can explore children's roles, challenges, and responsibilities close up. We will observe how child characters act themselves, how other characters interact with them, and how the children influence and react to their surroundings, situations, and relationships. These observations offer insight into how children were perceived, since these texts' writers operate with cultural expectations that they shared with their ancient audience.

## The Elisha Cycle: Literary Context and Genre

The Elisha cycle is a small part of a large collection of literary materials that scholars commonly call the Deuteronomistic History (DH). As proposed by Martin Noth, this extensive corpus extends from Deuteronomy through Kings and traces the formation, apex, division, and decline of Israel as a nation.[1] Widely disparate material coheres through charac-

---

1. Martin Noth, *Überlieferungsgeschichtliche Studien: Die sammelnden und bearbeitenden Geschichtswerke im Alten Testament* (Tübingen: Niemeyer, 1943). (For an English translation of pp. 1–110 of the 2nd edition [1957] see Martin Noth, *The Deuteronomistic History* [trans. and ed. David J. A. Clines; JSOTSup 15; Sheffield: JSOT Press, 1981].) Noth's work countered that of earlier scholars, notably Abraham Kuenen (who posited two editions of the Deuteronomistic History) and Julius Wellhausen (who basically agreed). Other academics prior to Noth (e.g., Gustav Hölscher and Otto Eissfeldt) saw the Yahwist and Elohist sources extending through Kings. For a discussion of Noth's legacy, see Steven L. McKenzie and M. Patrick Graham, eds., *The History of Israel's Traditions: The Heritage of Martin Noth* (JSOTSup 182; Sheffield: Sheffield Academic Press, 1994). For related essays, see Gary N. Knoppers and J. Gordon

ters, plot, and shared political and religious motifs. The writer/redactor of this material, according to Noth, shaped and framed his sources by the overarching narration and inserted easily discernible biases and beliefs, often through the characters' own words. These speeches serve to mark key sections of the work, as well as provide theological unity to the overall composition. Noth's conclusions, while still highly influential, no longer retain the iconic status they once enjoyed. Shortly after they were proposed, other scholars offered emendations.[2] These schemas recently have been called into question by Jan Gertz, Reinhard Müller, Reinhard Kratz, and Konrad Schmid, among others.[3] Extended review of this scholarship is beyond the purview of this book, as theories about the composition, dating, redaction, and authorship of the DH continue to prompt lively debate.[4] For our purposes, we will simply note that the Elisha cycle plays an important theological role in this wider literary collection.

---

McConville, eds., *Reconsidering Israel and Judah: Recent Studies on the Deuteronomistic History* (SBTS 8; Winona Lake, IN: Eisenbrauns, 2000).

2. For discussion of the revisions related to the book of Kings, see Frank Moore Cross, "The Themes of the Book of Kings and the Structure of the Deuteronomistic History," in *Canaanite Myth and Hebrew Epic: Essays in the History of the Religion of Israel* (Cambridge, MA: Harvard University Press, 1973), 274–78; André Lemaire, "Vers l'histoire de la rédaction des Livres des Rois," *ZAW* 98 (1986): 221–24; Steven L. McKenzie, *The Trouble with Kings: The Composition of the Book of Kings in the Deuteronomistic History* (VTSup 42; Leiden: E. J. Brill, 1991), 1–19; Richard D. Nelson, *The Double Redaction of the Deuteronomistic History* (JSOTSup 18; Sheffield: JSOT Press, 1981), 13–22; and Robert R. Wilson, "Unity and Diversity in the Book of Kings," in *"A Wise and Discerning Mind": Essays in Honor of Burke O. Long* (ed. Saul M. Olyan and Robert C. Culley; BJS 325; Providence, RI: Brown Judaic Studies, 2000), 295–301 (among others). For an overview discussion of scholarship regarding redaction and composition of the book of Kings, as well as an extensive bibliography, see Michael Avioz, "The Book of Kings in Recent Research (Part I)" *CBR* 4 (2005): 11–55.

3. See Jan Christian Gertz, *Die Gerichtsorganisation Israels im deuteronomischen Gesetz* (FRLANT 165; Göttingen: Vandenhoeck & Ruprecht, 1994); Reinhard Kratz, *Die Komposition der erzählenden Bücher des Alten Testaments: Grundwissen der Bibelkritik* (Göttingen: Vandenhoeck & Ruprecht, 2000); Reinhard Müller, *Königtum und Gottesherrschaft: Untersuchungen zur alttestamentlichen Monarchiekritik* (FAT 3; Tübingen: Mohr Siebeck, 2004); Markus Witte, Konrad Schmid, et al., eds., *Die deuteronomistischen Geschichtswerke: Redaktions- und religionsgeschichtliche Perspektiven zur "Deuteronomismus"-Diskussion in Tora und Vorderen Propheten* (BZAW 365; Berlin: de Gruyter, 2006). For further review of DH scholarship, see Thomas C. Römer, *The So-Called Deuteronomistic History: A Sociological, Historical, and Literary Introduction* (London: T&T Clark, 2007).

4. Questions of dating are not crucial for this study. Nonetheless, I agree with scholars who suggest that the Elijah and Elisha stories reflect northern pre-exilic material that was later incorporated into the Deuteronomistic History. See Römer, *The So-Called Deuteronomistic History*, 153–55. (Conversely, see Susanne Otto, "The Composition of the Elijah-Elisha Stories and the Deuteronomistic History," *JSOT* 27 [2003]: 504–8.) It seems plausible that the Elisha cycle has a northern provenance before the Assyrian conquest of Samaria, but was incorporated into the Deuteronomistic History in the exilic or post-exilic period. During the latter part of the eighth century, thousands of people from Israel escaped to Judah, with many locating in Jerusalem. Archeological remains from this time show that Jerusalem

Appearing toward the end of the Deuteronomistic History, the stories of Elisha concentrate on the prophet's wonder-working abilities, while forsaking salient themes of the DH (i.e., anger against apostasy, allegiance to the central sanctuary, election of the Israelites, prioritization of monotheism, keeping of the covenant, primacy of the Davidic dynasty, or distrust of foreigners).[5] The Elisha cycle nonetheless contributes to the theological goals of this wider literary corpus with stories of prophecy and fulfillment.[6] These narratives help to establish YHWH as the reigning deity in Israel by demonstrating the prowess of this prophet and his God.

---

grew in size and population at a dramatic rate. The population increased as much as fifteen times, and the small hill town of Jerusalem became an expansive urban center of 150 acres. Sprawling settlements also proliferated in the outlying agricultural areas, accompanied by an upsurge in building, trade, and manufacturing. In *The Bible Unearthed*, Israel Finkelstein and Neil Asher Silberman note increasingly sophisticated architecture in Jerusalem and suggest that this stemmed largely from Judah's incorporation into the Assyrian economy. See Israel Finkelstein and Neil Asher Silberman, *The Bible Unearthed: Archaeology's New Vision of Ancient Israel and the Origin of Its Sacred Texts* (New York: Free Press, 2001), 246. It also seems likely that the skills and abilities of northern refugees contributed to Jerusalem's renovation. Israel's capital of Samaria had had its own impressive urban accomplishments, boasting a superb royal acropolis, with advanced architectural styles, including intricate gates and exquisite engravings. See John S. Holladay, "The Kingdoms of Israel and Judah: Political and Economic Centralization in the Iron IIA-B (ca. 1000–750 BCE)," in *The Archaeology of Society in the Holy Land* (ed. Thomas E. Levy; New York: Facts on File, 1995), 368–98. See also Israel Finkelstein, "City-States to States: Polity Dynamics in the 10th-9th Centuries B.C.E.," in *Symbiosis, Symbolism, and the Power of the Past* (ed. William Dever and Seymour Gitin; Winona Lake, IN: Eisenbrauns, 2003), 80. Some of those who swelled Jerusalem's population must have fled from Samaria, bringing knowledge and labor. Usually the first people to leave a situation of impending disaster are those with the financial means to do so, further increasing the likelihood that some of Israel's educated populace were among the early refugees. For anthropological discussion of migration patterns, see Caroline Bretell, *Anthropology and Migration: Essays on Transnationalism, Ethnicity, and Identity* (Walnut Creek, CA: AltaMira, 2003). The trades that northern refugees from Israel brought to Judah likely involved building, but may have also included writing. This possible migratory scenario fuels speculation about the origin of the Elisha stories. These tales, situated in ninth-century Israel, may have been part of this influx of culture into the south in the late eighth century BCE, and provided some raw material for constructing a literary history of the northern kingdom.

5. For fuller discussion of these themes, see Moshe Weinfeld, *Deuteronomy and the Deuteronomic School* (London: Clarendon, 1972).

6. For examples of fulfilled prophecies from the Elisha cycle, see Ziony Zevit, *The Religions of Ancient Israel: A Synthesis of Parallactic Approaches* (London: Continuum, 2001), 484–85. However, not all of the prophetic material serves the narrative through the prophecy/fulfillment schema, and some even contradicts it. For example, in the story of the war with Moab, Elisha predicts that the Israelites will conquer the Moabites (2 Kgs 3:17–20), but the Israelites retreat (2 Kgs 3:27) (further discussion follows). For discussion of the fulfilled prophecy motif and its restricted role in Kings, see Robert R. Wilson, "The Former Prophets: Reading the Books of Kings," in *Old Testament Interpretation: Past, Present, and Future: Essays in Honor of Gene M. Tucker* (ed. James Luther Mays, David L. Petersen, and Kent Harold Richards; Nashville: Abingdon, 1995), 88–90.

As the institution of prophecy emerges in Israel's history, the episodes with Elisha provide dramatic and memorable accounts of prophetic ability and divine power. On a literary level, these stories in Kings also highlight the roles of prophets, which are further developed in the subsequent books of the writing prophets.

Scholars debate whether the narratives about Elijah or those of Elisha came first, as they share plots and phrases that correspond closely.[7] Some think the Elisha tales build upon the stories of Elijah, minimizing the conflict with Baal and favoring inspiring tales of wonder.[8] Others suggest that the Elisha stories are the foundation for the more theologically refined Elijah tales.[9] Building upon Rofé's work, Marsha White compares similar stories from the Elijah and Elisha cycles.[10] White incorporates variants from Septuagint manuscripts and examines misplaced narrative features to persuasively argue that Elijah's stories depend on those of Elisha.[11] The Elijah stories are also more compact, complicated, and overtly connected with YHWH than the Elisha versions. The text portrays Elisha as the prophetic successor, but Elijah is his textual heir.

Within the Elisha cycle, various inconsistencies surface. For example, the text offers no explanation for Israel's changed relationship with Aram, whether peaceful (2 Kgs 5:1) or hostile (2 Kgs 6:8). In one story, Elisha's servant Gehazi is rebuked (2 Kgs 5:25–26) and afflicted with a skin disease (2 Kgs 5:27), but in a subsequent episode he appears highly respected and perfectly fine (2 Kgs 8:4–5). For the most part, the order of the epi-

---

7. E.g., 1 Kgs 17:1, cf. 2 Kgs 3:24; 1 Kgs 17:8–16, cf. 2 Kgs 4:1–7; 1 Kgs 17:17–24, cf. 2 Kgs 4:27–37; 2 Kgs 2:12, cf. 2 Kgs 13:14.

8. See Benjamin Uffenheimer, *Early Prophecy in Israel* (Jerusalem: Magnes, 1999), 466–71.

9. Compare, for example, the conclusions of the stories about the boys whom Elijah and Elisha revive. In the Elisha account (2 Kgs 4:8–37), the Shunammite woman takes her risen son and exits wordlessly (v. 37). In the corresponding Elijah story (2 Kgs 17:17–24), the widow of Zarephath utters a profession of faith (v. 24). This theological addition may suggest that the Elijah account polishes the earlier Elisha tradition. This thesis was proposed by Gustav Hölscher, *Die Profeten: Untersuchungen zur Religionsgeschichte Israels* (Leipzig: J. C. Hinrichs, 1914), 177. For a more recent overview of this discussion, see Michael Avioz, "The Book of Kings in Recent Research (Part II)," *CBR* 5 (2006): 32–35.

10. See Marsha C. White, *The Elijah Legends and Jehu's Coup* (BJS 311; Atlanta, Scholars Press: 1997), 11–17. See also R. P. Carroll, "The Elijah-Elisha Sagas: Some Remarks on Prophetic Succession in Ancient Israel" *VT* 19 (1969): 400–415. Carroll suggests that Elijah and Elisha stories were built on existing prophetic traditions that largely centered on Moses. On parallels between Elisha and Joshua, see pp. 411–12.

11. For example, in 1 Kgs 17:10–24 the widow of Zarephath encounters Elijah. The prophet has a furnished upper room in the widow's house (v. 19), just like Elisha at the home of the wealthy Shunammite (2 Kgs 4:8–10). These accommodations seem oddly misplaced at the home of a destitute widow. The Greek versions of 1 Kgs 17:12–13 portray the widow with children (τέκνα), not one son. This discrepancy may reflect borrowing from 2 Kgs 4:1–7 since the widow in the Elisha story who receives a miracle of multiplication has two children. See White, *Elijah Legends*, 14.

sodes could be re-arranged without altering the meaning or confusing a plot. The Elisha cycle appears as a loose collection of tales focused on the wonder-working ability of this ninth-century prophet.

The stories that are the subject of this inquiry (2 Kgs 2:23–25; 3:26–27; 4:1–7; 4:8–37; 5:1–14; 6:24–31; 8:1–6) resist easy genre classification. Within the Elisha cycle, Rofé notes the prominence of the legendum: a simple, short, independent story with characters that function through their role. Legenda begin with a confounding crisis and end with a miraculous deliverance, orchestrated by the man of God.[12] The unfolding events do not carry political or national overtones and lack moral lessons. Rofé views legenda as developed condensations of earlier, oral versions of these stories, although this is difficult to prove.[13]

Following Rofé's lead, Burke Long limns loosely binding characteristics of the Elisha stories. Long offers a detailed review of genre classifications and categorizes nearly all the stories studied here (except 2 Kgs 3:26–27) under the broad rubric of "prophet legends."[14] He notes the challenge of imposing distinctions on material that does not easily meet specific genre criteria or incorporates various subgenres. For example, Long recognizes that the story of the Moabite battle (2 Kgs 3:4–27) has a historical character, but includes standard sayings that declare allegiance (v. 7), signal distress (v. 10), proclaim an oath (v. 14), and assure victory (v. 18).[15] Similarly, the story of Naaman's healing (2 Kgs 5:1–24) incorporates multiple elements, including scenarios with royalty and international relations (vv. 5–7) and indirect prophetic intervention (vv. 8–14). The story of the Shunammite (2 Kgs 4:8–37) combines passages of annunciation (vv. 16–17), petition (vv. 27–30), and prophetic power (vv. 32–35). Long includes the episode of the boys being eaten by their own mothers (2 Kgs 6:24–31) as part of a longer legend (2 Kgs 6:24–7:20; also 2 Kgs 4:8–37, 5:1–27).[16] The story of the boy restored to life (2 Kgs 8:1–6) is another prophet legend in Long's schema, even though the prophet is absent. Rather, Elisha's reputation is sufficiently powerful to accomplish goals (vv. 5–6). Long's discussion shows how interpretation can play a significant role in defining genre categorization.

Yael Shemesh offers a helpful summary and convincing critique of

---

12. For further discussion of this genre, see Alexander Rofé, *The Prophetical Stories: Narrative about the Prophets in the Hebrew Bible and Their Literary Types and History* (Jerusalem: Magnes, 1988), 13–22.

13. Of the seven tales that involve children in the Elisha cycle, only one—the story of the debt-collateral children (4:1–7)—neatly falls into Rofé's categorization of legendum.

14. Burke Long, *2 Kings* (FOTL 10; Grand Rapids, MI: Eerdmans, 1991), 32–99. The pericopes selected for this study (2 Kgs 2:23–25; 3:26–27; 4:1–7; 4:8–37; 5:1–14; 6:24–31; 8:1–6) do not always correspond to Long's division of passages.

15. Long, *2 Kings*, 45–46.

16. Long, *2 Kings*, 95.

various genre interpretations of the Elisha cycle.[17] According to Shemesh, these stories are saints' legends that intertwine the reputations of YHWH and Elisha. Shemesh rejects Leah Bronner's categorization of the Elijah and Elisha cycles as polemical stories against Baal, noting that the themes Bronner uses to determine cross-cultural correspondence (e.g., famine, childlessness, illness) are too general to have much relevance. Shemesh also disagrees with Burke Long's description of Elisha as a typical shaman, since he is such an extraordinary figure.[18] R. D. LaBarbera sees 2 Kings 5; 6:8–23; and 6:24–7:20 as social and political critiques against the ruling elite. However, Shemesh rightly points out that this position seems hard to sustain given the stories' plots.[19] Similarly, Rick Moore proposes that 2 Kings 5; 6:8–23; and 6:24–7:20 are didactic salvation stories that reflect tension between Aram and Israel. While these narratives do extol Elisha and YHWH, as Moore maintains, they do not consistently reflect a bitter historical rivalry.[20] Shemesh also questions David Marcus's assessment of 2 Kgs 2:23–25 as an anti-prophetic satire, disputing the suggestion that this story is critical of Elisha.[21] Instead Shemesh asserts that these stories express wonder, awe, reverence, and admiration for the prophet.

Shemesh makes a strong case for viewing these stories as saints' legends, which is ultimately persuasive. However, in Shemesh's understanding it appears that Elisha can do no wrong. When he causes the death of dozens of children (2 Kgs 2:23–25), Shemesh finds this justifiable since they have shown serious disrespect for the holy man of God.[22] When Elisha (arrogantly?) tells the Shunammite woman she will have a son she did not request (2 Kgs 4:16), Shemesh sees the prophet as generous and "supremely moral," as he repays her hospitality.[23] Shemesh maintains that Elisha is not overly proud when he refuses to see Naaman who has come to him for healing (2 Kgs 5:9–10); rather this expresses the prophet's humble attempt to magnify YHWH's role in the miraculous cure.[24] Although Elisha's advice has cost a woman her home and land (2 Kgs 8:1–3), Shemesh

---

17. Yael Shemesh, "The Elisha Stories as Saints' Legends," *JHS* 8, art. 5 (2008): 1–41, doi:10.5508/v.8.a5.

18. Shemesh, "Elisha Stories," 4–5. Long appears to have moved away from this idea himself to the views recounted above, as Shemesh remarks on p. 4 n. 9.

19. Shemesh, "Elisha Stories," 5–6. For example, in the story of the Israelite slave girl (2 Kgs 5:1–14) the lower and upper class live peaceably together. Servants make helpful suggestions to their superiors (2 Kgs 5:3, 13), who heed their underlings' advice (2 Kgs 5:4–9, 14).

20. Shemesh, "Elisha Stories," 7–8. The story of Naaman's healing questions this premise, as YHWH rewards the Aramean commander (2 Kgs 5:1), who then becomes a devoted follower (2 Kgs 5:17–18), reflecting positive relations between Aram and Israel.

21. Shemesh, "Elisha Stories," 9.

22. Shemesh, "Elisha Stories," 14.

23. Shemesh, "Elisha Stories," 18. For further discussion, see pp. 17–26.

24. Shemesh, "Elisha Stories," 26–30.

emphasizes that this loss is temporary and ultimately, through Elisha's reputation, all is restored (2 Kgs 8:4–6).[25] The story of Elisha's own death, where a dead man revives after touching his bones (2 Kgs 13:20–21), offers concluding affirmation of the prophet's sainthood, according to Shemesh.[26] Certainly these tales are so cryptic that portraits of Elisha remain open to readers' contrasting opinions. Yet Shemesh's analysis also illustrates how interpretations can bow to genre classification. We can legitimately read these stories as saints' legends that extol a holy man and his God, yet to be holy is not necessarily the same as morally perfect.

## Credibility, Child Characters, and the World of the Text

Having established that the Elisha cycle is a collection of saints' legends included in the DH to fulfill a theological purpose, we will now look at how this impacts our childist reading. For these legends to prove that Elisha is the designated conduit for YHWH's stunning power, the prophet needs to be the only extraordinary figure in each story. As Baruch Hochman notes, a character's range of accepted actions and attitudes varies according to literary genre. Within the expectations and confines of a particular genre, minimally stylized characters exhibit traits of plausibility and coherence, whereas maximally stylized characters take on features of caricature. Hochman explains that "minimal stylization involves the depiction of characters in more or less normative terms and in terms of the way we might perceive them if they really existed."[27] In saints' legends that extol a holy man, the other characters must behave naturally so that Elisha can inspire awe. The author works from the premise that YHWH can perform spectacular feats through this exceptional human being. The ordinary characters, including the children, are minimally stylized to conform to typical behavior and contrast the prophet's ability to transcend the bonds of convention. If these were fabulous tales filled with fantastic characters purely to entertain the reader, the ability to appreciate Elisha's extraordinary powers would be muddled or lost.[28]

---

25. Shemesh, "Elisha Stories," 30–32.
26. Shemesh, "Elisha Stories," 32–36.
27. Baruch Hochman, *Character in Literature* (Ithaca, NY: Cornell University Press, 1985), 93.
28. Astounding occurrences in the Elisha cycle display the parting of the river Jordan (2 Kgs 2:13–14), the instant purification of harmful spring waters (2 Kgs 2:19–22), bears responding to a prophet's curse (2 Kgs 2:24), an oil jar that fills vessels far beyond its own capacity (2 Kgs 4:1–7), a child rising from the dead (2 Kgs 4:32–35), the decontamination of a poisonous pot of stew (2 Kgs 2:39–41), the multiplication of loaves to feed a large crowd

The author therefore presents a narrative world that seems not only plausible, but authentic and enduring. Erich Auerbach explains, "The world of the Scripture stories is not satisfied with claiming to be a historically true reality—it insists that it is the only real world...."[29] To maintain this authority, the text presents its portrayals unapologetically. Accordingly, the narrator in the Elisha cycle assumes total credibility, even while describing seemingly impossible events.

We can therefore learn about how the writers thought about children by examining these stories. This is not the same as maintaining that these stories consistently show typical life for real children in antiquity. (For example, bears maul small children [2 Kgs 2:23–25], and a mother eats her own son [2 Kgs 6:24–31].) However, these narratives nonetheless are grounded in realistic settings and portray credible characters and relationships. The stories also raise social and historical issues that involved children in the larger society, as corroborated by additional biblical texts, extrabiblical sources, and historical scholarship. (For example, children risk becoming debt slaves [2 Kgs 4:1–7], and a child is taken as a captive for servitude [2 Kgs 5:2].) These legends in the Elisha cycle depict children in the narrative world while raising questions about children in the ancient world.

To notice the child characters we need to resist common reading strategies that assess a character's significance, often according to the length of his or her story. Adele Berlin, following E. M. Forster, outlines a typical hierarchy of characterization, starting at the bottom with "functionaries" or "agents," who perform a certain role in the story and then disappear. Next are the "flat characters" or "types," who do not develop in any way and often fulfill stereotypes, such as the faithful servant, dutiful wife, or powerful king. The most realized characters, called "round" or "full-fledged," show various aspects of their personality and, much like real people, may or may not conform to expectations.[30] The size and complex-

---

(2 Kgs 4:42–44), the healing of a person with a skin disease by immersion in water (5:1, 14), the transference of a skin affliction from one person to another (2 Kgs 5:25–27), an ax head rising to the top of the water (2 Kgs 6:5–7), Arameans being struck blind and then seeing again (2 Kgs 6:18–20), and a man being buried who springs back to life (2 Kgs 13:20–21). Some of these acts form the basis for Jesus' miracles in the New Testament, which Christians generally read as having actually transpired. For further discussion, see Raymond E. Brown, "Jesus and Elisha," *Perspective* 12 (1971): 85–104. Analogous to the stories of Elisha, the miracles of Jesus can only have the effect of extolling a prophet's extraordinary relationship with God if they are believed.

29. Erich Auerbach, *Mimesis: The Representation of Reality in Western Literature* (Princeton: Princeton University Press, 1953), 14–15.

30. Adele Berlin, *Poetics and Interpretation of Biblical Narrative* (Sheffield: Almond Press, 1983), 23–24. For discussion of characterization as understood by E. M. Forster, W. J. Harvey, Joseph Ewen, and A. J. Greimas, as well as a helpful bibliography, see D. F. Tolmie, *Narratology and Biblical Narratives: A Practical Guide* (San Francisco: International Scholars,

ity of a character's role are generally thought to correspond to her or his importance.³¹

Nonetheless, minor characters are compelling for many reasons. Solely studying the Bible's best-known characters can feed into a weary interpretive spiral that continually circles around the same luminaries, whereas concentrating on minor characters can shine new light on familiar texts. Further, as Uriel Simon notes, minor characters behave in ways that are consistent with their society as they provide background for the main characters or help to move the plot, and thereby offer cultural insights.³² Also, the distinction between a minor or major character can be subjective. Shimon Bar-Efrat observes, "It is not always possible to make a clear and unequivocal distinction between a primary and a secondary character."³³ Finally, each reader brings her or his own questions and interests to a text, which play a critical role in generating meaning.³⁴ A character who is entirely inconsequential for one reader may be stunningly significant for another. Who gets to determine which characters matter at the exclusion of others? Simon urges readers to focus on those with smaller roles in the biblical narrative and asserts that "it is the minor characters who often provide the key to the message of the story."³⁵

Instead of overlooking the children in the Elisha cycle, we understand them as characters in their own right, most of whose lives are not revealed to us. Gaps in the text are often laden with meaning, pulling in the reader to surmise what has transpired in the unexplained interim between events of reported sequence. Meir Sternberg notes that the narrator often refrains from providing details. Sternberg observes, "His [the narrator's] *ex-cathedra* judgments are valid as far as they go, but then they seldom go far below the surface of the narrative, where they find their qualification

---

1999), 54–61. See also Mark Allan Powell, *What Is Narrative Criticism?* (Minneapolis: Fortress, 1990), 54–55.

31. For example, Berlin describes how Bathsheba in 2 Samuel 11–12 helps to advance the plot, but shows no thoughts or feelings of her own and is thus "a complete non-person" (Berlin, *Poetics and Interpretation*, 27).

32. See Uriel Simon, "Minor Characters in Biblical Narrative," *JSOT* 46 (1990): 14–15.

33. Shimon Bar-Efrat, *Narrative Art in the Bible* (JSOTSup 70; Sheffield: Almond Press, 1989), 86.

34. As Danna Nolan Fewell and David Gunn point out, "Meaning is not something out there in the text waiting to be discovered. Meaning is always, in the last analysis, the reader's creation, and readers, like texts, come in an infinite variety." See Danna Nolan Fewell and David M. Gunn, *Narrative in the Hebrew Bible* (Oxford: Oxford University Press, 1993), xi. For lively debate on the role of the reader and the validity of interpretation, see Danna Nolan Fewell and David M. Gunn, "Tipping the Balance: Sternberg's Reader and the Rape of Dinah," *JBL* 110 (1991): 193–211; and Meir Sternberg, "Biblical Poetics and Sexual Politics: From Reading to Counterreading," *JBL* 111 (1992): 463–88.

35. Simon, "Minor Characters," 18.

and shading."[36] Readers search the text for clues about a character through the narrator's assessment or observing how the character acts, speaks, or functions. Yet our understanding of a character is not just a projection of our imagination, but limited by the text's parameters. In exploring the lives of child characters, we ask questions about them but do not transgress the boundaries of possibilities within the realm of the story.

To examine the children in the Elisha cycle requires commitment from the reader. While they may appear one-dimensional at first, these child characters can acquire multidimensional lives through concentrated attention. Hochman notes that characters do not simply reside in the text; they are created in the minds of the reader from the words on the page. He observes, "They [the characters], like everything else in the text, exist meaningfully only insofar as they come to exist in our consciousness."[37] By raising our awareness of these children, we contribute to their identity. The text provides basic material, but the reader gives the character his or her life.[38]

## Methodology for Childist Interpretation

Given the paucity of information about the children as they appear in the Elisha cycle, we need to develop strategies for learning about them. Toward this end, this book offers a systematic process to facilitate childist interpretation. Pericopes for discussion form around the children in the text, eschewing divisions suggested by liturgical readings, biblical commentaries, or published editions of the Bible. As Yairah Amit asserts, "The reader who defines the subject determines its scope."[39] Scenes begin when narrative elements appear that will involve the child character(s), and end when the narrative no longer relates to the child(ren). This helps the child characters to remain the focus of attention for the subsequent discussion.

---

36. Meir Sternberg, *The Poetics of Biblical Narrative: Ideological Literature and the Drama of Reading* (Bloomington: Indiana University Press, 1985), 51.

37. Hochman, *Character*, 32. Hochman notes that focusing on characters enriches our appreciation of the literature in which they appear. He suggests that "the possibility of abstracting or 'liberating' the characters and contemplating them as they are in themselves must be affirmed, for the sake of a full envisionment of the scope of individual texts and of the imaginative scope of literature itself" (p. 58).

38. For detailed discussion of the role of readers in building characters, especially minor characters, see Gina Hens-Piazza, *Nameless, Blameless, and without Shame: Two Cannibal Mothers before a King* (Collegeville, MN: Liturgical Press, 2003), 3–23. For further discussion of characters in narratives, see Yairah Amit, *Reading Biblical Narratives: Literary Criticism and the Hebrew Bible* (trans. Yael Lotan; Minneapolis: Fortress, 2001), 69–92. See also Robert Alter, *The Art of Biblical Narrative* (New York: Basic Books, 1981), 114–30.

39. Amit, *Reading Biblical Narratives*, 21.

All the child characters in the Elisha cycle lack names so the provided designations serve to facilitate commentary. These appellations also function as titles for each section of analysis, directing attention to the children. Ironically, the character's anonymity is part of his or her identity, so I refrain from bestowing proper names on unnamed characters.[40] Also, it can cause confusion if separate commentators create different proper names for the same character, whereas a designation is inherently descriptive.

Once passages and designations are in place, the discussion proceeds in six sections. Three steps of dissection (*Setting, Characters, Re-viewing the Plot from a Childist Perspective*) examine the story's details, before three steps of connection (*Childist Interpretation, Insights about Children, and Children and Textual Connections*) discuss its wider insights and implications. These divisions remain somewhat fluid, as discussion about one character involves another or the section on interpretation may include insights on children or connect to other texts. First, each analysis investigates the story's setting to provide a point of entry for the world of a given narrative. This grounds each episode, as the narrator paradoxically draws the reader into the text's world by feigning disinterest. Since narratives rarely provide background information before proceeding with the plot, a focus on the setting starts to explore the lives of the children through the location or circumstances of the story. Next, the analysis examines all the characters. As Bar-Efrat explains, characters invite more emotional involvement from the reader than other elements that comprise a story, such as location, time frame, and commentary. He notes, "Sometimes the characters arouse our sympathy, sometimes our revulsion, but we are never indifferent to them."[41] Special attention to the children's relationships with the characters around them shows how they influence each other. Subsequently, each discussion looks at the plot, which gives the story its shape as events unfold in a sequence that appears cohesive. How do the child characters help to form the narrative arc? The next section offers interpretations that highlight the children, who are commonly ignored in standard commentaries. How do readers understand the narrative differently with children at the center of attention? The focus then turns to children's involvement in the ancient world. How did the writers understand children and what does it mean to be a child in the world of the text? This section frequently includes information from various disciplines (such as archaeol-

---

40. For further discussion about approaches to naming, see Karla G. Bohmbach, "Names and Naming in the Biblical World," in *Women of Scripture: A Dictionary of Named and Unnamed Women in the Hebrew Bible, the Apocryphal/Deuterocanonical Books, and the New Testament* (ed. Carol Meyers, Toni Craven, and Ross S. Kraemer; Boston: Houghton Mifflin, 2000), 33–39.

41. Bar-Efrat, *Narrative Art*, 47.

ogy, anthropology, and sociology) as issues surface related to children's lives in ancient times. Finally, each story's analysis ends with connections between the child character(s) in that story and those who appear outside the Elisha cycle. Children in the Bible have lots of company, and noticing them offers avenues for future scholarship.

These analyses combine literary (synchronic) and historical-critical (diachronic) approaches with linguistic, sociological, anthropological, and archaeological insights.[42] The proposed methodology guides us to explore hidden complexities of this literature, the social-historical world it portrays, and the children within both. In addition to discovering new dimensions of ancient texts, we also gain and practice the skill of noticing and valuing the Bible's many children.

---

42. While scholars often understand historical-critical and literary approaches to the Bible as fiercely opposed, they share common ground and often complement each other. For example, as John Barton notes, both tactics seek to grasp the text's *Gestalt* by scrutinizing its details. Generally, literary critics look at the text as stemming from a specific ancient culture, and historical critics examine the words of the text to increase their knowledge. Barton suggests, "It is in the interest of all students of the Old Testament that historical and literary critics should somehow be brought to inhabit the same world, not to spend time staking out their own territory but to recognize that the whole land lies before them, and that most of the texts they interpret need both historical and literary skill if they are to be adequately interpreted." See John Barton, "Historical Criticism and Literary Interpretation: Is There Any Common Ground?" in *Israel's Past in Present Research: Essays on Ancient Historiography* (ed. V. Philips Long; Winona Lake, IN: Eisenbrauns, 1999), 437–38. For a more recent overview of this debate, see George Aichele, Peter Miscall, and Richard Walsh, "An Elephant in the Room: Historical-Critical and Postmodern Interpretations of the Bible," *JBL* 128.2 (2009): 383–404. Aichele, Miscall, and Walsh also call for a rapprochement between these two interpretative approaches.

# II

# Analyses of Stories—Children and Elisha

This book now delves into the stories containing children within the Elisha cycle. The following analyses assess who is a child on the basis of vocabulary and context, at points contradicting the opinion of commentators. Legends in the Elisha cycle could be re-arranged without seriously detracting from their purpose. However, this discussion treats passages in the order that they appear in the Bible, since the reader's encounter with each tale influences and informs her or his understanding of the next. Far from being insignificant minor characters, the children in the Elisha cycle are crucial to their stories, as these childist interpretations will prove.

The curious and troubling episode of 2 Kgs 2:23–25 fortuitously inaugurates our discussion while setting parameters and defining goals. To take these stories at face value and derive simple lessons from them would underestimate the text, as seen in 2 Kgs 2:23–25. While this passage portrays children being mauled by bears, it is not primarily about the dangers of wild animals in ancient Israel, particularly as a threat to children. Rather, this story offers surprising and troubling insights about children, Elisha, and their relationship to each other.

# 4

# The Mockers of Bethel
# (2 Kings 2:23–25)

In the tale of the mockers from Bethel, a group of children come from their town and jeer at Elisha, telling him to go away and calling him "bald." The prophet looks at these juvenile taunters and curses them in the name of YHWH. Instantly, two female bears come out of the woods and rip apart forty-two of these children. The prophet then continues on his way to Mount Carmel.

## Setting: Bethel

The Elisha cycle is packed with adventure; the day this prophet goes to Bethel may be the most exciting episode. The unpotable waters at Jericho have just been purified by Elisha's word so that they no longer cause sickness or death (2 Kgs 2:19–22). The prophet, assumed to be Elisha through context, then makes his way up into Israel's highlands from respectable Jericho to notorious Bethel.

Elisha must turn around to curse the children (ויפן אחריו, v. 24), creating an initial impression that they may have come from Jericho.[1] The narrator, however, seems intent on associating them with Bethel. About twenty kilometers separate Jericho from Bethel, so it is doubtful that such a large band of small children would follow Elisha this far. Further, after naming Bethel, the narrator interjects that the boys came out "from the town" (מן־העיר). A negative association with Bethel also serves a Deuteronomistic

---

1. Some scholars suggest the locale of v. 23 is Jericho, since that is the site from which Elisha has departed. Gwilym Jones suggests that the phrase "to go up" makes more sense if the prophet is leaving Jericho (*1 & 2 Kings* [vol. 2; NCB; Grand Rapids, MI: 1984], 389). David Marcus thinks that Elisha's turning around in v. 24 suggests the prophet was en route from Jericho (*From Balaam to Jonah: Anti-prophetic Satire in the Hebrew Bible* [BJS 301; Atlanta: Scholars Press, 1995], 55). But if the boys were from Jericho, why would they be so vindictive to one who had just made their town's tainted water safe?

*Weltanschauung* that views this cultic city with disdain (see 1 Kgs 12:28–30; 2 Kgs 10:29; 23:15–19).

Bethel may augur impending disaster. Along with Dan, this is a site of Jeroboam's shrine, erected in direct violation of the Deuteronomic insistence on worship in one place (e.g., Deut 12:13–14; 16:16; 17:10; 1 Kgs 12:26–33). Yet Bethel is familiar to both Elijah and Elisha (2 Kgs 2:1–3). Further, a group of the sons of the prophets, who are closely associated with Elisha, appears to reside here (v. 3).[2] Some commentators suggest that Bethel implies danger because of the erected shrine.[3] Others think that associating Bethel with Elijah and the sons of the prophets (2 Kgs 2:2–3) leaves a positive impression.[4] Regardless, Bethel is a site of thriving Yahwistic activity, with children as active and vocal members of this town.

## Characters

### נערים קטנים *and* ילדים

The narrator first describes the children who taunt Elisha as נערים קטנים (2 Kgs 2:23). Since נער is such a multivalent term, it is not surprising that scholars repeatedly suggest that these mockers are not children.[5]

---

2. David Petersen suggests there may have been multiple groups called the "sons of the prophets." Since one such group is found in Bethel (2 Kgs 2:3) and another in Jericho (2 Kgs 2:5), the text might understand similar associations to be located in several towns. See David L. Petersen, *The Roles of Israel's Prophets* (JSOTSup 17; Sheffield: JSOT Press, 1981), 48. For fuller discussion of the sons of the prophets aligned with this peripheral prophet (Elisha) and peripheral god (YHWH), see pp. 43–50. Robert Wilson agrees, "Seen from a sociological perspective, the sons of the prophets closely resemble members of a peripheral possession cult." See Robert R. Wilson, *Prophecy and Society in Ancient Israel* (Philadelphia: Fortress, 1980), 202; see also pp. 140–41. For another succinct overview, see T. R. Hobbs's excursus, *2 Kings* (WBC 13; Waco, TX: Word Books, 1985), 25–27.

3. E.g., Daniel Arnold, *Elisée: précurseur de Jésus—Christ: Commentaire de 2 Rois 2–9* (Saint-Légier: Emmaüs, 2002), 65.

4. E.g., Wesley J. Bergen, *Elisha and the End of Prophetism* (JSOTSup 286; Sheffield: Sheffield Academic Press, 1999), 69–70.

5. Peter J. Leithart reads these characters as older and reasons, "The phrase 'little boys' (נערים קטנים) in 2:23 can mean 'young men' or 'subordinates.' Bethel is the site of Jeroboam I's gold calf shrine, and the context suggests that these are not children, but 'Levites' of the idolatrous shrine." In a footnote, however, Leithart also offers the possibility that these characters are boys to be slain, citing Deut 20:10–18. See Peter J. Leithart, *1 & 2 Kings* (Grand Rapids, MI: Brazos, 2006), 175. Herbert Chanan Brichto reads קטן as a derogatory adjective and נער as referring to a subordinate. He ultimately translates (really, paraphrases) נערים קטנים as "mean-spirited rascals." See Herbert Chanan Brichto, *Toward a Grammar of Biblical Poetics: Tales of the Prophets* (New York: Oxford University Press, 1992), 198. While Solomon, as a grown man, calls himself a נער קטן in 1 Kgs 3:7, context makes clear that this is his

This interpretation also serves readers who would rather not see children ripped apart by YHWH's prophet. Nonetheless, the words נערים קטנים most likely convey small boys, as opposed to young men or servants. As discussed in Chapter 2, נער can designate a servant and/or a boy or youth, although not in a kinship relationship. The word נער connotes servitude in contexts that involve fulfilling a task to help another or in a profession of humility (e.g., 1 Kgs 3:7), which is hardly the case here. The qualifying adjective, קטן, also suggests that these are young children. Referring back to the נערים קטנים (v. 23), the term ילדים (v. 24) frequently indicates small children, confirming this impression.[6]

Since Hebrew uses the masculine plural to include females, we can allow for the possibility of girls among these mockers. We also do not see strict gender separation in the text, and with such a large group it seems reasonable to include girls in this crowd. The Hebrew Bible explicitly mentions ילדות only once (Zech 8:5), yet naturally girls were part of the ancient world. Thus, readers should make the effort to envision girls in situations and circumstances where their presence can be logically assumed, as in this passage.

---

(disingenuous) show of humility. Mark Mercer lifts up this example of Solomon to counter the impression that the נערים קטנים here are small children. By his own admission, Mercer notes, "the combination of these two words almost always refers to a young child . . ." but maintains that the example of Solomon shows "that the young people in 2 Kings 2 need not be young children as it is sometimes understood." Mercer instead suggests that "these youth were not children, but adolescents or young adults." See Mark Mercer, "Elisha's Unbearable Curse: A Study of 2 Kings 2:23–25," *AJET* 21 (2002): 172–73. The NIV and NKJV translate נערים קטנים as "youths," and the ASV translates "young lads." Rabbinic sages maintained that the instigators are "little of faith," not little people (*b. Sota* 46b). Understanding the mockers as older than "small boys" mitigates the severity of their punishment spurred by Elisha and YHWH.

6. For a contrasting view, see also Joel S. Burnett, "'Going Down' to Bethel: Elijah and Elisha in the Theological Geography of the Deuteronomistic History," *JBL* 129.2 (2010): 295–97. Burnett suggests that נערים קטנים and ילדים refer to grown men or older youth in the DtrH (1 Sam 16:11; 1 Kgs 3:7; 1 Kgs 11:14–17; 12). However, in the passages that Burnett cites the narrator provides context to indicate that the characters are not necessarily young, *despite* the use of terms that frequently portray children. Such context (not found in 2 Kgs 2:23–25) appears necessary to counter the impression of youth that would be derived from the words נערים קטנים and ילדים. Further, the Elisha cycle does not show clear evidence of Deuteronomistic editing. The other use of נער קטן in the Elisha cycle (2 Kgs 5:14) conveys distinguishing physical features of a *small child* (i.e., new, smooth, skin; cf. 2 Kgs 5:2). Burnett adopts Stager's understanding of a נער as a young man seeking to establish himself as a military or cultic functionary (p. 295), yet, as discussed in Chap. 2, this is at best only one possible meaning of נער. Instead of children, Burnett suggests that the נערים קטנים and ילדים are "young men of the royal and perhaps priestly establishment at Bethel" (p. 296), but this short narrative gives no indication that the mockers have any such status. What terms could the author use to convey a scene with pre-pubescent children if not נערים קטנים and ילדים?

## Elisha

Elisha's behavior is shocking. Instead of avoiding these children, he curses them in the name of YHWH and then ambles away as two female bears rip the children to shreds. Why would Elisha act this way? While the size of the young crowd might pose some threat, Elisha's reaction seems disproportionately harsh. He appears as an "unreliable" character of questionable mettle.[7] Is this prophet fearful, cruel, or both? Mostly, the writer conveys the idea that Elisha and his God are powerful. This legend is placed among the first of this collection and sends a warning: no matter how old you are, watch out for this prophet.

## Re-viewing the Plot from a Childist Perspective

The children are mean (think: *Lord of the Flies*), and Elisha is mean right back. The verb for "mocking," יתקלסו (v. 23b), suggests intense action.[8] The two other occurrences of קלס in the *hitpael* describe the rapacious war machine of the Chaldeans (Hab 1:10) and the bloody disgrace of Jerusalem (Ezek 22:5). This verbal form also connotes repeated taunting that seems like verbal malice intended to harm.

Still, why is Elisha so incensed? Perhaps he is infuriated by being called "bald." This description may contrast the hirsute master with the bald disciple, as Elijah is hairy (2 Kgs 1:8; see also Zech 13:4).[9] Yael Shemesh reviews multiple possibilities: baldness may have been a distinguishing feature for a prophet, perhaps showing ritual baldness before a purifying rite. Maybe Elisha shaved his head to mourn Elijah's death.[10] The children may be insulting Elisha as ugly.[11] Perhaps the mockers want to contrast the prophet's age and decline with their own youthful vigor.

---

7. This episode colors the characterization of Elisha, as his interaction with children here conveys him as an "unreliable character." Reliable characters share the narrator's own perspective and thereby earn inherent approval. Paul Kissling offers a comparative analysis between Elijah and Elisha, concluding that Elisha is far less reliable. Kissling suggests, "the reader would and should infer that Elisha is portrayed as a character with serious flaws and weaknesses." See Paul J. Kissling, *Reliable Characters in the Primary History: Profiles of Moses, Joshua, Elijah, and Elisha* (JSOTSup 224; Sheffield: Sheffield Academic Press, 1996), 200.

8. The Lucianic recension of the LXX further increases the severity of their behavior by adding καί ἐλίθαζον αὐτόν ("and they stoned him").

9. Since both Elijah and Elisha had been together in Bethel (2 Kgs 2:2), perhaps the children from Bethel had noticed the difference between hirsute and hairless prophets. Robert Cohn thinks this taunt may suggest an "invidious contrast" between prophet and disciple. See Robert L. Cohn, *2 Kings* (Berit; Collegeville, MN: Liturgical Press, 2000), 17.

10. Shemesh, "Elisha Stories," 12–13.

11. See Saul M. Olyan, *Disability in the Hebrew Bible: Interpreting Mental and Physical Differences* (Cambridge: Cambridge University Press, 2008), 20.

Some commentators think that telling the prophet to "go up" is a severe insult in itself, suggesting that Elisha is being derisively cajoled into imitating Elijah's ascent. Other scholars suggest the children are encouraging Elisha to offer sacrifices at Bethel and affront Deuteronomistic regulations, or, conversely, they want to prevent Elisha from visiting their forbidden cultic site.¹² Yet the jeer to "go up" probably does not anger the prophet, since he is already "going up" to Bethel. The narrator uses the same word, twice in this very verse, to describe Elisha's actions of his own volition (ויעל משם בית־אל והוא עלה בדרך, v. 23). Are the mockers antiphrastically telling Elisha to go away? Among his suffered insults, the prophet may be offended by receiving commands from children.

The turning point comes as Elisha turns around (ויפן אחריו, v. 24a). It appears his back had been to the children, maybe trying to get away from this large crowd. Elisha's looking at the hecklers (ויראם, v. 24a) confirms that they are the culprits, but also may be a prerequisite for prophetic spells (see Num 22:41; 23:13; 24:2, 20, 21). Just as the mockers have been making light of Elisha, he treats them with contempt and curses them (v. 24a). These children are the only people in the Hebrew Bible specifically cursed in YHWH's name.¹³ The vitriol that the small boys hurl at the prophet comes back at them with a vengeance.

While the text does not directly link Elisha's curse with the emergence of the bears, readers infer that the animals' violence against the children reflects divine punishment.¹⁴ The verbal form and number indicate that the bears are female (ותצאנה שתים דבים מן־היער, v. 24b), perhaps offering an ironic twist as mother bears who protect their own cubs now tear apart human offspring. The presence of two bears creates a trap, making it harder for the children to escape the bestial brutality. The verb ותבקענה is in the *piel*, connoting intensity, like the *hitpael* יתקלסו when the mockers accost the prophet. Some translators seek to soften the victims' mutilation, portraying the children as "mauled" (NIV, NKJV, NRSV), "savaged" (NJB), or "mangled" (NJPS). Yet the *piel* of בקע also depicts slashing the

---

12. For a review of various interpretations, see Mercer, "Unbearable Curse," 174–76. Mercer thinks the mockers want to coax the prophet to lead the people into "idolatrous" behavior, so the prophet will subsequently be punished for his action (p. 190). It seems curious, though, that the children would want to lead their own people (families?) into sinful ways. Terence Fretheim wonders if the instructions to "go up" might seek to keep Elisha from condemning the Bethel shrine. See Terence E. Fretheim, *First and Second Kings* (Louisville, KY: Westminster John Knox, 1999), 139.

13. As Brichto explains, the verb קלל carrying the sense of malediction or imprecation is rare in the Hebrew Bible. Brichto calculates that this exact verb (קלל, to be distinguished from its cognate קללה) appears four times (Deut 23:5; Josh 24:9; 1 Sam 17:43; 2 Kgs 2:24). Only 2 Kgs 2:24 has the phrase בשם יהוה. See Herbert Chanan Brichto, *The Problem of "Curse" in the Hebrew Bible* (JBLMS 13; Philadelphia: Society of Biblical Literature, 1963), 172–75.

14. The Hebrew Bible offers many instances when animals (esp. lions and bears) function as agents of YHWH. See Mercer, "Unbearable Curse," 189–91.

stomachs of pregnant women (2 Kgs 8:12; 15:16) and cleaving wood for a burnt offering (Gen 22:3), suggesting ripping apart or breaking into pieces.[15] Forty-two of the children are slashed—how many more escaped? Readers envision the hillsides of Bethel dotted with small, mutilated corpses, while other children scream and bleed.

If Elisha feels even the barest shred of remorse here, he hides it well. He continues to Mt. Carmel and then returns to Samaria (v. 25), without even a glance back toward Bethel. Were the insolent urchins taught the lesson they deserve? Some commentators see the children as threatening, suggesting that this miscreant behavior of children (especially boys) is both timeless and incorrigible.[16]

This motif of "the bad boys of Bethel" finds thorough review in Eric Ziolkowski's book, *Evil Children in Religion, Literature, and Art*. Ziolkowski recounts the opinions of scholars, some of whom think that this story was inspired by a genuine incident. He observes that commentators focus on many elements of the story, such as the town of Bethel, Elisha's baldness, the curse against the mockers, the brutality of the bears, or the role of YHWH in the punishment, but rarely discuss the children. This story raises troubling questions, Ziolkowski suggests, about the relationship between children (particularly boys) and holiness.[17] Ziolokowski correctly notices that commentators tend to neglect discussion *of* children in favor of a lesson *for* children.

## Childist Interpretation: Children as Agents and Victims

Many scholars read 2 Kgs 2:23–25 as a didactic story, possibly intended for a youthful audience. John Gray suggests that this tale recalled

---

15. BDB defines בקע in the *piel* as "cleave, cut to pieces, or rend open," noting the violence of the *piel* stem (BDB, 132). *HALOT* translates בקע in 2 Kgs 2:24 as "to tear to pieces" (*HALOT* 1:150). However, the NRSV (for example) translates בקע as "mauled" in this verse (as noted above) and as "rip up" and "ripped open" in 2 Kgs 8:12 and 2 Kgs 15:16, respectively.

16. Cogan and Tadmor note that harassment by "jeering urchins [is] a scene often repeated even today in the streets and markets of the Middle East, to the discomfort of the unwary traveler." See Mordechai Cogan and Hayim Tadmor, *II Kings* (AB 11; New York: Doubleday, 1988), 39. Bergen observes, "the seriousness with which stone-throwing Palestinian children are treated by Israeli troops might cause me to take their actions more seriously" (*Elisha*, 70).

17. Eric J. Ziolkowski, *Evil Children in Religion, Literature, and Art* (New York: Palgrave, 2001), 21. The first chapter (pp. 12–35) explores the theme of boys as evil (or at least reckless troublemakers) as portrayed in 2 Kgs 2:23–25; the rest of the book traces this motif from patristic views through the twentieth century. For a more concise discussion, see his article "The Bad Boys of Bethel: Origin and Development of a Sacrilegious Type," *HR* 30 (1991): 331–58.

a bygone disaster and was told by the locals "to awe their children."[18] Iain Provan notes that Bethel is notorious for its apostasy and observes, "It is no surprise to find its children adopting a disrespectful attitude towards a prophet. To treat a prophet with disrespect, however, is to treat God with disrespect and to risk immediate retribution. . . . Elisha shows himself to be a true prophet as he curses the children. . . ."[19] A. Graeme Auld implicitly instructs children in describing this tale as one of "punishing impertinent boys."[20] Additional commentators continue in this interpretive vein.[21]

Others offer less condemnatory readings. Alexander Rofé reads this as another short miracle story, along with the waters of Jericho that become safe to drink (2 Kgs 2:19–22), the widow and her children saved from slavery (2 Kgs 4:1–7), the purified pot of stew (2 Kgs 4:38–41), the feeding of a hundred people (2 Kgs 4:42–44), and the ax head that floats to the surface (2 Kgs 6:1–7). Structurally, 2 Kgs 2:23–25 seems to fit with the other legenda in Rofé's list, as a brief story describing straightforward events with anonymous characters. However, Rofé suggests these tales all depict a prophet who will "help ordinary people in their daily lives," exhibiting "minor deliverances, small acts of salvation."[22] However, far from being aided, the everyday characters in 2 Kgs 2:23–25, that is, the children, are killed. Rofé continues, "Those benefiting from the miracle are not particularly honest or righteous" but are "close to the Man of God."[23] The

---

18. John Gray, *I & II Kings* (OTL; Philadelphia: Westminster, 1970), 479.
19. Iain W. Provan, *1 & 2 Kings* (NIBCOT 7; Peabody, MA: Hendrickson, 1995), 175.
20. A. Graeme Auld, *I & II Kings* (Philadelphia: Westminster, 1986), 155.
21. T. R. Hobbs observes, "the ridicule of sacred persons is rewarded by the harshest of punishments" (*2 Kings*, 24). J. Robinson notes that while Elisha here acts as a "harsh tyrant," the editors retain this story "to instruct the people of the danger of turning away from their God." See J. Robinson, *The Second Book of Kings* (CBC; Cambridge: Cambridge University Press, 1976), 29. Richard Nelson comments on morals from earlier times: "The ancient reader, untroubled by our post-industrial revolution apotheosis of childhood, doubtlessly found this a satisfying story. Those juvenile delinquents got exactly what they deserved!" See Richard D. Nelson, *First and Second Kings* (IBC; Atlanta: John Knox Press, 1987), 161. Alexander Rofé notes the medieval rabbis' conclusions that the children had little faith (Rabbi Eleazar), or plaited hair like the Amorites (Rabbi Isaac the Smith), or were conceived on the Day of Atonement (Rabbi Samuel) (*Prophetical Stories*, 15 n. 3). Mordechai Cogan and Hayim Tadmor cite the medieval rabbi Isaac Abarbanel's rationalization, for the prophet "saw that the young boys were mocking not only him, but his master Elijah as well . . . and this at their parents' command" (*II Kings*, 39). Rashi adds that Elisha not only saw the children, but also successive generations. "He saw that neither in them nor in their descendants would there be any 'sap' of good deeds. " See A. J. Rosenberg, ed., *II Kings: Translation of Text, Rashi* (New York: Judaica, 1980), 251.
22. Rofé, *Prophetical Stories*, 14–15. Rofé implies that Elisha would be the ordinary person in this passage who is spared "the harassment of insolent youths" (*Prophetical Stories*, 14). However, one who performs all sorts of wonders is far from ordinary. Indeed, displaying Elisha's extraordinary powers as a man of God seems to be the point of the stories that Rofé explores.
23. Rofé, *Prophetical Stories*, 15.

children in 2 Kgs 2:23–25 are not close to the man of God and certainly do not benefit from any miracle. *Au contraire.*

Scholars strive to make sense of this gruesome scene. David Marcus suggests that 2 Kgs 2:23–25 is a parody, showing a fantastic situation complete with the participation of animals (see also Num 22:21–33; 1 Kgs 13:20–28; Jon 2:1–11 [Eng. 1:17–2:10]). He outlines various literary features of an artistic composition that has been carefully crafted.[24] Both in style and content, Marcus suggests, this short story is a satire. The goal is to criticize Elisha's actions and warn the audience about the inherent dangers of prophetic power.[25] Yael Shemesh understands the children are "punished for sacrilege," as is appropriate in this genre of saints' legends.[26] C. L. Seow proposes that this tale contradicts Elisha's action when he made Bethel's harmful waters potable (2 Kgs 2:19–22), and shows that this prophet continues the tradition of Mosaic prophets with the ability to curse or bless.[27] Yet Elisha's encounter with the mockers not only illustrates the prophet's powers, but also shows children as a serious threat to adults.

## Insights about Children and Power

The three short verses of this narrative offer multiple cultural insights about children. First, the size of the young group suggests that children may have assembled independently. More than forty-two mockers jeer the prophet or witness the taunting, raising questions about children's time and culture. While the society of the text appears to be essentially age-integrated, here no adult intervenes to stop the mockers or mediates with Elisha on their behalf. This story hints that children had their own pastimes and amusements, perhaps even on a large scale.

The children in this passage come out from the city when the prophet is going up to Bethel on the path (עלה בדרך, v. 23b). Perhaps the youngsters were looking for an activity or the prophet passing by has prompted their curiosity. They might have known him and disliked him after his previous sojourn in Bethel (cf. 2 Kgs 2:2–3). Regardless of their motivation, the children purposely spot their target (ויתקלסו־בו ויאמרו לו, v. 23b). These are

---

24. These satirical features include a set object of ridicule, and a short story saturated with exaggerated details, ironic touches, and various rhetorical devices. See Marcus, *Balaam to Jonah*, 45. For Marcus's textual diagram and discussion, noting careful attention to stylistic symmetry, see pp. 62–64.

25. Marcus, *Balaam to Jonah*, 64–65.

26. Shemesh, "Elisha Stories," 11.

27. C. L. Seow, "First and Second Books of Kings," in *The New Interpreter's Bible* (vol. 3; ed. Leander Keck et al.; Nashville: Abingdon, 1999), 178.

hardly milquetoast youngsters, squelching their spirits in an effort to be seen and not heard. Rather, they appear as loud, vehement, and rude.

Group dynamics become evident. Those who might not dare to ridicule a traveler, much less a man of God, find strength in a gang. The mockers may also (erroneously) think that their combined numbers will protect them against a solitary man. Only after the bloodshed does the reader realize that more than forty-two children were present (v. 24). Mercer asserts, "The size of the group and the fact that they came out to meet Elisha suggests that they were specifically organized to harass the prophet. This was not a group of children."[28] Yet Mercer's observation assumes that children could not be organized. Why not? Children often form groups for games or activities. The mockers may be teasing Elisha for fun, or perhaps they have a responsibility to keep away intruders. Yet the congregated children clearly have influence and thereby some authority.

The children insult Elisha and, by extension, YHWH. They combine their numbers, observation, energy, and knowledge of Elisha's vulnerability to rile him. Marcus argues that Elisha's provocateurs were small boys and therefore, "These were children who should *not* have been held responsible for their actions."[29] However, the text (along with Elisha and YHWH) holds them completely liable.

These children are a force to be reckoned with, although their threat would be different if they were adults. If the mockers were a large group of grown men, this would primarily be a story about justice: a large group of menacing adults harasses a prophet who acts in self-defense with YHWH's help. Indeed, many interpreters view the story the same way with the young mockers. But with small children as the offenders, 2 Kgs 2:23–25 offers a more nuanced message. Their behavior is not excused. These young offenders are not cherished innocents exempt from punishment, and the story becomes a comprehensive warning about YHWH and Elisha. No living being, not even children from a town or beasts from a forest, is beyond the scope of this duo's power.

## Children and Textual Connections

Facing threats is the thread of this story that leads to other texts including children. Elisha's succession parallels that of Joshua: both are successors to Mosaic prophets, and their names declare God's salvation (from ישע). Yet from a childist perspective, the monikers suggesting safety seem almost sardonic. Before going to Bethel in 2 Kgs 2:23, Elisha leaves

---

28. Mercer, "Unbearable Curse," 173–74.
29. Marcus, *Balaam to Jonah*, 51.

Jericho. This is the very city that Hiel *of Bethel* rebuilt at the cost of two children's lives (Abiram and Segub in 1 Kgs 16:34), under the curse of Joshua (Josh 6:26).[30] Violence done to two children of a city increases, as forty-two children of a city are made to bear a lethal prophetic curse. This number of forty-two appears one other time in Kings, when Jehu kills the kin of King Ahaziah (2 Kgs 10:13–14). Elijah orchestrated the annihilation of Ahaziah's men (2 Kgs 1:9–14); the king whom Elisha has had anointed (i.e., Jehu: 2 Kgs 9:1–13) kills forty-two of Ahaziah's descendants (2 Kgs 10:14).[31] Presumably, some among the murdered princes were children. In 2 Kgs 2:24, the bears cleave (תבקענה) the children, just as Abraham cleaves (יבקע) wood for the child sacrifice of Isaac (Gen 22:3). Both actions portend youthful death.

Elisha's reaction to the threat of children contrasts him with Elijah and the captains of units of fifty men (2 Kgs 1:9–14). As T. R. Hobbs points out, these two episodes parallel each other in syntax and content.[32] Both prophets face a large group of adversaries whom they destroy with an intervention from YHWH, but comparing these stories shows one prophet as superior to the other. Elijah faces captains acting on behalf of the king (2 Kgs 1:9, 11, 13). Elisha's adversaries are small children (2 Kgs 2:23). The military leaders respectfully acknowledge Elijah as a "man of God" (איש האלהים, 2 Kgs 1:9, 11, 13). The young boys derogatorily call Elisha "baldy" (קרח, 2 Kgs 2:23). Fifty men (cited fifteen times in the span of six verses)[33] accompany each commander who approaches Elijah. Forty-two children (mentioned once, 2 Kgs 2:24) are among those who threaten Elisha. Elijah expresses confident belief in his role as a man of God in response to his challenger (2 Kgs 1:10, 12). Elisha wordlessly glares and curses at his opponents (2 Kgs 2:24). Elijah twice summons the theophanic element of fire to descend from heaven and consume the men (2 Kgs 1:10, 12). Elisha's curse prompts bears to lumber out from the woods to rip apart the children (2 Kgs 2:24).[34] Comparing the children to the captains of units of fifty men further shows Elisha as inferior to Elijah.

YHWH's ursine punishment recalls other passages with beasts and children. In Lev 26:22 and Ezek 5:17, YHWH vows to unleash animals

---

30. While Abiram and Segub may connote a merism (the firstborn and youngest, respectively), the text names only these two children. Joshua 6:26 further mentions the firstborn and youngest as those who must perish in the rebuilding of the city. For further discussion of the connections between 1 Kgs 16:34 and 2 Kings 2, see Charles Conroy, "Hiel between Ahab and Elijah-Elisha: 1 Kgs 16,34 and Its Immediate Literary Context," *Bib* 77 (1996): 215–16.

31. While both ninth-century kings are named Ahaziah, Elijah's opponent is king of Israel and Jehu's foe is a slightly later king of Judah.

32. Hobbs, *2 Kings*, 18.

33. 2 Kgs 1:9 (2x), 10 (3x), 11 (2x), 12 (2x), 13 (4x), 14 (2x).

34. Hobbs charts the syntactical parallels here (*2 Kings*, 18).

who will bereave (שכל) the disobedient people of their children. In 2 Kgs 2:19–22, Elisha, with YHWH's help, makes harmful waters potable so that they no longer cause miscarriage (משכלת, v. 21). Yet Elisha's power can cause parents (who are entirely absent in the scene of 2 Kgs 2:23–25) bereavement through wild beasts who enter on the deity's cue. The bears and the parents share a bond, since bears too can be bereaved (שכול) of their cubs (Prov 17:12; Hos 13:8). Female bears seem an especially fearsome foe (2 Sam 17:8; Hos 13:8).[35]

Commentators' efforts to excuse Elisha's action by maintaining that these mockers are adults say more about modern scholars' sensibilities than the text. Here the children are held firmly accountable for their actions and drive the plot, impacting both Elisha and YHWH. These children have their own realm in which they operate, separate from adults. This unsettling short story shatters any idealization of children as innocent, prophets as beneficent, or YHWH as protective. Elisha appears to cause, and certainly does nothing to prevent, the violent mutilation of youngsters. His name—"God is Salvation"—is bitterly ironic for these children.

---

35. For further discussion on the functions of animals in the Hebrew Bible, see Yael Shemesh, "'And Many Beasts' (Jonah 4:11): The Function and Status of Animals in the Book of Jonah," *JHS* 10, art. 6 (2010): 5–8, doi:10.5508/jhs.2010.v10.a6.

# 5

# The Moabite Prince (2 Kings 3:26–27)

Chapter 3 of 2 Kings portrays a scene of battle that culminates in child sacrifice. Upon the death of Israel's King Ahab, King Mesha of Moab withholds tribute, provoking Israel's ire. In retaliation, King Jehoram of Israel, King Jehoshaphat of Judah, and the (anonymous) king of Edom muster their troops against the Moabites. As the allied forces advance toward Moab, they lack water and call upon Elisha for help. The prophet predicts a wadi of water and assures them of victory over Moab. Indeed, water does appear, and the Moabites ready themselves for battle. Upon seeing water reflecting the sun, the Moabites misinterpret this red water as the blood of slaughtered kings and attack the Israelite camp. However, their military advantage quickly reverses as the Israelites' counter-offense overtakes all of Moab, except Kir-hareseth. The slingers assault the city walls, and the king of Moab sends seven hundred fighters to stem the onslaught—to no avail. As a last resort, the Moabite king takes his firstborn son and offers him as a burnt offering on the wall. Wrath comes upon the Israelites, who immediately retreat. The father who sacrifices his son is Mesha (מישע); like Elisha (אלישע) his name carries connotations of salvation.[1] But again, this does not mean safety for children.

## Setting: The Battle at Moab

This narrative is epic in scope. The wide geographic area makes the story unusual in the Elisha cycle.[2] Four different nations comprise the setting as the focus shifts from Israel (vv. 1–3, 6), Moab (vv. 4–5), Judah (vv. 7), and Edom (v. 8), although most of the action appears to take

---

1. J. Andrew Dearman and Gerard Mattingly note, "There is little doubt that Mesha's name meant something like 'salvation' or 'redeemer,' though the exact etymology is uncertain." See J. Andrew Dearman and Gerard Mattingly, "Mesha Inscription," n.p., *ABD* on *CD-ROM*. Version 2.1. 1997.
2. For discussion of how 2 Kings 3 compares with the shorter miracle stories generally found in the Elisha cycle, see Uffenheimer, *Early Prophecy*, 421–29.

place on the frontier between Edom and Moab (vv. 9–27). Some scholars link this biblical narrative to the Mesha Inscription (MI) (also called the Moabite Stone), a stele unearthed in 1868 and dated to the mid-ninth century BCE. This inscription recounts the military victory of King Mesha of Moab, in service to his god, Kemosh,[3] boasting of the Moabite king's successful exploits. Some scholars reconcile the biblical narrative with the Moabite inscription as evidence of the Bible's historicity.[4] Others point out that any correspondence between the biblical and Moabite accounts do not ipso facto make either factual.[5] Here we simply recognize that the setting of this text, where a biblical scene of child sacrifice transpires, has a historical referent beyond the Hebrew Bible.

## Characters

### The Many

The narrative in 2 Kings 3 has a large cast of individual characters who are present simultaneously.[6] There are four kings (Jehoshaphat of Judah, Jehoram of Israel, Mesha of Moab, and the king of Edom) and multiple gods. Baal (v. 2) and YHWH (vv. 10–18) are named explicitly. Arguably,

---

3. This stele provides early archaeological attestation to YHWH (*l.* 18). For a general introduction to the Mesha Inscription (also called the Moabite Stone), see Dearman and Mattingly, "Mesha Inscription," n.p. See also the excursus in Hobbs, *2 Kings*, 39–41. For the dramatic history of the MI's discovery, see André Lemaire, "House of David Restored in Moabite Inscription," *BAR* 20 (1994): 30–37. For a more extensive account, see M. Patrick Graham, "The Discovery and Reconstruction of the Meshaʿ Inscription," in *Studies in the Mesha Inscription and Moab* (ed. Andrew Dearman; SBLABS 2; Atlanta: Scholars Press, 1989), 41–92. For complete text of the Moabite Stone, see Kent P. Jackson and J. Andrew Dearman, "The Text of the Meshaʿ Inscription" in *Mesha Inscription*, 93–95. For translation with notes, see Kent P. Jackson, "The Language of the Meshaʿ Inscription," in *Mesha Inscription*, 96–130.

4. John Bartlett explains 2 Kings 3 as factual in "The 'United' Campaign against Moab in 2 Kings 3:4–27," in *Midian, Moab and Edom: The History and Archaeology of Late Bronze and Iron Age Jordan and North-West Arabia* (ed. John F. A. Sawyer and David J. A. Clines; JSOTSup 24; Sheffield: JSOT Press, 1983), 135–46. More recently, Joe Sprinkle argues that the MI concurs with, and therefore verifies, many elements of the story in 2 Kings 3. He combines the two battle accounts into one historical incident. See Joe M. Sprinkle, "2 Kings 3: History or Historical Fiction," *BBR* 9 (1999): 247–70. J. A. Emerton responds to arguments of the minimalists, notably Thomas Thompson, who believes the MI itself is a later work of historical fiction and unreliable as a source of past information. See J. A. Emerton, "The Value of the Moabite Stone as an Historical Source," *VT* 52 (2002): 483–92.

5. See, for example, Brichto, *Biblical Poetics*, 204.

6. Uriel Simon points out, "Even in narratives with a long, involved plot, as for example in the story of Joseph or the book of Esther, no single scene has more than three active characters and the dialogue only rarely develops into a three-way conversation" ("Minor Characters," 11).

Elisha's (insulting) instruction that Jehoram turn to the prophets of his father and mother (v. 13a) is a veiled reference to Baal and Asherah, whose prophets Ahab and Jezebel supported according to 1 Kgs 18:19. Kemosh, the Moabite god, is not named here, but it seems logical that the Moabite king is sacrificing to him, and therefore it is Kemosh's wrath that comes upon the Israelites.[7] The prophet Elisha is also part of the scene, curiously accompanying the military entourage.[8] Even more enigmatic, a musician is also present. The expansive cast includes not only the troops and their supporting retinue, but many animals. Sheep, lambs, rams (v. 4) and horses (v. 7) receive mention, as well as the animals of the army (v. 9). The thirsty soldiers and servants, frustrated kings, and bellowing beasts on the plains of Edom join to create a scene of desperate pandemonium into which the prophet enters.

## Elisha

As the situation deteriorates, the king of Israel laments (2 Kgs 3:10) and the king of Judah seeks a solution (v. 11). Jehoshaphat asks if one of YHWH's prophets is here (פה, v. 11a), to inquire (דרש) of him (cf. 1 Kgs 22:7). The helpful response comes from one of the servants, who apparently (with how many others?) heard the king's question. The servant knows a prophet (i.e., Elisha) who can aid the situation (see also 2 Kgs 5:3). Furthermore, the nameless servant informs the kings that this seer is present (פה, v. 11b). It seems that the prophet is traveling among the support staff and not with the royal entourage, since the servant knew of Elisha's presence but the king did not. The attendant describes Elisha through a servile image: Elisha had poured water over the hands of Elijah.[9] This introduction both raises Elisha's status by associating him with a well-known prophet, while simultaneously lowering it by recounting his subordinate role. The connection between Elisha and water may also augur well for

---

7. This point is fiercely debated. Further discussion follows.

8. This is the only instance in the Hebrew Bible when a prophet acts as an on-site battle consultant (Cogan and Tadmor, *II Kings*, 49).

9. F. W. Farrar's commentary offers an anthropological anecdote in a footnote on this verse, sharing his own experience of Near Eastern hospitality: "Once, when driven by a storm into the house of the Sheykh of a tribe which had a rather bad reputation for brigandage, I was most hospitably entertained; and the old white-haired Sheykh, his son, and ourselves were waited on by the grandson, a magnificent youth, who immediately after the meal brought out an old richly chased ewer and basin, and poured water over our hands, soiled by eating out of the common dish, of course without spoons or forks." See Frederic William Farrar, *The Second Book of Kings* (New York: A. C. Armstrong and Son, 1902), 32 n. 1. Farrar's story illustrates how pouring water over hands is a custom demonstrating subservience and performed by a youth.

this parched people. Elisha enters to prove his power, which he (eventually) does.

Just as Elisha first refused a request, then relented with the sons of the prophets (2 Kgs 2:16–17), he repeats this pattern with kings (2 Kgs 3:13–15a). In the tradition of mediums,[10] Elisha requests a musician so that he might enter a trance and obtain divine insight (cf. 1 Sam 10:5–13).[11] Instantly the playing musician materializes causing the prophet to enter a possessed state (2 Kgs 3:15, ותהי עליו יד־יהוה—lit., "the hand of YHWH was upon him"). Elisha's oracle vacillates between YHWH's words foretelling of water (2 Kgs 3:16–17; cf. 1 Kgs 17:1; 18:1) and declaring victory over Moab (2 Kgs 3:18). Elisha assures the allied forces that their conquest will be complete (2 Kgs 3:19).[12] The very next day, the narrator reveals, the land is filled with water (v. 20). After this part of the prediction is realized, both the prophet and his deity disappear from the story. Elisha appears mysterious and omniscient, although his words can be later questioned.

## The Child Soldiers

Once Elisha is gone, other characters fill the void on the narrative stage (2 Kgs 3:21). To accommodate this crowd, the story's lens pulls back. The narrator specifies that *all* the Moabites hear of the kings making war against them (v. 21a). As a result, ויצעקו מכל חגר חגרה ומעלה: "they were summoned [to arms] from all who could wear a [military] belt [for a sword], and upward" (v. 21b). As noted in BDB and *HALOT*, both the verb צעק (in the *nifal*) and the noun חגרה carry militaristic overtones.[13] The preposition מן inclusively covers a range of agents.[14] As multiple transla-

---

10. Robert Wilson explains that the term "medium" broadly describes "anyone who acts as a channel of communication between the human and divine realms" (*Prophecy and Society*, 25). For distinctions among various types of prophetic roles, such as shaman, witch, priest, or mystic, see pp. 21–28.

11. David Petersen maintains that ecstasy was not a salient feature of Israelite prophecy (however, he does not discuss 2 Kgs 3:14–19 in this context) (*Roles of Israel's Prophets*, 25–30).

12. The scorched-earth policy that Elisha predicts (v. 19) violates Deut 20:19–20. Joe Sprinkle maintains that this Deuteronomic violation is the reason for Israel's retreat and defeat at the end of the story. See Joe M. Sprinkle, "Deuteronomic 'Just War' (Deut 20, 10–20) and 2 Kings 3, 27," *ZABR* 6 (2000): 285–301. See also Seow, "Kings," 185. However, this story does not presuppose, much less build upon, knowledge of Deuteronomic regulations.

13. BDB, 858 defines צעק in the *nifal* as "be summoned (i.e., to arms)," citing this verse, and *HALOT* 2:1043 offers "be called together, mustered." *HALOT* 1:291 renders the verb חגר as "**gird oneself** with weapons," and BDB, 292, defines חגרה in 2 Kgs 3:21 as "*belt* of warrior."

14. Ronald Williams's *Hebrew Syntax* cites this verse as an example of the inclusive use of the preposition מן and translates, "everyone who could wear armour and up." See Ronald J. Williams, *Hebrew Syntax: An Outline* (Toronto: University of Toronto Press, 1976), 57.

tions make clear, all who are physically capable of joining in the battle gird themselves for war, from the youngest possible on up.[15] Philip King and Lawrence Stager note that swords, the basic weapon worn on a belt, came in a wide range of sizes,[16] so these did not necessarily require great upper body strength to wield. Especially if *all* of Moab hears of the kings making war against them (v. 21a) and *all* who are able then proceed to gird themselves (v. 21b), we envision *all* the capable Moabites grabbing whatever arms may be available to them. There is no requirement issued regarding combatants' minimum age or sufficient weapon size, nor is there a gender specification. Indeed, all who are able are summoned to participate, with an allusion to younger recruits.[17]

John Gray offers a pertinent observation from Arab culture in the mid-twentieth century. Gray notes that words to describe youth in this Middle Eastern context are determined by their jobs and capacities, instead of numerical ages. For example, a young child below age five is described as "chasing the hens from the door of the house." A boy fit for military service, around age eleven or twelve, is designated as one who is old enough to wear a belt, instead of a loose shirt.[18] Gray's anthropological comparison, along with archaeological evidence and linguistic construction, enables readers to legitimately envision children and youth among the Moabites fighting against the Israelites (vv. 21–24). The prince sacrificed on the wall of Kir-hareseth likely is not the only youth to die in this battle.

## *The Prince and His Father*

Mesha's son becomes the bright center of attention in his moment of grisly glory. The narrator tersely reveals his place in his family, his relationship to his father, and his role in the kingdom (2 Kgs 3:27). Mesha's son is likely a boy, not an infant. It would seem strange if a king were to bring his baby to war, whereas children and youth were probably among the fighters. Perhaps Mesha was grooming his son for future battles. Yet

---

15. For example, the NRSV translates מכל חגר חגרה as "all who were able to put on armor, from the youngest to the oldest." See also the RSV and ESV.
16. King and Stager, *Life in Biblical Israel*, 224–25.
17. This call to arms evokes comparison with contemporary child soldiers. Children can be forced to join militias since they are more vulnerable and hence more easily manipulated than adults. Also children do not need to be especially large to wield certain weapons. The British Broadcasting Corporation (BBC) estimates that there are approximately 300,000 children being used as soldiers around the world with children as young as seven years old being forced into violent, militaristic groups (http://www.bbc.co.uk/worldservice/people/features/childrensrights/childrenofconflict/soldier.shtml; accessed January 2013).
18. Gray, *Kings*, 488–89.

regardless of his age and despite his brief appearance, the Moabite prince is the hinge upon which the story turns.

In language echoing young Isaac's description when he is about to be sacrificed (Genesis 22), the narrator introduces Mesha's son. In Gen 22:2a, YHWH commands Abraham: קח־נא את־בנך את־יחידך אשר־אהבת; in 2 Kgs 3:27a, the narrator relays Mesha's actions: ויקח את־בנו הבכור אשר־ימלך תחתיו. Each father takes (לקח) his son, as the text assumes both paternal power and filial surrender. Jon Levenson finds the parallels between these exceptional sons strikingly ominous. Isaac is (erroneously) described as Abraham's only son (את־יחידך).[19] Mesha's son may or may not be the sole male child in his family, but he is הבכור, suggesting youth and status. Isaac is not Abraham's "only" son (as second-born to Ishmael), but YHWH tells Abraham that this son is אשר־אהבת: the one whom you love (Gen 22:2). Mesha's scion is the king's firstborn and אשר־ימלך תחתיו: the one who is to reign in his stead (2 Kgs 3:27). Both sons are precious to their fathers—one personally, one politically.

Yet to be הבכור carries responsibilities as well as privileges. Traditionally a father's first son by his wife was entitled to an elevated position among the children. King and Stager assert, "He [the firstborn son] inherited a double portion of his father's property, received a special blessing from his father, and succeeded his father as head of the household, exercising authority over the other members."[20] Comparative ancient Near East literature, notably from Ugarit, indicates that this exalted role of the firstborn son existed beyond Israel.[21] While Victor Matthew and Don Benjamin rightly note that the oldest son did not always or automatically receive extra inheritance in ancient Israel and beyond, to be the בכור was nonetheless a noteworthy position in ancient Near Eastern family structures.[22] The connotations of youth, status, and deep regard afforded the בכור coalesce with the Moabite prince and his elevated social standing. As Mesha's heir apparent, the prince seems destined to fulfill his father's role as ruler. Levenson discusses the possibility that the prince replaces the

---

19. As Levenson notes, the word יחיד occurs twelve times in the Hebrew Bible, notably in stories of child sacrifice (Gen 22:2, 12, 16; Judg 11:34) and loss of a child (Amos 8:10; Jer 6:26). See Jon D. Levenson, *The Death and Resurrection of the Beloved Son: The Transformation of Child Sacrifice in Judaism and Christianity* (New Haven: Yale University Press, 1993), 27–28.

20. King and Stager, *Life in Biblical Israel*, 47.

21. Passages from Ugaritic narrative poetry reflecting desire for firstborn sons include KTU 1.14 vi 33–35; KTU 1.15 ii 23–25; KTU 1.15 v 21–22; KTU 1.17 i 16–22, 25–33, KTU 1.17 ii 1–8, 14–23.

22. Victor Matthews and Don Benjamin acknowledge this custom of primogeniture, yet observe, "But as is clear from the stories of Isaac and Rebekah in Genesis (Gen 27:1–45), the Code of Hammurabi, and even the *Iliad* of Homer from western Mediterreanean culture, primogeniture alone never exclusively determined who became the heir." See Victor H. Matthews and Don C. Benjamin, *Social World of Ancient Israel 1250–587 BCE* (Peabody, MA: Hendrickson, 1993), 111. See also my discussion of בכור in Chapter 2.

king within a royal theology that demands the ruler's own life, but will accept an heir as substitution (as the phrase אשר־ימלך תחתיו may suggest).[23] By sacrificing his son, King Mesha saves his kingdom from defeat while robbing it of its next ruler.

## Re-viewing the Plot from a Childist Perspective

King Mesha grows increasingly desperate before sacrificing his son. Unlike Abraham who gets up early to fulfill YHWH's foreboding instructions (Gen 22:2–3), King Mesha seems far more reluctant to take the life of his child (2 Kgs 3:26). First, Mesha assesses the situation and sees that the battle is strongly against him (v. 26a). His opening tactic commands seven hundred soldiers drawing swords (v. 26b),[24] presumably from among all the Moabites (including youth) who had girded themselves with military belts (v. 21b). The Moabite king directs these soldiers to break through to the king of Edom, aiming his forces at the weakest of the kings (v. 26b). After analyzing the battle, sending in a large battalion of armed troops, and directing them to a vulnerable point of entry, all without success, King Mesha finally takes his son and offers him as a burnt offering on the wall (v. 27a). As wrath comes upon them (v. 27a), the Israelites retreat and return to their land (v. 27b). The prince accomplishes in death what he will never have the chance to do in life, as his sacrifice rescues the Moabites from total defeat. The life of this one child accomplishes what seven hundred soldiers could not.

Mesha sets his son on fire as an act of extreme desperation, frantically seeking favor with his god, Kemosh. While the Hebrew Bible repeatedly disparages Kemosh (see 1 Kgs 11:7, 33; 2 Kgs 23:13; Jer 48:7, 13, 46), the Israelite and Moabite dieties exhibit striking similarities. The text of the Mesha Inscription depicts Kemosh as a god who becomes angry (יאנף, l. 5) with the Moabites and punishes them, resulting in their defeat (ll. 5–6).[25] YHWH shows anger (אף) against the Israelites when they are disobedient, leading to their destruction (e.g., Deut 7:4; 11:17) or conquest (e.g., Judg 2:12–14, 20–21; 3:8; 10:7). Kemosh also gives victory (l. 9),[26] like YHWH

---

23. Levenson, *Death and Resurrection*, 26–27.
24. The word איש in v. 26 need not signify adult males, as suggested by the translation "swordsmen" (ESV, NJPS, NIV, RSV, NRSV) or "[seven hundred] men" (ASV, JPS, KJV). BDB, 36, notes that this word can collectively mean "retainers, followers, soldiers," allowing for the possibility of youth among the combatants.
25. See the transciption from Jackson and Dearman, "Text of the Mesha' Inscription," 94–95.
26. Kent Jackson reads וישבה (ll. 8–9) as a *hiphil* imperfect 3rd masc. sg. from the root שוב, with a 3rd fem. sg. suffix: "he [Kemosh] returned it [the land of Mehadaba]." See the text-critical notes on line 8 in Jackson, "Language of the Meshaʿ Inscription," 110.

(e.g., Deut 20:4). The Moabites devote their vanquished enemies to destruction (החרמתה[27]) for Ashtar-Kemosh,[28] as the Israelites do for YHWH (חרם: e.g., 1 Sam 15:8–9). Within the texts of the Hebrew Bible, YHWH and Kemosh exhibit further similarities. Both gods appear to accept children as burnt offerings in exchange for defeating enemies (Judg 11:30–40; 2 Kgs 3:26–27).[29] Cultic practices among Yahwistic worshipers include burning children (Deut 12:31; 2 Kgs 17:31; Jer 7:31; 19:5) or making them "pass through the fire" (Deut 18:10; 2 Kgs 16:3; 17:17; 21:6; 2 Chr 33:6; Ezek 20:31),[30] and Kemosh is also a "god of infernal nature."[31] Gerald Mattingly further observes, "everything we know about the Moabites' perception of Kemosh finds its parallel in Hebrew religion."[32] This would include child sacrifice as a known practice among segments of the population. The sang-froid with which the narrator relays the immolation of the Moabite prince further underscores this likelihood.

While the sacrifice is efficacious, it is also confounding. As the Israelites leave Moab, they are denied total victory. This contradicts the sense of Elisha's prophecy in 2 Kgs 3:18–19, which predicts Israelite conquest. In v. 18b, Elisha foretells, ונתן את־מואב בידכם: "And he [YHWH] will give Moab into your hand [or power]." Scholars attempt to explain why the Israelites lose the battle after Elisha had predicted they would win. Raymond Westbrook maintains that Elisha's prophecy has been both fulfilled and misunderstood; Elisha foretold that the Israelites would strike every for-

---

27. Kent Jackson's translation ("I devoted it") understands החרמתה as a *hiphil* perfect 1st common sg. of חרם with a 3rd fem. sg. suffix. See the notes on line 17 in Jackson, "Language of the Meshaʿ Inscription," 115.

28. Lines 14–18 portray Kemosh commanding Mesha to seize Nebo from Israel. Mesha reports that he obeyed and slaughtered 7,000 inhabitants and "devoted it to 'Ashtar-Kemosh" (לעשתר כמש החרמתה, l. 17). Gerald Mattingly suggests that עשתר כמש is likely "another name of Moab's national god," who is mentioned eleven times in this insciption. See Gerald L. Mattingly, "Chemosh," n.p., *ABD* on *CD-ROM*. Version 2.1. 1997. However, it is also possible that the insertion of Ashtar distinguishes this deity from Kemosh and connotes a goddess (a form of Astarte [עשתרת]?) who is a consort of Kemosh. Regardless, the חרם is connected with Kemosh, either directly or by association.

29. On the similarities shared among the stories of Jephthah's daughter and Mesha's son, along with Isaac, see Levenson, *Death and Resurrection*, 12–17. While interpreters frequently suggest that the story of the *Aqedah* (Gen 22:1–19) functions as an etiology for the abolition of child sacrifice, Levenson notes, "it is passing strange to condemn child sacrifice through a narrative in which a father is richly rewarded for his willingness to carry out that very practice" (p. 13). For discussion of Levenson's analysis and Abraham's ethics, see Fretheim, "God Was with the Boy," 18–23.

30. For discussion of the terms that may suggest child sacrifice (including שחט, זבח, אכל, שרף, עבר, עלה, and נתן) see Stavrakopoulou, *King Manasseh and Child Sacrifice*, 141–48.

31. See Mattingly, "Chemosh," n.p.

32. See Mattingly, "Chemosh," n.p. For comparison of YHWH and Kemosh, see also Eric Wargo, "Everything You Always Wanted to Know about Kemosh (But Were Afraid to Ask)," *BAR* 28 (2002): 44–45.

tified city (v. 19), which they do (v. 25) (*hifil* of נכה). Jehoram interprets this initial onslaught as assurance of final victory only because he was unwittingly lured into a sense of false security by a prophet who cares little for Israel's king or his triumphs.[33] Jesse Long notes that the kings appear to be given over to Moab by their defeat at the end of the story, just as Jehoram had predicted (2 Kgs 3:10, 13). Long suggests that Elisha's prediction keeps the text in the tension of postponed judgment.[34] Ziony Zevit maintains that Elisha's prophecy is essentially accomplished; the sacrifice of the boy only caused the coalition of kings to withhold in that moment from conquering the Moabites.[35] Yet scholars' efforts to explain that Elisha's prediction was indeed fulfilled accentuate the conundrum of the Israelite retreat. It is entirely plausible to read 2 Kings 3 and conclude that Elisha was wrong: he predicted total victory for the allied forces over Moab (vv. 18–19), but, in the end, the Israelites withdraw from the battle (v. 27b). The text allows for the possibility that the fighting unfolds in a way that even Elisha did not foresee, defying his prediction. The prophet did not know that the Moabite king would sacrifice his son to his god and bring down the divine wrath upon the Israelites. Perhaps Elisha did not realize that Kemosh could be so powerful; yet the prophet, along with the reader, learns this shocking lesson through the sacrifice of a boy.

## Childist Interpretation: Wrath from Child Sacrifice

Many scholars bristle at the apostasy of such a suggestion. How could the Hebrew Bible possibly admit that another god besides YHWH has such power, essentially contradicting the *Weltanschauung* that defines the Deuteronomistic History? Herbert Chanan Brichto (somewhat flagrantly) outlines the problem. "The sacrifice of Mesha's son was efficacious! Why? To recommend such an expedient to us when all else fails? Absurd! To praise the power of Moab's god Chemosh? Equally absurd. Then the power that responded to the sacrifice was YHWH's!"[36] Terence Fretheim also surmises that "it seems unlikely that the larger narrative, so opposed to gods other than Yahweh, would ascribe such power to Chemosh or grant such an effect to child sacrifice. Hence it is best to see the wrath as having an origin from Israel's God."[37] Numerous scholars concur, reasoning that the writer or redactor simply would not allow Kemosh to

---

33. Raymond Westbrook, "Elisha's True Prophecy in 2 Kings 3," *JBL* 124 (2005): 530–32.
34. Jesse C. Long, Jr. "Elisha's Deceptive Prophecy in 2 Kings 3: A Response to Raymond Westbrook," *JBL* 126 (2007): 168–71.
35. Zevit, *Religions of Ancient Israel*, 485 n. 15.
36. Brichto, *Biblical Poetics*, 207.
37. Fretheim, *Kings*, 143.

retain this authority in a literary corpus that strives to portray other gods as impotent.[38] Iain Provan suggests the wrath is human, and the child sacrifice motivated the Moabites to push to victory.[39] However, the word קצף appears almost always in divine contexts.[40] Also, the text does not tell of invigorated Moabite troops. Again, we are left questioning the story's most plausible scenario.

Theologically the reader's hands are tied with the explanation that the wrath has come from YHWH. Why would the Moabite king offer an apotropaic sacrifice to a foreign and inimical god? Why would an opposing god take notice of a Moabite sacrifice? Even if YHWH were the divine agent here, it seems perplexing that YHWH would be incensed about this instance, given other accounts of child sacrifice. YHWH fulsomely rewards Abraham for his willingness to sacrifice a child (Gen 22:16–18). Jephthah sacrifices his daughter to YHWH with no objection from the deity or condemnation from the narrator (Judg 11:29–40). The prophet Micah includes the sacrifice of the firstborn in a list of YHWH's accepted offerings, along with calves, rams, and oil (Mic 6:6–7).[41] The text does repeatedly express anger about children being sacrificed, but only when this custom appears with other reviled cultic practices.[42] There is no sense of moral outrage regarding the lives of children, per se, nor is the practice condemned in 2 Kgs 3:27. Even if YHWH were angry about child sacrifice, why pour anger upon the Israelites (who merely witnessed the act) instead of the Moabite king (who set fire to his son) or his forces? Or, if YHWH is omnipotent and so adamantly opposed to child sacrifice, why not prevent the boy's holocaust? Why misdirect fury against his own people and contribute to their defeat? Why would YHWH undermine his own people and power?

In his article dealing with the question, "Why Did the Besieging Army Withdraw? (II Reg 3, 27)," John Barclay Burns reviews the gamut of

---

38. See, for example, Gina Hens-Piazza, *1–2 Kings* (AOTC; Nashville: Abingdon, 2006), 246; Leithart, *Kings*, 180; Jesse C. Long, Jr., and Mark Sneed, "'Yahweh Has Given These Three Kings into the Hand of Moab': A Socio-Literary Reading of 2 Kings 3," in *Inspired Speech: Prophecy in the Ancient Near East—Essays in Honor of Herbert B. Huffmon* (ed. John Kaltner and Louis Stulman; JSOTSup 378; London: T&T Clark, 2004), 261.

39. Provan, *Kings*, 186.

40. As John Barclay Burns notes, the word קצף appears twenty-eight times in the Hebrew Bible and refers to YHWH's anger in nearly every instance (save two). See J. B. Burns, "Why Did the Besieging Army Withdraw?" *ZAW* 102 (1990): 191–92. See also Cogan and Tadmor, *II Kings*, 47.

41. Repeated references to child sacrifice throughout the biblical corpus suggest this practice persisted, at least among some worshipers of YHWH. Susan Ackerman asserts that "the cult of child sacrifice was felt in some circles to be a legitimate expression of Yahwistic faith" (Ackerman, *Under Every Green Tree*, 137).

42. E.g., Lev 18:21–24; 20; Deut 18:9–12; 2 Kgs 16:2–4; 17:13–17; 21:1–9; 23:3–25; Isa 57:3–10; Jer 7:17–32; 19:3–6; 32:29–35; Ezek 16:15–26; 23:36–49.

interpretations.⁴³ One novel explanation comes from Philippe Derchain, who suggests that Mesha's son died by falling, not fire. Through comparison with Egyptian bas-reliefs depicting children dropped from a city wall in times of siege, Derchain notes that the city walls were not the place of burnt offerings. He underscores that the root sense of the verb עלה means "*élever, monter, faire monter.*"⁴⁴ Burns points out, however, that the bas-reliefs just show children being dangled, not completed sacrifices, and the pharaoh in these sieges remained unaffected.⁴⁵ Burns also discusses Baruch Margalit's suggestion that the קצף (which he translates as "indignation") that came upon the Israelites "denotes the psychological breakdown or trauma that affected the Israelite forces when they beheld the sign of human sacrifice atop the walls of Kir-Hareseth."⁴⁶ However, Burns counters that the mental/emotional analysis is anachronistic.⁴⁷ Burns discusses these and other examples of scholars' reluctance to attribute the קצף (and its power) to the Moabite god, but concludes that the wrath belongs to Kemosh.⁴⁸

Mesha's son upends the story of 2 Kings 3. Burke Long holds that the audience with Elisha earlier in the chapter is the indisputable "highpoint" of the chapter,⁴⁹ yet the story's blazing finale—featuring a child—seems far more stunning. The conflagration on the city wall is easily visible, able to horrify the opposing warrior witnesses. As Rick Dale Moore summarizes, "Here the outcome [of the battle] is seen to rest solely and mysteriously upon the Moabite king's sacrifice of his firstborn son (3.27)."⁵⁰ This Moabite prince may never reign, but he has his power. He casts doubt on a prophet's predictions. His sacrifice brings favor from his god, sending away armies. And through his death, Mesha's son continues to haunt readers with questions.

I can think of no other instance in the Hebrew Bible where a sacrifice to a god other than YHWH brings its desired effect. King Mesha sought to save Moab, and in the critical moment before capitulating, desperately

---

43. Burns, "Why Did the Besieging Army Withdraw?" 187–94.
44. Philippe Derchain, "Les plus anciens témoignages de sacrifices d'enfants chez les sémites occidentaux," *VT* 20 (1970): 354.
45. Burns, "Why Did the Besieging Army Withdraw?" 190.
46. Baruch Margalit, "Why King Mesha of Moab Sacrificed His Oldest Son," *BAR* 12 (1986): 63.
47. Burns, "Why Did the Besieging Army Withdraw?" 188–90. Margalit compares this sacrifice to Ugaritic and Carthaginian evidence, but Burns finds these comparisons baseless.
48. Burns finds the text to be straightforward: "The anger of Chemosh fell on the Israelites and drove them to seek the religious security of their own land. II Reg 3,27 is not a summons to pass moral judgement on nor to justify human sacrifice. It is the narration of one which was eminently effective" ("Why Did the Besieging Army Withdraw?" 193).
49. Burke O. Long, "2 Kings III and Genres of Prophetic Narrative," *VT* 23 (1973): 342.
50. Rick Dale Moore, *God Saves: Lessons from the Elisha Stories* (JSOTSup 95; Sheffield: Sheffield Academic Press, 1990), 140–41.

and successfully offers his firstborn son to his god. This young prince enters the text just to leave it, yet manages to push the theological boundaries of the entire Hebrew Bible.

## Insights about Children, War, and Sacrifice

This story shows children suffering the ravages of warfare as soldiers and victims. As suggested above, 2 Kgs 3:21 likely includes children and youth among the fighters. The word נער, often connoting youth, frequently appears in military contexts. Some of these נערים function in assistive capacities that seem naturally geared toward younger recruits, such as fetching arrows or bearing armor.[51] Judges 8:13–21 offers further examples of youth in situations of battle. Gideon captures a youth (וילכד־נער) from Succoth and interrogates him for information about the leaders of his hometown (v. 14). It appears that this נער was a young soldier from Succoth who became a prisoner. After trampling the people of Succoth (v. 16) and killing the men of Penuel (v. 17), Gideon confronts his brothers' killers (vv. 18–19). Incensed that these kings of Midian, Zebah[52] and Zalmunna, have murdered his kin, Gideon commands his firstborn son, Jether, to take action. "Then he [Gideon] said to Jether, his firstborn, 'Rise up! Slay them!' But the boy [נער] did not draw out his sword for he was afraid, since he was still a boy [נער]" (v. 20). Zebah and Zalmunna seem to understand why Jether hesitates, and they goad Gideon to fight them himself: "*You rise up and kill us, for as the man [איש] is, so is his strength*" (v. 21a). This story recognizes children as participants in war, while also realizing that children's abilities to fight are different from those of adults. Of the four characters who appear in Judg 8:18–21 (Gideon, Zebah, Zalmunna, and Jether), all but Gideon seem to know that certain tasks of battle—like sword-to-flesh slaughter—may be too much to ask of a child.

Both Mesha and Gideon assume control over their sons: the former kills his son; the latter commands him to kill. Jether does not voice his reluctance, showing submission, but he fails to follow orders, revealing his own limitations and silent objection. The reaction of Mesha's son is lost to us. F. W. Farrar speculates, "Doubtless the young prince gave himself up as a willing offering, for that was essential to the holocaust being valid and acceptable."[53] Yet it is hard to imagine the Moabite prince feeling anything but sheer terror. While the father might accommodate the child, as

---

51. For discussion of נערים functioning in various military capacities, see Leeb, *Away from the Father's House*, 68–124.

52. This king's name (זבח) ominously resembles the verb זבח: "to slaughter for sacrifice."

53. Farrar, *Second Kings*, 37.

Gideon does when he kills Zebah and Zalmunna himself (Judg 8:21b), the father also has the power of life or death over his child.

Human sacrifice in the Hebrew Bible is dominated by child sacrifice. Other ancient peoples, such as the Egyptians, would sacrifice children, but also foreigners, slaves, or captured royalty.[54] The Hebrew Bible, however, testifies to child sacrifices that were moreover offered by parents, and usually fathers.[55] This is not to suggest that child sacrifice was a prevalent Israelite worship custom.[56] No archaeological evidence from within Palestine confirms child sacrifice as a common rite.[57] However, the textual evidence suggests that child sacrifice was sporadically practiced, although often opposed in the text. As Francesca Stavrakopoulou observes, "the Hebrew Bible appears unintentionally to overturn its own insistence that child sacrifice is a foreign practice, for it offers, both implicitly and explicitly, a vivid portrayal of YHWH as a god of child sacrifice."[58]

It seems logical that children would be desirable for sacrifice on multiple levels. Theologically, to sacrifice a child honors YHWH's claim on

---

54. See Alberto Green, *The Role of Human Sacrifice in the Ancient Near East* (Ann Arbor, MI: University Microfilms International, 1973), 291–95.

55. Fathers can sacrifice children (e.g., Gen 22:1–19; Judg 11:30–40; 1 Kgs 16:34; 2 Kgs 3:26–27; 16:3; 21:6), or unspecified agents (inferably parents) can sacrifice their own sons and (often) daughters (e.g., Deut 12:31; 2 Kgs 17:17; Jer 7:31; 19:5; Ezek 16:20; 23:37; Ps 106:37). In ancient Carthage, where child sacrifice was an established practice, worshipers could purchase children of the poor. See Lawrence E. Stager and Samuel R. Wolff, "Child Sacrifice at Carthage—Religious Rite or Population Control? Archeological Evidence Provides Basis for a New Analysis," *BAR* 10 (1984): 47.

56. Scholars debate the issue of child sacrifice in the Hebrew Bible. Some deny that this practice existed among the ancient Israelites (e.g., Weinfeld, Albertz). Others cite the use of the term *mlk* in the text and suggest this was a kind of sacrifice (e.g., Eissfeldt), or an act of devotion to a Canaanite god, Molech (e.g., Heider, Day). Other scholars think child sacrifice was incorporated into popular Yahwism (e.g., Ackerman, Stavrakopoulou). Key works (in addition to those already cited) dealing with this subject include Albertz, *A History of Israelite Religion*, 191–94; John Day, *Molech: A God of Human Sacrifice in the Old Testament* (Cambridge: Cambridge University Press, 1989); Otto Eissfeldt, *Molk als Opferbegriff im Punischen und Hebräischen und das Ende des Gottes Moloch* (Halle: Niemeyer, 1935); Karin Finsterbusch, Armin Lange, K.F. Diethard Römheld, eds., *Human Sacrifice in Jewish and Christian Tradition* (Leiden: Brill, 2007); George B. Gray, *Sacrifice in the Old Testament: Its Theory and Practice* (New York: KTAV, 1971); George C. Heider, *The Cult of Molek: A Reassessment* (JSOTSup 43; Sheffield: JSOT Press, 1986); Roland de Vaux, *Studies in Old Testament Sacrifice* (Cardiff: University of Wales Press, 1964); and Moshe Weinfeld, "The Worship of Molech and of the Queen of Heaven and Its Background," *UF* 4 (1972): 133–54. For a refutation of Weinfeld that draws on comparative ancient Near Eastern material, see Morton Smith, "A Note on Burning Babies," *JAOS* 95 (1975): 477–79. Speaking of Akkadian texts and passages from the Hebrew Bible that portray child sacrifice, Smith concludes, "we may plausibly presume the texts mean what they say" (p. 479).

57. As Stager notes, the archaeological evidence for child sacrifice comes from Phoenician sites. See discussion and photos in King and Stager, *Life in Biblical Israel*, 359–62.

58. Stavrakopoulou, *Manasseh and Child Sacrifice*, 179. For more detailed discussion, see pp. 141–206.

the firstborn. Like the first fruits, the new life is prized so this sacrifice becomes a testimony of deep devotion. Economically, a child had limited working capacity, and the loss of labor incurred to the household might be felt less. Also, one less child would mean one less mouth to feed and (eventually) one less adult (especially if a son) to lay claim to the family's holdings. Practically, children depended on parents with little alternative besides living (or dying) under their control. Physically, parents could overpower their children, subduing them for sacrifice. Reproductively, a sacrificed child might ensure future fertility. A couple that was able to conceive would then have more children, making the first child expendable. The paradoxes accumulate: a child is precious, yet common—unique, but replaceable.

## Children and Textual Connections

Like Elisha's mockers, the Moabite prince highlights children's influence and vulnerability. Mesha's son and the children from Bethel evoke wrath from their god and, in the process, are destroyed. In 2 Kgs 2:24a, Elisha curses (from קלל in the *piel* [*qal*: to be slight]) the children of Bethel in the name of YHWH. In 2 Kgs 3:18, Elisha declares that handing over Moab into the Israelites' hand will be a trifle (from קלל in the *nifal*). Yet what may be a light matter for Elisha or YHWH bears crushing weight for the children.

Along with many other children in the Hebrew Bible, Mesha's son suffers due to war. In this scene, the Moabite prince has young company with the child soldiers fighting amid the battle. Beyond the Bible, the Mesha Inscription reports King Mesha's slaughter of all the people in Nebo (*ll.* 15–17), including young victims.[59] Mesha's boasts of his bloody conquests over young people in the Moabite Inscription; Mesha's child is

---

59. Lines 16–17 of the Mesha Inscription suggest youth among Mesha's victims: ואהרג כל[ה] שבעת אלפן ג[ב]רן ו[ג]רן וגברת ו[גר] (*l.* 16) (from Jackson and Dearman, "Text of the Mesha' Inscription," 94). W. F. Albright's translation of *ll.* 15–17 explicitly lists children among Mesha's victims: "So I went by night and fought against it from the break of dawn until noon, taking it and slaying all, seven thousand men, boys, women, girls and maid-servants, for I had devoted them to destruction for (the god) Ashtar-Chemosh." See "The Moabite Stone," translated by W. F. Albright (*ANET*, 320–21). Kent Jackson omits any reference to youth in his translation, rendering ג[ב]רן ו[ג]רן וגברת ו[גר] ת ורחמת as "native men, foreign men, native women, for[eign] women, and concubines" (Jackson, "Language of the Mesha' Inscription," 98). The Hebrew term גבר implies strength with concomitant youth (*HALOT* 1:175) and the term רחמת for "concubine" (or "maid-servants"), derived from רחם "womb," carries sexual overtones (cf. Judg 5:30). While these terms may not suggest someone as small as "boys" and "girls" (*contra* Albright), they do suggest youth.

burnt to death in the Hebrew Bible. Both texts testify to children as violated victims of conflict and combat.

King Mesha's son also calls attention to the persistent belief that ancient deities desired children. YHWH demands the life of the firstborn (Exod 13:2; 22:28 [Eng. 22:29]), with substitutions sometimes allowed (Exod 13:11–15; 34:20; Num 3:40–41; 18:15). Firstborn children are listed among offerings to YHWH (Mic 6:6–7). The repeated (but not ubiquitous) denunciation of this practice shows that it must have continued.[60] Other gods in the text also accept (or require?) child sacrifice.[61] Kings and commanders sacrifice their children hoping to win divine favor or deliverance (Judg 11:30–40; 2 Kgs 3:26–27; 16:3; 21:6 [2 Chr 33:6]). On the basis of textual evidence (see Isa 30:33; Jer 7:31–32; 19:1–5; 32:35), scholars infer there was a designated place for child sacrifice. This cult site, the Tophet of Ben Hinnom, appears to be south of Jerusalem from the seventh to the fourth century BCE, despite the text's report of Josiah's attempt to destroy it (2 Kgs 23:10).[62] The practice of child sacrifice seems tenacious.

As a child controlled by his authoritative father, Mesha's son finds poignant companions in the Hebrew Bible. Isaac (Gen 22:1–19) and Jether (Judg 8:20–21) (as discussed above) are not the only boys thrust into situations of life and death by a paternal potentate. The text shows King Ahab as consenting to hand over his children (along with his wives and silver and gold) to King Ben-Hadad of Aram (1 Kgs 20:1–4) and only objecting to unbridled plunder (1 Kgs 20:5–7); this scene portrays another way a father uses children to bargain for political ends. The Deuteronomists claim that Ahaz and Manasseh sacrifice their sons by making them pass through the fire (2 Kgs 16:2–3; 21:6, respectively). Like Mesha's son, the young Abijah, son of Jeroboam, is portrayed as caught in a conflict between a prophet, a king, and a god (1 Kgs 14:1–18), but in each story only the child dies (2 Kgs 3:27; 1 Kgs 14:17).[63]

Yet the character in the Hebrew Bible with greatest affinity to Mesha's son is Jephthah's daughter (Judg 11:29–40). Both are children of commanders in the heat of battle (2 Kgs 3:25–27; Judg 11:29–33). YHWH plays

---

60. E.g., Deut 18:10–12; 2 Kgs 17:17; Isa 57:5; Jer 7:31; Ezek 20:25–31; 23:36–39.

61. E.g., Lev 18:21; 20:2–4; Deut 12:31; 2 Kgs 3:26–27; 17:31; 23:10; Jer 19:5; 32:35; Ezek 16:20–21; Ps 106:37–38.

62. Eusebius's *Onomasticon* refers to *Thapheth* as a location near Jerusalem. Philip Schmitz deduces that the Tophet must have contained some sort of oven or kiln and been staffed with personnel to execute the prescribed rites. See Philip C. Schmitz, "Tophet," n.p., *ABD* on CD-ROM. Version 2.1. 1997. See also William G. Dever, *Did God Have a Wife? Archaeology and Folk Religion in Ancient Israel* (Grand Rapids, MI: Eerdmans, 2005), 218–19.

63. For further discussion of 2 Kgs 14:1–18 with focused attention on Jeroboam's wife, see Robin Gallaher Branch, *Jeroboam's Wife: The Enduring Contribution of the Old Testament's Lesser-Known Women* (Peabody, MA: Hendrickson, 2009), 83–106.

a dominant role in the context of these stories,[64] and Kemosh is also a divine presence (mentioned by name in Judg 11:24 and present by association with Moab in 2 Kgs 3:26–27). Jephthah's daughter is her father's only offspring, and Mesha's son is destined to replace his father. Fathers control the fate of both children while mothers are entirely absent. The outcome of Jephthah's and Mesha's military conflicts seems predicated on the lives of these children—one boy, one girl. Each child becomes a burnt offering as the sacrifice accomplishes the father's goals, seemingly in accordance with the will of their gods. In the stories of Jephthah's daughter and Mesha's son, the text offers no condemnation of child sacrifice.[65]

Yet perhaps the words of Jephthah's daughter might fill the reader with regret (Judg 11:36–37). She is discerning, articulate, noble, pious, and brave.[66] With magnanimity beyond her youth, Jephthah's daughter acquiesces gracefully to fulfill her father's rash vow. The girl gives a glimpse of the faithful leader she might have become, maybe, like Deborah, a judge in her own right. Instead another young life ends abruptly through war and sacrifice.

What might have become of the Moabite prince? What would he have said if he had had the chance to speak? What could he have accomplished if he had been allowed to live? At the end of the story in 2 Kings 3, YHWH, the prophet, and the prince are gone. Envisioning King Mesha standing on the wall, alone among his son's ashes, the reader recalls the words of the prophet Isaiah: "Therefore my innermost parts tremble like a lyre for Moab, and my insides for Kir-heres" (16:11).

---

64. See Judg 11:9, 10, 11, 21, 23, 24, 27, 29, 30, 31, 32, 35, 36 [2x]; and 2 Kgs 3:2, 10, 11 [2x], 12, 13, 14, 15, 16, 17, 18.

65. For discussion comparing Gen 22:1–19; Judg 11:29–40; and 2 Kgs 3:26–27, see Michel, *Gott und Gewalt*, 300–303. Michel suggests that these texts belong to early traditions that were established before the polemic against child sacrifice grows both within and beyond the DtrH (p. 303).

66. For feminist treatment of this young female protagonist, see Karla G. Bohmbach, "Daughter of Jephthah," in Meyers et al., *Women of Scripture*, 243–44. See also J. Cheryl Exum, "On Judges 11," in *A Feminist Companion to Judges* (ed. Athalya Brenner; FCB 4; Sheffield: Sheffield Academic Press, 1993), 131–44; and Phyllis Trible, *Texts of Terror: Literary-Feminist Readings of Biblical Narratives* (OBT; Philadelphia: Fortress, 1984), 92–116, among others.

# 6

## The Debt-Collateral Children
## (2 Kings 4:1–7)

After one narrative of children mutilated, followed by another of a child immolated, the Elisha cycle abruptly switches to stories of children who are saved. In 2 Kgs 4:1–7, a mother calls out to Elisha, explaining her predicament: her husband, one of the sons of the prophets, has died, and a creditor is about to take away her two children as slaves. The prophet asks her what he can do for her and what resources she has; she reveals that the only thing left in the house is some oil. Elisha instructs the woman to gather many vessels from her neighbors outside, shut the door behind her and her children, and then pour oil into the containers. Following the prophet's directive, the mother closes the door while she and her children are inside. The children keep bringing her vessels, and she keeps filling them, until her son proclaims that there are no more. Then the oil stops flowing. The prophet instructs the mother to sell the oil, pay her debts, and live off the remainder. This episode starts with emptiness and a threat, but ends with abundance and a miracle. Destitution denied becomes hope realized, and a story with children finally has a "happily-ever-after" ending.

Or does it?

## Setting: Situation, Not Site

Following directly after the retreat of the Israelite troops (2 Kgs 3:27),[1] 2 Kgs 4:1 returns back to Israel. Readers presume that the story of the debt-collateral children takes place in this land, although the text does not specify a distinct locale. However, the wider narrative obliquely offers various settings since the protagonist is a widow of one of the sons of

---

1. Second Kings 3:27bβ in the MT reads וישבו לארץ. The Lucianic recension of the Septuagint, the Peshitta, and the Vulgate add the third person plural suffix: "their land," further clarifying that the troops are back in Israel.

the prophets. This group appears to be organized in the hill country of Ephraim (2 Kgs 5:22) and near the Jordan (2 Kgs 6:1–4), with the specific mention of Bethel (2 Kgs 2:3), Jericho (2 Kgs 2:5, 15), and Gilgal (2 Kgs 4:38). It seems likely that the widow and her children hail from one of these areas, although the omission of this detail may be significant. The location (unknown) is not as important as the mood (desperation), and the lack of particularity suggests universality. The story becomes as catholic as any mother who has ever feared losing her children simply because she is so poor.

## Characters

### The Mother

The mother of the debt-collateral children is arguably the story's star.[2] She starts the episode, ends it, and is busy throughout this narrative. This woman juggles multiple roles simultaneously: widow, supplicant, mother, advocate, protector, worker, and reporter.[3] The woman's call to Elisha and her claim upon him, in the wake of her husband's death, may imply that the sons of the prophets relied on income from their prophetic activity (see 1 Sam 9:6–8; 1 Kgs 14:1–3; Amos 7:10–13).[4] Her position as a wife gives us information about the sons of the prophets, implying that this guild was organized around coenobitic (and not monastic) principles.[5]

Yet the woman is not described simply as the wife of a prophetic

---

2. Jan Fokkelman maintains that the woman is the indisputable hero of this tale because of her constant presence and persistence. For a discussion of her strength as a character, see J. P. Fokkelman, *Reading Biblical Narrative: A Practical Guide* (trans. Ineke Smit; Leiden: Deo, 1999), 18. While Fokkelman highlights the woman's role, he overlooks the children's agency.

3. While she remains anonymous, the mother is designated by Josephus (*Antiquities* 9.4.2) as the wife of Obadiah (עבדיה). Perhaps this comes from a paronomastic connection, since she describes her husband to Elisha as his servant (עבדך, 2 Kgs 4:1aα). The name may also come from Ahab's servant (עבדיה, 1 Kgs 18:1–16), who is twice described as one who fears YHWH (1 Kgs 18:3, 12; cf. 1 Kgs 4:1aβ). Cogan and Tadmor suggest that the designation as the wife of Obadiah "rescued the woman from biblical anonymity" (Cogan and Tadmor, *II Kings*, 55 n. 1). However, this only rescues her *husband* from nameless obscurity. She still does not have her own name.

4. See Marvin A. Sweeney, *I & II Kings* (OTL; Louisville, KY: Westminster John Knox, 2007), 288. Würthwein thinks this story provides evidence that the sons of the prophets lived in poverty, although various factors surrounding the husband's death could have led to the family's penury. See Ernst Würthwein, *Die Bücher der Könige: 1. Kön. 17–2. Kön. 25* (ATD 11,2; Göttingen: Vandenhoeck & Ruprecht, 1984), 288.

5. As Robert Wilson notes, the sons of the prophets appear to have lived in community, at least in some measure (2 Kgs 4:38–41; 6:1–2). However, this does not appear to have been a celibate or secluded group (*Prophecy and Society*, 202).

guild member. Rather, the text presents וְאִשָּׁה אַחַת מִנְּשֵׁי בְנֵי־הַנְּבִיאִים—lit., "one woman from the wives of the sons of the prophets" (2 Kgs 4:1a). This literal translation allows for the possibility that *the wives of the sons of the prophets* may have been its own organization (analogous to a "ladies auxiliary"?). With the sons of the prophets as a collective group, the women of this community might have created their own support structures. Perhaps a surrounding circle of women has instilled the advocacy skills that the children's mother deftly employs (cf. Judg 11:36–40).

The woman's status as a widow is a source of both weakness and power. Without sufficient finances or family ties, a widow might be forced to beg or prostitute herself in order to survive. If she has children to support (as in 2 Kgs 4:1–7), her situation is all the more bleak. The text frequently mentions the widow in contexts of oppression, often accompanied by the orphan and sojourner.[6] She becomes a portrait of helplessness, reliant upon the beneficence of the merciful deity, noble ruler, and charitable stranger.

Yet the widow's suffering ironically becomes the vehicle of her strength. She evokes sympathy. As a marginalized person whose condition reflects on the society at large, she has a claim upon those in positions of authority who can appear magnanimous by helping her.[7] YHWH's advocacy for the widow enhances his reputation as a champion of justice.[8] Those who harm this defenseless woman deserve their own suffering (Job 31:16–22). The widow has a unique relationship with the protective deity who hears her prayers and supplications (Exod 22:21–22 [Eng. 22:22–23]). However, the text also belies its own seemingly altruistic claims, as YHWH threatens to create widows in retaliation against those who abuse them (Exod 22:23 [Eng. 22:24]).

This stereotypical archetype of an abject widow likely reflected reality for some, but certainly not all, widows in ancient societies.[9] Younger widows probably remarried (Gen 38:6–26; 1 Sam 25:39–42; Ruth 4). Older widows probably lived with grown children (Ruth 1:1–5). Widows with money to support themselves no doubt mitigated many of the undesirable consequences of living without a husband. Without the restrictions of a man's control, some widows must have found unprecedented opportunity (and need) to speak in their own voices. Multiple widows in the text distinguish themselves as bright and articulate. In the Hebrew Bible, Tamar

---

6. E.g., Exod 22:20–21 [Eng. 22:21–22]; Deut 24:17; Job 24:3, 21; Ps 94:6; Isa 1:23.

7. For discussion of ancient Near Eastern texts that discuss rulers' and deities' obligations to the poor, see Fensham, "Widow, Orphan, and the Poor," 129–39.

8. See Deut 10:17–18; 24:19–21; 27:19; Isa 1:16–17; Jer 7:5–7; 22:3; Zech 7:9–10; Mal 3:5; Ps 146:9; Prov 15:25.

9. For fuller discussion of the widow's roles in the ancient Near East, see van der Toorn, "Torn between Vice and Virtue," 1–13.

(Gen 38:6–26) and Naomi (Ruth 3) devise plans for their own success. In the Apocrypha, Judith cleverly outwits and kills the Assyrian commander Holofernes (Jud 10:11–19; 11), then commands the Israelite troops to victory (Jud 14:1–9). Along with these widows, the unnamed woman in 2 Kgs 4:1–7 is a strategist. But unlike them, she speaks up to keep her children.[10]

## Elisha

As he interacts with this individual family, Elisha has a very different persona from his previous role as a prophetic commander (2 Kgs 3:11–20). Instead of disdaining kings (2 Kgs 3:13a), the powerful man listens to a widow (2 Kgs 4:1). Instead of asking for props so that he can enter a trance (2 Kgs 3:15a), the wonder-worker seeks resources for the family's material survival (2 Kgs 4:2a). Instead of telling many men what will happen (2 Kgs 3:16–19), the prophet informs one woman of what she must do (2 Kgs 4:3–4). Instead of predicting the fates of nations (2 Kgs 3:18), the seer focuses on the future of one family (2 Kgs 4:7). Instead of channeling information from a supernatural realm (2 Kgs 3:15–19), the man of God asks questions (2 Kgs 4:2a), receives information (2 Kgs 4:2b, 7a), and works an earthly wonder (2 Kgs 4:2–7). Elisha appears less omniscient, but more personable. He is also more effective in achieving the desired goal.[11]

Yet while Elisha rescues the debt-collateral children from becoming slaves, he makes inquiries and remains absent during the actual miracle. Mirroring his previous pattern, Elisha first asks a question before responding to the plea (2 Kgs 3:13–15; 4:1–2). This query could be a gracious way to invite the woman's input, a deliberate tactic to stall for time, a bewildered scramble to search for resources, or an initial denial before a change of heart. Since the prophet does not appear during the multiplication of oil (2 Kgs 4:2–5), the reader must fill in the cause-and-effect relationship between the words of the prophet and the situation's outcome, as with the mockers from Bethel (2 Kgs 2:23–24).[12] However, 2 Kgs 4:1–7 provides a much more positive angle from which to view Elisha's interactions with children.

---

10. Appropriately, the text never calls this articulate mother a "widow" (אלמנה), paranomastically (if not etymologically) connected with "mute" (אלם).

11. As discussed previously, Elisha's prediction that the Israelites will conquer Moab (2 Kgs 3:18–19) is thwarted by the battle at Kir-hareseth (2 Kgs 3:25) when the Israelites retreat (2 Kgs 3:27b).

12. Alexander Rofé suggests that 2 Kgs 4:1–7 may have directly succeeded 2 Kgs 2:23–25, since both stories involve children (*Prophetical Stories*, 50). However, Rofé does not notice a connection between the vulnerable child in 2 Kgs 3:26–27 and the subsequent story of children at risk in 2 Kgs 4:1–7.

## The Dead Husband and the Encroaching Creditor

The children's father and the debt collector are barely present in the text, although their specters loom large. The roles of these two men are intertwined, as the father's departure through death (מת, 2 Kgs 4:1a) has caused the creditor's arrival (בא, v. 1b). Twice the woman describes her husband to Elisha as "your servant" (עבדך, v. 1a); the creditor is going to take the two children as slaves (לעבדים, v. 1b) in place of what the father (עבדך, v. 1a) cannot pay.[13] The offspring of one man now risk belonging to the other, as the text emphasizes through the preposition לו (והנשה בא לקחת את־שני ילדי לו לעבדים, v. 1b). Both men have a claim on the children; here, like a father, the creditor is about to take (לקח) the children (see Gen 22:2–3; 2 Kgs 3:27a).

The family's father is the only character directly linked to YHWH. While the narrator describes the husband as one of the sons of the prophets, his wife describes him appositionally through relationships (2 Kgs 4:1). First she informs Elisha that this dead man was his servant (עבדך); he was also her husband (אישי) and a worshiper of YHWH (היה ירא את־יהוה, v. 1a). Even as a miracle comes to transpire, the husband's introduction is the narrative's only profession of Yahwistic faith. The story begins in tension, for the absence of the God-fearer brings the man whom the family fears.

The creditor represents the ominous fate that awaits the children. The text does not indicate if this man is a hired debt collector, a struggling landowner, or an exorbitant usurer. While Pentateuchal laws prohibit interest on loans (Exod 22:24 [Eng. 22:25]; Lev 25:36–37; Deut 23:21 [Eng. 23:20]), usury likely transpired nonetheless. As Siegfried Stein notes in relation to 2 Kgs 4:1–7 and Neh 5:1–5, "One is justified in concluding that if the major crime, the selling of children into slavery, took place, the minor crime of lending money on interest certainly did."[14] Regardless, the creditor's arrival infuses urgency into the scene. Prophet, mother, and children must act quickly.

---

13. The noun עבד bears broad connotations of subordination since Hebrew does not have separate words for "slave" or "servant." Helmer Ringgren explains that various meanings of עבד include "slave, servant, subject, official, vassal, or 'servant' or follower of a particular god." *TDOT* 10:387. For further discussion, see Muhammad A. Dandamayev, "Slavery: Old Testament," n.p., *ABD* on CD-ROM. Version 2.1. 1997.

14. Siegfried Stein, "The Laws on Interest in the Old Testament," *JTS* 4 (1953): 169. R. P. Maloney maintains that Israelite society barred usurious practices, although money lending with interest was prevalent throughout much of the ancient Near East. Typical interest rates hovered between 20 and 50 percent, depending on the culture and items borrowed (with grain generally exacting a higher interest than a loan of money). However, as Maloney notes, this information comes from official documentation, such as the Code of Hammurabi, and actual practices probably varied widely. See Robert P. Maloney, "Usury and Restrictions on Interest-Taking in the Ancient Near East," *CBQ* 36 (1974): 20.

## The Two Children

The mother introduces her two children as potential slaves (2 Kgs 4:1b). They may be two boys or, more likely, a boy and a girl. In 2 Kgs 4:1, the woman refers to her children as ילדי, and later Elisha instructs the mother to shut the door "behind you and behind your children (בניך)" (2 Kgs 4:4a). As discussed in Chapter 2, בנים and ילדים are relational words that can indicate "children" generally instead of solely male offspring. The text certainly allows for the possibility that one of the children is a girl, and indeed seems to support this reading. In v. 6 the narrator refers to one child as "her son," implying the other is a daughter. There is no reference to an "older" or "younger" son, which might distinguish one from another if both were boys. Just as the text allows for girls among the mockers (2 Kgs 2:23–25), it seems probable that a daughter is one of the debt-collateral children.

We do not know how old these two children are, but they are dependent on their mother. We also sense that they may be young because the woman is in charge. Neither the prophet nor the mother includes the children in making decisions or finding a strategy. Older children, especially the son, might have been consulted if on the cusp of adulthood. Instead, the widow states the problem, receives the prophet's commands, and follows his orders (vv. 3–5). The children seem eager to help, as both of them are bringing vessels to her, while she is pouring (הם מגשים אליה והיא מוצקת, v. 5b).[15] They are strong enough to carry vessels, perhaps experienced with fetching water. Perhaps they do not realize the intention of the debt collector and simply labor silently by way of habit. Perhaps they are only too aware of the creditor and work anxiously to avoid slavery and stay with their mother. The boy speaks briefly, answering his mother's question (v. 6a), showing his comprehension, involvement, and ability to articulate. As they toil away, the children inadvertently exhibit their potential value as slaves. They unobtrusively pour themselves into the task at hand and thereby avoid slavery by doing what slaves must do. They are the only characters in the Hebrew Bible who proactively work on their own behalf to stave off enslavement.

## Re-viewing the Plot from a Childist Perspective

While this narrative offers another example of the prophet's miraculous power, the goal within the story is to save the children from debt slavery. References to the two children frame the story, as the woman (2 Kgs

---

15. מוצקת follows the *qere*.

4:1) and the prophet (vv. 4, 7) and the narrator (vv. 5–6) all recognize the impending threat. The mother exhibits rhetorical skill as she cries out to Elisha about her plight, carefully crafting her words to emphasize relationship.[16] Through the pleonastic second person pronoun (ואתה ידעת), the woman highlights Elisha's awareness of her dead husband's God-fearing past and emphasizes the prophet's relationship with this member of the sons of the prophets (v. 1a). This beseeching wife further portrays herself as Elisha's servant (שפחתך, v. 2b), but makes no request. By intertwining Elisha as part of her familial nexus, the mother implies that he has an ethical obligation to help her and her children. The prophet instantly acquiesces, recognizing her claim upon him, and seeks her advice (v. 2a). The imperfect verb of Elisha's response מה אעשה־לך may suggest a future intention: "What shall I do for you?"; permission: "What can I do for you?"; or obligation: "What should I do for you?"[17] These modalities express the prophet's willingness to help, coupled with his need for direction.

Before the woman has the chance to respond, the prophet requests further information from her: הגידי לי מה־יש־לכי[18] בבית (v. 2a). She expresses her humility and desperation, as she is bereft of most everything: אין לשפחתך כל בבית כי אם־אסוך שמן (v. 2b). Her answer remains enigmatic, since אסוך (in construct with שמן) is a *hapax legomenon*. Most translations render this with a variation of "container."[19] Regardless of the exact definition, the overall impression remains: she does not have much.

Having discovered the meager resources available, Elisha formulates a plan. He tells the widow to go and ask for empty vessels from her neighbors (2 Kgs 4:3), underscoring that she is to collect as many as possible (אל־תמעיטי, v. 3b).[20] Then she is to shut the door behind her and her children, pour oil in all these vessels, and set the full ones aside (v. 4). The mother asks no questions, and follows the prophet's instructions closely, but not exactly. The

---

16. For literary analysis of this narrative with attention to symmetry, see Fokkelman, *Reading Biblical Narrative*, 9–19.
17. The expression מה־אעשה may also suggest futility (see Gen 27:37), but that seems unlikely here, given Elisha's follow-up question.
18. The use of the כי as marker of second person feminine possessive suffix appears repeatedly (but not always) in this passage (v. 3a: שכנכי; v. 7a: נשיכי; v. 7b: בניכי). Various Hebrew manuscripts amend the suffix to the usual ך in these occurences. See GKC § 91 *l*.
19. Translations include "pot" (ASV, JPS, KJV), "jar" (ESV, NJKV, NRSV, RSV), "pitcher" (GNV), "jug" (NAB, NJPS), or "flask" (NJB). The LXX renders אסוך with the similar-sounding ἀλείψομαι (from ἀλείφω, "to anoint") leading some late-nineteenth- and early-twentieth-century commentators to suggest that אסוך implied an "anointing amount" or single application of oil (e.g., C. F. Burney, *Notes on the Hebrew Text of the Books of Kings* [Oxford: Clarendon, 1903], 273). See Cogan and Tadmor, *II Kings*, 56 n. 2. HALOT 1:73 translates אסוך as "small jar" and "oil-jar."
20. For comparison between the collection of vessels in 2 Kgs 4:2–4 and the plunder of the Egyptians in Exod 3:21–22, see Yael Shemesh, "Elisha and the Miraculous Jug of Oil (2 Kgs 4:1–7)," *JHS* 8, art. 4 (2008):12, doi:10.5508/jhs.2008.v8.a4.

directives of v. 3 remain elliptically unfulfilled; the reader must infer that the widow has gone, asked the neighbors, and gathered all the vessels she could. Only the commands of v. 4 are reported in v. 5 as she closes the door behind her and her children and pours oil into the vessels.

Shutting the door may suggest the secrecy of the magical miracle. Here, curiously, the prophet is absent, perhaps to show that the wonder is from YHWH and not a trickster's illusion. The action of closing the door may also connote the security of being inside,[21] for the children's safety will flow from these proceedings.

The children appear briefly in this scene, yet their simple actions are significant. As the son and daughter work with their mother, the independent subject pronouns emphasize the characters' agency (הם מגשים אליה והיא מוצקת, 2 Kgs 4:5b). The participial verb forms suggest that they are laboring continuously. The children show initiative; all the prophet's commands (in the feminine singular) have been to the mother (vv. 3–4),[22] but the children nonetheless work wordlessly until the vessels are full. When the mother tells the son to bring her another vessel, he informs her that there are no more (v. 6a). At this point in the story, the children know more than any other character. The mother does not realize that all the containers have been used. The prophet is outside the shut door (v. 5a), and learns through the mother of all the proceedings inside (v. 7a). The creditor may have left, but is certainly not in the house, nor are the neighbors. The children play a crucial role in the miracle's unfolding as the boy reveals the latest development: the vessels have run out. The young son's words seem to trigger the end of the miracle; after he speaks, the flow of oil stops (v. 6b).[23] The mother informs the man of God, who issues his final commands to her (v. 7). She is to sell the oil, settle her debts, and live with her children on the rest. The creditor is to be paid with money, not minors, and silent thanks goes to Elisha for keeping this family together.

## Childist Interpretation: One Miracle and Two Questions

While this tale extols the wonders of the prophet Elisha, disquieting questions linger. Clearly, Elisha has acted with the (understood) aid of YHWH to help the indigent by transforming ordinary items into tools of temporal salvation. Yet, what actually happened to the debt-collat-

---

21. See Gen 19:10; Exod 12:22, 23; Judg 19:22–27; 2 Sam 13:17–18; 2 Kgs 4:21, 33; 6:32.
22. Verse 3: לכי, שאלי, תמעיטי; v. 4: תסיעי, יצקת, סגרת, באת.
23. As Yael Shemesh points out, the cessation of oil keeps the story miraculous. Had the oil kept flowing, the over-abundance of blessing would have become a messy curse ("Elisha and the Miraculous Jug," 14).

eral children? The narrator's attention moves onto new characters after the prophet's words in 2 Kgs 4:7, and the story remains ultimately unresolved. Readers infer that the woman does indeed sell the oil to save her children, although the narrative does not guarantee their safety. If she did sell the oil, would the sale generate enough income to cover the money owed? Did the miracle serve to keep the debt collector away for a while, only to have him return and take the son and daughter after Elisha had gone? Pessimistic possibilities persist.

Also, how should the last clause be interpreted? While 2 Kgs 4:7b ואת ובניך תחיי בנותר is consistently translated "you and your sons will live on the remainder" (or some variation thereof),[24] the text here is corrupt, prompting multiple emendations. The MT juxtaposes a masculine plural subject (בניך)[25] with a feminine singular verb (תחיי); this inconsistency is conveniently obscured in English translation (i.e., תחיי as "you will live"). Perhaps a scribe has emended an earlier text to insert the children, but did not change the verb form from the singular feminine to the masculine plural. *BHS* text critical note b on this verse offers ואת־בניכי תחיי as one possibility, pointing את as a direct object marker. The clause ואת־בניכי תחיי בנותר would then translate: "and as for your children, you will live with the remaining [ones]."[26] This interpretation hinges on the translation of ב, which can suggest either instrumentality ("you shall live *on* what is left over") or accompaniment ("you shall live *with* the remaining ones").[27] The Vulgate, Septuagint, and some Hebrew manuscripts emend the second person feminine singular verb (תחיי) to a second person masculine plural verb (תחיו) to clarify that all three characters—mother and two children—will live on the money procured from the sale of the oil. However, the singular verb retained by the MT accords with the other feminine singular forms used by Elisha as he directs his attention to the woman.[28] This would

---

24. E.g., ASV: "and live thou and thy sons of the rest"; JPS: "and live thou and thy sons of the rest"; KJV: "and live thou and thy children of the rest"; NIV: "You and your sons can live on what is left"; NJB: "you and your children can live on the remainder"; NKJV: "and you *and* your sons live on the rest"; NRSV, NJPS: "and you and your children can live on the rest"; RSV: " and you and your sons can live on the rest."

25. As with similar forms in this passage, this orthography follows the *qere* (בניך) not the *ketiv* (בניכי). Either reading portrays a plural noun.

26. T. R. Hobbs favors this reading, omitting the *shureq defectiva* before בניכי and reads ואת בניכי תחיי בנותר: "and you shall live with your remaining sons" (*2 Kings*, 43). This phrase also follows an inverted Hebrew word-order pattern with the subject preceding the verb, as previously exhibited in this passage (cf. v. 1a; see Long, *2 Kings*, 48).

27. Both BDB and *HALOT* offer pages of definitions for the multivalent ב. See BDB, 88–91, and *HALOT* 1:103–5. See also Williams, *Hebrew Syntax*, 44–45; and Bruce K. Waltke and M. O'Connor, *An Introduction to Biblical Hebrew Syntax* (Winona Lake, IN: Eisenbrauns, 1990), 196–99.

28. See v. 2: הגידי; v. 3: תמעיטי, שאלי, לכי; v. 4: תסיעי, יצקת, סגרת, באת; v. 7: שלמי, מכרי, לכי.

mean his instructions are to her, and the children are the antecedent to נותר, allowing for the translation "you will live with your remaining children."

If accepted, this reading would make the story bittersweet, hinting that Elisha knew of previous children whom the woman no longer has. Perhaps Elisha had been acquainted with this family in earlier days due to his association with the sons of the prophets and remembers when this woman had more children. Maybe the mother had older children who have already become slaves (see Neh 5:5). Some of the widow's offspring might be dead due to infant mortality or childhood illness. While such scenarios are speculative, the MT allows for the possibility that the widow's family has already suffered the loss of children.

Regardless of this conceivable interpretation for the story's end, the agency and fate of the children merit interpreters' attention. Scholars who look beyond prophetic power in this passage tend to follow Elisha's cue and direct their attention to the woman. Gina Hens-Piazza is typical in this regard as she observes, "Moreover, the miracle has come about by the woman acting to solve *her* own problem, thus empowering *her* to address *her* own crisis"[29] (emphasis added). Similarly, Yael Shemesh points out that Elisha helps a woman in 2 Kgs 4:1–7 and 2 Kgs 4:8–37, without initial mention of the three children whose lives are at stake in these stories.[30] Certainly the mother suffers in 2 Kgs 4:1–7, but the children have the most to lose. With little means of support, virtually no possessions, and without her children and their labor, the mother would find it extremely difficult (at best) to acquire the money necessary to pay the owed debt. This would leave the children enslaved indefinitely. The small children risk losing not only their family but also their home and their freedom. Seemingly to avoid this, they get busy working when Elisha offers a proposal. The boy reveals new information. These two small characters in 2 Kgs 4:1–7 play a pivotal role in a story that raises questions about poverty, debt, and child labor.

## Insights about Children and Debt Slavery

Second Kings 4:1–7 allows a glimpse into the personal cost of debt slavery, which was integral to ancient Near Eastern societies.[31] When

---

29. Hens-Piazza, *Kings*, 251. Conversely, Dorothy B. E. A. Akoto observes, "The faith of her [the widow's] children was also tested. They cooperated to receive the miracle of their own salvation." See Dorothy B. E. A. Akoto, "Women and Health in Ghana and the *Trokosi* Practice: An Issue of Women's and Children's Rights in 2 Kings 4:1–7," in *African Women, Religion, and Health: Essays in Honor of Mercy Amba Ewudziwa Oduyoye* (ed. Isabel Apawo Phiri and Sarojini Nadar; Maryknoll, NY: Orbis, 2006), 103. For Akoto's discussion of 2 Kgs 4:1–7 as it relates to modern Africa, see pp. 96–110.

30. Shemesh, "Elisha and the Miraculous Jug," 3.

31. For comparison between debt slavery in ancient Israel and the ancient Near East,

impoverished people had nothing left to sell, they would sell dependents, then themselves. This might be due to money already owed or new circumstances of poverty.[32] Debt slavery was arguably the most common method for procuring slaves.[33] Three different legislative passages (Exod 21:2–11; Lev 25:39–46; Deut 15:12–18) seek to regulate the acquisition of slaves (often through debt) and their treatment, calling attention to debt slavery as an accepted ancient Israelite institution.[34]

A closer look at the biblical law codes regulating slavery leads to insights regarding the enslavement of Israelites by their own people.[35]

---

see Chirichigno, *Debt-Slavery*, 30–144. For discussion of girls, women, and slavery in the ancient Near East, see Marsman, *Women in Ugarit and Israel*, 437–54. For discussion of laws regulating the treatment of slaves (with the context of debt slavery sometimes made explicit), see Raymond Westbrook, *Studies in Biblical and Cuneiform Law* (CahRB 26; Paris: J. Gabalda, 1988), 89–109.

32. John Van Seters notes that the laws about buying and selling slaves in Exod 21:2–6 cover business transactions without mention of debt. Similarly, Van Seters suggests, Exod 21:7–11 regulates the sale of daughters, suggesting poverty, but not specifying a context of money owed. See John Van Seters, "Law of the Hebrew Slave: A Continuing Debate," *ZAW* 119 (2007): 170–71. However, Raymond Westbrook observes that the stipulation requiring the slave go free "for nothing" (חנם, Exod 21:2b) suggests that a debt has been erased (Westbrook, *Biblical and Cuneiform Law*, 91).

33. See Isaac Mendelsohn, *Slavery in the Ancient Near East: A Comparative Study of Slavery in Babylonia, Assyria, Syria, and Palestine from the Middle of the Third Millennium to the End of the First Millennium* (New York: Oxford, 1949), 43. See also J. Andrew Dearman, "Prophecy, Property and Politics," SBLSP 23 (1984): 385.

34. In a lively exchange, Bernard Levinson and John Van Seters disagree about the order of these law codes and the effect each has on shaping the others. Focusing his attention on Lev 25:39–44, Levinson argues that the Holiness Code dates to the later Second Temple period. Through a series of subtle but traceable textual changes, Levinson outlines a proposed reworking from the Hebrew *Vorlage* through the Septuagint to various English translations that resulted in a misrepresentation of Lev 25:44–46 (in most English versions, save the KJV). The KJV renders Lev 25:46aβ לעלם בהם תעבדו as "they shall be your bondmen for ever" (referring to the children and clan members of the sojourners). Levinson maintains that the KJV properly recognizes לעלם as a technical term for permanent slavery. He then interprets these laws of the Holiness Code as intended to limit the regulations of Exod 21:2–11 by rejecting slavery of Israelites through the provision of jubilee release. See Bernard M. Levinson, "The Birth of the Lemma: The Restrictive Reinterpretation of the Covenant Code's Manumission Law by the Holiness Code (Leviticus 25:44–46)," *JBL* 124 (2005): 617–39 (esp. pp. 623–30). Van Seters, however, suggests that the laws of Exod 21:2–11 are later and instead comment on both the Holiness Code slave provisions (Lev 25:39–46) and those of Deuteronomy (Deut 15:12–18). By exempting the daughter sold as a wife from the release promised in Deut 15:12, Exod 21:7–11 keeps families intact. The slave wife is entitled to some measure of attention, and can be released if she does not receive basic care (Exod 21:10–11). Van Seters understands Exod 21:2–11 as providing a workable revision of the jubilee release in the Holiness Code, which is as unrealistic as it is unenforceable (Van Seters, "Law of the Hebrew Slave," 169–83).

35. Gregory Chirichigno draws distinctions between foreign chattel slaves and Israelite debt slaves, who are afforded different rights in the law codes. As Chirichigno notes, however, Hebrew does not have separate words to distinguish between debt slaves and chattel slaves

Deuteronomy 15:12–18 does not explicitly include children, but it does not exclude them as much as translations suggest. These regulations begin regarding העברי או העבריה — lit., "the male Hebrew or the female Hebrew." Since this phrase is awkward in English, translations consistently render העברי או העבריה "a Hebrew man or a Hebrew woman."[36] Yet עברי and העבריה indicate nationality and gender, but not age. This law does not preclude Hebrew children who were bought, sold, and taken as slaves, as the phrase "a Hebrew man or a Hebrew woman" implies. Children may also be obliquely referenced by the slave who voluntarily chooses to stay with the master (Deut 15:16–17), perhaps because this is the house in which he or she has grown up.

Exodus 21:2–11 incorporates regulations regarding children and youth more overtly into its stipulations. The male Hebrew slave of vv. 2–4 may be a youth or young man if he is unmarried (v. 3a) or given a wife during his servitude (v. 4a). It seems reasonable that he obtains a wife during his enslavement as he becomes old enough to be considered marriageable. If this acquired wife bears children to the male slave, the mother and children are to remain enslaved when the father is to be released in the seventh year (vv. 2–4). The male slave's immediate family members are, in effect, held hostage in exchange for a lifetime of slavery (vv. 4–6). (However, the text strategically has the slave first avow his love for his master, before his wife and children, as his motivation for refusing freedom [v. 5].) Children born into slavery stay enslaved. They appear to be exempt from the seventh year release since they were born into the master's household (v. 4), and not purchased (v. 2).

The second part of the slave laws in Exodus 21:7–11 bears more directly on young women and girls. Joseph Fleishman argues fathers could only sell daughters as concubines, who would be entitled to the rights of a secondary wife.[37] Their value as potential wives suggests that many female slaves were young and nubile.[38] A female slave (אמה) is not to be freed like a male slave (עבד) (v. 7), since slave girls and women become part of the family and therefore forfeit freedom. Being a female slave includes sexual obliga-

---

(both designated by עבד [for men]). Chirichigno suggests this distinction hinges on context as well as specialized use of the term עבד עברי, which he understands as referring to debt slaves in Exod 21:2 and Deut 15:12 (*Debt-Slavery*, 145–85). However, Hebrews may have been enslaved to one another through situations other than debt, such as selling a child due to general impoverishment or buying a Hebrew slave from a foreigner (see Van Seters, "Law of the Hebrew Slave," 170–76).

36. E.g., ASV, ESV, JPS, KJV, NRSV, RSV.

37. See Fleishman, "Law of Exodus 21:7–11," 47–64. For detailed discussion, see Fleishman, *Father-Daughter Relations in Biblical Law*, 7–92.

38. Carolyn Pressler notes that girls would be valued for their sexual capacity as potential mothers or concubines, as well as their working ability ("Wives and Daughters, Bond and Free," 155–56).

tion and pressure to please the master.³⁹ Exodus 21:8 explains that the slave owner is at liberty to sell his female slave (perhaps for a profit), although not to a foreign people. If she is pledged to his son, the father is to treat her like a daughter (v. 9). If the master takes another wife, the female slave already purchased is still entitled to food, clothes, and sexual intercourse (v. 10).⁴⁰ Failure to provide these should result in her release (v. 11), although to be set free as a rejected wife would bring its own societal challenges.

Leviticus 25:39–46 distinguishes between slaves from among the Hebrews and the foreigners. Verses 39–43 specify treatment of Hebrew slaves, using a term of lateral kinship (אחיך, v. 39). Treatment of the Hebrews' foreign slaves (ועבדך ואמתך, v. 44) is regulated in vv. 44–46, with both sets of laws noting the role of child slaves. According to these instructions, Hebrew children are to be released with their father in the year of jubilee and return to their family lands (v. 41), although the text omits the fate of the slave mother. Leviticus 25:45aα discusses foreign slave children and exhorts the slave purchaser, וגם מבני התושבים הגרים עמכם מהם תקנו: "Moreover, you may purchase them from among the children of the sojourners dwelling with you." To understand בני as meaning actual children in v. 45 corresponds to the use of this term in v. 41, where the children (בנים) are released with their father. If v. 45 were simply promoting the sale of the resident aliens (as suggested by the NRSV, among other translations⁴¹) there would be no need for the word בני. Further, the rest of v. 45 extends the list of those who can be purchased: וממשפחתם אשר עמכם אשר הולידו בארצכם והיו לכם לאחזה "and from their families that are with you, whom they begot in your land; they will be your possession." The children of the sojourners, as well as the other members of extended foreign families, are to be bought as property (v. 45). The master should give them to his children as an inheritance, and treat them as slaves forever (v. 46a).⁴² Only the Hebrew slaves, seen as kin (אחיו, אחיכם), escape

---

39. Exodus 21:8 describes the circumstances under which a female slave can be redeemed, although translations frequently shift the reason for rejection from the man's whim to the woman's failure. The phrase אם־רעה בעיני אדניה is generally translated with a variation of, "If she does not please her master" (ASV, JPS, KJV, NIV, NJB, RSV, NRSV) making the rejected (or victimized?) slave girl responsible for her own expulsion. For discussion of texts that depict a relationship between female slavery and sex, see Michel, "Sexual Violence," 56–57.

40. Translations euphemistically render ענה in Exod 21:10 as "duty of marriage" (KJV), "marital rites" (NRSV), or "conjugal rights" (NJPS). *HALOT* 1:855 cites this verse and defines ענה as "sexual intercourse." This word explicitly notes sex among the slave girl's responsibilities.

41. NRSV: "You may also acquire them from among the aliens residing with you." NIV: "You may also buy some of the temporary residents living among you." See also the RSV, ESV. However, the JPS and NJPS specifically mention children.

42. Levinson reads לעלם as "the technical formula for permanent indenture" ("Birth of the Lemma," 627).

harsh treatment (v. 46b) and have the hope of eventual manumission (Lev 25:39–41; Exod 21:2–4; Deut 15:12–14).

This portrayal of release from debt slavery may be deliberately misleading. Mark Sneed points out that the laws promoting the humane treatment of the poor and the marginalized may have served to bolster existing social hierarchies. Without enforceable (or even suggested) penalties for lack of compliance, the elite might have felt at liberty to ignore eleemosynary (but expensive) legislation.[43] If these charitable policies were followed, Marvin Chaney suggests that legal provisions for debt easement would have served the monarch's interest. Giving poor peasants eventual relief from their slavery would have won popular support, while undermining the upper class that might have otherwise posed a threat to the monarchy. While successive moneyed factions proposed various debt-easement policies over the centuries (see Neh 5:1–13), debt slavery appears to have persisted.[44]

Slavery in the Hebrew Bible undoubtedly involves children and youth, as 2 Kgs 4:1–7 illustrates and other texts also witness.[45] Due to the high percentage of children in the ancient population, selling dependents was both a desperate measure and practical recourse in dire situations. As a last resort, parents might sell some children in the struggle to keep a remnant of the family unit intact. This does not suggest they were cavalier about such action; rather, selling one's children was probably laden with feeling, as seen in 2 Kgs 4:1–7. Although parents would likely strive to acquire their own children back, Gregory Chirichigno maintains that this would have been difficult to impossible in many cases.[46] Children would be taken from their families with little hope of ever being reunited.

Children could also offer distinct advantages as slaves. Due to their young age and relatively small size, children generally would not pose a threat to slave owners. As a rule, children could be controlled with less effort than men or women and be malleable in learning tasks set before them. They cost less to feed than adults. Marvin Sweeney suggests that

---

43. Sneed, "Israelite Concern for the Alien, Orphan, and Widow," 504.

44. See Marvin L. Chaney, "Debt Easement in Israelite History and Tradition," in *The Bible and the Politics of Exegesis: Essays in Honor of Norman K. Gottwald on His Sixty-Fifth Birthday* (ed. David Jobling, Peggy L. Day, Gerald T. Sheppard; Cleveland: Pilgrim, 1991), 127–39.

45. E.g., Lev 25:41, 45; Exod 21:4–5, 7–11; Neh 5:5. Cuneiform texts also offer evidence of children as slaves in the ancient Near East. See, for example, Laws of Hammurabi ¶ 117, in Martha Roth, *Law Collections from Mesopotamia and Asia Minor* (SBLWAW 6; 2nd ed.; Atlanta: Scholars Press, 1997), 103. For comparative studies on the sale of daughters in ancient Near Eastern texts, see Pressler, "Wives and Daughters," 162–63; and Fleishman, *Father-Daughter Relations in Biblical Law*, 67–72.

46. Chirichigno notes that debt slavery was often a "surrender" of family members. He asserts, "Debt-slavery in Israel, as in Mesopotamia, demonstrates the mobility that existed between the free and unfree classes, since in many cases people were not able to redeem their dependents (cf. 2 Kgs 4.1; Jer. 34.8–16)" (*Debt-Slavery*, 141).

the young children in 2 Kgs 4:1–7 are "considered more economically viable than the woman herself."[47] Muhammad Dandamayev posits that most slaves did not perform highly skilled manufacturing jobs or intense agricultural work. Rather, he suggests that slave labor was generally concentrated on chores around the household,[48] which would be manageable for children. The boy and girl in 2 Kgs 4:1–7 naturally immerse themselves in such domestic work (v. 7), providing valuable labor.

As this story illustrates, children's work contributed to a household's survival. Children's efforts were not token gestures of "helping out"[49] as they toiled in the fields, gathered fuel, fetched water, tended to younger children, watched over animals, and learned skills, such as how to make pottery, process grains, cook, weave, build, plow, plant, and harvest.[50] Many of these jobs may have been divided along gender lines, but we need to be careful not to make assumptions based on modern biases.[51] Children's labor, whether slave or free, was incorporated into ancient economies. As Laurel Koepf asserts, "Ancient children are assets, not expenses."[52]

## Children and Textual Connections

The family of 2 Kgs 4:1–7 finds company in the lamentable ranks of those who sell themselves when they have nothing else left (see Gen 47:15–21). The children become a saleable commodity (see Exod 21:7; Lev 25:39; Deut 15:12; Jer 34:14; Neh 5:1–5) as they face being taken by a man who can control their lives (לקח: 2 Kgs 4:1b; see Gen 22:2–3; 2 Kgs 3:27). The widow joins other mothers who cry out, usually to powerful men, seeking justice or restitution (צעק: 2 Kgs 4:1a; see also 2 Kgs 6:26; 8:3; Neh 5:1). The prophet has the role of beneficent rescuer, helping those who are desperate (Isa 1:17, 23; 10:2) and providing relief for the widow (Job 29:13). Like YHWH, Elisha protects vulnerable children (e.g., Deut 10:18; 26:12–13; Mal. 3:5; Pss 68:6 [Eng. 68:5]; 146:9). Yet even YHWH traffics in humans (Isa 50:1).

---

47. Sweeney, *Kings*, 289.
48. Dandamayev, "Slavery," n.p.
49. For example, King and Stager claim that "boys were better help on the family farm than girls, who would assist their mothers around the house" (*Life in Biblical Israel*, 42). This appraisal relies on assumptions about the relative value of boys' and girls' work more than ancient evidence.
50. See Meyers, *Discovering Eve*, 148–52.
51. For example, while Gen 29:9 explicitly calls Rachel a shepherd (fem.) (רעה הוא), translators frequently withhold this title and note, "she kept them" (i.e., her father's sheep) (e.g., KJV, ASV, RSV, NRSV; JPS "she tended them"). Nehemiah 3:12 portrays Shallum's daughters as builders of Jerusalem's walls.
52. Koepf, "Give Me Children," 71.

Prophetic injunctions suggest that the abuses of the poor did not abate, despite protective legislation. Jeremiah 34:8–11 tells of masters who freed their Hebrew slaves when urged to do so by King Zedekiah, but then subjugated back these same people once again. Amos 2:6 reports poor people being sold for silver and sandals. Passages in Isaiah lament the plunder of the needy (Isa 3:14–15) and the acquisition of land by the rich (Isa 5:8), depicting practices that would render people vulnerable to becoming debt slaves.[53] Joel 4:3 [Eng. 3:3] voices YHWH's anger as a boy is traded for prostitution and a girl is sold for wine. And while texts suggest respect for keeping unfortunate families together (Lev 25:41; Exod 21:3–6), 2 Kgs 4:1–7 illustrates how debt slavery could (and probably often did) tear families apart.

The children of 2 Kgs 4:1–7 and Neh 5:5 find advocates in parents who petition those in power. In Neh 5:1–5, the people (with women specifically mentioned) protest the enslavement of their children, just like the mother in 2 Kgs 4:1. These parents have parted with all they have to keep from losing their children (2 Kgs 4:2; Neh 5:3–5), but are dejected by their inability to hold onto their offspring. Nehemiah 5:5 shows that these fears are well founded by noting children's increased vulnerability when away from their parents. The enslaved daughters are "ravished" (נכבשׁ, Neh 5:5b), with implications of sexual humiliation (see Esth 7:8). Both parents and slave owners desire the children, who carry emotional and economic value. Yet with few resources, destitute families struggle to stay intact.

Help can come from YHWH through the prophets. The narrative in 1 Kgs 17:8–15 shares many parallels with 2 Kgs 4:1–7. In the Elijah story, the prophet encounters a desperate widow who has a child; both mother and son face starvation. Elijah asks her to make him a cake before feeding her son, which she does. Miraculously her flour and oil do not run out so she and her household have a supply of food. In both the Elijah and Elisha stories, the prophets offer succor to poor widows with children. The mothers express concern about their sons (1 Kgs 17:12; 2 Kgs 4:1), and the prophets respond (1 Kgs 17:13; 2 Kgs 4:2–4). The children heighten the drama as they face desperate hunger (1 Kgs 17:12) or potential enslavement (2 Kgs 4:1). While only one boy says a few words (2 Kgs 4:6a), we imagine all three children in both stories as vulnerable, scared, and ultimately relieved. The prophets provide miracles of multiplied goods to keep the children alive (1 Kgs 17:15), free (1 Kgs 4:7), and with their widowed mothers.[54]

---

53. Dearman suggests that the loss of property was a critical factor in forcing people into debt slavery ("People, Property, and Politics," 385–86).

54. For extended comparison of these two stories, see Shemesh, "Elisha and the Miraculous Jug," 15–18.

Still, the happy endings of these stories in 1 Kgs 17:8–15 and 2 Kgs 4:1–7 in many ways belie ancient (and modern) realities. Debt slavery was (and is) a crushing problem for desperately impoverished people. The story in 1 Kgs 4:1–7 provides the most detailed example in the Hebrew Bible of the toll that debt slavery would take on a family, as this mother and her children take action to avoid this ruinous fate. The boy also speaks up, signaling the end of the unfolding miracle (2 Kgs 4:6). The widow's son and daughter in 2 Kgs 4:1–7 reveal how much children matter since the reputation of the prophet, and by extension, his God, hinges on them. Here the prophet's prowess relies on his ability to help children.

# 7

# The Shunammite's Son (2 Kings 4:8–37)

The story of the boy who is promised, born, dies, and is then resuscitated, showcases Elisha as one who can both give and restore life. This involved account weaves together separate scenes that cohere through the presence of the Shunammite woman and her relationship with the prophet. The tale begins with the great woman from Shunem who prevails upon Elisha to eat at her home. She and her husband build guest accommodations for the prophet, who seeks to repay her kindness with a child. The Shunammite woman declines the offer, but nonetheless bears a son as the prophet had predicted. One day when the boy is older he goes out to the fields, where he suffers from head pain, and soon dies. The Shunammite hurries to see Elisha and insists on his help. Elisha first sends his servant Gehazi to try to revive the boy, but Gehazi's efforts prove futile. Elisha comes to the Shunammite's house and sees the dead boy lying on the prophet's own bed. Elisha works to bring the child back to life by lying on his small body, and eventually the boy revives and sneezes. The Shunammite falls at the prophet's feet, presumably in gratitude, and leaves with her living son.

## Settings: Town, Home, Field, Road, Mountain, and Room

This tale begins with Elisha in the small town of Shunem. Located in Israel just north of Jezreel, Shunem dates back to the Middle Bronze age and is well positioned between the Transjordan and Mediterranean.[1] While Shunem receives relatively little mention in the Bible,[2] it provides

---

1. Sweeney, *I & II Kings*, 289. Shunem is attested in the Amarna letters, as well as in the conquest lists of Pharaohs Thutmose III and Sheshonk I. See Elizabeth F. Huwiler, "Shunem," n.p., *ABD* on CD-ROM. Version 2.1. 1997.

2. See Josh 19:18; 1 Sam 28:4; 2 Kgs 4:8. The only other biblical character to hail from

a few points of significance to this story. Shunem's location on a trade route might contribute to the woman's wealth, enabling her to build separate guest quarters. This town is also farther north than other places that Elisha has visited, perhaps hinting that his sphere of influence is creeping toward Phoenicia.[3] The prophet also designates the anonymous woman by the place from whence she comes (2 Kgs 4:12, 25, 36), and commentators generally follow his lead.[4]

Elisha stays and eats at the Shunammite's home. She suggests (and presumably implements) plans to construct a small guest room (עלית־קיר קטנה, 2 Kgs 4:10a)[5] for this holy man of God (vv. 9–11). With unusual attention to furniture, the text relates the contents of this upper chamber: a bed, table, chair, and lamp (v. 10).[6] Two pivotal scenes take place here: the conversation when Elisha, Gehazi, and the Shunammite discuss the possibility of her having a child (vv. 11–16), and the miracle when Elisha brings this child back to life (vv. 32–37). The interior of a bedroom pro-

---

Shunem is Abishag (1 Kgs 1:1–15; 2:13–25). Rabbinic interpretation, noticing the geographical connection between Abishag and the great woman of Shunem, suggests that the two women were sisters. See Rosenberg, *Kings 2*, 261. The character of Shulammite (Song 7:1 [Eng. 6:13]) also connects with the Shunammite paronomastically, and perhaps ethnographically as well.

3. Earlier in his travels, Elisha has been to Gilgal (2 Kgs 2:1), Bethel (2 Kgs 2:2–3, 23), Jericho (2 Kgs 2:4–5), Samaria (2 Kgs 2:25), along the Jordan (2 Kgs 2:6–7), Mt. Carmel (2 Kgs 2:25), and on the plains of Edom (2 Kgs 3:8–20). This extension of influence into Phoenicia (and Jezebel's territory) appears in the corresponding (and arguably later) adaptation of this story into the Elijah cycle (1 Kgs 17:8–24). On the chronological relationship between the Elijah and Elisha cycles, see White, *Elijah Legends*, 11–17.

4. Fokkelien van Dijk-Hemmes calls this character "Gedolah." See Fokkelien van Dijk-Hemmes, "The Great Woman of Shunem and the Man of God: A Dual Interpretation of 2 Kings 4:8–37," in *A Feminist Companion to Samuel and Kings* (FCB 5; ed. Athalya Brenner; Sheffield: Sheffield Academic Press, 1994), 230. A few scholars follow Dijk-Hemmes's lead, such as Jopie Siebert-Hommes, "The Widow of Zarephath and the Great Woman of Shunem: A Comparative Analysis of Two Stories," in *On Reading Prophetic Texts: Gender-Specific and Related Studies in Memory of Fokkelien van Dijk-Hemmes* (ed. Bob Becking and Meindert Dijkstra; Leiden: E. J. Brill, 1996), 250, and Timothy D. Finlay, *The Birth Report Genre in the Hebrew Bible* (FAT 12; Tübingen: Mohr Siebeck, 2005), 150. Others, such as Danna Nolan Fewell, prefer not to assign a name to the woman, asserting that doing so may limit our understanding of anonymous characters (*Children of Israel*, 85–86 n. 3). I agree that to bestow proper names upon anonymous characters seems contrived, and refer to the main protagonist simply as the Shunammite.

5. Lawrence Stager points out that the term עליה or "roof structure" can indicate a range of upper-room constructions, and here suggests an apartment, perhaps built on a casement of Shunem's city walls ("Archaeology of the Family," 16).

6. James Montgomery comments that these items offer basic necessities, and the account provides interior details befitting "a woman's story." See James A. Montgomery, *The Books of Kings* (ICC; New York: Scribner's, 1951), 367. Other commentators, such as Würthwein (*Könige 2*, 291) and Bergen (*Elisha*, 92), see these household items as notably commodious. The latter interpretation seems more likely since the text creates an impression of the host's generosity, which Elisha will want to reward (2 Kgs 4:13).

vides privacy for intimate scenes revolving around the promise, death, and life of a child.

Other settings change quickly. The boy goes out to the fields, where his father is among the reapers (v. 18). A servant brings the ailing child to his mother, who is apparently at the house (v. 20). After laying the child on the prophet's bed (v. 21), the Shunammite leaves to travel to Mount Carmel (v. 25). Before arriving at the mountain, she is intercepted by Gehazi (presumably on the road, vv. 25–26), but goes to the mountain (v. 27–28). Gehazi sets out again (v. 29), with the Shunammite and prophet not far behind (v. 30). Once the child has died, the settings follow a symmetrical pattern as the action moves from house to road to mountain to road and back to the house. The movement only slows when the prophet is with the lifeless child (vv. 32–37), who, lying motionless, has spurred the characters to move from place to place.

# Characters

## The Shunammite

The great woman of Shunem dominates this story. The text introduces her as an אשה גדולה (2 Kgs 4:8aα), signaling her power and importance.[7] Despite being married, she, not her husband, controls the action. This pattern is established at the outset of the story when the Shunammite prevails upon the prophet to eat at her home (ותחזק־בו לאכל־לחם, v. 8aβ). She speaks while her husband remains mute (vv. 9–10). Elisha recognizes her dominant role and asks Gehazi to summon the woman, not the couple (v. 12a). The prophet recognizes *her* (not their) efforts and asks what he can do for *her* (not them) (v. 13a). Upon receiving the prophet's annunciation (v. 16a), the Shunammite professes humility by calling herself his "maidservant" (שפחתך, v. 16b; see also 2 Kgs 4:2). She remains the focus throughout the story, as she bears the child (v. 17), cares for him while he is dying (v. 20), and takes action to advocate for his life after he is dead

---

7. Translations for אשה גדולה include "wealthy woman" (NRSV, RSV, ESV, NJPS), "great woman" (ASV, KJV, JPS), "notable woman" (NKJV), "woman of rank" (NJB), "well-to-do woman" (NIV), and "prominent woman" (NAS). Alternately, Josef Tropper views the Shunammite as old (Josef Tropper, "Elischa und die 'grosse' Frau aus Schunem [2 Kön 4,8–37]," *KUSATU* 3 [2002]: 80), and Robert Alter sees her as "large" and "simple" (Robert Alter, "How Convention Helps Us Read: The Case of the Bible's Annunciation Type-Scene," *Prooftexts* 3.2 [1983]: 125, 126). However, other characters described as גדל are frequently said to be rich and influential, attributes that the Shunammite woman shares (see the descriptions of Nabal, 1 Sam 25:2–3; Abner, 2 Sam 3:38; Barzillai, 2 Sam 19:33 [Eng. 19:32]; and Naaman, 2 Kgs 5:1). She is the only female character in the Hebrew Bible extolled as גדלה (Bergen, *Elisha*, 90).

(vv. 21–31).[8] After Elisha resuscitates her son (vv. 32–35), the Shunammite again comes before the prophet (v. 36) and falls at his feet, prostrating herself (v. 37a), apparently in gratitude. As she takes up her son and leaves (v. 37b), the Shunammite ends the story as she began it—by realizing her goals with the prophet (cf. v. 8).

This female character acts with astonishing authority as she commands, argues, dismisses, and prevails over male characters.[9] The elderly husband, presumably wealthy as well, defers to her (2 Kgs 4:9–10, 19, 23). While the Shunammite is highly assertive, the narrator never disparages her dominating demeanor.[10] This woman is strong, gracious, hospitable, effective, agreeable, independent, modest, prudent, knowledgeable, caring, determined, focused, pious, and grateful. Her impressive traits lead Richard Nelson to conclude, "She is one of the Old Testament's most attractive characters."[11]

## The Shunammite's Husband

The husband of the great woman of Shunem is identified by his relationship to her, making him unusual among biblical men.[12] His most conspicuous role is to highlight her power, as he consistently defers to his

---

8. In 2 Kgs 4:8a the Shunammite prevails upon Elisha to eat at her home (ותחזק־בו לאכל־לחם), and in v. 27a she grabs the prophet's feet (ותחזק ברגליו). The only other instances in the Hebrew Bible where a female character is the subject of the verb חזק are in Deut 25:11 (where a woman grabs a man's testicles) and Prov 7:13 (where the adulterous woman seizes her unsuspecting victim). Deuteronomy 25:11 and Prov 7:13 depict forceful women as dangerous, whereas the Shunammite remains both a powerful and positive female character.

9. The Shunammite summons her husband and commands him to send her servants and a donkey so she can embark on her mission (v. 22). His inquiry only receives her curt response (ותאמר שלום, v. 23b). She saddles the donkey, and instructs her servant to hurry as she travels to the man of God (vv. 24–25). The Shunammite challenges the prophet, grasping his feet (ותחזק ברגליו, v. 27a), objecting to his promise (לא תשלה אתי, v. 28b), and vowing not to leave him (חי־יהוה וחי־נפשך אם־אעזבך, v. 30a). Unlike Elisha, the Shunammite realizes that sending Gehazi will prove futile (vv. 29–31).

10. Commentators note similarities between the Shunammite woman and other biblical heroines, including Abigail and Esther (see Burney, *Notes on Kings*, 276) and the Woman of Valor in Prov 31:10–31 (see Marsman, *Women in Ugarit and Israel*, 311). The Shunammite is also associated with women who bear children despite challenges (Sarah, Rebekah, Rachel, Hannah, the mother of Samson, and Mary). Further discussion follows.

11. Nelson, *Kings*, 173. Claudia Camp agrees, "The portrayal of this unnamed woman is one of the most remarkable in the Bible. Both independent and maternal, powerful and pious, she brings to mind a number of other female characters, yet surpasses them all." See Claudia V. Camp, "1 and 2 Kings," in Newsom and Ringe, *Women's Bible Commentary*, 113.

12. Anonymous women are often identified by association with their husbands (e.g., Gen 39:1–20; Judg 13:1–24; 1 Sam 4:19–22). The Shunammite's husband bears closest textual resemblance to the husband of the Woman of Valor (Prov 31:10–31), who is also known by uxorial association. However, the text in Proverbs 31 confers more status upon the man,

wife.¹³ She suggests they build a room for the prophet and it is built (2 Kgs 4:9–11). Gehazi and Elisha ignore the husband as they seek to repay the Shunammite's hospitality (vv. 12–14a), suggesting that his participation has been minimal to nonexistent in this housing project. Gehazi introduces the husband into this discussion, only to describe him as old, implying he is unable to help produce a son (v. 14b). The wife is highly visible; the husband is often absent.

The Shunammite's husband gets a greater role when cast as the boy's father. Verses 18–19 portray a father/son scene as the boy goes to the field. When the child complains that his head is hurting (ראשי ראשי, v. 19a), the father seems flustered and inept. He hands his son over to a servant and passes the problem to his wife (v. 19b), who takes the boy on her knees and he dies (v. 20). When the Shunammite tells her husband to fetch a servant and donkey so she can hurry to the prophet (v. 22), his response seems callous or obtuse (v. 23a). Why does he not inquire about his sick child or infer any connection between the boy's suffering and her urgency? His lack of paternal interest contrasts her maternal dedication as a cursory "Shalom" (v. 23b) silences him for the rest of the story.¹⁴

## Elisha

Again we see Elisha as a surprising prophet. At the outset of the story, Elisha must exhibit some distinguishing characteristic(s) since the Shunammite immediately and unusually recognizes Elisha as holy (ידעתי כי איש אלהים קדוש הוא, 2 Kgs 4:9a).¹⁵ As he performs the ultimate act of healing, Elisha expands the possibilities for a man of God.

In contrast to the preceding story of the debt-collateral children, the prophet now appears less personable. Elisha asks the wife of the sons of the prophets what he can do for her (ויאמר אליה אלישע מה אעשה־לך, 2 Kgs 4:2a). However, he has Gehazi summon the Shunammite to have him pose her the same question (ויאמר לו אמר־נא אליה . . . מה לעשות לך, 2 Kgs 4:13a). While the situations are different, the widow is in a crisis and the Shunammite is not at this point in the story, the parallel suggests that the prophet

---

calling him בעלה (Prov 31:11, 23, 28) with connotations of "her lord" or "her owner" (BDB, 127). In 2 Kgs 4:9, 14, 22, the husband is simply אישה ("her man" or "her husband," BDB, 35).

13. As Daniel Arnold succinctly observes, "Le père est très passif" (*Elisée*, 101). It is also possible that the husband is supremely disinterested in the proceedings or the child.

14. Danna Nolan Fewell notes both the irony and the insight of the Shunammite's curt response. She is deeply vexed when she speaks of "peace," yet in the end "peace" will prevail (*Children of Israel*, 93 n. 17).

15. The phrase איש אלהים קדוש הוא is not found elsewhere in the Hebrew Bible, and this is the only instance where holiness is explicitly linked with a prophet. Cogan and Tadmor, *II Kings*, 56 n. 9.

makes a class distinction. Elisha repeatedly uses intermediaries when in the presence of powerful people (see 2 Kgs 3:13–15; 5:8–10), including the Shunammite (2 Kgs 4:12–14, 25–26, 29–31, 36). Having someone to do his bidding, Elisha establishes his own rank when among those who would also have servants at their behest (2 Kgs 3:11; 4:22–24; 5:13). Elisha's address to the Shunammite also hints of a derogatory tone. Despite visits to her home (4:8, 11) and making inquiries to Gehazi about her (4:13, 14, 26), the prophet only refers to her as "that Shunammite."[16] Elisha does express a desire to help the Shunammite (v. 13), but on his own terms (vv. 13–17; see 2 Kgs 2:2, 4, 6).

Elisha also volunteers a marked lack of prescience. As the distressed Shunammite seizes his feet, Elisha twice professes his ignorance about her situation (2 Kgs 4:27b). While Elisha makes no claim to omniscience (see 2 Kgs 4:2) and his predictions can be thwarted (2 Kgs 3:14–27), he seems surprised by his own lack of knowledge.[17] YHWH, his information conduit, has hidden the reason for the woman's urgency and not told him (ויהוה העלים ממני ולא הגיד לי, 4:27b). Her persistence (4:27–30) prompts him to reveal his powers. Elisha's actions had led to the loss of children's lives (2 Kgs 2:23–25), but now restore a child to life (2 Kgs 4:32–35).[18]

## Gehazi

Gehazi and the Shunammite's husband both serve as foils. Just as the husband's weakness contrasts his wife's strength, Gehazi's subordination

---

16. See 2 Kgs 4:12: השונמית הזאת; v. 25: השונמית הלז (cf. 1 Sam 17:26); v. 36: השונמית הזאת. English translations often omit this arguably derisive use of the demonstrative pronoun. The NRSV, for example, renders השונמית הזאת and השונמית הלז as "the Shunammite woman." Commentators frequently read Elisha's description of "that Shunammite" as a term of subtle belittlement. See, e.g., Cohn, *2 Kings*, 69; Hermann Gunkel, *Geschichten von Elisha* (Berlin: Karl Curtius, 1925), 19; Mary E. Shields, "Subverting a Man of God, Elevating a Woman: Role and Power Reversals in 2 Kings 4," *JSOT* 58 (1993): 61. This interpretation suggests that to call her "*that* Shunammite" instead of "*the* Shunammite" serves to distance her, not distinguish her; in context there are no other women from Shunem with whom she might be confused. However, Yael Shemesh points out that Elisha refers to "this Shunammite" in v. 13 and "this trouble" in v. 13, without any derogatory overtones. To the contrary, Shemesh sees Elisha as deeply respectful and appreciative of the woman throughout the episode ("Saints' Legends," 24). Uriel Simon contends that this is not a condescending form of address but simply reflects the loss of the woman's name from the tradition. See Uriel Simon, *Reading Prophetic Narratives* (trans. Lenn J. Schramm; Bloomington: Indiana University Press, 1997), 326 n. 14.

17. On this point, see Albert Šanda, *Die Bücher der Könige* (vol. 2; EHAT 9; Münster in Westfalen: Aschendorffsche, 1912), 32.

18. Commentators frequently interchange the terms "restoration," "revivification," and "resuscitation," with "resurrection." However, "resurrection" often implies that the revived person remains in a permanently altered state (i.e., "eternal life") and bears theological connotations better avoided in this context.

points to Elisha's authority. However, the interactions between Gehazi, the Shunammite, and Elisha are repeatedly muddled and marked by miscommunication.[19] Gehazi's ineffective actions highlight the determination of the Shunammite and the power of the prophet.

Gehazi appears by name in three episodes of the Elisha cycle,[20] making his debut here. Just as the Shunammite's husband surfaces in the narrative without prior introduction, Gehazi's name and appositional designation (גחזי נערו, 2 Kgs 4:12a) assume his presence in the narrative world. As a נער, he is outside the family structure with a subordinate role. Toward the outset of the story, the Shunammite talks directly to Elisha, despite Gehazi's address to her (vv. 12–16). Gehazi has what the prophet lacks: knowledge about the Shunammite and her sonless state (v. 14). This foreshadows Elisha's ignorance later when she is without a son again, this time due to the child's death (v. 27). The servant, like YHWH, has information that the prophet does not. But the prophet, with YHWH, has power that the servant lacks.

Gehazi places a staff on the child's face, perhaps to prevent the child from being buried until Elisha came or maybe to attempt reviving the boy himself (vv. 29–31). While bringing the dead back to life seems far beyond the capacity of a servant rebuked by his master (v. 27), Gehazi is only fulfilling Elisha's directives (v. 29). Did this servant believe that the prophet's powerful staff could complete the mission? Did Elisha think the same, or was he sending Gehazi on a doomed exercise to stress his own excep-

---

19. Although the Shunammite proposes building an upper room for the holy man of God (vv. 9–10), she apparently accommodates Gehazi too, since Elisha wants to repay all her trouble on *our* behalf (חרדת אלינו, v. 13a). Elisha has Gehazi call the Shunammite, and the prophet tries to communicate through his servant, but she is apparently standing in Elisha's presence (vv. 12–13a). The Shunammite responds, seemingly to Elisha (v. 13b), since Gehazi has not spoken. Elisha and Gehazi continue the conversation about the woman as if she were not there, although the text never reports her departure (v. 14). She is summoned again (v. 15), which seems strange since she never left (vv. 12–15), although now she is reported as standing in the doorway (v. 15). For various commentators' attempts to clarify this encounter see Bergen, *Elisha*, 94–95; and Simon, *Prophetic Narratives*, 239–43. When the Shunammite and Gehazi meet each other again (presumably on the road as she journeys to Mount Carmel), she answers Elisha's questions asked by Gehazi elliptically (vv. 25–26). When Gehazi attempts to push the Shunammite away, Elisha rebukes him (v. 27); and when Elisha sends Gehazi on a mission to save the boy, the Shunammite knows it will be fruitless (vv. 29–31). For more detailed discussion that notes Gehazi's ineffectiveness, see Mark Roncace, "Elisha and the Woman of Shunem: 2 Kings 4.8–37 and 8.1–6 Read in Conjunction," *JSOT* 91 (2000): 112–20.

20. Two of these scenes include the Shunammite and her son (2 Kgs 4:11–37; 8:1–6). The intervening episode with Gehazi involves his pursuit and acquisition of riches after Elisha has healed Naaman (2 Kgs 5:19–24), his lying about this encounter to Elisha (5:25–26), and his subsequent punishment by the prophet (5:27). This incident contributes to a negative portrayal of Gehazi, leading commentators to view him as "a rather tragic figure" (Hobbs, *2 Kings*, 51) and "gossipy, crude, violent, and in the end—a miserable failure" (Rofé, *Prophetical Stories*, 31–32).

tional ability? The Shunammite, however, instantly recognizes Gehazi's ineptitude and vows not to leave Elisha (v. 30). She is determined that the servant will not obstruct her mission and remains undeterred despite his continued intervention, directly addressing Gehazi only once (a brief שלום in v. 26, as she said to her husband in v. 23). Both the Shunammite's husband and Gehazi underscore the power of their superiors.

## Two Anonymous Servants

Two נערים enter the narrative just to do the bidding of their masters. One seems to be a fieldworker who carries the ailing child to his mother (2 Kgs 4:19–20). The other appears as a house servant who readies the donkey and accompanies the Shunammite on the journey to the prophet (vv. 22–24). The field servant reveals the father's ineptitude, taking over for the father in helping the child (vv. 19–20). Even if the Shunammite's husband were too old to carry the child himself, he makes no attempt to accompany his son or later ask what has happened to him. Conversely, the house servant enforces the Shunammite's image as competent and motivated. Even while with this servant, the Shunammite saddles the donkey herself (the only woman to do so in the Hebrew Bible), exhibiting confidence and self-reliance (cf. Prov 31:10–31). She also urges this servant to hurry on their mission and to hold back only if she so directs (v. 24), showing her sense of urgency. While the journey from Shunem to Mount Carmel (approximately twenty-five miles) is substantial, she is ready to withstand rigorous travel. The two anonymous servants emphasize the authority and drive of the Shunammite, contrasted with the lassitude and negligence of her husband.

## The Son

The anonymous child says and does little, while arguably remaining the center of attention. The stories of his birth and revival focus primarily on the mother and the prophet, who engage in power struggles while managing their underlings. However, the boy's birth shows the prophet's annunciatory ability in the first part of the story (2 Kgs 4:8–17), and the boy's revivification shows the prophet's restorative power in the second part (vv. 18–37). While the child is still through most of the narrative, he is important even in his passivity. Concern for his life steers the plot.

The Shunammite's son acts twice before dying and three times when he comes back to life. Once the boy is born (v. 17) according to the prophet's prediction (v. 16a), the narrative skips to his boyhood (v. 18a). The child goes out to his father and the reapers independently, yet seeks his father's presence (v. 18). There is no mention of the boy working in the fields, perhaps because he is too young for such labor, or perhaps due to his upper-class status. The boy's complaint of pain, "my head, my head" (ראשי ראשי, v. 19a), gives his only words, indicating that he dies of a malady and not malfeasance. This straightforward utterance may be a small child's simple pronouncement or an indication of agony.[21] Regardless, the boy appears relatively young since a servant lifts and brings him to his mother (v. 20) and she carries him out of the prophet's chamber at the end of the story (v. 37). When Elisha revives the child (vv. 32–35), the boy's flesh warms, he sneezes seven times, and opens his eyes (v. 35b), as he acts independently and dispels all doubt about his vitality.

The boy does not seem especially remarkable, and he is easy to gloss over, as indeed most commentators do. Yet each of the adults has a direct encounter with the boy and conveys his or her essence in the exchange. When faced with a crisis, the boy's father sends him to his mother, suggesting insouciance or ineptitude in dealing with the child (vv. 18–19). Gehazi fails to revive the child (v. 31), revealing his inferiority to his master (vv. 32–35) and calling attention to the difficulty of the prophet's miracle (vv. 33–35). The Shunammite's interactions with the child show her tenderness and fortitude as she conceives and bears her son (v. 17), holds the dying child on her lap (v. 20), gets help for her child (vv. 22–30), and carries her resuscitated son from the prophet's chamber (v. 37). Elisha, the wonder-worker par excellence, delivers an annunciation (vv. 16–17) and brings the dead to life (vv. 33–36). This boy inspires the strong characters and exposes the weak ones.

At the same time, the child prompts the commanding prophet and the independent Shunammite to acknowledge their own needs. On behalf of the boy, the Shunammite pleads with Elisha (vv. 27–30), and Elisha prays to YHWH (ויתפלל אל־יהוה, v. 33b). Both the Shunammite and the man of God accomplish goals by appealing to those greater than themselves. The determination of the mother, the effort of the prophet, and the power of YHWH all serve a nameless child.

The Shunammite's son has three designations in the narrative: ילד, בן, and נער. While these may appear interchangeable, the usage follows a subtle but consistent pattern. The living child with his mother is always called "son" (בן),[22] focusing on their close relational bond. One step removed, but still seeing the boy in relation to those around him, the prophet and narrator see him as a "child" (ילד).[23] When Elisha sees the Shunammite approaching, he sends Gehazi to ask if her "child" is well (השלום לילד,

---

21. For repeated words expressing anguish, see 2 Sam 19:5 [Eng. 19:4]; Jer 4:19; Lam 1:16. See Simon, *Prophetic Narratives*, 243.

22. Verse 14b: בן אין־לה; v.16a: אתי חבקת בן; v. 17a: ותהר האשה ותלד בן; v. 28a: ותאמר השאלתי ; v. 36b: בן מאת אדני; v. 37b: ויאמר שאי בנך; ותשא את־בנה ותצא.

23. Verse 18a: ויגדל הילד; v. 26a: השלום לילד; v. 34a: ויעל וישכב על־הילד; v. 34b: ויחם בשר הילד.

v. 26a), but she seeks help regarding her "son" (בן מאת אדני, v. 28a). Yet once the prophet infers that the child is dead (or at least that something is dreadfully wrong), Elisha instructs Gehazi to place his staff on the face of the נער (ושמת משענתי על־פני הנער, v. 29b). The dead child is called a "boy" (נער),[24] lacking the closeness of "son" or even "child," perhaps reflecting intentional distancing, as the boy leaves the realm of the living. While the narrator then designates the Shunammite as "the mother of the boy" (אם הנער, v. 30a), she never refers to her son as a נער. This may signal her refusal to accept his altered state as she resolutely seeks aid for her son.[25] To revive the child, Elisha places himself on top of the ילד (v. 34), showing their relationship and perhaps signaling the child's return to life. Surprisingly, the resuscitated boy is then twice called נער: (ויזורר הנער עד־שבע, פעמים ויפקח הנער את־עיניו, v. 35b). While contradicting the otherwise consistent pattern of word choice to indicate the child, the concluding use of נער may also emphasize the point of the narrative. The נער who was dead (vv. 29, 30, 31 [2x], 32) is now alive (v. 35), thanks to the prophet's power. As a final coda, the prophet tells the Shunammite to take up her son (בנך, v. 36b), harkening back to his first designation (vv. 14–17), while noting their restored relationship.

## Re-viewing the Plot from a Childist Perspective

Scholars divide the detailed plot of 2 Kgs 4:8–37 into various segments.[26] The narrative itself signals a tripartite division as scenes of increasing length begin with ויהי היום (vv. 8, 11, 18). These temporal demarcations

---

24. Verse 30a: ותאמר אם הנער; v. 31a: וישם את־המשענת על־פני הנער; v. 32b: והנה הנער מת.

25. See vv. 29–32. Carolyn Leeb also examines the shift in the use of these terms in this passage (*Away from the Father's House*, 107–9). She maintains that use of the term נער is tied to distance from the בית אב and the protection this implies. This position is hard to sustain here since the נער is in his father's (and mother's) house when this scene transpires and is being saved as a result of his mother's advocacy. Still, Leeb is right to note intentionality in the shifting use of these terms and observes, "Prior to his illness, the boy was always 'son' or 'child,' but as long as he is at risk, he is called נער, not once but seven times. Once healed, he is once again 'son,' never again נער" (p. 109).

26. For example, Simon (*Prophetic Narratives*, 235–53) divides the story into five scenes: 2 Kgs 4:8–10 (the Shunammite's hospitality); vv. 11–17 (Elisha seeks to reward her); vv. 18–24 (she persists in seeking help for her son); vv. 25–30 (Elisha sends Gehazi then goes himself); vv. 31–37 (Elisha saves the child). Hobbs (*2 Kings*, 46–48) finds four separate episodes: vv. 8–11 (the prophet's new "home away from home"); vv. 12–17 (reward for the Shunammite); vv. 18–28 (the boy and his death); and vv. 29–37 (resolution of the problem). Fritz sees two main parts, vv. 8–17 (the birth of the son) and vv. 18–37 (the child's revival), with subsidiary subplots (vv. 8–17, 18–19, 20–24, 25–31, 32–35, 36–37). See Volkmar Fritz, *1 & 2 Kings* (CC; trans. Anslem Hagedorn; Minneapolis: Fortress, 2003), 250–52. While the narrative coheres, its division into segments remains an interpretive choice.

note when Elisha first comes to Shunem and the Shunammite decides to build a room (vv. 8–10), when Elisha returns to Shunem and repays her hospitality with a son (vv. 11–17), and when the son falls sick, dies, and is eventually resuscitated (vv. 18–37).²⁷ This discussion focuses on the latter two episodes that revolve around the child.

The Shunammite is unusual among biblical women in that she expresses no desire for a son. When Elisha seeks to repay her hospitality, she responds בתוך עמי אנכי ישבת: "I live in the midst of my people" (v. 13b). This seems a like non sequitur, combining an affirmation of community with an assertion of self-sufficiency. Perhaps stymied by the Shunammite's refusal, the prophet (ironically?) turns to Gehazi for counsel, who informs Elisha that she has no son and her husband is old (v. 14). The prophet's ignorance seems odd; Elisha is staying in an upper chamber of the woman's house—why does he need Gehazi to inform him of her familial situation? Maybe the couple has daughters, so the prophet has simply observed a family with children without noticing a lack of sons. Perhaps the older husband has sons from a previous (or another) wife. Alternately, the prophet may have tried to distance himself from the Shunammite, resulting in isolation to the point of obliviousness. Once he has obtained this crucial information about her lack of sons, Elisha pronounces the birth and its timeline, למועד הזה כעת חיה אתי חבקת בן: "at this season, according to the time of life, you will embrace a son" (v. 16a).²⁸ Yet instead of reacting with joy, the Shunammite objects, אל־אדני איש האלהים אל־תכזב בשפחתך: "No, my lord, man of God, do not lie to your maidservant" (v. 16b). Her words surround an audacious command within a humble address. She twice acknowledges his lordly role (אדני איש האלהים) and finishes with an

---

27. As Rofé notes, these segments grow progressively longer as the plot gets increasingly complex (*Prophetical Stories*, 27–28).

28. This enigmatic phrase (כעת חיה) parallels Sarah's annunciation (Gen 18:10, 14). Commentators surmise that this indicates the renewal of life in the spring (Burney, *Notes on Kings*, 274–75; J. Skinner, *Kings* [Edinburgh: T. C. & E. C. Jack, ca. 1893], 292; Hobbs, *2 Kings*, 51). Montgomery, following a later interpretation of Skinner, reads למועד הזה as a gloss carried from Gen 18:14, euphemistically referring to pregnancy (Montgomery, *Kings*, 371–72). Cogan and Tadmor suggest this phrase has a positive volitive connotation, i.e., "good wishes for the year ahead" (Cogan and Tadmor, *II Kings*, 57 n. 16). The expression strengthens the connection between the Shunammite and Sarah. Both are powerful women who take control, especially with their husbands (2 Kgs 4:8–10, 22–23; Gen 16:1–6; 21:9–12). The phrase כעת חיה also creates a bond between Isaac and the Shunammite's son, as their births are foretold with the same verbatim annunciation. These stories also invite comparison between YHWH in Gen 18:10, 14 and Elisha in 2 Kgs 4:16. Leah Bronner suggests that Elisha's pronouncement here is intended to usurp YHWH over Baal as giver of fertility. See Leah Bronner, *The Stories of Elijah and Elisha as Polemics against Baal Worship* (Leiden: E. J. Brill, 1968), 98. For discussion of this phrase as a deviation from the standard annunciation pattern, see Finlay, *Birth Report Genre*, 150. Tikva Frymer-Kensky notes that the Shunammite's lack of desire for a child is *sui generis* among biblical portrayals of women ("Family in the Hebrew Bible," 58).

admission of her inferior status (שפחתך). Yet the Shunammite brazenly commands and accuses the prophet (אל־תכזב, v. 16b): "do not lie."[29] The prophet says nothing in response, as the narrator reports the promised child's conception and birth. The prophet is no liar; his prediction comes true at the appointed time and according to his word (v. 17).

The story of this seemingly inconceivable birth peaks interest in this child who goes on to miraculously survive death. When the boy dies on his mother's knees (v. 20), the prophet's prediction, "you shall embrace a child" (v. 16a), finds sad manifestation with this poignant pieta. Her flurry of activity then works toward saving him. As Amy Kalmanofsky points out, the Shunammite is a religious innovator who "acts as though the boundaries between life and death are permeable."[30] She lays the child down where responsibility lies, connecting him with the prophet by putting the boy on his bed (v. 21). When Elisha beholds the dead boy lying on his own bed (והנה הנער מת משכב על־מטתו, v. 32b), a scene of stunning intimacy unfolds. The narrator erases any ambiguity that the child might be sleeping, unconscious, or comatose by mentioning twice that he is dead (vv. 20, 32). Imitating the Shunammite (v. 21) and the mother of the debt-collateral children (2 Kgs 4:4–5), Elisha too shuts the door (v. 33), then prays to YHWH. Perhaps Elisha does not solely rely on (or trust?) the spirit of YHWH to resuscitate the child since he undertakes an arduous process. He places his own mouth, eyes, and palms directly on those of the child (v. 34a), as the child's flesh warms (v. 34b). As Elisha feels the heat of the small body, the text appeals to the tactile sense. After this glimmer of life, Elisha gets up and walks around the house (v. 35aα). Did he feel the life force draining out of himself? Was the miracle exhausting or scary, even for a man of God? He then crouches over the boy (v. 35aβ), who sneezes seven times (v. 35bα) (an auspicious biblical number), signaling revival through the auditory sense. Just as Elisha had put his mouth on the boy's, a sound comes from the child's mouth. Elisha had placed his eyes on the child's eyes, and the boy can see as he opens his eyes (v. 35bβ). The reader also envisions a dead child returned to life.

Elisha here assumes a prophetic role like that of a shaman.[31] These

---

29. Some translations mitigate the Shunammite's instructions, rendering אל־תכזב as "Don't mislead" (NIV), "do not deceive" (NRSV), and "do not delude" (NJPS). Mary Shields, however, notes the force of the Shunammite's words. Parallel constructions with אל repeated, first followed by a noun and then by a verb, are only found two other times in the Hebrew Bible, both in contexts of rape (see Judg 19:23; 2 Sam 13:12) (Shields, "Subverting a Man of God," 62).

30. Amy Kalmanofsky, "Women of God: Maternal Grief and Religious Response in 1 Kings 17 and 2 Kings 4," *JSOT* 36 (2011): 70.

31. The term "shaman" is borrowed from the Tungu tribe of Siberia, although shamans exist in both ancient and modern societies. For a brief introduction to the role of the shaman, see Lester Grabbe, "Ancient Near Eastern Prophecy from an Anthropological Perspective," in *Prophecy in Its Ancient Near Eastern Context: Mesopotamian, Biblical, and Arabian Perspectives*

divine-human intermediaries command spirits, showing great power and authority. As Robert Wilson notes, shamans differ from possessed prophets by controlling a spirit's influence. Potentially harmful forces can then be directed for a beneficial purpose intended by the shaman.[32] While acts of shamanism find wide cross-cultural comparison, they are unusual in the Hebrew Bible.[33] Thomas Overholt observes that 2 Kgs 4:31–37 and 1 Kgs 17:17–24 provide the only stories of resuscitation in the Hebrew Bible.[34] Both center on a child.

## Childist Interpretation: Paradigms Combined and Subverted

The story of the boy who comes back to life combines the typological scenes of a miraculous birth and a miraculous survival of a child. The annunciation type-scene involves a person (usually, but not always, a woman) without a son.[35] Frequently an obstacle prevents the birth. The future mother (or father) has proven worth, and is frustrated by being childless. She may take steps to increase her chances of having a child.

---

(SBLSymS 13; ed. Martti Nissinen; Atlanta: Society of Biblical Literature, 2000), 16–18. See also Thomas W. Overholt, *Prophecy in Cross-Cultural Perspective: A Sourcebook for Biblical Researchers* (SBLSBS 17; Atlanta: Scholars Press, 1986).

32. Wilson, *Prophecy and Society*, 23–24.

33. Thomas Overholt recounts numerous anthropological examples of shamanism with striking correspondences to this story. One account of an Ojibwa shaman describes a girl who was sick and then died. The shaman tied a piece of red yarn around the girl's wrist, so he could more easily identify her spirit. He then laid down her body and lay down next to her. Eventually the shaman started to move slightly, as did the child. After a while, the shaman sat up, and the girl also rose. Another story reports a case in Siberia in which a shaman went into a trance, crouched over a dying boy lying in a bed, and then worked to recapture the boy's spirit and jumped in bed with the child. See Thomas Overholt, "Elijah and Elisha in the Context of Israelite Religion," in *Prophets and Paradigms: Essays in Honor of Gene M. Tucker* (JSOTSup 229; ed. Stephen Breck Reid; Sheffield: Sheffield Academic Press, 1996), 104–7.

34. Overholt, "Elijah and Elisha," 104 n. 43. Overholt does not cite 2 Kgs 13:21, in which a man being buried is thrown into a grave and touches Elisha's bones, instantly reviving him. This brief story further testifies to Elisha's power, though the revival does not take place through the concerted action of an intermediary.

35. See the stories of Abraham and Sarah (Gen 15:2–4; 17:1–22; 18:1–15; 21:1–5), Isaac and Rebekah (Gen 25:21–26), Rachel (Gen 29:31–30:24), Samson's mother (Judges 13), and Hannah (1 Samuel 1). Second Kings 4:11–17 also parallels the Ugaritic tale of Aqhat in the lack of a son in a prominent family (*KTU* 1.17 i 18–33) and the announcement of that son (*KTU* 1.17 ii 1–8) (as noted by Simon, *Prophetic Narratives*, 34–35). (The actual birth of Danel's son, Aqhat, is missing from the existing tablets, but scholars surmise this would be reported on the bottom of the second tablet. See Parker, "Aqhat," in *Ugaritic Narrative Poetry* [SBLWAW 9; ed. Simon B. Parker; Atlanta: Scholars Press, 1997], 57.) In the New Testament, prominent annunciation stories of Elizabeth and Zechariah (Luke 1:7–25, 39–45, 57–80), and Mary (Luke 1:26–56; 2:1–20) foretell the arrivals of John the Baptist and Jesus, respectively.

A divine messenger intercedes and delivers an annunciation, prompting her reaction. The extraordinary birth takes place, usually followed by the name of the son and frequently an expression of thanksgiving. Almost always, the son goes on to garner fame in the biblical tradition.[36]

The birth of the Shunammite's son both reflects and subverts the annunciation typology. While commentators generally categorize the Shunammite as childless or barren, Mark Roncace notes that these assumptions are conjectural.[37] The Shunammite may have female children; to be without a son is not the same as lacking any child (see Gen 11:30).[38] Nowhere is the Shunammite called "barren" (עקרה, cf. Gen 11:30; 25:21; 29:31; Judg 13:2, 3). Also the blame for having no son veers toward the husband. The NRSV translates Gehazi's assessment אבל בן אין־לה ואישה זקן (2 Kgs 4:14b), "Well, she has no son, *and* her husband is old" (emphasis added).[39] This implies that the lack of a son is her problem, and he is no longer sufficiently virile. However, the *waw* here could also be translated, "She has no son *because* her husband is old,"[40] making only the man responsible for the couple's predicament; impregnating her is beyond his capacity.[41] The Shunammite does not seem bothered by her son-less state. When Elisha offers to repay her hospitality, the woman does not hint of any void in her life, much less ask for a baby boy. To the contrary, she eschews the prophet's offer of help (v. 13). This is an unusual story of a miraculous birth where neither parent has voiced a desire for a child and the woman is not described as barren.

Other elements of this story also vary significantly from the standard annunciation pattern.[42] Typically YHWH or his direct representative delivers the prediction of a child, as in the stories of Sarah (Gen 18:13–14; 21:1–2),

---

36. This outline follows the chart in Simon, *Prophetic Narratives*, 36–37. James G. Williams offers a slightly different schema: 1—a barren wife, 2—intervention of divine intermediary, 3—promise of a son, 4—confirmation despite doubt, 5—birth and naming of son. See James G. Williams, *Women Recounted: Narrative Thinking and the God of Israel* (Sheffield: Almond Press, 1982), 52. See also Long, *2 Kings*, 60, and Callaway, *Sing, O Barren One*, 17.

37. Roncace, "Elisha and the Woman of Shunem," 115.

38. Analeptic references to daughters reveal their existence without prior introduction. For example, Esau's daughters are assumed in Gen 36:6, even though they have not been mentioned previously. Jacob's family seems to have twelve sons and only one daughter (Dinah) (Gen 29:31–30:24, 35:16–26), but the text later refers to his daughters (46:7, 15). Girls who may be barely acknowledged in the text are nonetheless present.

39. Translations that render the *waw* as "and" include the ASV, ESV, JPS, KJV, NIV, RSV, and NJPS.

40. This phrase illustrates a continuous setting with circumstances specified in the second verbless clause. See Waltke and O'Connor, *Biblical Hebrew Syntax*, § 39.2.3.b.

41. This is the only instance in the Hebrew Bible where the blame for lack of children is laid solely with the man. See the chart in Simon, *Prophetic Narratives*, 36.

42. For fuller discussion of subversion of these elements, see Shields, "Subverting a Man of God," 63–64; and Roncace, "Elisha and the Woman of Shunem," 115–16.

Rebekah (Gen 25:21), Rachel (Gen 30:22–24), and Samson's mother (Judg 13:3–24). Here the man of God pronounces the child as a gift to a woman in direct return for her hospitality.[43] Also the annunciation in 2 Kgs 4:11–17 lacks any specific destiny for the child. Unlike other babies born of miracles, the son of the Shunammite disappears without acquiring biblical fame.

Commentators minimize the boy's significance, observing that he comes to life just to die.[44] The child also lacks a name, and perforce, any etymological explanation that might relate to his future greatness.[45] Yet these same commentators extol the Shunammite woman, who also is nameless and only resurfaces once more in the text—with her son (2 Kgs 8:1–6).[46] Clearly the woman has far greater agency than the boy, but naming and reappearance in the text are not the sole criteria for measuring a character's importance. While the child himself is not the main focus of the story, the action that pertains to him is.

Like better-known biblical boys, the Shunammite's son has stories of both annunciation and deliverance. Ishmael (Gen 21:8–21), Isaac (Gen 22:1–19), Moses (Exod 2:1–10), Gershom (Exod 4:23–26), and the son of the widow of Zarephath (1 Kgs 17:17–24) also face peril but do not perish.[47]

---

43. Abraham eagerly extends hospitality to divine guests, linking the Shunammite woman with him as well as Sarah (Gen 18:1–10). However, the meal with Abraham and his guests provides the setting, not the motivation, for the gift of a child. Esther Fuchs notes, "This type-scene [with the Shunammite] is the first to present Yahweh's intervention as *reward for woman's upright conduct*. . . . the Shunammite conceives, thanks to her selflessness, benevolence, humility, and loyalty to Yahweh's emissary." See Esther Fuchs, "The Literary Characterization of Mothers and Sexual Politics in the Hebrew Bible," in *Feminist Perspectives on Biblical Scholarship* (SBLBSNA 10; ed. Adela Yarbro Collins; Chico, CA: Scholars Press, 1985), 127. Robert Alter similarly observes the striking use of annunciation as a gift in return for a favor and suggests that exchange may provide "a satirical comment on the professionalization of the role of the man of God in the latter days when Elisha was active" ("How Convention Helps Us Read," 125).

44. E.g., Timothy Finlay points out, "The only other birth report that omits the name is the illegitimate child of Bathsheba and David in 2 Sam 11:27 and, like the son of the Shunammite woman, the next thing *it* does is die" (emphasis added) (*Birth Report Genre*, 150–51). Robert Alter remarks, "The most salient peculiarity of the Shunammite woman's annunciation may be what ultimately explains all the others: the fact that in this case the type-scene does not signal the birth of a hero at all but rather of an anonymous peasant boy whose sole functions in the narrative are to be born and then brought back from the brink of death" ("How Convention Helps Us Read," 126). Mary Shields agrees, "Finally, the last element does not appear at all—the child is not given a significant name because he himself is not significant" ("Subverting a Man of God," 63).

45. See the etymologies given for Isaac (Gen 21:6), Esau and Jacob (Gen 25:25–26), Joseph (Gen 30:24), and Samuel (1 Sam 1:20).

46. In contrast to their dismissal of the anonymous boy, Finlay describes the Shunammite woman as "the hero of the story" (*Birth Report Genre*, 149) and "remarkable" (*Birth Report Genre*, 150), and Shields notes that she is "a woman of means" with "independence and status in her own right" ("Subverting a Man of God," 60).

47. As outlined by Simon, features of this genre may include an ailment (or death), a

Among these accounts, the story of the Shunammite's son (not surprisingly) parallels the story of the son of the widow of Zarephath most closely, since the Elijah account is likely modeled on the Elisha story.[48] Yet after allowing for this corresponding exception, every boy in these type-scenes of annunciation and miraculous survival is named and noted (to varying degrees) in the history of Israel, except the Shunammite's son.[49]

The confluence of these typologies suggests that the Shunammite's son is remarkable in his own way. Rabbinic interpretation inferred that this important child's name got lost in the tradition, suggesting that he grew up to become the prophet Habakkuk.[50] Yet perhaps the real significance of this child is that he merits considerable attention without being renowned. Both the man of God and the great Shunammite undertake determined efforts to save this boy's life, without anticipating that he will achieve any greatness.[51] Rather, they seek to save the child for his own sake. Poetic images of parental devotion with YHWH as caring for a young child (Hos 11:3–4; Isa 46:3–4), comforting a child (Isa 66:12–13), and guarding an offspring's life (Job 10:11–12) find more extensive expression in the Shunammite's maternal dedication. As a further subversion of this type-scene, the Shunammite's son is noteworthy simply because—as a child—he has deep worth.

## Insights about Children and Their Worth

The Shunammite's son shows the value of children in the text and the culture that produced it, even when the offspring are not destined for fame. Other peoples from this wide region in the ancient world, such as the Babylonians, Assyrians, Greeks, and Romans, commonly exposed unwanted children, abandoning newborn infants outside to perish from cold or hunger.[52] If someone were to pick up a discarded baby, he or she

---

factor prompting the miracle, a response to the ailment, a reaction from the woman, a divine messenger and response (in the case of Ishmael), the future of the child predicted, a miracle performed, a bestowal of a name that is explained, and an act or profession of gratitude. See the chart in Simon, *Prophetic Narratives*, 38–39. As Alter points out, 2 Kgs 4:18–37 also shares features with a type-scene of "the life-threatening trial in the wilderness or field." The experience of the Shunammite's son then parallels the ordeals endured by Ishmael (Gen 21:8–21), Isaac (Gen 22:1–19), and Gershom (Exod 4:23–26) (Alter, "How Convention Helps Us Read," 126). The son of the widow of Zarephath also survives death (1 Kgs 17:17–24), although unlike Ishmael, Isaac, Gershom, and the Shunammite's son, the widow's son does not experience a threat to his life while outdoors.

48. See White, *Elijah Legends*, 11–17.
49. The sons whose birth is heralded by annunciation are Isaac, Esau, Jacob, Joseph, Samson, and Samuel. The sons who survive due to miraculous rescue are Isaac, Ishmael, Moses, and Gershom.
50. Rosenberg, *II Kings*, 262.
51. Cf. Gen 17:20, 21; 25:23; 45:4–8; Judg 13:3–5; 1 Sam 1:11, 22.
52. Cynthia Patterson examines infant exposure in ancient Greece and explains that

would likely raise this child as a slave.[53] However, the text gives little reason to suspect that ancient Israelites carried out—and much less condoned—the exposure of infants.[54] Children were appreciated for their work and participation in the household economy, but the Shunammite's son is prized for no discernible economic reason. We are not given information about the role of the child as a worker for the household farm, a potential heir for the family inheritance, or a future provider for the parents. Lacking any reference to the boy's intrinsic economic value or legacy, this narrative depicts a mother who simply cherishes her son.

The Shunammite's son reveals children's power to shape the lives of the adults. Even when child characters are not famous, forceful, or even especially noticeable, they can nonetheless stimulate responses and transform those around them through relationships. This boy changes the woman who had no interest in children into a devoted mother and advocate.[55] His death prompts the Shunammite to become a broker of divine power. The potential loss of this child motivates Elisha to exert himself physically and spiritually, showing his salvific abilities beyond any other miracle. The life of the child—both its giving and its restoring—creates a bond between far more visible characters. Even without taking action, a child can motivate concern and thereby exert influence.

## Children and Textual Connections

The boys of 2 Kgs 4:8–37 and 1 Kgs 17:8–24 are textual kin.[56] In the story of the widow of Zarephath, a poor widow with a son befriends,

---

this was not considered the same as killing a child, as reflected by the vocabulary. The terms for exposure (ἐκτίθημι, ἀποτίθημι, ἐκβάλλω) were different than the word for child-murder (παιδοκτονέω). Further, a newborn infant was called βρέφος, also the word for "fetus," and was not yet recognized or accepted as a family member. See Cynthia Patterson, "'Not Worth Rearing': The Causes of Infant Exposure in Ancient Greece," *TAPA* 115 (1985): 104–5.

53. For discussion of child exposure as a means to procure slaves in Mesopotamia, see Mendelsohn, *Slavery*, 5.

54. Exodus 2:1–10 offers a scene of infant exposure, but only under duress and performed to save, not destroy, the life of the child (i.e., Moses). Ezekiel 16:5–6 portrays infant exposure as an act of divine and deliberate punishment (metaphorically visited upon faithless Israel); however, YHWH commands the abandoned baby girl to live. Daniel Schwartz discusses this practice in Jewish culture during the Hellenistic and Roman periods and concludes that infant exposure undoubtedly occurred among Jews, although it was not sanctioned. See Daniel R. Schwartz, "Did the Jews Practice Infant Exposure and Infanticide in Antiquity?" *SPhilo* 16 (2004): 61–95.

55. For discussion of the Shunammite's transformation as a mother, see Bronner, *Stories of Biblical Mothers*, 34–35. For a feminist critique of exalting only women whose roles serve patriarchal ideologies, see Fuchs, "Literary Characterization," 130–36.

56. For further comparison of these two stories, see Shemesh, "Elisha Stories," 23–24; see also Kalmanofsky, "Women of God," 61–74.

feeds, and houses the prophet Elijah (1 Kgs 17:8–16). The boy becomes lifeless, but Elijah revives him (1 Kgs 17:17–24). Both boys' mothers provide a commanding presence in two encounters with the prophet (1 Kgs 17:8–16, 17–24; 2 Kgs 4:11–17, 18–37). Both children suffer from an unspecified affliction that results in their deaths (1 Kgs 17:17; 2 Kgs 4:19–20), although the word מת is only explicitly used with the Shunammite's son (2 Kgs 4:20, 32).[57] The plots are parallel as two unresponsive children lie on a bed while a prophet stretches out over each of them (1 Kgs 17:21; 2 Kgs 4:34) and the child is revived (1 Kgs 17:22; 2 Kgs 4:35). Both stories have satisfying endings.

However, some salient differences among the characters emerge. One mother is a poor, starving widow (1 Kgs 17:8–12), while the other is a wealthy, generous wife (2 Kgs 4:8–11). Elijah appears as the more devout prophet, since the name of YHWH appears six times as he revives the widow's son (1 Kgs 17:20 [2x], 21 [2x], 22, 24), whereas Elisha just prays to YHWH once to initiate his miracle (2 Kgs 4:33) and does not thank YHWH at the story's end. The Shunammite's boy grows (2 Kgs 4:18a), goes out to the reapers (v. 18b), speaks (v. 19a), sneezes (v. 35b), and opens his eyes (v. 35b). Unlike the widow's son, the Shunammite's son is not simply "the passive object of events."[58] Rather, he acts on his own accord at the beginning of the story and physically revives at the end. Without a voiced theological profession (cf. 1 Kgs 17:24), the Shunammite's son, by his action, offers the evidence for YHWH's restorative power.

The Shunammite's son also shares elements of his story with other boys in the Hebrew Bible. Like Isaac, the Shunammite's son faces an unlikely birth and is born to an elderly father (Gen 18:10–14; 21:1–5; 2 Kgs 4:14–17). Both Isaac and the Shunammite's son are endangered while being outside with their fathers, who offer no protection (Gen 22:1–10; 2 Kgs 4:18–19). Like Ishmael, the Shunammite's son is close to death (Gen 21:14–15; 2 Kgs 4:19). The mother's persistent presence contrasts the father's absence from the time of peril until the assurance of rescue (Gen 21:16–19; 2 Kgs 4:20–37). Like Esau and Jacob, the Shunammite's son is born to a woman without sons (Gen 25:21; 2 Kgs 4:14, 17), and YHWH is called upon for help regarding the offspring (Gen 25:22–23; 2 Kgs 4:33). Like Joseph, the Shunammite's son has a mother who is resourceful as she

---

57. Alexander Rofé notes that the boy from Zarephath has lost his breath, a phrase that can indicate an altered state (such as being comatose or unconsciousness) without dying (see Dan 10:17). Judges 15:19; 1 Sam 30:12; and 1 Kgs 10:5 portray characters losing or regaining their רוח while remaining alive (*Prophetical Stories*, 134). Marvin Sweeney points out that the overt declaration that the child is dead indicates YHWH's ability to control life, much like Inanna and Ishtar in ancient Near Eastern myths (*Kings*, 290).

58. This assessment is from Uriel Simon (*Reading Prophetic Narratives*, 231), who describes the Shunammite's son as "similarly inconsequential," not unlike the nameless servants.

seeks either to get a son (Gen 30:1, 14–16, 22–24) or get her son back (2 Kgs 4:20–30). Like Samuel, the Shunammite's son has his birth foretold by a religious figure (1 Sam 1:17; 2 Kgs 4:16). Like Moses and his son Gershom, the Shunammite's son faces death but is saved through female initiative (Exod 1:22–2:10; 4:23–26; 2 Kgs 4:20–37). Like Samson, the Shunammite's son has a perceptive mother who recognizes and understands the presence of one who is holy (Judg 13:6–7, 21–23; 2 Kgs 4:9). While all these stories highlight the desire for sons in a culture biased toward males, they also illustrate the value of children in the narrative world.

The Shunammite's son who comes back to life makes a tripartite return. He is the only person in the Hebrew Bible who is overtly pronounced dead and is then brought back to life.[59] Just as the prophet made three points of contact with the boy (hands, mouth, eyes) who thrice manifests his return to life (his flesh warms, he sneezes, he opens his eyes), this child also comes alive in the text three times. The first is its most obvious manifestation in this story (2 Kgs 4:34–35) when the power of the prophet conquers death. The second is the boy's return to the text, as he later reappears in the Elisha cycle (2 Kgs 8:1–6). The third is the reworking of his account in later Christian tradition as Jesus revives Jairus's daughter (Mark 5:22–23, 35–43; Luke 8:41–42, 49–56; see also Matt 9:23–26) and the son of the woman at Nain (Luke 7:11–15).[60] The Shunammite's son is revived and his story lives on long after this episode has past.

---

59. Two other instances of revivification do not mention death per se. In 2 Kgs 13:20–21, a band of Moabites is burying a man who is thrown into Elisha's grave and revives upon touching the prophet's bones. Readers infer the man was dead, but this is not stated directly. In 1 Kgs 17:17, the son of the widow of Zarephath no longer has any breath (לא־נותרה־בו נשמה), prompting his mother to seek out Elijah for help. She asks why he has allowed the death of her son (ולהמית את־בני, v. 18b), and Elijah asks the same of YHWH (להמית את־בנה, v. 20b). However, some commentators interpret this as describing the boy's extreme weakness. John Gray points out, "Neither in this verse [v. 19] nor the sequel to it is it said that the lad was actually dead" (Kings, 342). Marvin Sweeney also interprets this passage as a restoration to health. He summarizes, "YHWH enables Elijah to restore the widow's son to life when he nearly dies as the result of the drought" (Kings, 209). For further discussion of the word נשמה and its meanings as "breath of God," "breath of man," or "breath of everything," see T. C. Mitchell, "The Old Testament Usage of $N^E\check{S}\bar{A}M\hat{A}$," VT 11 (1961): 177–87.

60. For more detailed discussion about the correspondence between the Elijah/Elisha stories and the Gospel accounts of the life of Jesus, see Brown, "Jesus and Elisha," 85–104. See also Thomas L. Brodie, "Luke 7,36–50 as an Internalization of 2 Kgs 4,1–37: A Study in Luke's Use of Rhetorical Imitation," Bib 64 (1983): 457–85; and Philippe Guillaume, "Miracles Miraculously Repeated: Gospel Miracles as Duplication of Elijah-Elisha's," BN 98 (1999): 21–23.

# 8

# The Israelite Slave Girl
# (2 Kings 5:1–14)

The slave girl in Naaman's household is a young child kidnapped from Israel. She serves Naaman's wife and speaks of a desire for her master's healing, triggering the subsequent chain of events. After procuring a letter of introduction from the Aramean king, Naaman journeys to Israel laden with riches. The king of Israel misinterprets the missive, thinking he himself should attempt to cure Naaman. Mysteriously, Elisha hears of these proceedings and requests Naaman's presence. When the commander arrives, Elisha sends out a messenger with instructions for Naaman to wash in the Jordan seven times. Outraged by the presence of a lackey who issues mundane instructions, Naaman refuses. Yet Naaman's servants coax their commander into trying the cure, which he does, and it proves efficacious. The leader with a skin disease has his flesh restored to that of a little boy (נער קטן, v. 14b), thanks to the suggestion of a little girl (קטנה נערה, v. 2a).

## Setings: Houses, Palaces, and Rivers

This story illustrates the fluctuating relationship between Israel and Aram.[1] Along with YHWH, Elisha serves the leaders of both nations,

---

1. For detailed historical analysis of the territory of Aram, see Sigurður Hafþórsson, *A Passing Power: An Examination of the Sources for the History of Aram-Damascus in the Second Half of the Ninth Century B.C.* (Stockholm: Almqvist & Wiksell, 2006). Evidence suggests that Aram probably reached its political zenith in the middle of the ninth century BCE, corresponding with the textual chronology of Elisha's career in the second half of the ninth century. This state at Israel's northern border would then prove a useful ally in the face of the encroaching Assyrian threat. Assyrian records attest to an alliance between Aram and Israel in Shalmaneser III's accounts of exploits against the Aramean coalition. This Assyrian king lists the military retinue of 1,200 chariots, 1,200 cavalrymen, and 20,000 foot soldiers that came from Damascus and combined with the 2,000 chariots and 10,000 foot soldiers from Israel (among others) to oppose Shalmaneser (*ANET*, 278–79). While these numbers are obviously unverifiable, they indicate the relative perceived strength of these forces in

showing the frequent crossover of theological and political grounds.[2] The kings of Israel and Aram first appear respectful of each other (2 Kgs 5:5–6), but then their bond becomes tense (2 Kgs 5:7), epitomizing the cooperation and conflict between these two nations.

While the narrative involves international relations, it largely takes place in internal spaces. The story glides from house to palace to palace to house, and ends outside at the Jordan. The Israelite slave girl serves Naaman's wife, and appears to be a house servant, speaking to her mistress while in Naaman's home (2 Kgs 5:3). The story then moves to Naaman's encounters with kings (vv. 4–7), who presumably reside in their royal residences. Elisha sends a message to the king of Israel, prompting Naaman to come to the prophet's house (vv. 8–9). While the exchange between the kings is marked by miscommunication (vv. 4–7), the slave girl and the prophet are clear about steps for Naaman's cure (v. 3, vv. 8–10). The settings then show palaces as containing confusion, but houses with Israelites as having healing knowledge.

Naaman's transformation takes place outside. The commander's initial refusal to wash in the Jordan is fueled by blatant disdain for this river (2 Kgs 5:12). Naaman scornfully compares the Jordan with the rivers of Damascus, Abana and Pharpar, which scholars generally take to be the Barada and Awaj rivers in Syria.[3] These rivers run swiftly through mountains and connect with oases, whereas the Jordan is often slow, shallow, and feeds into the Dead Sea. The rivers, then, reflect the characters of their lands. While Abana and Phapar, like the Aramean king and commander, may seem outwardly remarkable, the Jordan, like the Israelite prophet and slave girl, holds the real power. Elisha initially received YHWH's sign

---

the eyes of their enemy, and testify to an alliance between Israel and Aram. Biblical accounts show Aram, at times, fighting Israel and Judah (1 Kgs 11:23–25; 20:1–29; 2 Kgs 6:24–25; 9:14–15; 12:18–19 [Eng. 12:17–18]). Both Israel and Aram also individually form alliances with Judah (1 Kgs 15:18–22; 20:30–34; 22:1–4, 29–36), as separate kingdoms vie for control of northern territories. Yet even when the Arameans and Israelites fight (1 Kgs 20:1–30, 2 Kgs 6:8–19, 24; 13:3–7), reconciliation may ensue (1 Kgs 20:31–34; 2 Kgs 6:20–23). Peace among the nations also can endure for long periods (1 Kgs 22:1) and be purchased through tribute (2 Kgs 12:18–19 [Eng. 12:17–18]). YHWH uses Aram as an instrument of affliction (2 Kgs 13:3, 17) and delivers the Israelites from the Arameans (2 Kgs 13:4–5, 22–23). Carl-Johan Axskjöld suggests that Israel and Judah were more closely linked with Aram than other surrounding nations. Axskjöld notes that Aram acts as an instrument of YHWH in some contexts, including 2 Kings 5. For his discussion of this story, see Carl-Johan Axskjöld, *Aram as the Enemy Friend: The Ideological Role of Aram in the Composition of Genesis–2 Kings* (ConBOT 45; Stockholm: Almqvist & Wiksell, 1998), 112–24.

2. See 2 Kgs 5:1–14; 6:15–23; 8:7–15; 13:14–19. For detailed discussion of the theological implications of Elisha's role in combating the Aramean threat, see Moore, *God Saves*, 128–47.

3. Hafþórsson, *Passing Power*, 154. See Ray Lee Roth, "Abana," and Henry O. Thompson, "Pharpar," n.p., *ABD* on CD-ROM. Version 2.1. 1997.

of approval at the river Jordan (2 Kgs 2:13–14); now these waters further display their abiding and potent relationship (2 Kgs 5:10, 14).

## Characters

### Naaman

Naaman commands much of this narrative. His name, meaning "pleasant" (נעם), augurs well for success, although it may be tinged with irony for a man who commands armies that kill people.[4] Yet the text extols him as a highly respected man who serves the king of Aram (2 Kgs 5:1a).[5] Naaman is an איש גדול, implying status, riches, and power (see 2 Kgs 4:8), and the text recounts his bravery and prowess as a man of valor (גבור חיל, v. 1b). Further, YHWH favors Naaman, who grants him victory for Aram (כי־בו נתן־יהוה תשועה לארם, 2 Kgs 5:1aβ). Even in Israelite literature, this Aramean military hero is popular in human, royal, and divine realms.

The narrator then reveals Naaman's weakness: He is a מצרע (v. 1b). Generally translated in the context of being "leprous," this *pual* participle more accurately portrays a skin disease with an unsightly manifestation such as a rash, severe dryness, flaking scales, or a scabby condition.[6] The more severe symptoms of modern-day leprosy (Hansen's disease), such as disfigurement, blindness, and loss of limbs, are not relevant to Naaman, who appears vigorous and energetic. While מצרע may be associated with ritual uncleanness and divine reprobation,[7] Naaman does not suffer from any communal condemnation. While ill, he remains robust. While looking

---

4. This anthroponym was known north of Israel, as testified in Ugaritic literature. The adjective *n'mn* (f. *n'mnt*) is translated as "good-looking," "gracious" (*DLU*, 314–15), "fine" (from "Aqhat," in Parker, *Ugaritic Narrative Poetry*, 62, 65), and "pleasant" (from Edward Greenstein, "Kirta," in Parker, *Ugaritic Narrative Poetry*, 13). In the masculine form, this adjective describes the heroes Keret (*KTU* 1.14 i 40) and Aqhat (*KTU* 1.17 iv 45; 1.18 iv 14) in laudatory contexts. As a proper name, *n'mn* also occurs outside of narrative poetry (*DLU*, 315). Yet as Jacques Ellul notes, "In spite of the meaning of his name, he [Naaman] is a man of war, a man of blood." See Jacques Ellul, *The Politics of God and the Politics of Man* (trans. Geoffrey W. Bromiley; Grand Rapids, MI: Eerdmans, 1972), 25. Josephus specifically credits Naaman with the slaying of Israel's notorious king Ahab (*Antiquities* 8.15.5).

5. The phrase נשא פנים (v. 1, literally suggesting raised faces) connotes being "graciously received, held in honor" (BDB, 670; see Isa 3:3; 9:14 [Eng. 9:15]; Job 22:8). John Gray suggests this idiom derives from a king extending his scepter to a prostrated supplicant, inviting him or her to look up (Gray, *Kings*, 452; see Esth 8:3–5).

6. In the biblical context, מצרע connotes a repulsive, visible skin disorder characterized by scaly skin and carrying ritual contamination. For fuller discussion, see Jacob Milgrom, *Leviticus 1–16* (AB 3; New York: Doubleday, 1991), 816–20.

7. See Provan, *Kings*, 194. See Lev 13–14; 22:4–6; Num 5:1–4; 12:1–15; 2 Sam 3:26–29; 2 Kgs 15:5; 2 Chr 26:19–23.

repulsive, he stays haughty. The commander continues in control, despite his crusty condition.

Naaman then becomes a paradoxical character – both mighty and sick. Similarly, he consults those who have positions of strength and weakness. He heeds the words of his servants (2 Kgs 5:3–4, 13–14), while disdaining the long-sought advice of the prophet (vv. 5–12). He also listens to the king of Aram, who urges him to see the prophet (vv. 5–6), but offers no response to the anguished king of Israel who thinks he is expected to cure Naaman himself (v. 7). Naaman shows the license afforded to powerful people, as well as the confidence and confusion that buoy and plague a person seeking transformation.

## Raiding Bands

A group of anonymous raiders (גדודים) quickly bursts on the scene to capture a young girl, then disappears (2 Kgs 5:2a). Their role serves the narrative by explaining how a child who knows about Elisha ends up in Naaman's house. The text repeatedly portrays groups of marauders that descend into neighboring lands to steal, kidnap, and kill.[8] Here these raiders present Naaman as an overseer of violent military operations. They also show the powerlessness of a little girl whom they likely wrenched from her home to bring to a foreign land. Serving as a bridge between Naaman and the slave girl, the גדודים transport one character to the other and set up their perfect contrast.

## The Israelite Slave Girl

Among all the children in the Elisha cycle, the young slave in this story is the only one directly described as a girl, yet she is more articulate than all the boys combined.[9] She not only holds a unique place in the Elisha cycle, but indeed she is the only character explicitly called a "little girl" who takes initiative and speaks in any narrative of the Hebrew Bible. Other girls and young women certainly have roles in biblical stories, but she is the only ילדה or נערה described as קטנה, erasing ambiguity about the possibility of her being a young woman. As a little girl, sexual ele-

---

8. See 1 Sam 30:1–3; 2 Sam 3:22; 2 Kgs 6:23; 13:20, 21; 24:2; Jer 18:22; Hos 6:9; 7:1; 2 Chr 22:1.

9. She speaks ten words (אחלי אדני לפני הנביא אשר בשמרון אז יאסף אתו מצרעתו, 2 Kgs 5:3). The mockers of Bethel share four words (עלה קרח עלה קרח, 2 Kgs 2:23), one of the debt-collateral children utters three words (אין עוד כלי, 2 Kgs 4:6), and the Shunammite's son also has two words (ראשי ראשי, 2 Kgs 4:19). Other children who die or hide in fear (2 Kgs 3:27; 6:28–29) remain mute.

ments of her servitude and capture are minimized. Without parents, she essentially appears as an orphan, joining the ranks of other young, noble, likeable orphans in literature (such as Harry Potter, Little Orphan Annie, or Oliver Twist). This small, enslaved girl is alone in a foreign country, yet her words prompt the action of kings and a commander.

Naaman and this slave girl are paradoxically bound through their differences. Both present themselves before someone whom they serve, yet they serve on very different levels. Naaman comes before his lord (לפני אדניו, 2 Kgs 5:1a), the most visible and powerful person in the land (i.e., the king). The little girl comes before Naaman's wife (לפני אשת נעמן, v. 2b) in the private and humble role of domestic servant. In their cultural hierarchy, each is one rung from the end. The commander's role in society is just below the monarch. The slave girl's place is at the bottom of the social pyramid, just above a baby girl or toddler, whose life might be considered less valuable (see Lev 27:5–6). The military leader has valuable connections and lavish riches. One king serves as Naaman's advocate (2 Kgs 5:4–5), and another king receives his request (vv. 6–7). Naaman has family (v. 2), money (v. 5b), horses and chariots (v. 9), and servants (v. 13) to accommodate his wishes. The slave girl lacks the security of kin and possessions as she tends to others. Naaman, the named Aramean, is a great, adult, male, ruling conqueror. She, the anonymous Israelite, is a small, young, female, submissive slave.

The Israelite slave girl nonetheless possesses the courage of conviction. Her age is a mystery, although she is young enough to be described as "little," and old enough to remember the prophet in Samaria. This girl may have met Elisha or perhaps she heard about his power, since she knows of his healing ability. Yet if the prophet's reputation is widespread, it did not cross national lines. The girl's words about the prophet present new information to the Arameans. While poor, the Israelite slave girl has intangible resources: the knowledge of a prophet, faith in his ability, communication skills, and kindness toward her owner. This small, foreign, captive female child incarnates vulnerability, and yet acts with the compassion and magnanimity that befit greatness.

## Naaman's Wife

The woman of the house is defined by her relationships, being described as Naaman's wife (אשת נעמן, 2 Kgs 5:2b) and the girl's mistress (גברתה, v. 3a). She creates the link between the worlds of a servant girl and a military leader. As mentioned above, Naaman and the slave girl are opposites in many ways. Similarly, Naaman's wife offers a pointed contrast to the raiding parties. She is one woman, the mistress of a rich household, presumably cultured and refined. They are many men, looters and thieves, who kidnap, steal, and murder for a living. Yet just as the raiders provided the link that brought the girl to Naaman, his wife transports the girl's words to her husband.

The slave girl voices an unsolicited suggestion to her mistress. Perhaps they share a respectful closeness from their working relationship (v. 2b). At minimum, their interaction does not hint of any animosity, fear, or jealousy between them (cf. Gen 16:1–9; Prov 30:23). This re-enforces the impression of the slave girl as young and not posing any threat as a sexual rival. It seems likely that the mistress of the house rules over her slave fairly (see Ps 123:2; Prov 31:15), fostering trust that allows for meaningful exchanges between those of different statuses.

The role of the woman of the house varies among ancient translations. The MT uses a masculine verb form in v. 4 that portrays someone going to his lord and relaying the words of the slave girl (ויבא ויגד לאדניו לאמר כזאת וכזאת דברה הנערה אשר מארץ ישראל, v. 4). Many English translations, along with the Vulgate, insert Naaman's name here as the subject of the masculine verbs, implying that he is talking to the king.[10] However, the Hebrew text does not mention Naaman or the king specifically. This verse could also portray an unknown character, perhaps a servant, speaking to Naaman, having overheard the conversation between the slave girl and her mistress.[11] If Naaman is the subject of ויגד and ויבא in v. 4, explaining to *his* lord what the girl has said, how would he know the content of her words? The text gives no indication that he was there when the slave girl spoke to Naaman's wife (v. 3), suggesting his absence. If Naaman were present, the girl would have been rude, bordering on insubordinate, not to acknowledge him. The Septuagint changes the genitive suffix to feminine in v. 4a, "her lord" (LXX: τῷ κυρίῳ ἑαυτῆς; cf. MT: לאדניו). This reading implies that Naaman's wife relays the girl's suggestion leading to her husband's physical healing (v. 14), and ultimately resulting in his embrace of YHWH as his god (v. 15).

## *The Kings of Aram and Israel*

The kings of Aram and Israel, like the slave girl and Naaman's wife, are anonymous but significant.[12] Yet the kings seem more concerned

---

10. E.g., ESV, NAB, NIV, NJB, NJPS, NRSV, and RSV, perhaps following the Vulgate: *ingressus est itaque Naaman ad dominum suum et nuntiavit ei dicens sic et sic locuta est puella de terra Israhel* ("then Naaman went into his lord and told him, saying, Thus and thus said the girl from the land of Israel").

11. The KJV and ASV remain ambiguous with "And one went in, and told his lord . . . ," and the JPS closely translates, "And he went in, and told his lord . . . ," without specifying an agent for the action. The Peshitta also keeps the subject vague. See Burney, *Notes on Kings*, 279.

12. Scholars speculate that the king of Aram may be a precursor to Ben-Hadad I, and

about their position vis-à-vis each other than with Naaman and his healing. Naaman reports the words of the Israelite girl to the Aramean king, who immediately offers to write a letter to the king of Israel (v. 5a). Is the Aramean king executing proper protocol by showing due respect or looking for an excuse to fight a rival? The latter option appears more likely given the content of the letter. Naaman is being sent, the king of Israel reads, "so that *you* might cure him of his skin disease" (emphasis added; v. 6b, ואספתו מצרעתו). The king of Israel is threatened by this challenge, rending his garments and asking, "Am I God, to kill or to bring to life, that this man sends to me to cure a man of his skin disease? Surely look and see how he is seeking a quarrel against me!" (v. 7).[13] The king of Aram seems sly and conniving, appearing altruistic while being bellicose. The king of Israel emerges as insecure and histrionic, ranting that he cannot restore the dead. Both monarchs suffer in comparison to servile characters who lack power, but retain composure.

## Elisha and His Messenger

When the kings are at their nadir, Elisha saves them from their squabble. He somehow hears of the king of Israel's anguish and asks why he has torn his clothes (2 Kgs 5:8). The ruler's ineptitude is further highlighted by his ignorance of the prophet who resides in his own capital of Samaria (v. 4). The king is subject to Elisha's command: "Now let him come to me, and he will know that there is a prophet in Israel" (v. 8b). Elisha seems focused on establishing his superior status, as he instructs a king and commander. An unnamed messenger acts as an intermediary, issuing the prophet's instructions to Naaman (v. 10), illustrating the prophet's lack of need or desire to greet the commander personally. When surrounded by those in the upper echelons of society, Elisha asserts his own place as equal or above them.

The portrait of the prophet that emerges from this story is similar to those discussed previously as Elisha commands others (2 Kgs 3:14–15; 4:3, 7, 12, 36), uses assistants (2 Kgs 3:15; 4:12–15, 25–26, 29–31), and performs wonders (2 Kgs 2:14, 24; 4:3–6, 16–17, 32–35). However, instead of journey-

---

the king of Israel might be identified with Jehoram. T. R. Hobbs makes these conclusions tentatively, realizing that the chronological sequence of the Elisha cycle is far from secure (*2 Kings*, 61–62). Some scholars, such as Gina Hens-Piazza, associate the king of Israel with Jehoram on the basis of literary portrayal "because he acts like Jehoram." Hens-Piazza asserts, "When he was marching out with the kings of Judah and Edom to attack Moab and was confronted with a lack of water for the troops, Jehoram acted similarly (3:10). He was negative and blaming, the same way he is here" (*Kings*, 260; see also Fretheim, *Kings*, 152).

13. Georg Hentschel maintains that this request reflects a widespread ancient belief in kings' curative abilities. See Georg Hentschel, *2 Könige* (Würzburg: Echter, 1985), 23.

ing with Elijah (2 Kgs 2:1–10), consorting with a band of prophets (2 Kgs 2:1–7, 15–18), or working with Gehazi in different locales (2 Kgs 4:12–15, 25–32, 36), the peripatetic prophet becomes stationary. Elisha seems to hold a prophetic office with a business address. Naaman has brought astounding riches (2 Kgs 5:5b), which seem intended for Elisha (2 Kgs 5:15). Is the healer operating an expensive enterprise?

The messenger (מלאך) who issues Elisha's command to Naaman (2 Kgs 5:10) serves as the prophet's subordinate, although he does not seem to be Gehazi. When Gehazi appears later in this chapter (vv. 20–27) he is introduced as Elisha's נער, suggesting he has not had a previous role in this story.[14] The messenger elevates the prophet's importance by relaying his boss's instructions. Like the slave girl, the messenger gives information that can lead to Naaman's healing, if only he will regard the subordinates' words.

### Naaman's Servants

Naaman's underlings also serve as vehicles of transformation. After Naaman angrily spurns the prophet's simple directive to wash in the Jordan seven times (vv. 10–12), his servants respectfully approach him (v. 13). Just as the king had called Naaman his servant (את־נעמן עבדי, v. 6b), these attendants are Naaman's servants (עבדיו, v. 13a). Their salutation to their master, אבי (v. 13a), is strikingly intimate. This address seems congruous with the servants' general behavior. They show gentle concern for their master, appealing to his greatness of character and pointing out that this small act of ablution is worth undertaking (v. 13). Calling Naaman "my father" reflects the tenderness of their reasoning. Perhaps the slaves in Naaman's house—the girl who serves his wife and the group that serves him—are treated well by their mistress and master. All of these servants seem to have a genuine desire to help Naaman be freed of his infirmity, and they play a pivotal role in his healing.

## Re-viewing the Plot from a Childist Perspective

The story of Naaman's skin disease in 2 Kgs 5:1–14 is part of a larger narrative that progresses from a miracle story to a conversion account.

---

14. The narrator consistently describes Gehazi appositionally as Elisha's נער (2 Kgs 4:12, 25; 5:20; 8:4), even when he acts as a messenger (2 Kgs 4:12–13, 25–26). Only Gehazi uses a different designation for himself, (obsequiously?) suggesting he is Elisha's slave (עבדך, 2 Kgs 5:25b), perhaps trying to appear deferential after deceptively exacting riches from Naaman (2 Kgs 5:20–24).

In the first seven verses of this chapter, Elisha does not appear, and is obliquely referenced only once (v. 3). The Israelite slave girl, however, features prominently in this section, as she speaks and prompts the ensuing action (v. 3). She arrives in the story by force, snatched from her home, her family, her land, and her culture (v. 2a). This girl is the only reported booty from the Arameans' raid, perhaps implying that the motive for their plundering foray was to acquire slaves. Yet despite the trauma she has endured, this girl is faithful, respectful, and considerate.

She begins with a simple utterance of appeal: אחלי (v. 3aβ). This interjection shows volition and frequent translations include "Would that" (ASV, JPS, RSV), "If only" (NIV, NRSV), or "I wish" (NJPS).[15] The slave girl is skilled in the art of approach. Appropriately for a servant, she refers to Naaman as "my lord" (אדני, v. 3aβ). Naaman has gone before his lord (לפני אדניו, v. 1a), and she serves before Naaman's wife (לפני אשת נעמן, v. 2b). The girl's words to her mistress introduce a new figure who merits deference—Naaman should go before the prophet (לפני הנביא, v. 3aβ). Wisely, the slave girl couches her suggestion as a nonthreatening desire. She voices her hope and specifies that this prophet is in Samaria (v. 3a), although she does not mention Elisha specifically. Perhaps this girl knew of the wonder-worker only by reputation, or maybe she has forgotten his name during her time of captivity. Presumably, Elisha is the only prophet in Samaria.

The servant girl explains that the prophet would make Naaman better (אז יאסף אתו מצרעתו, v. 3b). The word אסף means "to gather" but in this

---

15. The word אחלי appears only one other time in the Hebrew Bible (Ps 119:5) in a plea for faithfulness to keep God's statutes. While most scholars assign a late date to Psalm 119, Mitchell Dahood suggests a pre-exilic setting. See Mitchell Dahood, *Psalms* III (AB 17A; Garden City, NY: Doubleday, 1970), 173. Regardless of dating, this Psalm seems relevant to the situation of the Israelite slave girl as the speaker self-identifies as a faithful servant. Verses that seem especially apt include v. 9: "How can a young servant [נער; cf. 2 Kgs 5:2] keep his way pure? By keeping according to your word"; v. 19: "I live as a stranger in the land; do not hide your commandments from me"; v. 23: "Even though princes [שרים; cf. 2 Kgs 5:1a] sit talking against me, your servant thinks about your decrees"; v. 110: "The wicked laid a trap for me, but I did not wander away from your precepts"; v. 141: "I am small and despised, but I have not forgotten your precepts." As Marc Brettler notes, the masculine language of the Psalm does not preclude a female speaker. Various women in the Hebrew Bible, Apocrypha, and New Testament offer songs with no alteration to feminine language (Miriam in Exod 15:21; Deborah in Judg 5:1–31; Hannah in 1 Sam 2:1–10; Judith in Jud 16:1–17; and Mary in Luke 1:46–55). For fuller discussion, see Marc Zvi Brettler, "Women and Psalms: Toward an Understanding of the Role of Women's Prayer in the Israelite Cult," in *Gender and Law in the Hebrew Bible and the Ancient Near East* (ed. Victor H. Matthews, Bernard M. Levinson, and Tikva Frymer-Kensky; JSOTSup 262; Sheffield: Sheffield Academic Press, 1998), 25–56. The Ugaritic cognate for אחלי (*aḥl*) is translated "would that" or "I pray." This translation was first proposed by Cassuto and has been widely adopted. (*DLU*, 16, renders *aḥl* as "ojalá"!) For further discussion, see Meindert Dijkstra and Johannes C. de Moor, "Problematic Passages in the Legend of Aqhâtu," *UF* 7 (1975): 204.

passage is generally translated as "recover" or "cure."[16] Gwilym Jones contends, "It is impossible to derive the meaning cure from the Heb. verb *'āsap*, 'to gather,' which does not occur anywhere else with this meaning."[17] Yet the Israelite girl appears to suggest that Naaman be gathered from his affliction, that is, the skin disease will be removed from him. The commander, like the girl, is also captive. If he is taken from his sickness, he will be released from what constricts him. The girl is under Naaman's control, as he is subject to his disease. The text offers her no hope of freedom, yet still she wishes liberation for her captor.

As the Israelite girl speaks of Naaman being gathered from his illness, the kings and commander quote her. The narrator vaguely summarizes Naaman's report to his king (כזאת וכזאת דברה הנערה, v. 4b; cf. 2 Sam 17:15; 2 Kgs 9:12), but apparently the girl's term אסף was included in the recapitulation. The king of Aram repeats the girl's word choice (ואספתו מצרעתו, v. 6b), as do the king of Israel (לאסף איש מצרעתו, v. 7aβ), and Naaman (ואסף המצרע, v. 11b). The phrasing of this little girl frames Naaman's quest as kings and the commander follow her lead.

Remarkably, none of the most powerful people in the land eschews the suggestion of a foreign slave girl. Naaman reveals her as the source of this idea (הנערה אשר מארץ ישראל, v. 4b), perhaps to appear blameless should the mission fail. Yet, when speaking with the king of Aram, Naaman alters the narrator's introduction of the girl slightly, omitting the adjective "little" (cf. v. 2a, נערה קטנה). Admitting that this suggestion came from a small female slave girl may be too embarrassing. Alternatively, she may not seem so diminutive, having garnered esteem in his eyes. No one disparages the girl or questions her reliability. As *the* servant girl from the land of Israel (v. 4b), she appears to be the only known female Israelite slave in the area, or she already has an established reputation.

Initially, it may appear that Naaman follows her advice because he has nothing to lose except his ailment. However, it later becomes apparent that he also can lose riches since cures may be very expensive. As Naaman journeys to Israel, he takes along ten talents of silver and six thousand shekels of gold, along with ten sets of garments (v. 5b).[18] While the sum may seem more like a present for a king than a fee for a prophet (see 1 Sam 9:7–8; 1 Kgs 14:2–3; 2 Kgs 4:42), Naaman gives only the letter to the king of Israel (2 Kgs 5:6). The extravagant treasure seems intended for the prophet

---

16. E.g., "recover": ASV, JPS, KJV; "cure": NIV, RSV, NRSV, NJPS. Usual terms for healing take a form of רפא.

17. Jones, *Kings*, vol. 2, 415. Jones cites Gray (*Kings*, 453) and Montgomery (*Kings*, 378), who equate אסף with the Akkadian *ašāpu, meaning "to exorcise." Cogan and Tadmor, however, note that only nominal forms are attested in Akkadian (*āšipu*, "exorcist") (*II Kings*, 64). See also *āšiptu* "sorceress, female magician," and *āšipūtu* "exorcism" [*CDA*, 28]).

18. T. R. Hobbs calculates the cumulative weight of these treasures as 750 pounds of silver and nearly 200 pounds of gold (*2 Kings*, 63–64).

(v. 15), showing how precious this recovery is to Naaman. As a political figure, Naaman realizes that paying for services relieves him of personal indebtedness (cf. 2 Kgs 4:11–17). He invests heavily in the possibility of being healed, because of the girl's words.

As Naaman shows power through riches and royal access, Elisha has miraculous ability and royal demeanor. The prophet knows that the Israelite king has ripped his clothes in anguish (v. 8) and also seems aware of the Israelite girl's wish. With Naaman in the capital city, Elisha expands his prophetic realm and (self-aggrandizingly?) wants Naaman to learn that there is a prophet in *Israel* (v. 8), not just Samaria (cf. v. 3). The girl told Naaman where to go (v. 3a); Elisha tells what Naaman must know (וידע כי יש נביא בישראל, v. 8bβ). As Robert Cohn points out, the prophet behaves like a king by withholding an audience from the important man who shows up at his door (vv. 9–10). Elisha acts with regal reserve.[19]

In contrast, both Naaman and the king are quick to anger. Arriving at Elisha's house with his horses and chariots, Naaman must first stand at the prophet's door (v. 9). Elisha sends his messenger forth with the instructions to wash in the Jordan seven times (v. 10),[20] but Naaman becomes enraged (v. 11a). This commander expected the prophet to wave his hand over the spot and gather Naaman's skin disease (v. 11b), instead of having an insignificant envoy tell him to wash in Israel's inferior waters (v. 12). Naaman's internal character is revealed, showing neediness beyond his exterior ailment. His servants reason with the great man (איש גדול, v. 1a), noting that he would have done a great deed (דבר גדול, v. 13a) and convincing Naaman to follow the prophet's instructions (v. 13b). The mighty man's physical descent to the Jordan, according to the word of the prophet (v. 14a), embodies his spiritual submission. Naaman's flesh is restored to that of a נער קטן (v. 14b) as he becomes like the נערה קטנה (v. 2a) who knows of the prophet's powers.

## Childist Interpretation: Insight and Irony

The story of Naaman's healing brims with irony, much of it related to the Israelite girl.[21] The passage begins with the odd admission that YHWH

---

19. Robert L. Cohn, "Form and Perspective in 2 Kings V," *VT* 33 (1983): 177. On Elisha's demeanor, see also Wesley Bergen, "The Prophetic Alternative: Elisha and the Israelite Monarchy," in *Elijah and Elisha in Socioliterary Perspective* (ed. Robert B. Coote; Atlanta: Scholars Press, 1992), 131.

20. The Shunammite's son sneezes seven times (2 Kgs 4:35), perhaps revealing a connection between the number seven, prophetic power, and complete signs of restoration.

21. For discussion of irony and its function in relationship to foreigners and power, see Carolyn J. Sharp, *Irony and Meaning in the Hebrew Bible* (Bloomington, IN: Indiana University

gives deliverance to Aram because of Naaman (כי־בו נתן־יהוה תשועה לארם, v. 1a). It seems ironic that YHWH would give victory to those who frequently oppose his own people.[22] Yet while Naaman can deliver all of Aram, it takes a small slave girl to deliver him. She is the first one who points toward his own salvation (תשועה), and he is saved from his illness by Elisha (אלישע). Naaman only later comes to realize the power of this deity who had been with him all along (v. 1), as he fully confesses his faith in YHWH's ability (vv. 15–17). If YHWH gave Naaman military victory at the outset of the story, YHWH might have also given him healing earlier, had he just known enough to ask. Instead, Naaman embarks on a costly journey after confusing encounters with kings. The small slave girl, however, has insight and vision leading to restoration.

Her knowledge and demeanor also contrast ironically with that of the Israelite king. The anonymous slave girl and the anonymous king show that names do not equal power and that prodigious wisdom is not limited to outwardly impressive people. The Israelite slave girl lives in an alien land and recommends the prophet in Samaria (v. 3), but the Israelite king, with all his retinue and resources, seems unaware of the prophet in his own town (v. 7). This counters the expectation of the Aramean king, who, having heard of the slave girl's wish, sends a letter to Israel's ruler (vv. 5–7). The king of Aram evidently assumes that such prophetic services must be under royal auspices (see 1 Kgs 22:1–28). Yet upon receiving the letter, the Israelite king does not respond in a way befitting a monarch, which might involve proclaiming a search for the prophet or commanding Elisha to come forward. Instead he explodes, assuming total powerlessness and highlighting his inabilities (v. 7). The frustration and helplessness he expresses are more appropriate for a slave than a king. The Israelite girl speaks politely of her Aramean master, referring to Naaman as "my lord" (אדני, v. 3aβ). The Israelite king, who sees the king of Aram as a threat (v. 7b) and therefore more powerful, speaks of his royal counterpart only as "this [man]" (זה, v. 7aβ). As the girl seems to realize, but the king does not, to risk public offense of a social superior is dumb and can be danger-

---

Press, 2009), 43–83. Sharp reveals how the Hebrew Bible ironically portrays its own leaders (e.g., Joseph, David, Solomon, Hezekiah) and uses irony to skewer foreign rulers (e.g., Pharaoh, Abimelech, Belshazzar, Darius, and Ahasuerus). She observes, "At stake in all of these narratives is the question of maintaining Israelite integrity when faced with the threat of a foreign power" (p. 83). The Israelite slave girl shows this integrity on a personal level. She expresses her faith while captive to a foreign commander who reveals his foolishness before heeding an Israelite prophet. Even a powerless Israelite slave girl can exceed a mighty foreign leader in maturity, wisdom, and insight.

22. As Philip Satterthwaite observes, YHWH consistently gives victory (נתן תשועה) to Israel (see Judg 15:18; Isa 46:13; Ps 144:10). The use of this phrase in relation to another nation is found only here. See Philip E. Satterthwaite, "The Elisha Narratives and Coherence of 2 Kings 2–8," *TynBul* 49 (1998): 16 n. 42.

ous. The Israelite girl is a paragon of respect, composure, knowledge, and wisdom, whereas the Israelite king exhibits disrespect, agitation, ignorance, and foolishness.

The ironic twists in the story continue with Elisha and Naaman (vv. 8–12).[23] The Aramean commander assembles his retinue and riches to journey to a foreign land and arrives at Elisha's house (while the prophet is not known by his own king). The commander has brought presents to bestow upon the prophet, who does not bestow his presence upon the commander. The priceless gifts become worthless as Elisha declines to receive Naaman (v. 10) or his largesse (v. 16). When Naaman hears the messenger's instructions for a cure, he refuses to follow them (vv. 10–12). Ironically, Naaman has heeded the unsolicited words of the lowly slave girl, but rejects the suggestion of the powerful prophet whose advice he sought. Naaman's servants intervene to urge their master to follow Elisha's simple directives (v. 13). They note the irony of Naaman's refusal: why favor a hard process over an easy remedy? In the end, the slaves' sagacity matters more than the commander's riches or the kings' posturing. Lai Ling Ngan summarizes, "It is ironic that those with power throw up obstacles while those who are without power move efficiently toward the desired goal."[24]

The words of the slave girl (אחלי אדני לפני הנביא אשר בשמרון, v. 3a) find their fulfillment as Naaman stands before the prophet (ויבא ויעמד לפניו, v. 15a). He has been cured of his illness (וישב בשרו כבשר נער קטן ויטהר, v. 14b; cf. v. 3b, יאסף אתו מצרעתו) and resembles a child (v. 14b, נער קטן; cf. v. 2, נערה קטנה). Just as she was the little girl brought back (וישבו, v. 2a) from Israel, his skin has been returned (וישב, v. 14b) to that of a little boy, as the prophet promised his flesh would be restored (וישב בשרך לך, v. 10b). Naaman takes on physical characteristics and acquires new knowledge like that which the slave girl already possesses, to his betterment. He discovers that there is not only a prophet in Israel (v. 8), but more important, there is a God in Israel (v. 15). The paths of the slave's and commander's journeys have crossed as she goes from Israel to Aram and he goes from Aram to Israel. She leaves freedom to captivity, and he goes from being captive to his disease to being freed from it. As Gerhard von Rad notes, she is the story's first instrument of salvation.[25] The least significant character in this narrative—a poor, captive, slave girl—arugably becomes the most influential of all.

---

23. For discussion of irony in this scene, see Terence E. Fretheim, *Deuteronomic History* (Nashville: Abingdon, 1983), 151.

24. Lai Ling Elizabeth Ngan, "2 Kings 5," *RevExp* 94 (1997): 591. See also Moore, *God Saves*, 71–84.

25. Gerhard von Rad, *God at Work in Israel* (trans. John H. Marks; Nashville: Abingdon, 1980), 48.

## Insights about Children and Captivity

While this story may offer uplifting literary reversals of character portrayal, it also raises troubling historical issues about children and slavery.[26] The Israelite slave girl is captured and used as a slave, but the text does not criticize her kidnapping.[27] Slavery was an established institution in the ancient world, although practices varied widely.[28] Historically, the first slaves in the ancient Near East were foreigners, who were usually prisoners of war.[29] Often children exiled into new lands as part of mass deportations became slaves. The Neo-Assyrians were especially skilled in using forced exile as an effective tool of foreign domination. As attested in accounts of deportations and further corroborated by Neo-Assyrian bas-reliefs, families were exiled intact. As Bustenay Oded explains, this practice discouraged men from trying to escape back to their homeland. Further, people were more productive laborers if allowed to be with their family.[30] Children are explicitly listed in documents recording exilic conquests.[31] While the exploitation of foreign slaves was condoned, kid-

---

26. The Israelite girl is never explicitly called a female slave or servant (אמה or שפחה), yet it is clear from the context that this is the capacity in which she serves. The more general term for "slave" (עבד) does not have a feminine form.

27. See Andreas Michel, "Gewalt gegen Kinder im alten Israel. Eine sozialgeschichtliche Perspektive," in Kunz-Lübcke and Lux, *"Schaffe Mir Kinder,"* 149.

28. Dexter Callender points out that slavery in the ancient Near East was very different from modern slavery. Slavery in the ancient Near East also differed from slavery in the Greco-Roman world, where large numbers of slaves posed a constant threat to the existing social structure. Greco-Roman slaves were also subject to degrading treatment, which was not necessarily the case in the ancient Near East. For comparison of slavery in classical antiquity and ancient Near Eastern cultures, see Dexter E. Callender, Jr., "Servants of God(s) and Servants of Kings in Israel and the Ancient Near East," *Semeia* 83/84 (1998): 67–72. For discussion of slavery in Jewish households during the Greco-Roman period, see Dale B. Martin, "Slavery and the Ancient Jewish Family," in Cohen, *Jewish Family in Antiquity*, 113–29.

29. Isaac Mendelsohn notes that the progression of slavery in the ancient Near East began with foreign captives of war, then foreigners who were imported, and finally natives heavily indebted being sold into slavery. The Sumerian signs for slave were *nita + kúr* "male of a foreign country," and *munus + kúr* "female of a foreign country" (Mendelsohn, *Slavery*, 1).

30. Bustenay Oded, *Mass Deportations and Deportees in the Neo-Assyrian Empire* (Wiesbaden: Ludwig Reichert, 1979), 23–24. Assyrian bas-reliefs portray women and children riding on animals as they are carted into captivity. See M. A. Littauer and J. H. Crouwel, *Wheeled Vehicles and Ridden Animals in the Ancient Near East* (HO 7; Leiden: E. J. Brill, 1979), 139. For a photo of a bas-relief depicting entire families sent into exile, see David Ussishkin, *The Conquest of Lachish by Sennacherib* (Tel Aviv: Institute of Archaeology, 1982), 77 (esp. slabs 4, 5).

31. For textual and inscriptional evidence, see Oded, *Mass Deportations*, 2–11. A typical list of captives would include the number taken, then the description of the deportees who were *ṣeḫer rabi zikar u sinniš* "young and old, male and female." The term *ṣeḫer* specifically indicates "(time of) youth" (*CDA*, 335) (*Mass Deportations*, 3, 23).

napping is condemned by the Hammurabi Code (¶ 14).[32] Nonetheless this profitable practice persisted.[33] Children would be defenseless when captured by bandits and skirted off to a far-away land. As Susan Niditch points out, children were valuable as malleable workers, easily inculcated in the ways of slavery.[34] Most slaves worked in domestic service, doing tasks accessible to children, and many did not have names. Private households would have a few slaves, usually not more than four. Slaves also might be branded or tattooed.[35]

According to Israelite law codes, slaves are considered chattel (Exod 21:21); they can be bought (Exod 21:2), sold (Deut 15:12), and left as part of an inheritance (Lev 25:46).[36] Native people who became slaves, often due to excessive debt, are of greater concern to biblical legislation and are afforded (at least in theory) time lines for their manumission (Exod 21:2–3; Deut 15:12–15).[37] Foreign slaves, however, receive no such promises. Laws restrict slaveholders from treating their fellow Israelites harshly, but no similar safeguard exists for the foreign slave (Lev 25:45–46). The perception of people from another land as "alien" renders them defenseless in these legal codes, and thereby legitimates their exploitation.

Slaves who were especially vulnerable could also prove especially valuable. Yehudah Kaplan documents Assyrians' use of foreigners to serve society's upper echelons, including the king. Kaplan explains that captive soldiers would not have enough support to harbor their own political ambitions. Slaves' access to power could come through gaining favor with their master, often resulting in fierce loyalty.[38] Similarly, the

---

32. For discussion of children and infants in Mesopotamia succumbing to slavery through kidnapping and exposure, see Mendelsohn, *Slavery*, 5. Hammurabi's Code specifically prohibits the kidnapping of the young child of another man (*mār awīlim ṣiḫram*; Law of Hammurabi ¶ 14; Roth, *Law Collections from Mesopotamia*, 84). Biblical law codes that offer corresponding protection are focused on Israelites and do not specify youth (Exod 21:16; Deut 24:7). The penalty for kidnapping in all three law codes is death.

33. Roland de Vaux asserts that slave trade was common and likely promulgated by the Phoenicians, known as travelers and traders (*Ancient Israel*, 81–82).

34. Susan Niditch, *War in the Hebrew Bible: A Study in the Ethics of Violence* (New York: Oxford University Press, 1993), 84.

35. Mendelsohn, *Slavery*, 121–22. While Mendelsohn's study covers a wide period of time, he notes that the institution of slavery remained essentially constant due to the persistence of basic economic structures.

36. For further discussion of these law codes and their implications for the lives of slaves, see Hans Walter Wolff, "Masters and Slaves: On Overcoming Class-Struggle in the Old Testament," *Interp* 27.3 (1973): 266–71.

37. For discussion of the freeing of slaves, see de Vaux, *Ancient Israel*, 87–88. The failure of such legislation is revealed in Jer 34:8–16, in which slaves are released, then re-captured.

38. Yehuda Kaplan, "Recruitment of Foreign Soldiers into the Neo-Assyrian Army during the Reign of Tiglath-pileser III," in *Treasures on Camels' Humps: Historical and Literary Studies from the Ancient Near East Presented to Israel Eph'al* (ed. Mordechai Cogan and Dan'el Kahn; Jerusalem: Magnes, 2008), 139.

Israelite slave girl, whose precarious existence depends on her owner's favor, shows strong devotion to his household.

The girl's desire to help her master may also be an attempt to help herself. As a female slave, she risked eventual sexual exploitation. Isaac Mendelsohn notes that slave girls frequently served both mistress as an attendant and master as a concubine (see Gen 16:1–6).[39] A young slave girl might be sold into prostitution, which Mendelsohn describes as "the inevitable fate of the female slave."[40] A slave girl's best hope for avoiding rape might be the mercy—or better, the indebtedness—of her master. Naaman has shown that he does not like to remain in another's debt (2 Kgs 5:5b, 15), yet the Israelite slave girl has done him a big favor. She is both strategic and savvy.

## Children and Textual Connections

This child joins the ranks of countless girls and women whose efforts undergird lives brought to light in the text, while they themselves are barely noticed. Other נערות appear fleetingly in the Hebrew Bible, hinting at the presence of many more young female servants. These nameless servant girls are generally grouped together, attending to the needs of their moneyed mistress (Gen 24:61; Exod 2:5; 1 Sam 25:42; 2 Kgs 5:2; Prov 9:3; 27:27; 31:15; Esth 4:4, 16) or master (Ruth 2:22, 3:2). When נערות are not under someone's aegis, they often still travel together (1 Sam 9:11; Job 40:29 [Eng. 41:5]).[41] This may point to the need for security, as illustrated by the vulnerability of the lone נערה. A נערה is frequently in a sexual situation (Gen 34:1–12; 1 Kgs 1:2–4; Amos 2:7; Esth 2:9–13) or facing an impending sexual threat (Deut 22:15–29; Judg 19:3–9 [19:22–26]; Ruth 2:5–9),[42] although safety in numbers may offer some protection (Ruth 2:6–8). In Judg 21:12–14; 1 Kgs 1:3; and Esth 2:2–4, the נערה (alone or in a group) is sought specifically for sexual purposes. The נערה in Naaman's house-

---

39. Mendelsohn, *Slavery*, 8–9.

40. Mendelsohn, *Slavery*, 11–12. Mendelsohn here refers to Nuzi contracts involving the sale of a daughter, in which parents would try help daughters avoid prostitution (see Exod 21:7–11).

41. For further discussion of young women's vulnerability, see Kunz-Lübcke, *Kind in den antiken Kulturen*, 110–14.

42. Rebekah is a נערה who appears by herself and is not threatened sexually (Gen 24:14, 16). However, a servant appraises her as a potential bride for his master's son, with clear sexual implications. Rebekah leaves her home and family (Gen 24:55–58), and like the Israelite slave girl shows both the vulnerability and agency that a נערה could have. For more detailed discussion of Rebekah and other נערות, see Leeb, *Away from the Father's House*, 125–50.

hold is described as "little" (2 Kgs 5:2), mitigating sexual expectations. Yet freedom from sexual use would likely end as she grew older (see Neh 5:5).

As a girl acting on her own initiative, the Israelite slave girl keeps company with better-known female characters. Like Dinah, she is out on her own among foreign people (Gen 34:1; 2 Kgs 5:2). Like Rebekah, she extends kindness to a man who is her senior (Gen 24:17–20; 2 Kgs 5:3). More noticeably, the Israelite slave girl parallels the portrayal of Moses' sister in Exod 2:4–9.[43] Both girls reach across lines of class and nationality to help a male figure, as Moses' sister saves her baby brother (Exod 2:4–9) and the slave girl's words lead to Naaman's healing (2 Kgs 5:2–3, 14). Each of the young slaves approaches a female social superior, as Moses' sister offers a suggestion to Pharaoh's daughter (Exod 2:7) and the Israelite slave girl initiates conversation with Naaman's wife (2 Kgs 5:3). These scenes have girls and women talking to each other without intervening male voices, which is rare in the Hebrew Bible. Yet the anonymous females' conversations benefit known males, focusing on rescuing Moses from death (Exod 1:22) or healing Naaman from disease (2 Kgs 5:1–3). Both the Israelite slave girl and Moses' sister are servants on multiple levels: they serve the narrative they are in, the female characters they are under, the male characters they save, and the patriarchal ideology that courses through the text. Yet these girls are also mavericks, pushing the confines of their sanctioned roles to determine the course of events.

Esther Menn finds striking similarities between the Israelite slave girl and David, who is perhaps the most beloved character in the Hebrew Bible. Comparing the portrayal of young David (1 Sam 16–17) with that of the slave girl (delineated as 2 Kgs 5:1–19), Menn notes how they play key roles crossing political boundaries. She observes, "Both stories depict young people finding solutions to problems, intervening when adults are threatened and ineffectual, offering theological insights into God's way, and acting within the context of international conflict and tensions between cultures and national identities."[44] These youth have profound influence in an adult world, while the adults themselves have not offered solutions amid problematic scenarios. Heroic young David is anointed king (1 Sam 16:1–13), soothes troubled Saul (1 Sam 16:14–23), and slays menacing Goliath (1 Samuel 17). The Israelite slave girl is considerate and selfless, daring to voice a hope for her captor's healing (2 Kgs 5:3). However, as Menn points out, these young characters also highlight children's relative defenselessness, as they are away from their families due to

---

43. As discussed in Chapter 2, the narrator refers to this anonymous sister as an עלמה (Exod 2:8), indicating a girl or teenager.

44. Esther M. Menn, "Child Characters in Biblical Narratives: The Young David (1 Samuel 16–17) and the Little Israelite Servant Girl (2 Kings 5:1–19)," in Bunge, *Child in the Bible*, 325.

national conflicts.[45] Young David and the Israelite slave girl epitomize the surprising influence and sheer vulnerability of children's lives.

The Israelite slave girl presents a child character who is both familiar and unique. She is typical of many children in the Bible in that she is barely noticed in the story itself or in many modern commentaries. She works in a servile role, no doubt involved in the support jobs that enable quotidian survival. Yet this Israelite slave is the only little girl in the entire Hebrew Bible who speaks in her own voice. Despite being a captive slave living far from her family, she shows a remarkable sense of self and maintains her belief in the prophet, bringing hope to the narrative. The small slave girl utters a wish, and formidable characters act on her words. Influential kings engage in international exchanges. A wonder-working prophet offers healing. A sick commander is cured. A parade of potentates proceeds through this passage . . . and a little child has led them.

---

45. Menn, "Child Characters," 351.

# 9

# The Sons of the Starving Mothers (2 Kings 6:24–31)

The two boys in this shocking story become prey for their own mothers. This passage begins with Samaria under a siege that starves the inhabitants. While the king of Israel is walking on the city walls, a woman cries out to him for help. He asks what he can do for her, and mentions the threshing floor or the wine press, implying that neither has any stores left. The woman explains that another mother had suggested that they eat one of their sons one day and then the other son the next day. She recounts that they boiled her son and ate him, but the next day the other mother hid her son. Upon hearing this, the king rends his garments. Since he is on the city wall, the people see that he is wearing sackcloth underneath. Somewhat enigmatically, the king vows to have Elisha killed, perhaps viewing him as responsible for the fate of the children as victims and victuals.

## Setting: Samaria under Siege

This story is set on the walls of Israel's capital city. Biblical accounts describe Samaria as established by Omri (1 Kgs 16:23–24) with an ivory palace built by his son, Ahab (1 Kgs 22:39). Constructed on a hill, Samaria's name may be related to שמר "to guard or watch."[1] This adds irony to this narrative since the city is unable to guard itself against invaders. Hermann Niemann explains that Samaria functioned primarily as a home for the Israelite king before the Assyrian invasion.[2] Since the king is so closely

---

1. Samaria had a strategic location, standing approximately three hundred feet above the surrounding valleys. For background information on Samaria, see James D. Purvis, "Samaria," n.p., *ABD* on *CD-ROM*. Version 2.1. 1997. For a succinct archaeological overview of this city, with attention to the walls and the city's role as a royal acropolis, see Volkmar Fritz, *The City in Ancient Israel* (Sheffield: Sheffield Academic Press, 1995), 128–31.

2. See Hermann Michael Niemann, "Royal Samaria—Capital or Residence? or: The Foundation of the City of Samaria by Sargon II," in *Ahab Agonistes: The Rise and Fall of the Omri Dynasty* (ed. Lester L. Grabbe; LHB/OTS 421; London: T&T Clark, 2007), 184–207. Niemann

associated with the capital city, Samaria's military weakness reflects the monarch's powerlessness. This sets the stage for the conflict between monarch and prophet (2 Kgs 6:30–31).

This passage begins with the Arameans effectively laying siege to Samaria, a common strategy for conquering walled cities (which the Assyrians perfected). At the sight of oncoming attackers, a town might negotiate with the enemy or pre-emptively surrender. Refusal to capitulate could have severe consequences if the enemy triumphed.[3] To gain entry to a city, the attackers could scale the surrounding walls, try to break them down, or dig underneath. However, these tactics took time and resources, including siege engines and materials to build ramps. The attacking army might also gain entry through a water duct or cut off access to water and food supplies, a process called circumvallation, ravaging the population.[4] Multiple biblical texts, including 2 Kgs 6:24–31,[5] testify to how horrendous and deadly siege warfare could prove to be for a city's residents.

## Characters

### Two Kings

The name given to the king of Aram, Ben-Hadad, appears to suggest a general title,[6] although he is sometimes identified as Ben-hadad III, son of Hazael.[7] The theophoric element in the king's name invokes the storm

---

summarizes, "Samaria was no traditional capital city. It was merely a mountain stronghold (Heb. עיר) for the court and family of a mobile warrior king" (p. 199). He concludes that Sargon was responsible for establishing Samaria as a military and economic center, so the Assyrian king ironically deserves credit as the city's true founder (pp. 202–3).

3. For further detail, see Jacob L. Wright, "Warfare and Wanton Destruction: A Reexamination of Deuteronomy 20:19–20 in Relation to Ancient Siegecraft," *JBL* 127.3 (2008): 423–58, esp. pp. 430–32.

4. For further information about siege warfare, especially during the Neo-Assyrian period, see Duncan B. Campbell, *Besieged: Siege Warfare in the Ancient World* (Oxford: Osprey, 2006), 7–13. For a wider historical survey of this military strategy, see Paul K. Davis, *Besieged: An Encyclopedia of Great Sieges from Ancient Times to the Present* (Santa Barbara, CA: ABC-CLIO, 2001). For an overview of ancient siege machinery, see Stager and King, *Life in Biblical Israel*, 237–39. For discussion of Assyrian siege warfare accompanied by agricultural destruction, see Jeremy D. Smoak, "Assyrian Siege Warfare Imagery and the Background of a Biblical Curse," in *Writing and Reading War: Rhetoric, Gender, and Ethics in Biblical and Modern Contexts* (ed. Brad E. Kelle and Frank Ritchel Ames; SBLSymS 42; Leiden: Brill, 2008), 83–91.

5. See also 2 Kgs 18:9–11; 25:1–3; Jer 32:24; 52:5–6; 2 Chr 32:9–11.

6. See Moore, *God Saves*, 96 n. 1; and Jones, *1 and 2 Kings*, 339.

7. Robinson (*Second Kings*, 65), Hens-Piazza (*Kings*, 270), Cogan and Tadmor (*II Kings*, 79), and Gray (*Kings*, 470) make the historical connection to Ben-Hadad III due to Aram's political advantage during his reign, when this kingdom could impose a prolonged siege. However, the chronology of Ben-Hadad III does not neatly correspond with this biblical

god, Hadad, underscoring the theological overtones of this political conflict.[8] The Aramean king is a victorious military leader who enacts a crippling siege upon Samaria (v. 24), before disappearing from the story.

Embodying the conflict between the nations, the anonymous and weakened king of Israel appears both helpless and angry. Most scholars infer this is Jehoram (also called Joram), son of Ahab and Jezebel (2 Kgs 3:1–2), since this story is set during the account of his reign (2 Kgs 3:1–8:15).[9] Others speculate it might be Jehoahaz or Joash,[10] but as with the Aramean king, the narrator does not provide names.

The king undergoes a striking transformation. As the story opens, he wanders on the city walls, perhaps surveying the wracked Samaria. When the woman first calls to him, he seems annoyed, incorrectly anticipating that she has come seeking food (2 Kgs 6:26–27). By citing the store houses (v. 27b), obviously drained of all supplies, the ruler seems almost sardonic. Yet upon hearing this supplicant's gruesome story (vv. 28–29), the king is moved. He demonstrates humility (v. 30), then turns on Elisha seeking vengeance (v. 31). In this short episode, the king moves from being uncaring or paralyzed to sarcastic, then contrite, and finally irate. The fate of two hapless boys has turned the king's rancor into rage.[11]

## Two Mothers

Like the kings, the mothers in this story are anonymous. Commentators tend to refer to them as "cannibal mothers." However, as Gina Hens-

---

account. For further discussion and a chart of the kings of Aram with corresponding biblical passages, see "The Ben-Hadads of the Old Testament" in Hafþórsson, *A Passing Power*, 178–81. For additional analysis on the identity of the king, see Wayne T. Pitard, "Ben-Hadad," n.p., *ABD on CD Rom*. Version 2.1. 1997.

8. While Hadad is frequently viewed as another name for Baal, J. C. Greenfield notes that the two gods are distinct deities in the time that this story is set: Baal has become the Canaanite manifestation and Hadad is the primary god of the Arameans. See J. C. Greenfield, "Hadad," in *Dictionary of Deities and Demons in the Bible* (ed. Karel van der Toorn, Bob Becking, and Pieter W. van der Horst; Leiden: Brill, 1999), 379.

9. See Sweeney, *Kings*, 310 and Bergen, *Elisha*, 136, among others. Stuart Lasine argues that this king is undoubtedly Jehoram because the literary portrayal of him here is consistent with the passages in which he appears named. See Stuart Lasine, "Jehoram and the Cannibal Mothers (2 Kings 6.24–33): Solomon's Judgment in an Inverted World," *JSOT* 50 (1991): 42–44. Ingo Kottsieper, however, thinks 2 Kgs 6–7 was originally a story about Ahab, later connected with the prophet Elisha. See Ingo Kottsieper, "The Tel Dan Inscription (*KAI* 310) and the Political Relations between Aram-Damascus and Israel in the First Half of the First Millennium BCE," in Grabbe, *Ahab Agonistes*, 123–24.

10. Gray, *Kings*, 471; Uffenheimer, *Early Prophecy*, 458.

11. T. R. Hobbs notes this transformation: "The king of Israel emerges as a real threat for the prophet and assumes strength as a character" (Hobbs, *2 Kings*, 75). C. L. Seow comments that the king's threat heaps more death into the scene of famine ("Kings," 204).

Piazza notes, this characterization is laden with condemnation.[12] Those who never know starvation should be slow to judge actions provoked by wretched desperation.

Nonetheless, the woman who appeals to the king fails to garner sympathy. She recounts, in a strikingly straightforward manner, that she has boiled and eaten her own son (2 Kgs 6:29a). If she feels any remorse, she hides it well. She does not confess any wrongdoing, ask for food, or testify to her suffering. Rather, her complaint centers on a lack of justice: the woman who proposed the bargain (v. 28b) has hidden her son, cheating the other mother, whose son *was* eaten, out of a subsequent meal (v. 29b). Guilt, shame, sorrow, and regret are overtaken by the drive to survive as this character challenges ideas of what it means to be a mother.

The other mother seems to be present but silent. The supplicant mother refers to "this woman" (האשה הזאת, v. 28b), perhaps suggesting that both women appear before the king (cf. 1 Kgs 3:16–28). One woman recounts that the other woman has reneged on the bargain by hiding her son. Was this a reaction of disgust after eating the first macabre meal? Or was this her nefarious plan all along—to get some food and then abscond before fulfilling her end of the deal? The second mother emerges as a minor but complex character who initiates one plan, then follows another.

## *Two Sons*

The sons in this story are barely there, yet their ephemerality is haunting. They seem to be young, since their mothers still retain great power over their lives. Are they alive at the outset of the story? This changes the maternal violation if the eaten child has been killed for food.

The text suggests that the boys are not corpses when the story begins. Hugh Pyper notes that both women issue the identical demand, "Give up your son" (תני את־בנך, vv. 28b, 29b) suggesting that the boys were in the same condition (living or dead) at the story's start.[13] If the sons had already died before the one was eaten, the woman who calls to the king would likely have mentioned this to diminish her crime. Also, a day transpires between eating one boy and hiding the second son (v. 29), and a rot-

---

12. Gina Hens-Piazza observes, "In the case of these biblical women their only identity, 'cannibal mothers,' makes them particularly objectionable and ensures their 'otherness.' Portraying the women as eaters of their own children effectively obscures their status as victims and immunizes almost everyone against the sympathies their plight evoke" (*Nameless, Blameless, and without Shame*, 87). However, while Hens-Piazza blames the women's plight on the surrounding power structures, she nonetheless consistently calls these women "cannibal mothers" instead of adopting a more empathetic designation.

13. Hugh S. Pyper, "Judging the Wisdom of Solomon: The Two-Way Effect of Intertextuality," *JSOT* 59 (1993): 33.

ting cadaver would barely be edible, if at all. Most important, the second mother would have much more motivation to protect a living child than to hide a dead body, prompting her refusal. It therefore appears that the child who is eaten had been alive before the two women boiled and ate him. The fate of this boy is steeped in the water that cooks his bones, and in the betrayal of his own flesh and blood.

## People of Samaria

The people of Samaria turn a private matter between a ruler and two subjects into a public display of suffering. The starving populace witnesses the stricken king on the wall and notices his bare skin (2 Kgs 6:30). Perhaps the king is mourning for the child who has died (see Gen 37:34), repenting for his own inadequacy (see 1 Kgs 21:27), or lamenting over the city's utter misery (see 2 Kgs 19:1–2). As Wesley Bergen points out, the king makes himself available to the people by this public presence.[14] They look up to him and behold a monarch overcome with grief.

## Elisha

The prophet who cursed forty-two children leading to their lethal suffering (2 Kgs 2:24), now receives a death threat because of the lethal suffering of two children (2 Kgs 6:31). Perhaps the king wants to blame the only one who might have access to some relief through YHWH. As the king's anger rises, Elisha's status falls until the esteemed man of God is reduced to a fugitive hiding behind a door (2 Kgs 6:32). T. R. Hobbs observes, "He [Elisha] quickly becomes a victim rather than controller of circumstance, and every vestige of the confident prophet is lost by the end of the chapter."[15] In face of the crisis of 2 Kgs 6:24–31, Elisha failed to act. He has not shown any prescient knowledge related to a military conflict (cf. 2 Kgs 3:16–19), used his abilities to help impoverished children (cf. 2 Kgs 4:1–7), performed any salvific miracles (cf. 2 Kgs 4:32–35), or taken steps to ameliorate someone's suffering (cf. 2 Kgs 5:8–14). The king's oath reveals that he views the prophet to have power in the face of this predicament. The threat becomes a vitriolic testimony to the king's faith in

---

14. Bergen, *Elisha*, 139 n. 258. Bergen suggests that the presence of the people helps the readers to see the king "through the eyes of his adoring subjects" (p. 139). Yet the text simply portrays the people's presence, and any assessment of admiration is speculative. Conversely, in 1 Kgs 3:28 all of Israel witnesses Solomon's wisdom and stands in awe of his judgment, but no similar justice has been executed here.

15. Hobbs, *2 Kings*, 81.

Elisha and his God. The inclusion of Elisha's patronymic, בן־שפט (2 Kgs 6:31b), might sarcastically call attention to Elisha's lack of judgment (Heb. שפט). This story of the starving mothers and their sons offers a mordant portrayal of Elisha as unaware, unconcerned, or inept.

## Re-viewing the Plot from a Childist Perspective

Second Kings 6:24–31 is part of a larger plot (2 Kgs 6:24–7:20) that weaves together various episodes on the same day. Earlier in this chapter, the Arameans have tried to capture Elisha, only to be captured by Elisha. With YHWH's help, the Arameans are struck with blindness and led into Samaria, where they are easy prey (2 Kgs 6:8–20). The Israelite king asks Elisha if he should kill the Arameans (v. 21). Instead Elisha counsels the king to feed the enemy troops and let them return to their master (v. 22). Going beyond this instruction, the king of Israel provides a lavish feast for these captured Arameans, thereby ending their attacks (v. 23). In the next verse, however, the king of Aram musters all his forces to lay siege to Samaria (v. 24). While the narrative allows for a gap between the peace and hostility (ויהי אחרי־כן, v. 24a), the transition is nonetheless awkward.[16] Still, the theme of food takes the reader from feast to famine to morbid meal.

The narrator shows the increasing severity of the situation in Samaria. Even disgusting "food" is prohibitively expensive. A donkey's head is fetching eighty pieces of silver (2 Kgs 6:25b). A quarter of a kab of dove's dung (רבע הקב דביונים, v. 25b),[17] most likely indicating a (carob?) husk,[18]

---

16. Some commentators see this juxtaposition of peace and war as entirely congruous. T. R. Hobbs suggests that the Aramean king responds violently in retaliation for the shame suffered by the Arameans who were fed and released (2 *Kings*, 79). Peter Leithart thinks the change between v. 23 and v. 24 may contrast two distinct military strategies: sending raiding parties vs. laying siege. He also proffers the possibility that several years have transpired between these two verses, and the famine of this passage is the same as 2 Kgs 8:1 (*Kings*, 207–8). More likely is Leah Bronner's assessment that the material is simply arranged loosely (*Elijah and Elisha*, 28; similarly, see Skinner, *Kings*, 306).

17. This follows the *qere*. See BDB, 179; *HALOT* 1:208.

18. This item is otherwise unknown in the Hebrew Bible. While commentators generally agree that one-fourth of a kab roughly equals a pint, the significance of the "dove's dung" is elusive. Josephus hypothesized that this substance was used like salt (*Antiquities* 9.4.4) and Rashi thought the dung might be sought for kindling (Rosenberg, *II Kings*, 284). Hens-Piazza suggests that the seeds in dove's dung would be valued to plant (*Kings*, 271), but seedlings would take a long time to yield a harvest, making this interpretation unlikely. All of these readings, however, overlook the fact that to collect a pint of droppings from a small bird would be very time-consuming and provide a commodity that would be understandably, and not surprisingly, expensive. Different foods have been suggested, such as "roasted chick

is being sold for five silver coins. People are paying high prices to eat garbage, and the food in Samaria will become even worse, moving from repulsive to horrifying.

The scene then focuses on the king of Israel upon the city wall and the woman who calls to him. She likely raises her voice,[19] while addressing the king appropriately (הושיעה אדני המלך, v. 26b). Ironically, the woman shows her regard for social decorum although she has just eaten her own child; she is both courteous and depraved. Her words may suggest a source of help, as her appeal (הושיעה) rings with an echo of Elisha's name.

The king refuses his respectful subject's request. As Burke Long points out, this violates the topos of a person [usually a woman] seeking help from a king or prophet who grants her petition.[20] The king's answer raises theological questions as he shifts the blame for responsibility from himself to YHWH (אל־יושעך יהוה, v. 27aα). Literal renderings of this phrase "Let not YHWH help you" or "No, let YHWH help you" render the king noticeably callous, bordering on mean. English translations frequently combine this clause (אל־יושעך יהוה, v. 27aα) with the subsequent one (מאין אושיעך, v. 27aβ) to suggest that if YHWH has not helped the woman, the king is unable to do so.[21] The king assumes that the woman wants something to eat; by mentioning the threshing floor and wine press (see also Num 18:27, 30; Deut 15:14; 16:13), he highlights that there is neither grain nor grape. Yet he seems to have heard her plea, using the verb ישע twice in his denial (אל־יושעך יהוה מאין אושיעך, v. 27a). The king's words also evoke the presence, and perhaps power, of Elisha (אלישע).

Immediately after admitting his lack of resources, the king seems to change his mind and ask the woman what he can do for her (ויאמר־לה

---

peas" (Farrar, *Second Kings*, 77) and "white meal" (see Jones, *Kings*, vol. 2, 432), but these seem inappropriately appetizing. Most convincing is the interpretation endorsed by Cogan and Tadmor (*II Kings*, 79) that this term is related to the Akkadian "dove's dung" (*ḫalla/zē summāti*) indicating inedible husks. Like a donkey's head, this barely consumable item is normally discarded.

19. Ziony Zevit notes this passage among a list of addresses in the Elijah and Elisha cycles that signal the start of direct discourse with the verb צעק (see also Kgs 20:39; 2 Kgs 2:12; 4:1, 40; 6:5). He suggests that this use of צעק is 'odd' because "there is no pragmatic reason to assume that any shouting is involved" (*Religions of Ancient Israel*, 487 n. 34). However, in 2 Kgs 6:26 the woman must call loudly to be heard by the king on the wall.

20. Desperate women seek assistance from a king (2 Sam 14:4–11; 1 Kgs 3:16–28; 2 Kgs 8:5–6) or a prophet (2 Kgs 4:1–7). Only in 2 Kgs 6:26–31 does the supplicant not receive any help. See Long, *2 Kings*, 92, 96.

21. Reading אל־יושעך יהוה (v. 27aα) as a negative protasis with a jussive verb (GKC §109h), combined with מאין אושיעך (v. 27aβ), the KJV and JPS translate, "If the Lord do not help thee, whence shall I help thee?" Similarly, the NJB reads, "'If Yahweh does not help you,' he retorted, 'where can I find help for you?'" See Burney, *Notes on Kings*, 289 and Gray, *Kings*, 467 n. d.

המלך מה־לך, v. 28a). The woman responds with an unflinching account of another woman's dire plan. The mother is to give her son (תני את־בנך, v. 28b) for food. She acquiesces, seemingly without compunction, and matter-of-factly relates, "So we boiled my son and we ate him" (v. 29a).[22] When the woman who has eaten her son becomes hungry the next day, she focuses on the boy she wants to eat, and not the boy she once had.

In a gesture equated with contrition and mourning, the king rends his garments to reveal sackcloth underneath (v. 30).[23] However, the king does not directly address the women's degenerate action or morose destitution. He does not confront or comfort either mother, nor does he take steps to protect the child who is hiding. Kings were responsible for protecting the weak,[24] but this king prefers to place the blame squarely on Elisha. Violence continues as the death of a child leads to a death threat against a prophet (v. 31).[25] In addition to expecting help from the prophet, the king may also be enraged because Elisha had previously instructed him to feed the captured Arameans and set them free (2 Kgs 6:20–23), and they returned to besiege the city. Once the king had power and used it for peace, but now he is impotent in time of war.

Although this story relates the ghastly demise of one child and suggests the fearful cowering of another, some scholars categorize it as comedic. Alexander Rofé views this incident as part of the larger story of Samaria's siege and remarks, "While displaying a broad epic perspective, it [2 Kgs 6:24–7:20] integrates its folkloristic elements into a single unit, in which humor, though macabre, is the dominant vein."[26] Stuart Lasine similarly describes the mother before the king in 2 Kgs 6:24–31 as a comic character, who clings to her desire with a rigid focus that obscures all else. Citing H. Bergson, Lasine notes that the audience is prompted to laugh as a social corrective to the objectionable behavior that disappears

---

22. In recounting this plot, Robert LaBarbera summarizes, "Then he [the king of Israel] learns that the woman is suffering because she had been tricked by another woman into eating her own child." See Robert LaBarbera, "The Man of War and the Man of God: Social Satire in 2 Kings 6:8–7:20," *CBQ* 46 (1984): 645. However, she acted with full awareness that she was eating her son.

23. Commentators suggest various reasons for this royal response, ranging from genuine contrition and a humble appeal for divine aid to a false piety and selfish desire to divert attention away from any royal culpability. See Sweeney, *Kings*, 311. Gina Hens-Piazza (*Kings*, 272) suggests that the king's sackcloth reveals him as choosing to fast (see 1 Kgs 21:27; Jonah 3:5–8), while everyone else is forced to starve. Ernst Würthwein (*Könige,* vol. 2, 311) reads the rending of garments as theological, as the king appeals for divine aid.

24. See Fensham, "Widow, Orphan, and the Poor," 129–39.

25. Hens-Piazza views the king's action as one of moral indignation, as spiraling violence continues. See Gina Hens-Piazza, "Forms of Violence and the Violence of Forms: Two Cannibal Mothers before a King (2 Kings 6:24–33)," *JFSR* 14 (1998): 99.

26. Rofé, *Prophetical Stories*, 66.

before its ramifications are ever explored.²⁷ The characters enter, exit, and act quickly, as in comedy. Also, comedy often appeals to base—and even violent—instincts.²⁸

Yet the tragedy of this tale overtakes any chilling humor. People are starving and children are viewed as food, provoking reactions of shock, pity, and grief. Both monarch and prophet have failed to prevent a child's death. This story fits the definition of tragedy as "a dramatization of an individual's sense of life and society as constantly under threat from the arbitrary chances of fate and humanity's own innate savagery."²⁹ Even worse, the boys might have been spared this terror if the famine had ended just one day earlier (2 Kgs 7:16).

## Childist Interpretation: Motherhood Deconstructed and Childhood Destroyed

The fleeting but gripping story in 2 Kgs 6:24–31 subverts common expectations of mothers. More typically, the Bible portrays women who desperately yearn for children, especially sons (e.g., Gen 16:1–2; 29:31–30:24; 1 Sam 1:1–20), assuring the women's places in society. Commentators often pass subtle judgment on women who are not mothers. As Leah Bronner observes, "No other biblical woman, whether wife, sister or daughter, seems to enjoy the same status and power as the mother. As the mother of the Bible cares for her clan, she does so with wisdom and purpose, acquiring authority and position within the household and beyond."³⁰ Other female characters, notably Miriam (Exodus 15; Numbers 12; 20:1; 26:59; Deut 24:9; Mic 6:4; 1 Chr 5:29 [Eng. 6:3]), Deborah (Judges 4–5), and Huldah (2 Kgs 22:14–20 [2 Chr 34:22–28]), indeed play important roles in Israel's tradition with no reference to their having children. However, most biblical women come to light as they birth and nurture sons.

---

27. Lasine, "Jehoram and the Cannibal Mothers," 33. Lasine further compares this to the story of the Levite's concubine in Judges 19, where he also finds comedy in a tragic tale. "The Levite's absurd lack of awareness and his narrow focus on the petty goal of beginning the journey home serve the same function as the comic obliviousness and social myopia of the cannibal mother of 2 Kings 6. In both stories grotesque humor conveys the essence of an inverted world in which social relations have totally broken down" (p. 39). For further discussion of the elements of humor in this story, see Harald Schweizer, *Elischa in den Kriegen* (SANT 37; Munich: Kösel, 1974), 423–24.

28. For discussion of comedy in literature and drama, see "Comedy," in *The Routledge Dictionary of Literary Terms* (ed. Peter Childs and Roger Fowler; London: Routledge, 2006), 28–29.

29. See "Tragedy," in *The Routledge Dictionary of Literary Terms* (ed. Peter Childs and Roger Fowler; London: Routledge, 2006), 241.

30. Bronner, *Biblical Mothers*, ix.

Ideas about mothers are held sacred, from ancient times through modern society. Societies commonly assume that a mother will be her child's primary caretaker. Once a child is born, the woman's main concerns are expected to shift (instantly and naturally) to her offspring. A limitless drive to protect and provide for children, even at the expense of the mother's own health or safety, is often viewed as a "maternal instinct."[31] The story of the starving mothers strikingly deconstructs maternal ideologies that many people, spanning millennia, view to be natural.[32]

The women in 2 Kgs 6:24–31 raise questions about a mother's choice to put herself before her children. Is it fair to expect self-abnegation that leads to death, even if children are involved? Gina Hens-Piazza argues that the women are blamed for their actions, but the text uses them to divert responsibility from the patriarchal power structure that created the siege and surrounding structures of oppression.[33] Raw hunger leads a mother to cook her son, showing how unpredictable all people (including mothers) can become under extreme duress. The traits traditionally associated with motherhood—love, loyalty, protection, and advocacy—disappear in this story, just like grain in times of famine.

Does any sense of childhood exist for these boys? If motherhood is a cultural amalgamation of shared ideas that accrue to birthing and raising a child, what are the expectations regarding childhood here? Clearly, modern assumptions about children's entitlements are entirely absent for these two boys whose story is shrouded in famine, fear, and death. Yet the

---

31. Historical, sociological, and anthropological studies call these "natural" assumptions about motherhood into question. Like childhood, motherhood is a social construct that varies widely in different places, times, and cultures. For a historical overview of motherhood beginning with the Enlightenment, see Aminatta Forna, *Mother of All Myths: How Society Moulds and Constrains Mothers* (London: HarperCollins, 1998), 25–45. For an anthropological cross-cultural study that includes discussion of mother-child relationships, see Whiting, *Six Cultures*.

32. Sociologist Sharon Hays notes that the presumption of mothers caring for children is largely unquestioned, but *how* mothers should do this is fiercely debated (with mothers and opinions of them at the focus). She recounts the strong reactions that motherhood evokes and wryly observes, "I sometimes believe that my public presentations would meet with equal levels of success and failure if I simply stood before the audience and chanted the word *mothering* over and over. It seems that the word itself, without any embellishments on my part, is a highly provocative one." See Sharon Hays, *The Cultural Contradictions of Motherhood* (New Haven: Yale University Press, 1996), ix.

33. Hens-Piazza suggests, "The women do not so much represent social and moral decay as they stand as victims of these parasitic conditions. They and their children represent an expiatory offering bearing the iniquities of the whole society" ("Forms of Violence," 102). However, as W. Brian Aucker points out, other women in the text find ways to strategize and resist deadly forces in efforts to save children (e.g., Exod 1:8–2:10; 2 Kgs 11:1–4). See W. Brian Aucker, review of Gina Hens-Piazza, *Nameless, Blameless, and without Shame: Two Cannibal Mothers before a King*, RBL 6 (2004): 234.

text underscores the intimate relationship of the parent-child bond by reiterating the word "son" five times in a span of two verses (2 Kgs 6:28–29), even as this relationship becomes grotesquely twisted.[34] The consumed son and his starving mother know macabre union, as once again he becomes bone of her bone and flesh of her flesh.

## Insights about Children: Defenseless unto Death

The boys in this story call attention to children's dependence on adults (usually parents) and their vulnerability. The boy who is not eaten can survive because his mother hides him. Even starving children may have hope with a parental advocate. The consumed son embodies a child's helplessness. While children can devise survival strategies, often they lack the knowledge or ability to find the security and supplies that are necessary to save their own lives.

The shock in this narrative stems from a mother eating her offspring intentionally.[35] This raises questions about the motivation for cannibalism, which varies widely in different historical and anthropological contexts. Cannibalism (or anthropophagy) may be prompted by famine, although extreme hunger can be met by many responses.[36] Cannibalism can also be a ritual practice, a violation of a taboo, or an act of enemy aggression.[37] Anthropologists caution against using cannibalism to draw clear distinctions among cultures, viewing cannibals as savage, primitive, crude, base,

---

34. The word "son" appears in rapid succession, each time with a possessive suffix. The first four instances form a chiasm between "my son" and "your son," linguistically mirroring the women's wrangling (v. 28bα, בנך; v. 28bβ, בני; v. 29aα, בני; v. 29bα, בנך). The last reference is to "her son" (v. 29bβ, בנה), as the hidden boy is one step removed from this tug of war.

35. Mario Liverani reads 2 Kgs 6:24–31 as an example of actual cannibalism as part of a legalized practice in time of siege. See Mario Liverani, *Israel's History and the History of Israel* (trans. Chiara Peri and Philip R. Davies; London: Equinox, 2005), 126–27.

36. The text shows various recourses to extreme poverty, often prompted by famine. These include the sale of possessions or land (Gen 47:15–20; Neh 5:3), migration (Gen 12:10; 26:1; Gen 42:1–5; Ruth 1:1; 2 Kgs 8:1–2), selling or relinquishing one's children (Exod 21:7; 2 Kgs 4:1–7; Neh 5:5) or oneself (Lev 25:39) into slavery, and appeals for help (2 Kgs 4:1, 38–41).

37. Peggy Reeves Sanday notes the many potential meanings of cannibalism, including responses to famine or as tools of social formation. "In many cases, ritual cannibalism physically enacts a cultural theory (of order and chaos, good and evil, death and reproduction) that enables humans to regulate desire, to build and maintain social order. As a symbol of chaos, cannibalism is equated with all that must be dominated, controlled, or repressed in the establishment of the social order." See Peggy Reeves Sanday, *Divine Hunger: Cannibalism as a Cultural System* (Cambridge: Cambridge University Press, 1986), 214.

or evil.³⁸ While this is not to condone cannibalism, modern, Western cultures are not entirely devoid of such tendencies, as histories of cannibalism amply document.³⁹

Cannibalism in the Hebrew Bible portrays Israelites eating one another. Generally, this punishment is threatened or meted directly by YHWH (Lev 26:29; Deut 28:53–57; Isa 49:26; Jer 19:9; Ezek 5:10) or results from the destruction that YHWH has allowed (Lam 2:20; 4:10).⁴⁰ A majority of these texts use language that implies children are the victims (בשר את בשר בניהם: Deut 28:53; בשר בניך ובנתיך: Lev 26:29; בניכם ובשר בנתיכם); עללי טפחים: Ezek 5:10; בנים: Deut 28:53; פרי־בטנך: Jer 19:9; ואת בשר בנתיהם Lam 2:20; ילדיהן: Lam 4:10).⁴¹ Deuteronomy 28:53–57 warns of covenant violations that result in inhabitants of besieged towns eating their children (Deut 28:53), refusing to share their grisly meals, and begrudging even family members (Deut 28:54–57). The appalling threat of Deut 28:53–57 finds fulfillment in 2 Kgs 6:24–31. The consumed son is the only individual child actually eaten within a narrative, outside of general portrayals or warnings.

The cooking and consuming of the boy is graphic: ונבשל את־בני ונאכלהו "then we boiled my son and we ate him" (v. 29a). The verb בשל in the *piel* means "to boil, cook, fry." In nearly every other instance where בשל appears in this stem, it pertains to food.⁴² Humans are the object of this verb in Lam 4:10, which also portrays mothers cooking and eating their own children. The women in Lam 4:10 are explicitly called compassionate (רחמניות),⁴³ showing that good people are capable of such acts (see also

---

38. In the foreword to *Eating Their Words: Cannibalism and the Boundaries of Cultural Identity*, Maggie Kilgour explains that the label of "cannibal" has been used to brand and demonize cultures. This has made cannibalism "a myth constructed about others that cultures have used to justify hate and aggression." Yet, she maintains, "that difference is illusory: the cannibal is us. For a post-holocaust culture especially, the question of whether one can distinguish civilization from barbarism seems especially urgent, yet difficult." See Kristen Guest, ed., *Eating Their Words: Cannibalism and the Boundaries of Cultural Identity* (Albany: State University of New York Press, 2001), vii, viii. For further discussion, see Guest's introductory essay, pp. 1–9.

39. For a history of cannibalism that focuses primarily on Western culture, see Mark P. Donnelly and Daniel Diehl, *Eat Thy Neighbor: A History of Cannibalism* (Phoenix Mill, England: Sutton, 2006). For reference to 2 Kgs 2:24–31, see p. 6. See also Moira Martingale, *Cannibal Killers: The History of Impossible Murders* (New York: Carroll & Graf, 1993).

40. For discussion of cannibalism in the Bible as an indicator of greater social destruction, see Lasine, "Jehoram and the Cannibal Mothers," 32–33.

41. For comparison of these texts in their literary contexts, see Michel, *Gott und Gewalt*, 213–45. Michel notes that *teknophagie* (i.e., the eating of children) surfaces in times of crisis throughout ancient Near Eastern literature, pp. 200–213.

42. See *HALOT* 1:164. See Exod 12:9; 16:23; 23:19; 34:26; Lev 6:21 [Eng. 6:28]; Num 6:19; 11:8; Deut 14:21; 16:7; 1 Sam 2:13, 15; 2 Sam 13:8; 1 Kgs 19:21; 2 Kgs 4:38; Ezek 46:20, 24; Zech 14:21; 2 Chr 35:13.

43. The association between the "compassionate women" (רחמניות) and "womb" (רחם)

Deut 28:53–57). In these passages, as elsewhere, human meat is children's flesh.[44]

The upsetting image of mothers and fathers eating their sons and daughters may paradoxically indicate children's worth. These descriptions frequently function as warnings to scare the intended audience. For fear of being reduced to parental cannibals, the people are to obey YHWH. Stuart Lasine notes that child cannibalism has societal ramifications. "In the biblical context, the eating of children is both cultural and religious suicide, for it is through the children that the covenant with Yahweh is kept alive."[45] Violence against children continues as the text fails to offer any defense or recourse to the starving mothers' sons.

## Children and Textual Connections

Second Kings 6:24–31 recalls the prostitutes' dispute and appeal to King Solomon in 1 Kgs 3:16–28. In both stories, mothers lacking the aegis of a husband or father beseech a king to provide mediation regarding their sons (1 Kgs 3:16; 2 Kgs 6:26). One son has died due to maternal action (1 Kgs 3:19; 2 Kgs 6:28–29a) and the other comes perilously close to death (1 Kgs 3:24–25; 2 Kgs 6:29b). The woman calling to the king portrays herself as wronged by another woman's deception (1 Kgs 3:17–21; 2 Kgs 6:29b). Both kings respond (1 Kgs 3:23–27; 2 Kgs 6:30–31), although justice may remain elusive (2 Kgs 6:31).

While scholars direct their attention to the women and kings in comparing these two stories,[46] the children also merit scrutiny. The sons of the prostitutes are infants, just a few days old (1 Kgs 3:17–18); the sons of the starving mothers are young but not necessarily babies. Under Solomon's

---

links the children's death with their birth. For detailed discussion of this metaphor, see Phyllis Trible, *God and the Rhetoric of Sexuality* (OBT; Philadelphia: Fortress, 1978), 31–59.

44. The only other instance where a specific kind of person is eaten is Zech 11:9: תאכלנה אשה את־בשר רעותה "let a woman eat the flesh of her friend [fem.]." This portrays a woman as both perpetrator and victim of cannibalism, although English translations tend to erase the female agents, despite the feminine subject, verb form, and object. See, for example, the ASV: "let them that are left eat every one the flesh of another"; KJV: "let the rest eat every one the flesh of another"; JPS: "let them that are left eat every one the flesh of another"; RSV, NRSV: "let those that are left devour the flesh of one another"; and NJPS: "let the rest devour each other's flesh!" Isaiah 49:26; Mic 3:3; and Ps 14:4 also portray cannibalism without specific reference to children. As noted above, Lev 26:29; Deut 28:53; 2 Kgs 6:29; Jer 19:9, Ezek 5:10; and Lam 2:20; 4:10 all suggest children as cannibals' food.

45. Lasine, "Jehoram and the Cannibal Mothers," 35.

46. For a lively exchange of different interpretations of these two stories, see Lasine, "Jehoram and the Cannibal Mothers"; Pyper, "Judging the Wisdom of Solomon"; and Stuart Lasine, "The Ups and Downs of Monarchical Justice: Solomon and Jehoram in an Intertextual World," *JSOT* 59 (1993): 37–53. See also, Michel, *Gott und Gewalt*, 218–19.

rule, two boys know peace, and one child's death is accidental. Under Samaria's siege, two boys know war, and one child's death is intentional. The harlot's baby who remains alive gets returned to his rightful mother.[47] The son who escapes the cannibalistic pact survives due to his mother's protection. Children's fates—in war or peace—often depend on their parents.

The boy who narrowly escapes a cannibalistic demise shares similarities with the young prince Joash (2 Kgs 11:1–4). When Athaliah's son, Ahaziah, is killed in Jehu's coup, Athaliah murders the remaining heirs to the throne and rules as queen for six years. Only the one-year-old Joash survives, hidden by his aunt Jehosheba and cared for by his nurse. Jehosheba is the daughter of Jehoram, arguably the same king who walks on Samaria's wall in 2 Kgs 6:26. Both the hidden son in 2 Kgs 6:29 and young Joash in 2 Kgs 11:1–3 are saved by one woman as they escape the homicidal intentions of another. Joash (also called Jehoash) is returned to the throne by the priest Jehoiada, and becomes king of Judah (2 Kgs 11:4–21). His legacy is assured in biblical tradition (2 Kgs 12:1–22 [Eng. 11:21–12:21]; 2 Chr 22:10–12; 23–24) and he reigns for forty years (2 Kgs 12:1). Women working together to save the life of a child rescue the Davidic line from extinction (cf. Exod 1:15–2:10). Two boys are hidden (2 Kgs 6:29; 2 Kgs 11:2), but only the prince has a legacy (2 Kgs 11:21–12:2).

The consumed son finds grim company with other children eaten by their parents as victims (Lam 2:20, 4:10) or part of a threatening curse (Lev 26:29; Deut 28:53–57; Jer 19:9; Ezek 5:10). None of these passages specifies that the children are dead prior to consumption, although commentators may presume this to be the case.[48] Indeed, if such violence intends to jolt the reader with unimaginable behavior, the level of atrocity reaches its pinnacle when killing one's own child to eat him or her. Deuteronomy 28:53–57 cautions against dismissing child cannibalism because even the most refined person can succumb to ingesting his or her offspring. If no parent is immune from such behavior, then no child is completely safe.

---

47. Adele Reinhartz notes how 1 Kgs 3:16–28 defines motherhood, even as it deconstructs it, as one mother is willing to chop a baby in half. A reconstructed view of motherhood has the woman who advocates for the child's life as his mother, regardless of biological attachment. Reinhartz's interpretation, while compelling, overlooks the physical connection between mother and son in the text as (lit.) her womb grows warm for her son (כי־נכמרו רחמיה על־בנה, v. 26aα). For comparison of 1 Kgs 3:16–28 and 2 Kgs 6:26–30, see Adele Reinhartz, "Anonymous Women and the Collapse of the Monarchy: A Study in Narrative Technique," in *A Feminist Companion to Samuel and Kings* (ed. Athalya Brenner; FCB 5; Sheffield: Sheffield Academic Press, 1994), 52–55.

48. E.g., Johan Renkema comments on the mothers in Lam 4:10, "These very [maternal] feelings, however, are the source of the enormous tension set up by what the famine is forcing them to do: to cook the flesh of their dead offspring." See Johan Renkema, *Lamentations* (Leuven: Peeters, 1998), 519. Likewise, Hobbs, *2 Kings*, 80. However, the text does not state that the children are already dead.

Like Isaac, the consumed son is to be killed by a parent (Gen 22:1–19). But no angel halts the murder. Like Moses, the consumed son is a victim of politics far beyond his control (Exod 1:15–2:10). But no royal personage comes to his rescue. Like Jephthah's daughter, the consumed son dies as the result of a parental pact (Judg 11:29–40). But no one remembers his sacrifice. From a childist perspective, the story of 2 Kings 6:24–31 is a juvenile text of terror.

In *Texts of Terror*, Phyllis Trible's feminist analysis of selected stories in the Hebrew Bible, Trible maintains that the Levite's concubine of Judges 19 stands out among biblical characters for her unsurpassed powerlessness. This raped woman is without name, speech, power, or friends. She is used by the text and the people around her. Her humanity is denied and no one mourns her death.[49] The consumed son of 2 Kgs 6:24–31 suffers all this and more. The Levite's concubine tries to save herself (Judg 19:26). The consumed son is deprived of action. The dismembered body of the Levite's concubine serves as a violent remembrance (Judg 19:29–30). The digested body of the consumed son disappears. The Levite's concubine, in Trible's debt, has a story that is widely known. The consumed son has been swallowed into biblical obscurity. He is the least of all characters in the Hebrew Bible.

---

49. Trible, *Texts of Terror*, 80–81.

# 10

# Epilogue: The Boy Restored to Life (2 Kings 8:1–6)

The boy whose birth the prophet foretold (2 Kgs 4:12–17), and whose death the prophet reversed (2 Kgs 4:32–37), now reappears in a subsequent story. Elisha tells the mother of this revived boy (i.e., the Shunammite) to leave the land because a famine is approaching that will last for seven years. She follows his advice and goes with her family to Philistia, and remains there for the duration. Upon returning home, the woman beseeches the king for her house and her field back. Coincidentally, the king had been asking Gehazi about Elisha's great deeds. Just as Gehazi is recounting the story of the boy whom Elisha brought back from death, this very mother appears making her appeal to the king. Gehazi exclaims that this is the woman and her son whom Elisha revived. The king and woman converse, prompting the king to send an official to ensure that everything be returned to her, including the income from the land during the time she had been away. Filial and terrestrial restoration come to this woman through association with Elisha.

## The Boy Restored to the Text

Second Kings 8:1–6 invites reflection on the tales of Elisha and children. Of the forty-nine children who have appeared in the Elisha cycle, only this boy reemerges later in the text. His story serves as a postscript to the tale of the Shunammite (2 Kgs 4:8–37) with recurring characters and a plot that recalls the previous episode. In the second act, the king asks to hear about all the wonders the prophet has performed (2 Kgs 8:4). Since this story has an inherent retrospective quality, 2 Kgs 8:1–6 offers an opportunity to review multiple points of correspondence with stories already discussed, rounding out this portrayal of children in the Elisha cycle.

This tale begins as Elisha's career wanes, although he does not disappear immediately after this story. He continues to be involved in political affairs, consulting with kings (2 Kgs 8:7–15; 13:14–18), instructing prophets (2 Kgs 9:1–3), and foretelling the future (2 Kgs 13:19). In a final scene that echoes Elijah's ascent (2 Kgs 2:12), Elisha dies (2 Kgs 13:14–21).[1] The wonder-worker's astounding power remains strong even in death, as a man being buried (presumably dead) revives after touching Elisha's bones (2 Kgs 13:20–21). Yet, as Robert Cohn notes, in these final stories Elisha has "a rather different prophetic persona."[2] He no longer focuses on performing impressive feats, and he deals with kings and prophets more than with average people.

## From Destruction to Deliverance (2 Kings 2:23–25)

In our first tale, Elisha showed little sympathy for children. When the children from Bethel taunt the bald prophet, he curses them in YHWH's name (2 Kgs 2:23). After two female bears tear up the children (v. 24), Elisha continues on his way (v. 25), exhibiting blithe indifference or vindictive *Schadenfreude*. Either way, the prophet exhibits no concern for the children's well-being and indeed appears to instigate their destruction.

The story of the boy brought back to life can be read as a corrective, or at least a critique, of the earlier (and less experienced?) Elisha. The prophet who had cursed children now looks out for the life of a child. Second Kings 8:1–6 underscores the prophet's connection to the child as his mother (previously called "that Shunammite" in 2 Kgs 4:12, 25, 36) is now known as "the woman whose son he had restored to life" (האשה אשר־החיה את־בנה, 2 Kgs 8:1, 5). When the mother and son appear before the king, Gehazi calls attention to them (זאת האשה וזה־בנה אשר־החיה אלישע, v. 5b), extolling the prophet's miracle.

The prophet now seems to understand how much children can matter. When Elisha instructs the woman to seek refuge during the seven years of the famine, he instructs her, "get up and go—you and your household" (קומי ולכי את וביתך[3], 2 Kgs 8:1a). The prophet's reference to her household (ביתך) includes her son, perhaps remembering him, and delivers an unsolicited warning about the impending famine. Elisha has gone from destroying children to delivering a child to safety. As the Elisha cycle ends, the prophet's name—"God is salvation"—seems authentic.

---

1. Marsha White maintains that Elijah imitates Elisha here, since Elisha's declaration makes more sense in context (*Elijah Legends*, 14–15).

2. Cohn, *2 Kings*, 55.

3. This reading follows the *qere*, with את instead of אתי (*ketiv*), reflecting an earlier form of the feminine pronoun. See GKC § 32 *h*.

## The Power of One Child (2 Kings 3:26–27)

In the stories of the Moabite prince and the boy restored to life, Elisha functions as a seer. As a famine imperils the woman and her son (2 Kgs 8:1–6), the prophet issues a warning (v. 1). Similarly, before the battle with Moab when the kings of Judah, Israel, and Edom seek prophetic insight (2 Kgs 3:9–15), Elisha foretells what will occur (vv. 16–19). The prophet is not present at the time of conflict (2 Kgs 3:20–26) or in the court (2 Kgs 8:4) when the child enters the scene (2 Kgs 3:27; 8:5).

These two narratives show the influence a child can have on a king. The Moabite king offers his son as a holocaust, and the Israelites withdraw from battle (2 Kgs 3:26–27), giving King Mesha his victory. The Israelite king sees the woman's son as a tribute to power of Elisha (2 Kgs 8:4–6). Neither king's god, Kemosh or YHWH respectively, is directly named, but the incidents that involve children reflect the power of these deities. In 2 Kgs 3:26–27, a child loses his life and disappears. In 2 Kgs 8:4–6, a child who had lost his life re-appears. The sacrifice of Mesha's son accomplishes the goal his father desires: military retreat of the enemy (2 Kgs 3:26–27). The witness of the boy brought back to life accomplishes the goal his mother desires: restitution of her home and property (2 Kgs 8:6). Each story's denouement relies on a child.

## Advocating Mothers—Rescued Sons (2 Kings 4:1–7)

The debt-collateral children and the boy restored to life have maternal advocates. Both women have a male relative linked to Elisha (2 Kgs 4:1; 8:1), although they encounter the prophet directly themselves. Each woman faces loss: one fears relinquishing her children (2 Kgs 4:1), the other loses her house and land (2 Kgs 8:1–5). In their distress, the women call out to powerful figures (צעק: 2 Kgs 4:1, 8:5; see also 2 Kgs 6:26). The mothers heed the prophet's advice (2 Kgs 4:3–5; 8:1–2), driven by the hope of his help. Both stories end with restitution for families (2 Kgs 4:7; 8:6).

However, the role of the prophet differs markedly. In 2 Kgs 4:1–7, the prophet miraculously solves a difficult situation by saving the debt-collateral children from slavery. In 2 Kgs 8:1–6, the prophet causes problems that are temporary but distressing by sending the woman and her family away from their home.[4] His advice to sojourn (to an unspecified place) for seven years causes the woman to go with her household to the land of the Philistines (v. 2). Her time there and her trip back remain a

---

4. For discussion of a diminished portrayal of Elisha and an elevated understanding of the woman in 2 Kgs 8:1–6, see Roncace, "Elisha and the Woman of Shunem," 109–27.

mystery. Yet upon her return, she apparently discovers that her home has been taken over (v. 3). Further, the land appears to have yielded produce in the time she was away (v. 6), raising questions about the severity of the famine and the credibility of the prophet. Not surprisingly, this woman turns to the king (and not the prophet) for assistance. Elisha's glory already comes less through action than by reputation.

Both 2 Kgs 4:1–7 and 2 Kgs 8:1–6 show similar bonds between mothers and children. Mothers are the children's providers and protectors. Children are the mothers' helpers and hope. The widow's children contribute to the miracle of unending oil by gathering vessels to be filled (2 Kgs 4:5). The son brought back to life presumably accompanies his mother on her journey to Philistia as part of her household (2 Kgs 8:2) and appears with her before the king (2 Kgs 8:5). As the likely heir to the family property, this boy would have a keen interest in the king's response. Like the debt-collateral children, the restored boy has a future that depends on a powerful man. The presence of the children increases the tension of the story as their fates hang in the balance.

## New Incarnations and Relations (2 Kings 4:8–37)

Second Kgs 8:1–6 reintroduces the Shunammite woman and her son (2 Kgs 4:8–37). Most commentators view 2 Kgs 8:1–6 as a separate tale that was adjusted to link with the earlier story in 2 Kgs 4:8–37.[5] This seems likely due to the altered portrayals of the characters in this second story. Nowhere, for example, is the woman in 2 Kgs 8:1–7 called "that Shunammite," as the prophet consistently calls her in 2 Kgs 4:8–37 (vv. 12, 36: השונמית הזאת; v. 25: השונמית הלז). The woman wordlessly follows directions and seems relatively compliant in 2 Kgs 8:1–2, contrasting her previous assertiveness (2 Kgs 4:8–10, 13–17, 22–30). In the first act, the Shunammite is forthright and articulate (2 Kgs 4:9–10, 13, 16, 22–24, 28, 30). In the second act, the woman's words are cryptically hidden from the reader (2 Kgs 8:5–6). Gehazi, who had been brushed aside by the Shunammite (2 Kgs 4:25–26), rebuked by Elisha (4:27), and unable to revive the child (4:31), later appears as a *bona fide* confidante of the king (8:4–5). The boy speaks (briefly) in the first story (2 Kgs 4:19a), but remains silent in the second. In the initial episode, Elisha concerns himself with the personal affairs of the Shunammite, including matters of home (2 Kgs 4:8–13), family (4:14–17, 26–28), and restoration (4:29–37). Yet later when the woman is concerned about her home, family, and restoration (2 Kgs 8:3–5), Elisha is nowhere to be found.[6] None-

---

5. For an overview of different positions and their adherents, see Long, *2 Kings*, 98.
6. Some scholars suggest that this is because Elisha has died, although the text does not

theless, the text presents these characters as the same cast making another appearance.

The relatively long story of the Shunammite's son showcases the prophet's most impressive miracle. The king asks Gehazi to recount את כל־הגדלות "all the great things" (2 Kgs 8:4b) Elisha has performed, recalling the great woman (אשה גדלה, 2 Kgs 4:8a) of Shunem. Perhaps reminded of her by the king's use of the term גדלה, Gehazi only speaks about this woman and her son (2 Kgs 8:5). The effects of Elisha's miracles endure. Since the raised son is still alive, readers have reason to think that Elisha's miracles retain their power. As his career nears its end, the prophet focuses on politics (2 Kgs 8:7–15; 9:1–10; 13:14–21) while the story of the boy restored to life affirms Elisha's relationship with the populace.

The woman's relationship with the prophet also comes full circle. In 2 Kgs 4:11–13, the prophet offers to speak to the king or commander on her behalf, yet she refuses this assistance. He then gives her divine aid in the form of a son, for which she expressed no desire (2 Kgs 4:14–17). In the second story, the woman needs and wants divine and human help. She heeds the warning of the prophet (2 Kgs 8:1) and seeks a word with the king (8:5–6), which she had formerly eschewed (4:13). The gift that she had refused—her son—enables her restoration.

The boy appears in 2 Kgs 8:1–6, whereas his father does not. His absence causes some commentators to infer that the wife from 2 Kgs 4:8–37 is now a widow.[7] However, the husband's absence could be the result of various untold possibilities, death only one among them. When the mother and child appear before the king (2 Kgs 8:5), the son, not the father, has a silent but significant role. He is the flesh-and-blood evidence of the past miracle and a witness to present process.

## Living Testimonies to Prophetic Power (2 Kings 5:1–14)

The boy restored to life and the Israelite slave girl both contrast and coincide as characters. The boy remains silent (2 Kgs 8:5); the girl speaks

---

relay Elisha's death until 2 Kgs 13:14–21. See Hugo Gressmann, *Die älteste Geschichtsschreibung und Prophetie Israels (von Samuel bis Amos und Hosea)* (Göttingen: Vandenhoeck & Ruprecht, 1921), 295; Martin Rehm, *Die Bücher der Könige* (Würzburg: Echter, 1949), 27, 82.

7. S. Joy Osgood confidently asserts, "That the woman is now a widow seems beyond question: her husband was already old in the earlier incident (4:14), and only his death in the intervening period sufficiently accounts for his absence at this juncture." See S. Joy Osgood, "Women and Inheritance in the Land of Early Israel," in *Women in the Biblical Tradition* (ed. George J. Brooke; Lewiston, NY: Edwin Mellen, 1992), 29. See also Farrar, *Second Kings*, 88; Gray, *Kings*, 475; Hobbs, *2 Kings*, 100; Jones, *Kings*, vol. 2, 440; and Robinson, *Second Kings*, 69, among others.

(2 Kgs 5:3). He has parental protection (2 Kgs 8:2–6); she has none (2 Kgs 5:2). He presumably stands to inherit arable land (2 Kgs 8:5–6); she is a captive slave (2 Kgs 5:2). Both know foreign regions: he journeys from Israel to Philistia (2 Kgs 8:2), and she is brought from Israel to Aram (2 Kgs 5:2). The future looks bright for a young boy with a strong mother from a family with resources. The future for a foreign slave girl is bleak. These characters can be read as foils to each other, offering a range of possibilities for children's lives.

Yet the children's actions invert this relationship. The little slave girl exercises authority, speaking her mind and voicing her hope (2 Kgs 5:3). She must be known and respected since she is cited as a source of information (v. 4), and powerful people follow her suggestion (vv. 5–6). By contrast, the heir apparent to a house and revenue-producing farm is barely present. In 2 Kgs 8:5a, the woman "whose son he had revived" comes in to the king. Is the boy even there? The narrator has overlooked him, although Gehazi notes his presence: "this is the woman and this is her son whom Elisha revived" (2 Kgs 8:5b). This scion (and heir?) accompanies his mother wordlessly. The little Israelite slave girl has had to learn to speak up on her own.

Despite their differences, this boy and girl are both vehicles of restoration. The girl is small but brave, voicing an original idea that draws on her memory, affirms her beliefs (2 Kgs 5:3), and leads to Naaman's healing (2 Kgs 5:14). Without this girl, the commander might have remained afflicted. The revived boy proves Elisha's power. Seeing him and his mother, the king is convinced that their property and revenue should be restored (2 Kgs 8:6). Without this boy, the mother might have lost her land. These two children have critical roles in the plot as they enable Elisha and YHWH to prove their power.

## Starvation and Salvation (2 Kings 6:24–31)

The story of the boy restored to life answers some questions that remained open at the end of the story of the sons of the starving mothers. In 2 Kgs 6:31 when the Israelite king discovers that one mother had eaten her own child, he rends his garments and asks for Elisha's head. Why is Elisha blamed? Second Kings 8:1 provides one possibility, as Elisha warns a mother that a famine is coming and instructs her to leave the land with her family. Unlike the cannibal mothers, she is able to stave off starvation. Perhaps the prophet has learned to take responsibility for women with children, motivated by the king's death threat.

The change in Elisha's action may alter the king's attitude. The monarch who was earlier outraged with the prophet (2 Kgs 6:31) now appears as his ardent admirer (2 Kgs 8:4–6). The declaration of Gehazi, the account of the woman, and the witness of the boy convince the king to appoint an official to meet the woman's demands. Even without being present, Elisha's impact is strong.

For the child eaten by his own mother, the prophet offers no salvific power. How much of the king's anger in 2 Kgs 6:31 was prompted by his sympathy for children? The death of this boy who suffered from the siege might have been prevented. The starving mothers were not forced to come up with the plan to eat their own children, but they execute it intentionally (2 Kgs 6:28–29). Whereas the mother of the restored boy took steps to stay alive with her son (2 Kgs 8:2), another mother proceeded to boil hers (2 Kgs 6:29). Famine can prompt various responses, as the story of the boy brought back to life shows. The prophet serves the people, the king, and his own reputation when he saves lives.

## Insights about Children and Elisha

This reflective discussion has applied the last two steps of the prior analyses (*Children and Textual Connections* and *Childist Interpretation*) to the final story with a child in the Elisha cycle. In this overview, we have observed that children can remain victims, as with the sons of the starving mothers, but usually the adults interact meaningfully with the children. Elisha acts quickly when threatened by small children (2 Kgs 2:23–24). King Mesha of Moab believes that his son's sacrifice can bring victory (2 Kgs 3:26–27). The widow of the sons of the prophets finds a way to keep her children, who are at risk of being enslaved (2 Kgs 4:1–7). The Shunammite reacts with immediate concern for her son's illness and death (2 Kgs 4:18–37). Commanders and kings heed the implicit suggestion of a small girl (2 Kgs 5:1–6). Children also initiate events. The boys from Bethel incite Elisha without provocation (2 Kgs 2:23). The debt-collateral children act on their own motivation (2 Kgs 4:5). The Israelite slave girl offers an unsolicited solution for Naaman's affliction (2 Kgs 5:3). The Shunammite's son is a living witness to Elisha's power, prompting the king to restore the family's lands (2 Kgs 8:5–6). Children are vital characters in the Elisha cycle.

A comprehensive childist interpretation of this collection also deepens our understanding of Elisha. Read from this perspective, three of these stories—the Mockers from Bethel, the Moabite Prince, and the Sons of Starving Mothers—are tales of destruction. Four stories—the Debt-Collateral Children, the Shunammite's Son, the Israelite Slave Girl, and the Boy Restored to Life—are tales of restoration. All of the children face slavery, danger, or death, but Elisha is no simple saint. Rather, he is complex prophet whose power can be lethal, helpful, or absent, as revealed in his interactions with children.

# Conclusions

Childist biblical interpretation encourages resistant reading of both the Bible and commentaries, replacing the tendency to ignore child characters with focused attention on them. When I began analyzing the Elisha cycle, the textual material on the children seemed promising but thin. For the most part, biblical scholarship offered little information about the child characters, prompting the development of the demonstrated six-step process. Other scholars might find it productive to exclude the first two steps (*Setting, Characters*), which tend to be general, and concentrate on the latter four (*Reviewing the Plot from a Childist Perspective, Childist Interpretation, Insights about Children,* and *Children and Textual Connections*), which focus more overtly on the children. However, the full approach builds grounded understandings of narratives and paves the way for new discoveries about child characters.

As discussed in Part I, various words used to portray children and youth show the nuanced understandings that the writers had about young people. This vocabulary serves as an index for the culture's ideas, noting attention to children's growth, relationship, role, status, and security. Concepts of children as coddled innocents and romantic notions of childhood as a period of entitlement are anachronistic, ethnocentric, and inappropriate for biblical understanding. Rather, the text reveals awareness of children's value and vulnerablity as they progress through stages of development and assume cultural roles of increasing responsibility.

Just as the ancient society that produced these texts needed children for physical and cultural survival, the stories of the Elisha cycle rely on children to generate specific meanings. Hearing the story of the mockers of Bethel, the audience may be shocked that the prophet and his God react so violently to small children, sending the message that even children (and beasts) know Elisha's power. The effective sacrifice of the Moabite king's son relies on the preciousness and powerlessness of a child prince. The son and daughter of the impoverished widow need to be children since they depend on their mother and the prophet to save them. The parent-child bond between the Shunammite and her son stirs sympathy and fosters hope that the prophet will succeed in reviving the small boy. The youth of the Israelite slave girl highlights the strength of the prophet's reputation: even a little girl knows about the prophet in Samaria. The sons of the starving mothers must be small for the plot to proceed; how could the mothers eat grown sons, who would defend themselves or be just as capable of eating them? The biblical writers clearly recognized children as different from adults and used these understandings to create and nuance the messages of these narratives.

While the children in the Elisha cycle have minor roles, they are pivotal. Of course, the children fulfill a function in the story, giving rise to their textual existence. However, that purpose may directly relate to the children, as when the debt-collateral children must be saved from slavery or the Shunammite's son comes back to life. Even, and especially, when the children suffer, this divulges expectations that the writer shared with the early audience about children's separate status as those at risk needing protection and care to survive. At the same time, children are fully integrated participants in their surrounding culture who work to help sustain their society.

These stories show children contributing to economic, religious, and military spheres. The debt-collateral children and the Israelite slave girl help sustain household economies as workers in domestic settings. The immolation of the Moabite prince shows a child's stunning sacrifice as successful in maintaining relations between deities and mortals. Children also can be envisioned among the combatants in the battle at Moab. The text reveals children as vital to the ancient world on many levels, without necessarily anticipating the adults that they will become.

These child characters also call attention to the critical role of family in determining destiny. The Shunammite holds her dying boy, but will not accept his death and acts with undaunted determination to secure prophetic intervention. Similarly, the debt-collateral children have a mother who acts on their behalf, underscoring the children's worth. However, in the stories of the Moabite prince and the sons of the starving mothers, parents destroy their children. Yet these parents take these drastic measures amidst desperate circumstances. The loss of the boys' lives brings other gains: the Moabites win their battle, and two famished women survive another day. Here children's lives are esteemed for what their deaths can accomplish.

Children who appear without families seem independent, while influenced by their surroundings. The insolent mockers from Bethel rouse a prophet's ire and are penalized severely. The respected Israelite slave girl is far from her family, but her voiced hope becomes a commander's mission. Both stories portray small children as highly effective agents.

All of the children in the Elisha cycle are susceptible to forces beyond their control. Readers of this collection witness children who are mauled by bears, burnt as a sacrifice, nearly sold into debt slavery, die from illness, are captured and taken into slavery, risk perishing amidst siege and starvation, and relocate in times of famine. Yet children can also be appreciated, and not just for their economic value or role in perpetuating the family line. Some scenes portray genuine tenderness and concern for children's health and safety, as one mother saves her children from debt slavery, another perseveres so her child will be revived, and a third hides her son to keep him from being eaten. Adults can be advocates or adversaries. Children can be beloved or butchered.

The children are vulnerable, valuable, and sometimes both; indeed, these two estimations can be intertwined. Since children, especially the very young, are relatively defenselessness and dependent, they require resources and protection to survive. The sharing of supplies and outpouring of effort, often accompanied by emotion, increases parental and communal investment in the children. This value, in turn, can heighten the children's vulnerability, since they are desired. Children are needed for cultural survival, but may be used or exploited through slavery or sacrifice. On personal and societal levels, the girls and boys in the Elisha cycle illustrate the woes and worth of children in the Hebrew Bible.

Just like the young characters discussed here, many children in the Hebrew Bible have been overlooked in biblical interpretation. Opportunities for childist interpretation await. In addition to analyzing other passages that include neglected child characters, interpreters might focus on the youthful portrayal of well-known biblical figures. For example, how do episodes from the childhood or youth of Isaac, Rebekah, Joseph, Moses, Miriam, Samuel, or David impact the portrayal of that character? Words that designate children should be studied in further depth along chronological trajectories to discover how thoughts about children and childhood may have altered over time. Texts that raise aspects of children's lives (e.g., adoption, abandonment, work, play, sibling rivalry, and filial relationships) can be gathered and analyzed to inform our understanding of these issues. Questions of boundaries and dimensions of childhood should be investigated to see what signs of demarcation between phases of growing might be present in the text. More generally, scholarship focused on life in ancient Israel should include explicit discussion of children. Like children themselves, childist biblical interpretation is young but holds great potential.

# Bibliography

Aasgaard, Reidar. "Children in Antiquity and Early Christianity: Research History and Central Issues." *Familia* 33 (2006): 23–46.

———. "Paul as a Child: Children and Childhood in the Letters of the Apostle." *Journal of Biblical Literature* 126.1 (2007): 129–59.

Ackerman, Susan. *Under Every Green Tree: Popular Religion in Sixth-Century Judah*. Harvard Semitic Monographs 46. Atlanta: Scholars Press, 1992.

———. "Household Religion, Family Religion, and Women's Religion in Ancient Israel." Pages 127–209 in *Household and Family Religion in Antiquity*. Edited by John Bodel and Saul M. Olyan. Oxford: Blackwell, 2008.

Aichele, George, Peter Miscall, and Richard Walsh. "An Elephant in the Room: Historical-Critical and Postmodern Interpretations of the Bible." *Journal of Biblical Literature* 128.2 (2009): 383–404.

Akoto, Dorothy B. E. A. "Women and Health in Ghana and the *Trokosi* Practice: An Issue of Women's and Children's Rights in 2 Kings 4:1–7." Pages 96–110 in *African Women, Religion, and Health: Essays in Honor of Mercy Amba Ewudziwa Oduyoye*. Edited by Isabel Apawo Phiri and Sarojini Nadar. Maryknoll, NY: Orbis, 2006.

Albertz, Rainer. *A History of Israelite Religion in the Old Testament Period. Volume I: From the Beginnings to the End of the Monarchy*. Translated by John Bowden. Old Testament Library. Louisville, KY: Westminster/John Knox, 1994.

———. "Family Religion in Ancient Israel and Its Surroundings." Pages 89–112 in *Household and Family Religion in Antiquity*. Edited by John Bodel and Saul M. Olyan. Oxford: Blackwell, 2008.

Albright, W. F. "The Moabite Stone." Pages 320–21 in *Ancient Near Eastern Texts Relating to the Old Testament*. Edited by James B. Pritchard. 2nd ed. Princeton: Princeton University Press, 1958.

Alexandre-Bidon, Danièle, and Didier Lett. *Children in the Middle Ages: Fifth – Fifteenth Centuries*. Translated by Jody Gladding. Notre Dame, IN: University of Notre Dame Press, 1999.

Alter, Robert. *The Art of Biblical Narrative*. New York: Basic Books, 1981.

———. "How Convention Helps Us Read: The Case of the Bible's Annunciation Type-Scene." *Prooftexts* 3.2 (1983): 115–30.

Amit, Yairah. *Reading Biblical Narratives: Literary Criticism and the Hebrew Bible*. Translated by Yael Lotan. Minneapolis: Fortress, 2001.

Archard, David. *Children: Rights and Childhood*. London: Routledge, 1993.
Ariès, Philippe. *L'enfant et la vie familiale sous l'ancien régime*. Paris: Plon, 1960. English: *Centuries of Childhood: A Social History of Family Life*. Translated by Robert Baldick. New York: Vintage, 1962.
Arnold, Daniel. *Elisée: précurseur de Jésus—Christ: commentaire de 2 Rois 2–9*. Saint-Légier: Emmaüs, 2002.
Aucker, W. Brian. Review of Gina Hens-Piazza, *Nameless, Blameless, and without Shame: Two Cannibal Mothers before a King*. *Review of Biblical Literature* 6 (2004): 229–36.
Auerbach, Erich. *Mimesis: The Representation of Reality in Western Literature*. Princeton: Princeton University Press, 1953.
Auld, A. Graeme. *I & II Kings*. Philadelphia: Westminster, 1986.
Avioz, Michael. "The Book of Kings in Recent Research (Part I)." *Currents in Biblical Research* 4 (2005): 11–55.
———. "The Book of Kings in Recent Research (Part II)." *Currents in Biblical Research* 5 (2006): 11–57.
Axskjöld, Carl-Johan. *Aram as the Enemy Friend: The Ideological Role of Aram in the Composition of Genesis–2 Kings*. Coniectanea biblica: Old Testament Series 45. Stockholm: Almqvist & Wiksell, 1998.
Axtell, James L. *The Educational Writings of John Locke*. Cambridge: Cambridge University Press, 1968.
Badinter, Elisabeth. *Mother Love: Myth and Reality; Motherhood in Modern History*. Translated by Roger DeGaris. New York: Macmillan, 1981.
Baker, Jane. "Disabled Children." Pages 244–48 in *Childhood Studies: An Introduction*. Edited by Dominic Wyse. Malden, MA: Blackwell, 2004.
Baker, Mary. "Invisibility as a Symptom of Gender Categories." Pages 183–91 in *Invisible People and Processes: Writing Gender and Childhood into European Archaeology*. Edited by Jenny Moore and Eleanor Scott. London: Leicester University Press, 1997.
Bakke, O. M. *When Children Became People: The Birth of Childhood in Early Christianity*. Translated by Brian McNeil. Minneapolis: Augsburg Fortress, 2005.
Barclay, John M. G. "The Family as the Bearer of Religion in Judaism and Early Christianity." Pages 66–80 in *Constructing Early Christian Families: Family as Social Reality and Metaphor*. Edited by Halvor Moxnes. London: Routledge, 1997.
Bar-Efrat, Shimon. *Narrative Art in the Bible*. Journal for the Study of the Old Testament: Supplement Series 70. Bible and Literature Series 17. Sheffield: Almond Press, 1989.
Barr, James. *The Semantics of Biblical Language*. Oxford: Oxford University Press, 1961.
Bartlett, John. "The 'United' Campaign against Moab in 2 Kings 3:4–27." Pages 135–46 in *Midian, Moab and Edom: The History and Archaeology of Late Bronze and Iron Age Jordan and North-West Arabia*. Edited by

John F. A. Sawyer and David J. A. Clines. Journal for the Study of the Old Testament: Supplement Series 24. Sheffield: *JSOT* Press, 1983.

Barton, John. "Historical Criticism and Literary Interpretation: Is There Any Common Ground?" Pages 427–38 in *Israel's Past in Present Research: Essays on Ancient Historiography*. Edited by V. Philips Long. Winona Lake, IN: Eisenbrauns, 1999.

Baxter, Jane Eva. *The Archaeology of Childhood: Children, Gender, and Material Culture*. Walnut Creek, CA: AltaMira, 2005.

Beedham, Christopher. *Language and Meaning: The Structural Creation of Reality*. Amsterdam: John Benjamins, 2005.

Bendor, Shunya. *The Social Structure of Ancient Israel: The Institution of the Family (beit 'ab) from the Settlement to the End of the Monarchy*. Jerusalem: Simor, 1996.

Bennett, Harold V. *Injustice Made Legal: Deuteronomic Law and the Plight of Widows, Strangers, and Orphans in Ancient Israel*. Grand Rapids, MI: Eerdmans, 2002.

Bergen, Wesley J. "The Prophetic Alternative: Elisha and the Israelite Monarchy." Pages 127–37 in *Elijah and Elisha in Socioliterary Perspective*. Edited by Robert B. Coote. Atlanta: Scholars Press, 1992.

———. *Elisha and the End of Prophetism*. Journal for the Study of the Old Testament: Supplement Series 286. Sheffield: Sheffield Academic Press, 1999.

Berlin, Adele. *Poetics and Interpretation of Biblical Narrative*. Bible and Literature Series 9. Sheffield: Almond Press, 1983.

Bernstein, Robin. *Racial Innocence: Performing American Childhood from Slavery to Civil Rights*. New York: New York University Press, 2011.

Berquist, Jon L. "Childhood and Age in the Bible." *Pastoral Psychology* 58 (2009): 521–30.

Bird, Phyllis. "Poor Man or Poor Woman? Gendering the Poor in Prophetic Texts." Pages 37–51 in *On Reading Prophetic Texts: Gender-Specific and Related Studies in Memory of Fokkelien van Dijk-Hemmes*. Edited by Bob Becking and Meindert Dijkstra. Biblical Interpretation Series 18. Leiden: E. J. Brill, 1996.

———. *Missing Persons and Mistaken Identities: Women and Gender in Ancient Israel*. Minneapolis: Fortress, 1997.

Blenkinsopp, Joseph. "The Family in First Temple Israel." Pages 48–103 in *Families in Ancient Israel*. Edited by Leo G. Perdue, Joseph Blenkinsopp, John J. Collins, and Carol Meyers. Louisville, KY: Westminster John Knox, 1997.

Block, Daniel I. "Marriage and Family in Ancient Israel." Pages 33–102 in *Marriage and Family in the Biblical World*. Edited by Ken M. Campbell. Downers Grove, IL: InterVarsity, 2003.

Bodel, John, and Saul M. Olyan, eds. *Household and Family Religion in Antiquity*. Oxford: Blackwell, 2008.

Bohmbach, Karla G. "Names and Naming in the Biblical World." Pages 33–39 in *Women of Scripture: A Dictionary of Named and Unnamed Women in the Hebrew Bible, the Apocryphal/Deuterocanonical Books, and the New Testament*. Edited by Carol Meyers, Toni Craven, and Ross S. Kraemer. Boston: Houghton Mifflin, 2000.

———."Daughter of Jephthah." Pages 243–44 in *Women of Scripture: A Dictionary of Named and Unnamed Women in the Hebrew Bible, the Apocryphal/Deuterocanonical Books, and the New Testament*. Edited by Carol Meyers, Toni Craven, and Ross S. Kraemer. Boston: Houghton Mifflin, 2000.

Borowski, Oded. *Daily Life in Biblical Times*. Society of Biblical Literature Archaeology and Biblical Studies 5. Atlanta: Society of Biblical Literature, 2003.

Boswell, John. *The Kindness of Strangers: The Abandonment of Children in Western Europe from Late Antiquity to the Renaissance*. New York: Pantheon, 1988.

Branch, Robin Gallaher. *Jeroboam's Wife: The Enduring Contribution of the Old Testament's Lesser-Known Women*. Peabody, MA: Hendrickson, 2009.

Brennan, Patrick McKinley, ed. *The Vocation of the Child*. Grand Rapids, MI: Eerdmans, 2008.

Bretell, Caroline. *Anthropology and Migration: Essays on Transnationalism, Ethnicity, and Identity*. Walnut Creek, CA: AltaMira, 2003.

Brettler, Marc Zvi. "Women and Psalms: Toward an Understanding of the Role of Women's Prayer in the Israelite Cult." Pages 25–56 in *Gender and Law in the Hebrew Bible and the Ancient Near East*. Edited by Victor H. Matthews, Bernard M. Levinson, and Tikva Frymer-Kensky. Journal for the Study of the Old Testament: Supplement Series 262. Sheffield: Sheffield Academic Press, 1998.

Brichto, Herbert Chanan. *The Problem of "Curse" in the Hebrew Bible*. Journal of Biblical Literature Monograph Series 13. Philadelphia: Society of Biblical Literature, 1963.

———. *Toward a Grammar of Biblical Poetics: Tales of the Prophets*. New York: Oxford University Press, 1992.

Brodie, Thomas L. "Luke 7,36–50 as an Internalization of 2 Kgs 4,1–37: A Study in Luke's Use of Rhetorical Imitation." *Biblica* 64 (1983): 457–85.

Bronner, Leila Leah. *The Stories of Elijah and Elisha as Polemics against Baal Worship*. Pretoria Oriental Series 6. Leiden: E. J. Brill, 1968.

———. *Stories of Biblical Mothers: Maternal Power in the Hebrew Bible*. Dallas: University Press of America, 2004.

Brown, Raymond E. "Jesus and Elisha." *Perspective* 12 (1971): 85–104.

Browning, Don S. and Marcia J. Bunge, eds. *Children and Childhood in World Religions: Primary Sources and Texts.* New Brunswick, NJ: Rutgers University Press, 2009.
Browning, Don S., and Bonnie J. Miller-McLemore, eds. *Children and Childhood in American Religions.* New Brunswick, NJ: Rutgers University Press, 2009.
Brueggemann, Walter. "Vulnerable Children, Divine Passion, and Human Obligation." Pages 399–422 in *The Child in the Bible.* Edited by Marcia J. Bunge. Grand Rapids, MI: Eerdmans, 2008.
Buckingham, David. "Television and the Definition of Childhood." Pages 79–96 in *Children's Childhoods: Observed and Experienced.* Edited by Berry Mayall. London: Falmer, 1994.
———. "New Media, New Childhoods? Children's Changing Cultural Environment in the Age of Digital Technology." Pages 108–22 in *An Introduction to Childhood Studies.* Edited by Mary Jane Kehily. Maidenhead, NY: Open University Press, 2004.
Bühler-Niederberger, Doris. "Introduction: Childhood Sociology—Defining the State of the Art and Ensuring Reflection." *Current Sociology* 58 (2010): 155–64.
Bunge, Marcia J. "The Child, Religion, and the Academy: Developing Robust Theological and Religious Understandings of Children and Childhood." *Journal of Religion* 86.4 (2006): 549–79.
———, ed. *The Child in the Bible.* Grand Rapids, MI: Eerdmans, 2008.
———, ed. *Children, Adults, and Shared Responsibilities: Jewish, Christian, and Muslim Perspectives.* Cambridge: Cambridge University Press, 2012.
Burke, Catherine. "Theories of Childhood." Pages 818–26 in vol. 3 of *Encyclopedia of Children and Childhood: In History and Society.* Edited by Paula S. Fass. 3 vols. New York: Macmillan, 2004.
Burnett, Joel S. "'Going Down' to Bethel: Elijah and Elisha in the Theological Geography of the Deuteronomistic History." *Journal of Biblical Literature* 129.2 (2010): 281–97.
Burney, C. F. *Notes on the Hebrew Text of the Books of Kings.* Oxford: Clarendon, 1903.
Burns, John Barclay. "Why Did the Besieging Army Withdraw?" *Zeitschrift für die alttestamentliche Wissenschaft* 102.2 (1990): 187–94.
Cahan, Emily, Jay Mechling, Brian Sutton-Smith, and Sheldon H. White. "The Elusive Historical Child: Ways of Knowing the Child of History and Psychology." Pages 192–223 in *Children in Time and Place: Developmental and Historical Insights.* Edited by Glen H. Elder, Jr., John Modell, and Ross D. Parke. Cambridge: Cambridge University Press, 1993.
Callaway, Mary. *Sing O Barren One: A Study in Comparative Midrash.* Society of Biblical Literature Dissertation Series 91. Atlanta: Scholars Press, 1986.

Callender, Dexter E., Jr., "Servants of God(s) and Servants of Kings in Israel and the Ancient Near East." *Semeia* 83/84 (1998): 67–82.
Camp, Claudia V. "1 and 2 Kings." Pages 102–16 in *The Women's Bible Commentary*. Edited by Carol A. Newsom and Sharon H. Ringe. Louisville, KY: Westminster John Knox, 1998.
Campbell, Duncan B. *Besieged: Siege Warfare in the Ancient World*. Oxford: Osprey, 2006.
Carasik, Michael. "Why Did Hannah Ask for 'Seed of Men'?" *Journal of Biblical Literature* 129.3 (2010): 433–36.
Carr, David McLain. *Writing on the Tablet of the Heart: Origins of Scripture and Literature*. New York: Oxford University Press, 2005.
Carroll, John T. "Children in the Bible." *Interpretation* 55.2 (2001): 121–34.
Carroll, R. P. "The Elijah-Elisha Sagas: Some Remarks on Prophetic Succession in Ancient Israel." *Vetus Testamentum* 19 (1969): 400–415.
Chamberlain, Andrew T. "Commentary: Missing Stage of Life—Towards the Perception of Children in Archaeology." Pages 248–50 in *Invisible People and Processes: Writing Gender and Childhood into European Archaeology*. Edited by Jenny Moore and Eleanor Scott. London: Leicester University Press, 1997.
———. "Minor Concerns: A Demographic Perspective on Children in Past Societies." Pages 206–12 in *Children and Material Culture*. Edited by Joanna Sofaer Derevenski. London: Routledge, 2000.
Chaney, Marvin L. "Debt Easement in Israelite History and Tradition." Pages 127–39 in *The Bible and the Politics of Exegesis: Essays in Honor of Norman K. Gottwald on His Sixty-Fifth Birthday*. Edited by David Jobling, Peggy L. Day, Gerald T. Sheppard. Cleveland: Pilgrim, 1991.
Childs, Peter, and Roger Fowler, eds. *The Routledge Dictionary of Literary Terms*. London: Routledge, 2006.
Chirichigno, Gregory C. *Debt-Slavery in Israel and the Ancient Near East*. Journal for the Study of the Old Testament: Supplementary Series 141. Sheffield: Sheffield Academic Press, 1993.
Chudacoff, Howard P. *How Old Are You? Age Consciousness in American Culture*. Princeton: Princeton University Press, 1989.
Clarke, John. "Histories of Childhood." Pages 3–12 in *Childhood Studies: An Introduction*. Edited by Dominic Wyse. Malden, MA: Blackwell, 2004.
Classen, Albrecht. "Philippe Ariès and the Consequences: History of Childhood, Family Relations, and Personal Emotions: Where Do We Stand Today?" Pages 1–65 in *Childhood in the Middle Ages and the Renaissance: The Results of a Paradigm Shift in the History of Mentality*. Edited by Albrecht Classen. Berlin: de Gruyter, 2005.
Cleverley, John, and D. C. Phillips. *From Locke to Spock: Influential Models of the Child in Modern Western Thought*. Carlton, Australia: Melbourne University Press, 1976.

Cluysenaar, Anne. "Text." Pages 237–38 in *The Routledge Dictionary of Literary Terms*. Edited by Peter Childs and Roger Fowler. London: Routledge, 2006.
Cogan, Mordechai, and Hayim Tadmor. *II Kings*. Anchor Bible 11. Garden City, NY: Doubleday, 1988.
Cohen, Shaye J. D., ed. *The Jewish Family in Antiquity*. Brown Judaic Studies 289. Atlanta: Scholars Press, 1993.
Cohn, Robert L. "Form and Perspective in 2 Kings V." *Vetus Testamentum* 33 (1983): 171–84.
———. *2 Kings*. Berit Olam: Studies in Hebrew Narrative and Poetry. Collegeville, MN: Liturgical Press, 2000.
Conroy, Charles. "Hiel between Ahab and Elijah-Elisha: 1 Kgs 16,34 and Its Immediate Literary Context." *Biblica* 77 (1996): 210–18.
Cooper, John. *The Child in Jewish History*. Northvale, NJ: Jason Aronson, 1996.
Coote, Robert B. "Tribalism—Social Organization in the Biblical Israels." Pages 35–49 in *Ancient Israel: The Old Testament in Its Social Context*. Edited by Philip F. Esler. Minneapolis: Fortress, 2006.
Cornill, Carl Heinrich. *The Culture of Ancient Israel*. Translated by W. H. Carruth. Chicago: Open Court, 1914.
Coveney, Peter. *The Image of Childhood*. Baltimore: Penguin, 1967.
———. *Poor Monkey: The Child in Literature*. London: Rockliff, 1957.
Cross, Frank Moore. "The Themes of the Book of Kings and the Structure of the Deuteronomistic History." Pages 274–89 in *Canaanite Myth and Hebrew Epic: Essays in the History of the Religion of Israel*. Cambridge, MA: Harvard University Press, 1973.
Cunningham, Hugh. *Children and Childhood in Western Society since 1500*. London: Longman, 1995.
———. "Work." Pages 892–99 in vol. 3 of *Encyclopedia of Children and Childhood: In History and Society*. Edited by Paula S. Fass. 3 vols. New York: Macmillan, 2004.
———. *The Invention of Childhood*. London: BBC Books, 2006.
Cutler, B., and John MacDonald. "Identification of the *Na'ar* in the Ugaritic Texts." *Ugarit-Forschungen* 8 (1976): 27–35.
Dahood, Mitchell. *Psalms* III. Anchor Bible 17A. Garden City, NY: Doubleday, 1970.
Dandamayev, Muhammad A. "Slavery: Old Testament." *The Anchor Bible Dictionary on CD-ROM*. Logos Library System Version 2.1. 1997. Print ed.: David Noel Freedman, ed. *Anchor Bible Dictionary*. 6 vols. New York: Doubleday, 1992.
Davis, Paul K. *Besieged: An Encyclopedia of Great Sieges from Ancient Times to the Present*. Santa Barbara, CA: ABC-CLIO, 2001.

Day, John. *Molech: A God of Human Sacrifice in the Old Testament*. Cambridge: Cambridge University Press, 1989.

Day, Peggy L. "From the Child Is Born the Woman: The Story of Jephthah's Daughter." Pages 58–74 in *Gender and Difference in Ancient Israel*. Edited by Peggy L. Day. Minneapolis: Fortress, 1989.

———. "Anat." Pages 36–43 in *Dictionary of Deities and Demons in the Bible*. Edited by Karel van der Toorn, Bob Becking, and Pieter W. van der Horst. Leiden: E. J. Brill, 1999.

Dearman, J. Andrew. "Prophecy, Property and Politics." *Society of Biblical Literature Seminar Papers* 23 (1984): 385–97.

———. "The Family in the Old Testament." *Interpretation* 52.2 (1998): 117–29.

——— and Gerard Mattingly. "Mesha Inscription." *The Anchor Bible Dictionary on CD-ROM*. Logos Library System Version 2.1. 1997. Print ed.: David Noel Freedman, ed. *Anchor Bible Dictionary*. 6 vols. New York: Doubleday, 1992.

DeMause, Lloyd, ed. *The History of Childhood*. Northvale, NJ: Jason Aronson, 1974.

Derchain, Philippe. "Les plus anciens témoignages de sacrifices d'enfants chez les sémites occidentaux." *Vetus Testamentum* 20 (1970): 351–55.

Derevenski, Joanna Sofaer, ed. *Children and Material Culture*. London: Routledge, 2000.

Dever, William G. *Did God Have a Wife? Archaeology and Folk Religion in Ancient Israel*. Grand Rapids, MI: Eerdmans, 2005.

Devitt, Michael, and Richard Hanley, eds. *The Blackwell Guide to the Philosophy of Language*. Malden, MA: Blackwell, 2006.

Dieckmann, Detlef, and Dorothea Erbele-Küster, eds. *"Du hast mich aus meiner Mutter Leib gezogen": Beiträge zur Geburt im Alten Testament*. Neukirchen-Vluyn: Neukirchener, 2006.

Dijk-Hemmes, Fokkelien van. "The Great Woman of Shunem and the Man of God: A Dual Interpretation of 2 Kings 4:8–37." Pages 218–30 in *A Feminist Companion to Samuel and Kings*. Edited by Athalya Brenner. Feminist Companion to the Bible 5. Sheffield: Sheffield Academic Press, 1994.

Dijkstra, Meindert, and Johannes C. de Moor. "Problematic Passages in the Legend of Aqhâtu." *Ugarit-Forschungen* 7 (1975): 171–215.

Donnelly, Mark P., and Daniel Diehl. *Eat Thy Neighbor: A History of Cannibalism*. Phoenix Mill, England: Sutton, 2006.

Doody, Margaret Anne. "Infant Piety and the Infant Samuel." Pages 103–22 in *Out of the Garden: Women Writers on the Bible*. Edited by Christina Büchmann and Celina Spiegel. New York: Fawcett Columbine, 1994.

Dutcher-Walls, Patricia. "The Clarity of Double-Vision: Seeing the Family in Sociological and Archaeological Perspective." Pages 1–15 in *Fam-*

*ily in Life and in Death: The Family in Ancient Israel: Sociological and Archaeological Perspectives*. Edited by Patricia Dutcher-Walls. Edinburgh: T&T Clark, 2009.

Ebeling, Jennie R. *Women's Lives in Biblical Times*. London: T&T Clark, 2010.

Eissfeldt, Otto. *Molk als Opferbegriff im Punischen und Hebräischen und das Ende des Gottes Moloch*. Halle: Niemeyer, 1935.

Elkind, David. *The Hurried Child: Growing Up Too Fast Too Soon*. Reading, MA: Addison-Wesley, 1981.

Ellul, Jacques. *The Politics of God and the Politics of Man*. Translated by Geoffrey W. Bromiley. Grand Rapids, MI: Eerdmans, 1972.

Emerton, J. A. "The Value of the Moabite Stone as an Historical Source." *Vetus Testamentum* 52 (2002): 483–92.

Eng, Milton. *The Days of Our Years: A Lexical Semantic Study of the Life Cycle in Biblical Hebrew*. Library of Hebrew Bible/Old Testament Studies 464. New York: T&T Clark, 2011.

Ennew, Judith. *The Sexual Exploitation of Children*. Cambridge: Polity, 1986.

———. "Time for Children or Time for Adults?" Pages 125–43 in *Childhood Matters: Social Theory, Practice and Politics*. Edited by Jens Qvortrup, Marjatta Bardy, Giovanni Sgritta, and Helmut Wintersberger. Aldershot, England: Avebury, 1994.

Esser, Annette, Andrea Günter, and Rajah Scheepers, eds. *Kinder haben, Kind sein, Geboren sein: Philosophische und theologische Beiträge zu Kindheit und Geburt*. Königstein/Taunus: Ulrike Helmer, 2008.

Exum, J. Cheryl. "On Judges 11." Pages 131–44 in *A Feminist Companion to Judges*. Edited by Athalya Brenner. Feminist Companion to the Bible 4. Sheffield: Sheffield Academic Press, 1993.

Farrar, Frederic William. *Second Book of Kings*. Expositor's Bible. New York: A. C. Armstrong and Son, 1902.

Fass, Paula S., ed. *Encyclopedia of Children and Childhood: In History and Society*. 3 vols. New York: Macmillan, 2004.

———. "Social History and the History of Childhood." Pages 16–17 in the *Society for the History of Children and Youth Newsletter* 13 (Winter 2009).

———. "Viviana Zelizer: Giving Meaning to the History of Childhood." *Journal of the History of Childhood and Youth* 5.3 (2012): 457–61.

Fechter, Friedrich. *Die Familie in der Nachexilszeit: Untersuchungen zur Bedeutung der Verwandtschaft in ausgewählten Texten des Alten Testaments*. Beihefte zur Zeitschrift für die alttestamentliche Wissenschaft 264. Berlin: de Gruyter, 1998.

Fensham, F. Charles. "Widow, Orphan, and the Poor in Ancient Near Eastern Legal and Wisdom Literature." *Journal of Near Eastern Studies* 21 (1962): 129–39.

Feucht, Erika. "Kinderarbeit und Erziehung im Alten Ägypten." Pages 89–117 in *"Schaffe Mir Kinder . . .": Beiträge zur Kindheit im alten Israel und in seinen Nachbarkulturen*. Edited by Andreas Kunz-Lübcke and Rüdiger Lux. Arbeiten zur Bibel und ihrer Geschichte 21. Leipzig: Evangelische Verlagsanstalt, 2006.

Fewell, Danna Nolan. *The Children of Israel: Reading the Bible for the Sake of Our Children*. Nashville: Abingdon, 2003.

———, and David M. Gunn. "Tipping the Balance: Sternberg's Reader and the Rape of Dinah." *Journal of Biblical Literature* 110 (1991): 193–212.

———. *Narrative in the Hebrew Bible*. Oxford: Oxford University Press, 1993.

Finkelstein, Israel, and Neil Asher Silberman. *The Bible Unearthed: Archaeology's New Vision of Ancient Israel and the Origin of Its Sacred Texts*. New York: Free Press, 2001.

Finkelstein, Israel. "City-States to States: Polity Dynamics in the 10th–9th Centuries B.C.E." Pages 75–83 in *Symbiosis, Symbolism, and the Power of the Past*. Edited by William Dever and Seymour Gitin. Winona Lake, IN: Eisenbrauns, 2003.

Finlay, Timothy D. *The Birth Report Genre in the Hebrew Bible*. Forschungen zum Alten Testament 12. Tübingen: Mohr Siebeck, 2005.

Finsterbusch, Karin, Armin Lange, and K. F. Diethard Römheld, eds. *Human Sacrifice in Jewish and Christian Tradition*. Numen Book Series 112. Leiden: Brill, 2007.

Fischer, Irmtraud. "Über Lust und Last, Kinder zu haben: Soziale, genealogische und theologische Aspekte in der Literatur Alt-Israels." *Jahrbuch für biblische Theologie* 17 (2002): 56–82.

Fleishman, Joseph. "The Age of Legal Maturity in Biblical Law." *Journal of Ancient Near Eastern Studies* 21 (1992): 35–48.

———. *Parent and Child in Ancient Near East and the Bible*. Jerusalem: Magnes, 1999.

———. "Does the Law of Exodus 21:7–11 Permit a Father to Sell His Daughter to Be a Slave?" *Jewish Law Annual* 13 (2000): 47–64.

———. "A Daughter's Demand and a Father's Compliance: The Legal Background to Achsah's Claim and Caleb's Agreement." *Zeitschrift für die alttestamentliche Wissenschaft* 118 (2006): 354–73.

———. "The Delinquent Daughter and Legal Innovation in Deuteronomy xxii 20–21." *Vetus Testamentum* 58 (2008): 191–210.

———. *Father-Daughter Relations in Biblical Law*. Bethesda, MD: CDL Press, 2011.

Fokkelman, Jan. *Reading Biblical Narrative: A Practical Guide*. Translated by Ineke Smit. Tools for Biblical Study 1. Leiden: Deo, 1999.

Forna, Aminatta. *Mother of All Myths: How Society Moulds and Constrains Mothers*. London: HarperCollins, 1998.

Fortes, Meyer. "Age, Generation, and Social Structure." Pages 99–122 in *Age and Anthropological Theory*. Edited by David I. Kertzer and Jennie Keith. Ithaca, NY: Cornell University Press, 1984.
Francis, James M. M. *Adults as Children: Images of Childhood in the Ancient World and the New Testament*. Oxford: Peter Lang, 2006.
French, Valerie. "Children in Antiquity." Pages 14–29 in *Children in Historical and Comparative Perspective: An International Handbook and Research Guide*. Edited by Joseph M. Hawes and N. Ray Hiner. Westport, CT: Greenwood, 1991.
Fretheim, Terence E. *Deuteronomic History*. Nashville: Abingdon, 1983.
———. *First and Second Kings*. Westminster Bible Companion. Louisville, KY: Westminster John Knox, 1999.
———. "God Was with the Boy." Pages 3–23 in *The Child in the Bible*. Edited by Marcia J. Bunge. Grand Rapids, MI: Eerdmans, 2008.
Fritz, Volkmar. *The City in Ancient Israel*. Sheffield: Sheffield Academic Press, 1995.
———. *1 & 2 Kings*. Continental Commentaries. Translated by Anselm Hagedorn. Minneapolis: Fortress, 2003.
Frymer-Kensky, Tikva. *In the Wake of the Goddesses: Women, Culture, and the Biblical Transformation of Pagan Myth*. New York: Free Press, 1992.
———. "The Family in the Hebrew Bible." Pages 55–73 in *Religion, Feminism, and the Family*. Edited by Anne Carr and Mary Stewart Van Leeuwen. Louisville, KY: Westminster John Knox, 1996.
———. "Virginity in the Bible." Pages 79–96 in *Gender and Law in the Hebrew Bible and the Ancient Near East*. Edited by Victor H. Matthews, Bernard M. Levinson, Tikva Frymer-Kensky. Journal for the Study of the Old Testament: Supplement Series 262; Sheffield: Sheffield Academic Press, 1998.
Fuchs, Esther. "The Literary Characterization of Mothers and Sexual Politics in the Hebrew Bible." Pages 117–36 in *Feminist Perspectives on Biblical Scholarship*. Edited by Adela Yarbro Collins. Society of Biblical Literature Biblical Scholarship in North America 10. Chico, CA: Scholars Press, 1985.
Furniss, Tom. "Rousseau: Enlightened Critic of the Enlightenment?" Pages 596–609 in *The Enlightenment World*. Edited by Martin Fitzpatrick, Peter Jones, Christa Knellwolf, and Iain McCalman. London: Routledge, 2004.
Garroway, Kristine Sue Henriksen. "The Construction of 'Child' in the Ancient Near East: Towards an Understanding of the Legal and Social Status of Children in Biblical Israel and Surrounding Cultures." Ph.D. diss., Hebrew Union College, 2009.
Gertz, Jan Christian. *Die Gerichtsorganisation Israels im deuteronomischen Gesetz*. Göttingen: Vandenhoeck & Ruprecht, 1994.

Gies, Kathrin. *Geburt—ein Übergang: Rituelle Vollzüge, Rollenträger und Geschlechterverhältnisse*. Arbeiten zu Text und Sprache im Alten Testament 88. St. Ottilien: Erzabtei St. Ottilien, 2009.

Gillis, John R. "Life Course and Transitions to Adulthood." Pages 547–52 in vol. 2 of *Encyclopedia of Children and Childhood: In History and Society*. Edited by Paula S. Fass. 3 vols. New York: Macmillan, 2004.

Giroux, Henry A. *Stealing Innocence: Youth, Corporate Power, and the Politics of Culture*. New York: St. Martin's Press, 2000.

Gittins, Diana. "The Historical Construction of Childhood." Pages 25–38 in *An Introduction to Childhood Studies*. Edited by Mary Jane Kehily. Maidenhead, NY: Open University Press, 2004.

Goldberg, P. J. P., Felicity Riddy, and Mike Taylor. "Introduction: After Ariès." Pages 1–10 in *Youth in the Middle Ages*. Edited by P. J. P. Goldberg and Felicity Riddy. York: York Medieval Press, 2004.

Golden, Mark. *Children and Childhood in Classical Athens*. Baltimore: Johns Hopkins University Press, 1990.

———. "Childhood in Ancient Greece." Pages 13–29 in *Coming of Age in Ancient Greece: Images of Childhood from the Classical Past*. Edited by Jennifer Neils and John H. Oakley. New Haven: Yale University Press, 2003.

Gowan, Donald E. "Wealth and Poverty in the Old Testament: The Case of the Widow, the Orphan, and the Sojourner." *Interpretation* 41.4 (1987): 341–53.

Grabbe, Lester L. "Ancient Near Eastern Prophecy from an Anthropological Perspective." Pages 13–32 in *Prophecy in Its Ancient Near Eastern Context: Mesopotamian, Biblical, and Arabian Perspectives*. Edited by Martti Nissinen. Society of Biblical Literature Symposium Series 13. Atlanta: Society of Biblical Literature, 2000.

Graham, M. Patrick. "The Discovery and Reconstruction of the Mesha' Inscription." Pages 41–92 in *Studies in the Mesha Inscription and Moab*. Edited by Andrew Dearman. Society of Biblical Literature Archaeology and Biblical Studies 2. Atlanta: Scholars Press, 1989.

Gray, George B. *Sacrifice in the Old Testament: Its Theory and Practice*. New York: KTAV, 1971.

Gray, John. *I & II Kings*. Old Testament Library. Philadelphia: Westminster, 1970.

Green, Alberto. *The Role of Human Sacrifice in the Ancient Near East*. Ann Arbor, MI: University Microfilms International, 1973.

Greenfield, J. C. "Hadad." Pages 377–82 in *Dictionary of Deities and Demons in the Bible*. Edited by Karel van der Toorn, Bob Becking, and Pieter W. van der Horst. 2nd ed. Leiden: Brill, 1999.

Greenspahn, Frederick E. *When Brothers Dwell Together: The Preeminence of Younger Siblings in the Hebrew Bible*. New York: Oxford University Press, 1994.

Greenstein, Edward. "Kirta." Pages 9–48 in *Ugaritic Narrative Poetry*. Edited by Simon B. Parker. Society of Biblical Literature Writings from the Ancient World 9. Atlanta: Scholars Press, 1997.

Gressmann, Hugo. *Die älteste Geschichtsschreibung und Prophetie Israels (von Samuel bis Amos und Hosea)*. Göttingen: Vandenhoeck & Ruprecht, 1921.

Grossman, Jonathan. "'Gleaning among the Ears'—'Gathering among the Sheaves': Characterizing the Image of the Supervising Boy [Ruth 2]," *Journal of Biblical Literature* 126.4 (2007): 703–716.

Gruber, Mayer I. "Breast-Feeding Practices in Biblical Israel and in Old Babylonian Mesopotamia." *Journal of the Ancient Near Eastern Society* 19 (1989): 61–83.

Guest, Kristen, ed. *Eating Their Words: Cannibalism and the Boundaries of Cultural Identity*. Albany: State University of New York Press, 2001.

Guillaume, Philippe. "Miracles Miraculously Repeated: Gospel Miracles as Duplication of Elijah-Elisha's." *Biblische Notizen* 98 (1999): 21–23.

Gundry-Volf, Judith M. "The Least and the Greatest: Children in the New Testament." Pages 29–60 in *The Child in Christian Thought*. Edited by Marcia J. Bunge. Grand Rapids, MI: Eerdmans, 2001.

Gunkel, Hermann. *Geschichten von Elisha*. Berlin: Karl Curtius, 1925.

Haas, Louis. *The Renaissance Man and His Children: Childbirth and Early Childhood in Florence 1300–1600.* New York: St. Martin's Press, 1998.

Hafþórsson, Sigurður. *A Passing Power: An Examination of the Sources for the History of Aram-Damascus in the Second Half of the Ninth Century B.C.* Stockholm: Almqvist & Wiksell, 2006.

Hallo, William W., ed. *Canonical Compositions from the Biblical World*. Vol. 1 of *The Context of Scripture*. 3 vols. Leiden: E. J. Brill, 1997.

Harrison, Eveleen. *Little-Known Young People of the Bible*. New York: Round Table, 1937.

Hasan, Raqaiya, and J. R. Martin, eds. *Language Development: Learning Language, Learning Culture. Meaning and Choice in Language: Studies for Michael Halliday*. Advances in Discourse Processes 50. Norwood, NJ: Ablex, 1989.

Hawes, Joseph M., and N. Ray Hiner. *Children in Historical and Comparative Perspective: An International Handbook and Research Guide*. Westport, CT: Greenwood, 1991.

Hays, Sharon. *The Cultural Contradictions of Motherhood*. New Haven: Yale University Press, 1996.

Heider, George C. *The Cult of Molek: A Reassessment*. Journal for the Study of the Old Testament: Supplement Series 43. Sheffield: JSOT Press, 1986.

Hens-Piazza, Gina. "Forms of Violence and the Violence of Forms: Two Cannibal Mothers before a King (2 Kings 6:24–33)." *Journal of Feminist Studies in Religion* 14 (1998): 91–104.

———. *Nameless, Blameless, and Without Shame: Two Cannibal Mothers before a King*. Collegeville, MN: Liturgical Press, 2003.

———. *1–2 Kings*. Abingdon Old Testament Commentaries. Nashville, TN: Abingdon, 2006.

Henten, Jan Willem van, and Athalya Brenner, eds. *Families and Family Relations as Represented in Early Judaisms and Early Christianities: Texts and Fictions*. Studies in Theology and Religion 2. Leiden: Deo, 2000.

Hentschel, Georg. *2 Könige*. Würzburg: Echter, 1985.

Herzog, Kristin. *Children and Our Global Future: Theological and Social Challenges*. Cleveland: Pilgrim, 2005.

Hiner, N. Ray, and Joseph M. Hawes. "History of Childhood: The United States." Pages 426–30 in vol. 2 of *Encyclopedia of Children and Childhood: In History and Society*. Edited by Paula S. Fass. 3 vols. New York: Macmillan, 2004.

Hobbs, T. R. *2 Kings*. Word Biblical Commentary 13. Waco, TX: Word Books, 1985.

Hochman, Baruch. *Character in Literature*. Ithaca, NY: Cornell University Press, 1985.

Holladay, John S. "The Kingdoms of Israel and Judah: Political and Economic Centralization in the Iron IIA-B (ca. 1000–750 BCE)." Pages 368–98 in *The Archaeology of Society in the Holy Land*. Edited by Thomas E. Levy. New York: Facts on File, 1995.

Hölscher, Gustav. *Die Profeten: Untersuchungen zur Religionsgeschichte Israels* Leipzig: J. C. Hinrichs, 1914.

Hoof, Dieter. "Das Evidenzproblem in der althistorischen Kindheitsforschung." Pages 19–43 in *"Schaffe Mir Kinder . . .": Beiträge zur Kindheit im alten Israel und in seinen Nachbarkulturen*. Edited by Andreas Kunz-Lübcke and Rüdiger Lux. Arbeiten zur Bibel und ihrer Geschichte 21. Leipzig: Evangelische Verlagsanstalt, 2006.

Hübner, Ulrich. *Spiele und Spielzeug im antiken Palästina*. Orbis biblicus et orientalis 121. Göttingen: Vandenhoeck & Ruprecht, 1992.

Hutton, Patrick H. *Philippe Ariès and the Politics of French Cultural History*. Amherst: University of Massachusetts Press, 2004.

Huwiler, Elizabeth F. "Shunem." *The Anchor Bible Dictionary on CD-ROM*. Logos Library System Version 2.1. 1997. Print ed.: David Noel Freedman, ed. *Anchor Bible Dictionary*. 6 vols. New York: Doubleday, 1992.

Hymowitz, Kay S. *Ready or Not: Why Treating Children as Small Adults Endangers Their Future—and Ours*. New York: Free Press, 1999.

Jackson, Kent P. "The Language of the Meshaʿ Inscription." Pages 96–130 in *Studies in the Mesha Inscription*. Edited by Andrew Dearman. Society of Biblical Literature Archaeology and Biblical Studies 2. Atlanta: Scholars Press, 1989.

———, and J. Andrew Dearman. "The Text of the Meshaʿ Inscription." Pages 93–95 in *Studies in the Mesha Inscription*. Edited by Andrew

Dearman. Society of Biblical Literature Archaeology and Biblical Studies 2. Atlanta: Scholars Press, 1989.

James, Allison. "Understanding Childhood from an Interdisciplinary Perspective: Problems and Potentials." Pages 25–37 in *Rethinking Childhood*. Edited by Peter B. Pufall and Richard P. Unsworth. New Brunswick, NJ: Rutgers University Press, 2004.

———, and Adrian L. James. *Constructing Childhood: Theory, Policy and Social Practice*. New York: Palgrave Macmillan: 2004.

———, Chris Jenks, and Alan Prout. *Theorizing Childhood*. Cambridge: Polity, 1998.

Janata, Jaromír. *Masochism: The Mystery of Jean-Jacques Rousseau*. Danbury, CT: Rutledge, 2001.

Jensen, David H. *Graced Vulnerability: A Theology of Childhood*. Cleveland: Pilgrim, 2005.

Jones, Gwilym H. *1 & 2 Kings*. Volume 2. New Century Bible. Grand Rapids, MI: Eerdmans, 1984.

Jones, Janet, Sandra Gollin, Helen Drury, and Dorothy Economou. "Systemic-Functional Linguistics and Its Application to the TESOL Curriculum." Pages 257–328 in *Language Development: Learning Language, Learning Culture. Meaning and Choice in Language: Studies for Michael Halliday*. Edited by Raqaiya Hasan and J. R. Martin. Norwood, NJ: Ablex, 1989.

Jones, Russell. "Ethnicity and Race." Pages 239–43 in *Childhood Studies: An Introduction*. Edited by Dominic Wyse. Malden, MA: Blackwell, 2004.

Kaiser, Otto. "Erziehung und Bildung in der Weisheit des Jesus Sirach." Pages 223–51 in *"Schaffe Mir Kinder . . .": Beiträge zur Kindheit im alten Israel und in seinen Nachbarkulturen*. Edited by Andreas Kunz-Lübcke and Rüdiger Lux. Arbeiten zur Bibel und ihrer Geschichte 21. Leipzig: Evangelische Verlagsanstalt, 2006.

Kalmanofsky, Amy. "Women of God: Maternal Grief and Religious Response in 1 Kings 17 and 2 Kings 4." *Journal for the Study of the Old Testament* 36 (2011): 55–74.

Kamp, Kathryn A. "Where Have All the Children Gone?: The Archaeology of Childhood." *Journal of Archaeological Method and Theory* 8.1 (2001): 1–34.

Kaplan, Yehuda. "Recruitment of Foreign Soldiers into the Neo-Assyrian Army during the Reign of Tiglath-pileser III." Pages 135–52 in *Treasures on Camels' Humps: Historical and Literary Studies from the Ancient Near East Presented to Israel Eph'al*. Edited by Mordechai Cogan and Dan'el Kahn. Jerusalem: Magnes, 2008.

Keatinge, M. W., translator. *The Great Didactic of John Amos Comenius*. London: Adam & Charles Black, 1896. Repr., New York: Russell & Russell, 1967.

Kehily, Mary Jane, ed. *An Introduction to Childhood Studies*. 2nd ed. Maidenhead, NY: Open University Press, 2009.

Kemmer, Suzanne, and Michael Barlow. "Introduction: A Usage-Based Conception of Language." Pages vii–xxviii in *Usage-Based Models of Language*. Edited by Michael Barlow and Suzanne Kemmer. Stanford, CA: Center for the Study of Language and Information, 2000.

Kilgour, Maggie. "Foreword." Pages vii–viii in *Eating Their Words: Cannibalism and the Boundaries of Cultural Identity*. Edited by Kristen Guest. Albany: State University of New York Press, 2001.

King, Philip J., and Lawrence E. Stager. *Life in Biblical Israel*. Louisville, KY: Westminster John Knox, 2001.

Kirk-Duggan, Cheryl A., and Tina Pippin, eds. *Mother Goose, Mother Jones, Mommie Dearest: Biblical Mothers & Their Children*. Semeia Studies 61. Atlanta: Society of Biblical Literature, 2009.

Kissling, Paul J. *Reliable Characters in the Primary History: Profiles of Moses, Joshua, Elijah and Elisha*. Journal for the Study of the Old Testament: Supplement Series 224. Sheffield: Sheffield Academic Press, 1996.

Kitzinger, Jenny. "Defending Innocence: Ideologies of Childhood." *Feminist Review* 28 (January 1988): 77–87.

Knoppers, Gary N., and J. Gordon McConville, eds. *Reconsidering Israel and Judah: Recent Studies on the Deuteronomistic History*. Sources for Biblical and Theological Study 8. Winona Lake, IN: Eisenbrauns, 2000.

Koepf, Laurel W. "Give Me Children or I Shall Die: Children and Communal Survival in Biblical Literature." Ph.D. diss., Union Theological Seminary, 2012.

Komensky (Comenius), John Amos. *Labyrinth of the World and the Paradise of the Heart*. Translated by Count Lützow. New York: E. P. Dutton, 1901.

Konner, Melvin. "Infancy among the Kalahari Desert San." Pages 287–328 in *Culture and Infancy: Variations in Human Experience*. Edited by P. Herbert Leiderman, Steven R. Tulkin, and Anne Rosenfeld. New York: Academic Press, 1977.

Korbin, Jill E. "'Good Mothers,' 'Babykillers,' and Fatal Child Maltreatment." Pages 253–76 in *Small Wars: The Cultural Politics of Childhood*. Edited by Nancy Scheper-Hughes and Carolyn Sargent. Berkeley: University of California Press, 1998.

Kottsieper, Ingo. "The Tel Dan Inscription (*KAI* 310) and the Political Relations between Aram-Damascus and Israel in the First Half of the First Millennium BCE." Pages 104–34 in *Ahab Agonistes: The Rise and Fall of the Omri Dynasty*. Edited by Lester L. Grabbe. Library of Hebrew Bible/Old Testament Studies 421. London: T&T Clark, 2007.

Kraemer, David. "Images of Childhood and Adolescence in Talmudic Literature." Pages 65–80 in *The Jewish Family: Metaphor and Memory*. New York: Oxford, 1989.

Kraemer, Ross S. "Jewish Mothers and Daughters in the Greco-Roman World." Pages 89–112 in *The Jewish Family in Antiquity*. Edited by Shaye J. D. Cohen. Brown Judaic Studies 289. Atlanta: Scholars Press, 1993.

———. "Implicating Herodias and Her Daughter in the Death of John the Baptizer: A (Christian) Theological Strategy?" *Journal of Biblical Literature* 125.2 (2006): 321–49.

Kratz, Reinhard. *Die Komposition der erzählenden Bücher des Alten Testaments: Grundwissen der Bibelkritik*. Göttingen: Vandenhoeck & Ruprecht, 2000.

Kunz-Lübcke, Andreas, and Rüdiger Lux, eds. *"Schaffe Mir Kinder . . .": Beiträge zur Kindheit im alten Israel und in seinen Nachbarkulturen*. Arbeiten zur Bibel und ihrer Geschichte 21. Leipzig: Evangelische Verlagsanstalt, 2006.

Kunz-Lübcke, Andreas. "Wahrnehmung von Adoleszenz in der Hebräischen Bibel und in den Nachbarkulturen Israels." Pages 167–95 in *"Schaffe Mir Kinder . . .": Beiträge zur Kindheit im alten Israel und in seinen Nachbarkulturen*. Edited by Andreas Kunz-Lübcke and Rüdiger Lux. Arbeiten zur Bibel und ihrer Geschichte 21. Leipzig: Evangelische Verlagsanstalt, 2006.

———. *Das Kind in den antiken Kulturen des Mittelmeers: Israel, Ägypten, Griechenland*. Neukirchen-Vluyn: Neukirchener, 2007.

———. "Gotteslob aus Kindermund: Zu einer Theologie der Kinder in Psalm 8." Pages 84–106 in *Mensch und König: Studien zur Anthropologie des Alten Testaments Rüdiger Lux zum 60. Geburtstag*. Edited by Angelika Berlejung and Raik Heckl. Herders Biblische Studien 53. Freiburg: Herder, 2008.

LaBarbera, Robert. "The Man of War and the Man of God: Social Satire in 2 Kings 6:8–7:20." *Catholic Biblical Quarterly* 46 (1984): 637–51.

Lareau, Annette, ed. *Unequal Childhoods: Class, Race, and Family Life*. Berkeley, CA: University of California Press, 2003.

Lasine, Stuart. "Jehoram and the Cannibal Mothers (2 Kings 6.24–33): Solomon's Judgment in an Inverted World." *Journal for the Study of the Old Testament* 50 (1991): 27–53.

———. "The Ups and Downs of Monarchical Justice: Solomon and Jehoram in an Intertextual World." *Journal for the Study of the Old Testament* 59 (1993): 37–53.

Leeb, Carolyn S. *Away from the Father's House: The Social Location of na'ar and na'arah in Ancient Israel*. Journal for the Study of the Old Testament: Supplement Series 301. Sheffield: Sheffield Academic Press, 2000.

Leithart, Peter J. *1 & 2 Kings*. Brazos Theological Commentary on the Bible. Grand Rapids, MI: Brazos, 2006.

Lemaire, André. "Vers l'histoire de la rédaction des Livres des Rois." *Zeitschrift für die alttestamentliche Wissenschaft* 98 (1986): 221–36.

———. "House of David Restored in Moabite Inscription." *Biblical Archaeology Review* 20 (1994): 30–37.

Levenson, Jon D. *The Death and Resurrection of the Beloved Son: The Transformation of Child Sacrifice in Judaism and Christianity.* New Haven: Yale University Press, 1993.

LeVine, Robert A. "Child Rearing as Cultural Adaptation." Pages 15–27 in *Culture and Infancy: Variations in the Human Experience.* Edited by P. Herbert Leiderman, Steven R. Tulkin, and Anne Rosenfeld. New York: Academic Press, 1977.

Levinson, Bernard M. "The Birth of the Lemma: The Restrictive Reinterpretation of the Covenant Code's Manumission Law by the Holiness Code (Leviticus 25:44–46)." *Journal of Biblical Literature* 124 (2005): 617–39.

Littauer, M. A., and J. H. Crouwel. *Wheeled Vehicles and Ridden Animals in the Ancient Near East.* Handbuch der Orientalistik 7. Leiden: E. J. Brill, 1979.

Liverani, Mario. *Israel's History and the History of Israel.* Translated by Chiara Peri and Philip R. Davies. London: Equinox, 2005.

Logan, Alice. "Rehabilitating Jephthah." *Journal of Biblical Literature* 128.4 (2009): 665–85.

Long, Burke O. "2 Kings III and Genres of Prophetic Narrative." *Vetus Testamentum* 23 (1973): 337–48.

———. *2 Kings.* Forms of the Old Testament Literature 10. Grand Rapids, MI: Eerdmans, 1991.

Long, Jesse C., Jr. "Elisha's Deceptive Prophecy in 2 Kings 3: A Response to Raymond Westbrook." *Journal of Biblical Literature* 126 (2007): 168–71.

———, and Mark Sneed. "'Yahweh Has Given These Three Kings into the Hand of Moab': A Socio-Literary Reading of 2 Kings 3." Pages 253–75 in *Inspired Speech: Prophecy in the Ancient Near East—Essays in Honor of Herbert B. Huffmon.* Edited by John Kaltner and Louis Stulman. Journal for the Study of the Old Testament: Supplement Series 378. London: T&T Clark, 2004.

Lux, Rüdiger. "Die Kinder auf der Gasse. Ein Kindheitsmotiv in der prophetischen Gerichts- und Heilsverkündigung." Pages 197–221 in *"Schaffe Mir Kinder . . .": Beiträge zur Kindheit im alten Israel und in seinen Nachbarkulturen.* Edited by Andreas Kunz-Lübcke and Rüdiger Lux. Arbeiten zur Bibel und ihrer Geschichte 21. Leipzig: Evangelische Verlagsanstalt, 2006.

MacDonald, John. "The Status and Role of the *Na'ar* in Israelite Society." *Journal of Near Eastern Studies* 35.3 (1976): 147–70.

———. "Untersuchungen zum Begriff נער im Alten Testament." Review of Hans-Peter Stähli, *Knabe-Jüngling-Knecht*. *Journal of Biblical Literature* 99.4 (1980): 594–95.
Maier, Christl M. *Daughter Zion, Mother Zion: Gender, Space, and the Sacred in Ancient Israel*. Minneapolis: Fortress, 2008.
Maloney, Robert P. "Usury and Restrictions on Interest-Taking in the Ancient Near East." *Catholic Biblical Quarterly* 36 (1974): 1–20.
Mandelbaum, David G., ed. *Selected Writings of Edward Sapir in Language, Culture, and Personality*. Berkeley: University of California Press, 1951.
Marcus, David. *From Balaam to Jonah: Anti-prophetic Satire in the Hebrew Bible*. Brown Judaic Studies 301. Altanta: Scholars Press, 1995.
Marcus, Ivan G. *Rituals of Childhood: Jewish Acculturation in Medieval Europe*. New Haven: Yale University Press, 1996.
———. *The Jewish Life Cycle: Rites of Passage from Biblical to Modern Times*. Seattle: University of Washington Press, 2004.
Maretzki, Thomas, and Hatsumi Maretzki. "Taira: An Okinawan Village." Pages 367–539 in *Six Cultures: Studies of Child Rearing*. Edited by Beatrice B. Whiting. New York: John Wiley & Sons, 1963.
Margalit, Baruch. "Why King Mesha of Moab Sacrificed His Oldest Son." *Biblical Archaeology Review* 12 (1986): 62–63.
Marsman, Hennie J. *Women in Ugarit and Israel: Their Social and Religious Position in the Context of the Ancient Near East*. Oudtestamentische Studiën 49. Leiden: Brill, 2003.
Martin, Dale B. "Slavery and the Ancient Jewish Family." Pages 113–29 in *The Jewish Family in Antiquity*. Edited by Shaye J. D. Cohen. Brown Judaic Studies 289. Atlanta: Scholars Press, 1993.
Martingale, Moira. *Cannibal Killers: The History of Impossible Murders*. New York: Carroll & Graf, 1993.
Marty, Martin. *The Mystery of the Child*. Grand Rapids, MI: Eerdmans, 2007.
Matthews, Victor H., and Don C. Benjamin. *Social World of Ancient Israel 1250–587 BCE*. Peabody, MA: Hendrickson, 1993.
Matthews, Victor H., Bernard M. Levinson, and Tikva Frymer-Kensky, eds. *Gender and Law in the Hebrew Bible and the Ancient Near East*. Journal for the Study of the Old Testament: Supplement Series 262. Sheffield: Sheffield Academic Press, 1998.
Mattingly, Gerald L. "Chemosh." *The Anchor Bible Dictionary on CD-ROM*. Logos Library System Version 2.1. 1997. Print ed.: David Noel Freedman, ed. *Anchor Bible Dictionary*. 6 vols. New York: Doubleday, 1992.
Mayall, Berry, ed. *Children's Childhoods: Observed and Experienced*. London: Falmer, 1994.
McConnell, Douglas, Jennifer Orona, and Paul Stockley, eds. *Understanding God's Heart for Children: Toward a Biblical Framework*. Colorado Springs: Authentic, 2007.

McKenzie, Steven L. *The Trouble with Kings: The Composition of the Book of Kings in the Deuteronomistic History*. Vetus Testamentum Supplements 42. Leiden: E. J. Brill, 1991.

——— and M. Patrick Graham, eds. *The History of Israel's Traditions: The Heritage of Martin Noth*. Journal for the Study of the Old Testament: Supplement Series 182. Sheffield: Sheffield Academic Press, 1994.

Medforth, Nicholas. "Children Working." Pages 262–68 in *Childhood Studies: An Introduction*. Edited by Dominic Wyse. Malden, MA: Blackwell, 2004.

Mendelsohn, Isaac. *Slavery in the Ancient Near East: A Comparative Study of Slavery in Babylonia, Assyria, Syria, and Palestine from the Middle of the Third Millennium to the End of the First Millennium*. New York: Oxford University Press, 1949.

Menn, Esther M. "Child Characters in Biblical Narratives: The Young David (1 Samuel 16–17) and the Little Israelite Servant Girl (2 Kings 5:1–19)." Pages 324–52 in *The Child in the Bible*. Edited by Marcia J. Bunge. Grand Rapids, MI: Eerdmans, 2008.

Mercer, Mark. "Elisha's Unbearable Curse: A Study of 2 Kings 2:23–25." *Africa Journal of Evangelical Theology* 21 (2002): 165–98.

Meyers, Carol. *Discovering Eve: Ancient Israelite Women in Context*. New York: Oxford University Press, 1988.

———. "Everyday Life: Women in the Period of the Hebrew Bible." Pages 251–59 in *The Women's Bible Commentary*. Edited by Carol A. Newsom and Sharon H. Ringe. Louisville, KY: Westminster John Knox, 1998.

Michel, Andreas. *Gott und Gewalt gegen Kinder im Alten Testament*. Forschungen zum Alten Testament 37. Tübingen: Mohr Siebeck, 2003.

———. "Sexual Violence against Children in the Bible." Pages 51–60 in *The Structural Betrayal of Trust*. Translated by John Bowden. Edited by Regina Ammicht-Quinn, Hille Haker, and Maureen Junker-Kenny. Concilium. London: SCM, 2004.

———. "Gewalt gegen Kinder im alten Israel. Eine sozialgeschichtliche Perspektive." Pages 137–63 in *"Schaffe Mir Kinder . . .": Beiträge zur Kindheit im alten Israel und in seinen Nachbarkulturen*. Edited by Andreas Kunz-Lübcke and Rüdiger Lux. Arbeiten zur Bibel und ihrer Geschichte 21. Leipzig: Evangelische Verlagsanstalt, 2006.

Milgrom, Jacob. *Leviticus 1–16*. Anchor Bible 3. New York: Doubleday, 1991.

Mintz, Steven. "Why the History of Childhood Matters." *Journal of the History of Childhood and Youth* 5.1 (2012): 17–28.

Mitchell, T. C. "The Old Testament Usage of $N^{E}\check{S}\bar{A}M\hat{A}$." *Vetus Testamentum* 11 (1961): 177–87.

Montgomery, James A. *The Books of Kings*. International Critical Commentary. New York: Scribner's, 1951.

Moore, Jenny, and Eleanor Scott, eds. *Invisible People and Processes: Writing Gender and Childhood into European Archaeology*. London: Leicester University Press, 1997.
Moore, Rick Dale. *God Saves: Lessons from the Elisha Stories*. Journal for the Study of the Old Testament: Supplement Series 95. Sheffield: Sheffield Academic Press, 1990.
Müller, Reinhard. *Königtum und Gottesherrschaft: Untersuchungen zur alttestamentlichen Monarchiekritik*. Tübingen: Mohr Siebeck, 2004.
Neils, Jenifer, and John H. Oakley, eds. *Coming of Age in Ancient Greece: Images of Childhood from the Classical Past*. New Haven: Yale University Press, 2003.
Nelson, Richard D. *First and Second Kings*. Interpretation: A Bible Commentary for Teaching and Preaching. Atlanta: John Knox Press, 1987.
———. *The Double Redaction of the Deuteronomistic History*. Journal for the Study of the Old Testament: Supplement Series 18. Sheffield: JSOT Press, 1981.
Neumann, Josef N. "Kindheit in der griechisch-römischen Antike. Entwicklung –Erziehung – Erwartung." Pages 119–33 in *"Schaffe Mir Kinder . . .": Beiträge zur Kindheit im alten Israel und in seinen Nachbarkulturen*. Edited by Andreas Kunz-Lübcke and Rüdiger Lux. Arbeiten zur Bibel und ihrer Geschichte 21. Leipzig: Evangelische Verlagsanstalt, 2006.
Ngan, Lai Ling Elizabeth. "2 Kings 5." *Review and Expositor* 94 (1997): 589–97.
Nicholas, David. "Childhood in Medieval Europe." Pages 31–52 in *Children in Historical and Comparative Perspective: An International Handbook and Research Guide*. Edited by Joseph M. Hawes and N. Ray Hiner. Westport, CT: Greenwood, 1991.
Niditch, Susan. *War in the Hebrew Bible: A Study in the Ethics of Violence*. New York: Oxford University Press, 1993.
———. *Oral World and Written Word*. Louisville, KY: Westminster John Knox, 1996.
Niemann, Hermann Michael. "Royal Samaria – Capital or Residence? or: The Foundation of the City of Samaria by Sargon II." Pages 184–207 in *Ahab Agonistes: The Rise and Fall of the Omri Dynasty*. Edited by Lester L. Grabbe. Library of Hebrew Bible/Old Testament Studies 421. London: T&T Clark, 2007.
Noth, Martin. *Überlieferungsgeschichtliche Studien: Die sammelnden und bearbeitenden Geschichtswerke im Alten Testament*. Tübingen: Niemeyer, 1943. English: Martin Noth, *The Deuteronomistic History*. Translation supervised and edited by David J. A. Clines. Journal for the Study of the Old Testament: Supplementary Series 15. Sheffield: JSOT Press, 1981.

Nydegger, William F., and Corinne Nydegger. "Tarong: An Ilocos Barrio in the Philippines." Pages 697–867 in *Six Cultures: Studies of Child Rearing*. Edited by Beatrice B. Whiting. New York: John Wiley & Sons, 1963.

Oakley, Ann. "Women and Children First and Last: Parallels and Differences between Children's and Women's Studies." Pages 13–32 in *Children's Childhoods: Observed and Experienced*. Edited by Berry Mayall. London: Falmer, 1994.

Oded, Bustenay. *Mass Deportations and Deportees in the Neo-Assyrian Empire*. Wiesbaden: Ludwig Reichert, 1979.

Olyan, Saul M. "Family Religion in Israel and the Wider Levant of the First Millennium BCE." Pages 113–26 in *Household and Family Religion in Antiquity*. Edited by John Bodel and Saul M. Olyan. Oxford: Blackwell, 2008.

———. *Disability in the Hebrew Bible: Interpreting Mental and Physical Differences*. Cambridge: Cambridge University Press, 2008.

Osgood, S. Joy. "Women and Inheritance in the Land of Early Israel." Pages 29–52 in *Women in the Biblical Tradition*. Edited by George J. Brooke. Studies in Women and Religion 31. Lewiston, NY. Edwin Mellen, 1992.

Osiek, Carolyn, and David L. Balch, eds. *Families in the New Testament World: Households and House Churches*. Louisville, KY: Westminster John Knox, 1997.

Otto, Susanne. "The Composition of the Elijah-Elisha Stories and the Deuteronomistic History." *Journal for the Study of the Old Testament* 27 (2003): 487–508.

Overholt, Thomas W. *Prophecy in Cross-Cultural Perspective: A Sourcebook for Biblical Researchers*. Society of Biblical Literature Sources for Biblical Study 17. Atlanta: Scholars Press, 1986.

———. "Elijah and Elisha in the Context of Israelite Religion." Pages 94–111 in *Prophets and Paradigms: Essays in Honor of Gene M. Tucker*. Edited by Stephen Breck Reid. Journal for the Study of the Old Testament: Supplementary Series 229. Sheffield: Sheffield Academic Press, 1996.

Parker, Simon B. "Aqhat." Pages 49–80 in *Ugaritic Narrative Poetry*. Edited by Simon B. Parker. Society of Biblical Literature Writings from the Ancient World 9. Atlanta: Scholars Press, 1997.

Patterson, Cynthia. "'Not Worth Rearing': The Causes of Infant Exposure in Ancient Greece." *Transactions of the American Philological Association* 115 (1985): 103–23.

Payne, George Henry. *The Child in Human Progress*. New York: Putnam, 1916.

Perdue, Leo G., Joseph Blenkinsopp, John J. Collins, and Carol Meyers. *Families in Ancient Israel*. Louisville, KY: Westminster John Knox, 1997.
Petersen, David L. *The Roles of Israel's Prophets*. Journal for the Study of the Old Testament: Supplementary Series 17. Sheffield: Journal for the Study of the Old Testament Press, 1981.
Piaget, Jean."Jean Amos Comenius." *Prospects* 23, no. 1/2 (1993): 173–96.
Pitard, Wayne T. "Aram." *The Anchor Bible Dictionary on CD-ROM*. Logos Library System Version 2.1. 1997. Print ed.: David Noel Freedman, ed. *Anchor Bible Dictionary*. 6 vols. New York: Doubleday, 1992.
———. "Ben-Hadad." *The Anchor Bible Dictionary on CD-ROM*. Logos Library System Version 2.1. 1997. Print ed.: David Noel Freedman, ed. *Anchor Bible Dictionary*. 6 vols. New York: Doubleday, 1992.
Plotz, Judith. *Romanticism and the Vocation of Childhood*. New York: Palgrave, 2001.
Pollock, Linda A. *Forgotten Children: Parent-Child Relations from 1500 to 1900*. Cambridge: Cambridge University Press, 1983.
Postman, Neil. *The Disappearance of Childhood*. New York: Delacorte, 1982.
Powell, Mark Allan. *What is Narrative Criticism?* Minneapolis: Fortress, 1990.
Pressler, Carolyn. "Wives and Daughters, Bond and Free: Views of Women in the Slave Laws of Exodus 21.2–11." Pages 147–72 in *Gender and Law in the Hebrew Bible and the Ancient Near East*. Edited by Victor H. Matthews, Bernard M. Levinson, and Tikva Frymer-Kensky. Journal for the Study of the Old Testament: Supplement Series 262. Sheffield: Sheffield Academic Press, 1998.
Pritchard, James B., ed. *Ancient Near Eastern Texts Relating to the Old Testament*. Princeton: Princeton University Press, 1958.
Provan, Iain W. *1 & 2 Kings*. New International Biblical Commentary on the Old Testament 7. Peabody, MA: Hendrickson, 1995.
Purvis, James D. "Samaria the City." *The Anchor Bible Dictionary on CD-ROM*. Logos Library System Version 2.1. 1997. Print ed.: David Noel Freedman, ed. *Anchor Bible Dictionary*. 6 vols. New York: Doubleday, 1992.
Pyper, Hugh S. "Judging the Wisdom of Solomon: The Two-Way Effect of Intertextuality." *Journal for the Study of the Old Testament* 59 (1993): 25–36.
Qvortrup, Jens. "Childhood Matters: An Introduction." Pages 1–23 in *Childhood Matters: Social Theory, Practice and Politics*. Edited by Jens Qvortrup, Marjatta Bardy, Giovanni Sgritta, and Helmut Wintersberger. Aldershot, England: Avebury, 1994.
———, William A. Corsaro, and Michael-Sebastian Honig, eds. *The Palgrave Handbook of Childhood Studies*. New York: Palgrave Macmillan, 2009.

Rad, Gerhard von. *God at Work in Israel*. Translated by John H. Marks. Nashville, TN: Abingdon, 1980.

Rehm, Martin. *Die Bücher der Könige*. Würzburg: Echter, 1949.

Reinhartz, Adele. "Parents and Children: A Philonic Perspective." Pages 61–88 in *The Jewish Family in Antiquity*. Edited by Shaye J. D. Cohen. Brown Judaic Studies 289. Atlanta: Scholars Press, 1993.

———. "Anonymous Women and the Collapse of the Monarchy: A Study in Narrative Technique." Pages 43–65 in *A Feminist Companion to Samuel and Kings*. Edited by Athalya Brenner. Feminist Companion to the Bible 5. Sheffield: Sheffield Academic Press, 1994.

Renkema, Johann. "Does Hebrew *ytwm* Really Mean 'Fatherless'?" *Vetus Testamentum* 45.1 (1995): 119–22.

———. *Lamentations*. Historical Commentary on the Old Testament. Leuven: Peeters, 1998.

Revell, E. J. *The Designation of the Individual: Expressive Usage in Biblical Narrative*. Kampen: Kok Pharos, 1996.

Richardson, Alan. *Literature, Education, and Romanticism: Reading as Social Practice, 1780–1832*. Cambridge: Cambridge University Press, 1994.

Richardson, Laurel Walum. *The Dynamics of Sex and Gender: A Sociological Perspective*. Boston: Houghton Mifflin, 1981.

Ringgren, Helmer. "Some Observations on the Text of the Psalms." *Maarav* 5–6 (Spring 1990): 307–09.

Roberts, Benjamin B. "History of Childhood: Europe." Pages 422–26 in vol. 2 of *Encyclopedia of Children and Childhood: In History and Society*. Edited by Paula S. Fass. 3 vols. New York: Macmillan, 2004.

Robinson, J. *The Second Book of Kings*. Cambridge Bible Commentary. Cambridge: Cambridge University Press, 1976.

Rofé, Alexander. *The Prophetical Stories: The Narratives about the Prophets in the Hebrew Bible Their Literary Types and History*. Jerusalem: Magnes, 1988.

Rogerson, John. "The Family and Structures of Grace in the Old Testament." Pages 25–42 in *The Family in Theological Perspective*. Edited by Stephen C. Barton. Edinburgh: T&T Clark, 1996.

Römer, Thomas C. *The So-Called Deuteronomistic History: A Sociological, Historical, and Literary Introduction*. London: T&T Clark, 2007.

Roncace, Mark. "Elisha and the Woman of Shunem: 2 Kings 4.8–37 and 8.1–6 Read in Conjunction." *Journal for the Study of the Old Testament* 91 (2000): 109–127.

Rosenberg, A. J., ed. *II Kings: Translation of Text, Rashi*. New York: Judaica, 1980.

Roth, Martha. *Law Collections from Mesopotamia and Asia Minor*. Society of Biblical Literature Writings from the Ancient World 6. 2nd ed. Atlanta: Scholars Press, 1997.

Roth, Ray Lee. "Abana." *The Anchor Bible Dictionary on CD-ROM*. Logos Library System Version 2.1. 1997. Print ed.: David Noel Freedman, ed. *Anchor Bible Dictionary*. 6 vols. New York: Doubleday, 1992.

Rousseau, Jean-Jacques. *Emile* or *On Education*. Translated by Allan Bloom. New York: Basic, 1979.

Rundin, John S. "Pozo Moro, Child Sacrifice, and the Greek Legendary Tradition." *Journal of Biblical Literature* 123.3 (2004): 425–47.

Sadler, John E. *Comenius*. London: Macmillan, 1969.

Šanda, Albert. *Die Bücher der Könige*. Vol. 2. Exegetisches Handbuch zum Alten Testament 9. Münster in Westfalen: Aschendorffsche, 1912.

Sanday, Peggy Reeves. *Divine Hunger: Cannibalism as a Cultural System*. Cambridge: Cambridge University Press, 1986.

Sapir, Edward. *Selected Writings in Language, Culture, and Personality*. Edited by David G. Mandelbaum. Berkeley: University of California Press, 1985.

Satterthwaite, Philip E. "The Elisha Narratives and Coherence of 2 Kings 2–8." *Tyndale Bulletin* 49 (1998): 1–28.

Saussure, Ferdinand de. *Course in General Linguistics*. Translated and annotated by Roy Harris. London: Duckworth, 1983.

Schmitz, Philip C. "Tophet." *The Anchor Bible Dictionary on CD-ROM*. Logos Library System Version 2.1. 1997. Print ed.: David Noel Freedman, ed. *Anchor Bible Dictionary*. 6 vols. New York: Doubleday, 1992.

Schwartz, Daniel R. "Did the Jews Practice Infant Exposure and Infanticide in Antiquity?" *Studia philonica* 16 (2004): 61–95.

Schweizer, Harald. *Elischa in den Kriegen*. Studien zum Alten und Neuen Testaments 37. Munich: Kösel, 1974.

Seow, Choon-Leong. "First and Second Books of Kings." Pages 1–295 in vol. 3 of *The New Interpreter's Bible*. 12 vols. Edited by Leander E. Keck et al. Nashville: Abingdon, 1999.

Shahar, Shulamith. *Childhood in the Middle Ages*. London: Routledge, 1990.

Sharp, Carolyn J. *Irony and Meaning in the Hebrew Bible*. Bloomington, IN: Indiana University Press, 2009.

Shemesh, Yael. "Elisha and the Miraculous Jug of Oil (2 Kgs 4:1–7)." *Journal of Hebrew Scriptures* 8, art. 4 (2008): 1–18. doi:10.5508/jhs.2008.v8.a4.

———. "The Elisha Stories as Saints' Legends." *Journal of Hebrew Scriptures* 8, art. 5 (2008): 1–41. doi:10.5508/jhs.2008.v8.a5.

———. "'And Many Beasts' (Jonah 4:11): The Function and Status of Animals in the Book of Jonah." *Journal of Hebrew Scriptures* 10, art. 6 (2010): 1–26. doi:10.5508/jhs2010.v10.a.6.

Shields, Mary E. "Subverting a Man of God, Elevating a Woman: Role and Power Reversals in 2 Kings 4." *Journal for the Study of the Old Testament* 58 (1993): 59–69.

Shilling, Chris. *The Body and Social Theory*. London: Sage, 1993.
Shorter, Edward. *The Making of the Modern Family*. New York: Basic, 1977.
Siebert-Hommes, Jopie. "The Widow of Zarephath and the Great Woman of Shunem: A Comparative Analysis of Two Stories." Pages 231–50 in *On Reading Prophetic Texts: Gender-Specific and Related Studies in Memory of Fokkelien van Dijk-Hemmes*. Edited by Bob Becking and Meindert Dijkstra. Leiden: E. J. Brill, 1996.
Siegel, David, Timothy Coffey, and Gregory Livingston. *The Great Tween Buying Machine: Capturing Your Share of the Multi-Billion-Dollar Tween Market*. Chicago: Dearborn Trade, 2004.
Simon, Uriel. *Reading Prophetic Narratives*. Translated by Lenn J. Schramm. Indiana Studies in Biblical Literature. Bloomington: Indiana University Press, 1997.
———. "Minor Characters in Biblical Narrative." *Journal for the Study of the Old Testament* 46 (1990): 11–19.
Skinner, J. *Kings*. Century Bible. Edinburgh: T. C. & E. C. Jack, ca. 1893.
Smoak, Jeremy D. "Assyrian Siege Warfare Imagery and the Background of a Biblical Curse." Pages 83–91 in *Writing and Reading War: Rhetoric, Gender, and Ethics in Biblical and Modern Contexts*. Edited by Brad E. Kelle and Frank Ritchel Ames. Society of Biblical Literature Symposium Series 42. Leiden: Brill, 2008.
Sneed, Mark. "Israelite Concern for the Alien, Orphan, and Widow: Altrusim or Ideology?" *Zeitschrift für die alttestamentliche Wissenschaft* 111 (1999): 498–507.
Spinka, Matthew. *John Amos Comenius: That Incomparable Moravian*. Chicago: University of Chicago Press, 1943.
Sprinkle, Joe M. "2 Kings 3: History or Historical Fiction." *Bulletin for Biblical Research* 9 (1999): 247–70.
———. "Deuteronomic 'Just War' (Deut 20, 10–20) and 2 Kings 3, 27." *Zeitschrift für altorientalische und biblische Rechtsgeschichte* 6 (2000): 285–301.
Stager, Lawrence E., and Samuel R. Wolff. "Child Sacrifice at Carthage—Religious Rite or Population Control? Archeological Evidence Provides Basis for a New Analysis." *Biblical Archaeology Review* 10 (1984): 31–51.
Stager, Lawrence. "The Archaeology of the Family in Ancient Israel." *Bulletin of the American Schools of Oriental Research* 260 (1985): 1–35.
Stähli, Hans-Peter. *Knabe-Jüngling-Knecht: Untersuchungen zum Begriff* נער *im Alten Testament*. Beiträge zur biblischen Exegese und Theologie 7. Frankfurt am Main: Peter Lang, 1978.
Stavrakopoulou, Francesca. *King Manasseh and Child Sacrifice: Biblical Distortions of Historical Realities*. Beihefte zur Zeitschrift für die alttestamentliche Wissenschaft 338. Berlin: de Gruyter, 2004.

Stein, Siegfried. "The Laws on Interest in the Old Testament." *Journal of Theological Studies* 4 (1953): 161–70.
Steinberg, Naomi. "Sociological Approaches: Toward a Sociology of Childhood in the Hebrew Bible." Pages 251–69 in *Method Matters: Essays on the Interpretation of the Hebrew Bible in Honor of David L. Petersen.* Edited by Joel M. LeMon and Kent Harold Richards. Atlanta: Society of Biblical Literature, 2009.
Stephens, Sharon, ed. *Children and the Politics of Culture.* Princeton: Princeton University Press, 1995.
Sternberg, Meir. *The Poetics of Biblical Narrative: Ideological Literature and the Drama of Reading.* Bloomington: Indiana University Press, 1985.
———. "Biblical Poetics and Sexual Politics: From Reading to Counterreading." *Journal of Biblical Literature* 111 (1992): 463–88.
Stone, Lawrence. *The Family, Sex and Marriage in England 1500–1800.* New York: Harper & Row, 1977.
Strawn, Brent A. "Jeremiah's In/Effective Plea: Another Look at נער in Jeremiah I 6." *Vetus Testamentum* 55.3 (2005): 366–77.
Sweeney, Marvin A. *I & II Kings.* Old Testament Library. Louisville, KY: Westminster John Knox, 2007.
Syrén, Roger. *The Forsaken First-Born: A Study of a Recurrent Motif in the Patriarchal Narratives.* Journal for the Study of the Old Testament: Supplement Series 133. Sheffield: Sheffield Academic Press, 1993.
Theis, Joachim. "Participatory Research with Children in Vietnam." Pages 99–109 in *Children and Anthropology: Perspectives for the 21st Century.* Edited by Helen B. Schwartzman. Westport, CT: Bergin & Garvey, 2001.
Thompson, E. P. "Happy Families." Review of Lawrence Stone, *The Family, Sex and Marriage in England, 1500–1800. New Society* 41 (1977): 499–501.
Thompson, Geoff. "M. A. K. Halliday." Pages 116–22 in *Key Thinkers in Linguistics and the Philosophy of Language.* Edited by Siobhan Chapman and Christopher Routledge. Oxford: Oxford University Press, 2005.
Thompson, Henry O. "Pharpar." *The Anchor Bible Dictionary on CD-ROM.* Logos Library System Version 2.1. 1997. Print ed.: David Noel Freedman, ed. *Anchor Bible Dictionary.* 6 vols. New York: Doubleday, 1992.
Thuesen, Peter J. *In Discordance with the Scriptures: American Protestant Battles over Translating the Bible.* New York: Oxford, 1999.
Tolmie, D. F. *Narratology and Biblical Narratives: A Practical Guide.* San Francisco: International Scholars Press, 1999.
Toorn, Karel van der. *From Her Cradle to Her Grave: The Role of Religion in the Life of the Israelite and Babylonian Woman.* Translated by Sara J. Denning-Bolle. Sheffield: JSOT Press, 1994.

———. "Torn between Vice and Virtue: Stereotypes of the Widow in Israel and Mesopotamia." Pages 1–13 in *Female Stereotypes in Religious Traditions*. Edited by Ria Kloppenborg and Wouter J. Hanegraaff. Studies in the History of Religions 66. Leiden: E. J. Brill, 1995.

———. *Family Religion in Babylonia, Syria, and Israel: Continuity and Change in the Forms of Religious Life*. Leiden: E. J. Brill, 1996.

———. "Nine Months among the Peasants in the Palestinian Highlands: An Anthropological Perspective on Local Religion in the Early Iron Age." Pages 393–410 in *Symbiosis, Symbolism, and the Power of the Past: Canaan, Ancient Israel, and Their Neighbors from the Late Bronze Age through Roman Palaestina*. Edited by William G. Dever and Seymour Gitin. Winona Lake, IN: Eisenbrauns, 2003.

———. *Scribal Culture and the Making of the Hebrew Bible*. Cambridge, MA: Harvard University Press, 2007.

Trible, Phyllis. *God and the Rhetoric of Sexuality*. Overtures to Biblical Theology. Philadelphia: Fortress, 1978.

———. *Texts of Terror: Literary-Feminist Readings of Biblical Narratives*. Overtures to Biblical Theology. Philadelphia: Fortress, 1984.

Tropper, Amram. "Children and Childhood in Light of the Demographics of the Jewish Family in Late Antiquity." *Journal for the Study of Judaism in the Persian, Hellenistic, and Roman Periods* 37.3 (2006): 299–343.

Tropper, Josef. "Elischa und die 'grosse' Frau aus Schunem (2 Kön 4,8–37)." *Kleine Untersuchungen zur Sprache des Alten Testaments und seiner Umwelt* 3 (2002): 71–80.

Uffenheimer, Benjamin. *Early Prophecy in Israel*. Jerusalem: Magnes, 1999.

Ussishkin, David. *The Conquest of Lachish by Sennacherib*. Tel Aviv: Institute of Archaeology, 1982.

Van Seters, John. "Law of the Hebrew Slave: A Continuing Debate." *Zeitschrift für die alttestamentliche Wissenschaft* 119 (2007): 169–83.

Vann, Richard T. "The Youth of *Centuries of Childhood*." *History and Theory* 2 (1982): 279–97.

Vaux, Roland de. *Ancient Israel: Its Life and Institutions*. Translated by John McHugh. New York: McGraw-Hill, 1961.

———. *Studies in Old Testament Sacrifice*. Cardiff: University of Wales Press, 1964.

Volk, Konrad. "Von Findel-, Waisen-, verkauften und deportierten Kindern. Notizen aus Babylonien und Assyrien." Pages 47–87 in *"Schaffe Mir Kinder . . .": Beiträge zur Kindheit im alten Israel und in seinen Nachbarkulturen*. Edited by Andreas Kunz-Lübcke and Rüdiger Lux. Arbeiten zur Bibel und ihrer Geschichte 21. Leipzig: Evangelische Verlagsanstalt, 2006.

Vos, Clarence. *Woman in Old Testament Worship*. Amsterdam: Delft, Judels, and Brinkman, 1968.

Wall, John. "Childhood Studies, Hermeneutics, and Theological Ethics." *Journal of Religion* 86.4 (2006): 523–48.
———. *Ethics in Light of Childhood*. Washington, DC: Georgetown University Press, 2010.
Walls, Neal H. *The Goddess Anat in Ugaritic Myth*. Society of Biblical Literature Dissertation Series 135. Atlanta: Scholars Press, 1992.
Waltke, Bruce K., and M. O'Connor. *An Introduction to Biblical Hebrew Syntax*. Winona Lake, IN: Eisenbrauns, 1990.
Wargo, Eric. "Everything You Always Wanted to Know about Kemosh (But Were Afraid to Ask)." *Biblical Archaeology Review* 28.1 (2002): 44–45.
Watson, W. G. E. "The PN *yṣb* in the Keret Legend," *Ugarit Forschungen* 11 (1979): 807–9.
Weinfeld, Moshe. "The Worship of Molech and of the Queen of Heaven and Its Background," *Ugarit-Forschungen* 4 (1972): 133–54.
———. *Deuteronomy and the Deuteronomic School*. London: Clarendon, 1972.
Wenham, Gordon J. "*B^ETÛLĀH* 'A Girl of Marriageable Age.'" *Vetus Testamentum* 22 (1972): 326–48.
West, Heather C., and William J. Sabol. "Prisoners in 2007." *Bureau of Justice Statistics Bulletin*. December 2008.
Westbrook, Raymond. *Studies in Biblical and Cuneiform Law*. Cahiers de la Revue biblique 26. Paris: J. Gabalda, 1988.
———. "Elisha's True Prophecy in 2 Kings 3" *Journal of Biblical Literature* 124 (2005): 530–32.
White, Lynn K., and David B. Brinkerhoff. "Children's Work in the Family: Its Significance and Meaning." *Sociological Review* 43 (November 1981): 789–98.
White, Marsha C. *The Elijah Legends and Jehu's Coup*. Brown Judaic Studies 311. Atlanta: Scholars Press, 1997.
Whiting, Beatrice B., ed. *Six Cultures: Studies of Child Rearing*. New York: John Wiley & Sons, 1963.
Wierzbicka, Anna. *Understanding Cultures Through Their Key Words: English, Russian, Polish, German, and Japanese*. New York: Oxford University Press, 1997.
Williams, James G. *Women Recounted: Narrative Thinking and the God of Israel*. Bible and Literature Series 6. Sheffield: Almond Press, 1982.
Williams, Margaret. "The Jewish Family in Judaea from Pompey to Hadrian—the Limits of Romanization." Pages 159–82 in *The Roman Family in the Empire: Rome, Italy, and Beyond*. Edited by Michele George. Oxford: Oxford University Press, 2005.
Williams, Ronald J. *Hebrew Syntax: An Outline*. Toronto: University of Toronto Press, 1976.

Wilson, Robert R. *Prophecy and Society in Ancient Israel.* Philadelphia: Fortress, 1980.

———. "The Former Prophets: Reading the Books of Kings." Pages 83–96 in *Old Testament Interpretation: Past, Present, and Future: Essays in Honor of Gene M. Tucker.* Edited by James Luther Mays, David L. Petersen, and Kent Harold Richards. Nashville, TN: Abingdon, 1995.

———. "Unity and Diversity in the Book of Kings." Pages 293–310 in *"A Wise and Discerning Mind": Essays in Honor of Burke O. Long.* Brown Judaic Studies 325. Edited by Saul M. Olyan and Robert C. Culley. Providence, RI: Brown Judaic Studies, 2000.

Witte, Marcus, Konrad Schmid, Doris Prechel, and Jan Christian Gertz, eds. *Die deuteronomistischen Geschichtswerke: Redaktions- und religionsgeschichtliche Perspektiven zur "Deuteronomismus"-Diskussion in Tora und Vorderen Propheten.* Beihefte zur Zeitschrift für die alttestamentliche Wissenschaft 365. Berlin: de Gruyter, 2006.

Wolff, Hans Walter. "Masters and Slaves: On Overcoming Class-Struggle in the Old Testament." *Interpretation* 27.3 (1973): 266–71.

Wright, Jacob L. "Warfare and Wanton Destruction: A Reexamination of Deuteronomy 20:19–20 in Relation to Ancient Siegecraft." *Journal of Biblical Literature* 127.3 (2008): 423–58.

Würthwein, Ernst. *Die Bücher der Könige: 1. Kön. 17 – 2. Kön. 25.* Das Alte Testament Deutsch 11,2. Göttingen: Vandenhoeck & Ruprecht, 1984.

Wyse, Dominic, ed. *Childhood Studies: An Introduction.* Malden, MA: Blackwell, 2004.

Yarbrough, O. Larry. "Parents and Children in the Jewish Family of Antiquity." Pages 39–59 in *The Jewish Family in Antiquity.* Edited by Shaye J. D. Cohen. Brown Judaic Studies 289. Atlanta: Scholars Press, 1993.

Zelizer, Viviana A. *Pricing the Priceless Child: The Changing Social Value of Children.* New York, Basic, 1985.

———. "The Priceless Child Turns Twenty-Seven." *Journal of the History of Childhood and Youth* 5.3 (2012): 449–56.

Zevit, Ziony. *The Religions of Ancient Israel: A Synthesis of Parallactic Approaches.* London: Continuum, 2001.

———. "Three Debates about Bible and Archaeology." *Biblica* 83 (2002): 1–27.

Ziolkowski, Eric J. *Evil Children in Religion, Literature, and Art.* New York: Palgrave, 2001.

———. "The Bad Boys of Bethel: Origin and Development of a Sacrilegious Type." *History of Religions* 30 (1991): 331–58.

Zuck, Roy B. *Precious in His Sight: Childhood and Children in the Bible.* Grand Rapids, MI: Baker, 1996.

Zwilling, Anne-Laure. *Frères et sœures dan la Bible: Les relations fraternelles dans l'Ancien et le Nouveau Testament.* Paris: Éditions du Cerf, 2010.

# Index of Biblical Passages

Page references in bold under 2 Kings (see 2 Kings 2:23-25; 3:26-27; 4:1-7; 4:8-37; 5:1-14; 6:24-31; 8:1-6) should also be consulted for the individual verses within the range of verses.

| Hebrew Bible/ Old Testament | | 19:4 | 60, 63 | 22:2 | 108 |
|---|---|---|---|---|---|
| | | 19:7 | 49 | 22:3 | 96, 100 |
| | | 19:8 | 58 | 22:10 | 48 |
| Genesis | | 19:10 | 126 | 22:12 | 108 |
| 1:27–28 | 41 | 19:31–38 | 52 | 22:13 | 51 |
| 3:16 | 7, 46 | 19:31–32 | 51 | 22:16–18 | 112 |
| 5 | 47 | 19:31 | 51 | 22:16 | 108 |
| 9:7 | 41 | 19:33 | 51 | 22:17–18 | 42 |
| 11:10–32 | 47 | 19:34 | 51 | 22:17 | 57 |
| 11:30 | 150 | 19:37 | 51 | 24 | 57 |
| 11:31 | 46 | 19:38 | 51 | 24:10–67 | 10 |
| 12:2–3 | 42 | 21:1–8 | 7 | 24:14–61 | 62 |
| 12:10 | 185 | 21:1–5 | 149, 154 | 24:14 | 63 |
| 13:14–15 | 41 | 21:1–2 | 150 | 24:16 | 58, 62, 63 |
| 14:16 | 49 | 21:4 | 41 | 24:17–20 | 173 |
| 15:2–4 | 149 | 21:5 | 25 | 24:23 | 46 |
| 15:5 | 42 | 21:6 | 151 | 24:28 | 62, 63 |
| 15:12 | 42 | 21:7 | 68 | 24:43 | 56 |
| 16:1–9 | 162 | 21:8–21 | 151, 152 | 24:50–51 | 62 |
| 16:1–6 | 147, 172 | 21:8–11 | 49 | 24:55–58 | 172 |
| 16:1–2 | 42, 183 | 21:8 | 43, 64, 69, 70 | 24:55 | 62, 63 |
| 16:10 | 42 | 21:9–20 | 10 | 24:57 | 62, 63 |
| 17:1–22 | 149 | 21:9–12 | 147 | 24:59 | 68 |
| 17:4–8 | 42 | 21:12 | 61, 63 | 24:60 | 42, 50 |
| 17:9–27 | 41 | 21:14–15 | 154 | 24:61 | 172 |
| 17:12 | 46 | 21:14 | 54 | 25:20 | 25, 55 |
| 17:17 | 25, 55 | 21:15 | 54 | 25:21–26 | 149 |
| 17:20 | 152 | 21:16–19 | 154 | 25:21 | 42, 150, 151, 154 |
| 17:21 | 152 | 21:16 | 43 | | |
| 17:23–27 | 41 | 21:17–19 | 63 | 25:22–23 | 154 |
| 18:1–16 | 7 | 21:21 | 55 | 25:23–26 | 68 |
| 18:1–15 | 149 | 22:1–19 | 10, 115, 117, 118, 151, 152, 189 | 25:23 | 152 |
| 18:1–10 | 151 | | | 25:25–26 | 151 |
| 18:1–8 | 57 | | | 25:27 | 62 |
| 18:10–14 | 154 | 22:1–14 | 48 | 26:1 | 185 |
| 18:10 | 147 | 22:1–13 | 15 | 26:3–4 | 42 |
| 18:13–14 | 150 | 22:1–10 | 154 | 26:34 | 25, 55 |
| 18:14 | 147 | 22:2–3 | 108, 123, 133 | 27:1–45 | 108 |

233

## 234  Index of Biblical Passages

| Genesis (continued) | | 43:29 | 49 | 4:23 | 51, 52 |
|---|---|---|---|---|---|
| 27:37 | 125 | 43:30 | 49 | 6:16 | 46 |
| 28:13–14 | 42 | 43:33 | 11, 49, 52, 73 | 6:20 | 43 |
| 29:4 | 49 | 44:2 | 49 | 10:9–10 | 66 |
| 29:6 | 46 | 44:12 | 49 | 10:9 | 47, 60, 63 |
| 29:9 | 133 | 44:20 | 43, 49, 52, 49 | 10:10 | 67 |
| 29:15 | 49 | 44:22–34 | 62 | 10:24 | 67 |
| 29:23 | 46 | 44:23 | 49 | 11:5 | 51 |
| 29:26 | 51, 52 | 44:26 | 49 | 12:5 | 46 |
| 29:31–30:24 | 149, 150, 183 | 44:30 | 49 | 12:7–11 | 129 |
| | | 44:31 | 49 | 12:9 | 186 |
| 29:31 | 150 | 44:32 | 49 | 12:12 | 51 |
| 30:1 | 42, 155 | 44:33 | 49 | 12:22 | 126 |
| 30:14–16 | 155 | 44:34 | 49 | 12:23 | 126 |
| 30:21 | 46, 64 | 45:4–8 | 152 | 12:29 | 51 |
| 30:22–24 | 151, 155 | 45:19 | 67 | 12:37 | 66 |
| 30:24 | 151 | 46:5–7 | 68 | 12:43–48 | 41 |
| 33:2 | 64 | 46:5 | 67 | 13:2 | 117 |
| 33:5 | 43 | 46:7 | 47 | 13:11–15 | 51, 117 |
| 33:13–14 | 43, 74 | 46:34 | 63, 73 | 15 | 183 |
| 34 | 50 | 47:12 | 66, 67 | 15:21 | 165 |
| 34:1–12 | 172 | 47:15–21 | 133 | 16:23 | 186 |
| 34:1 | 173 | 47:15–20 | 185 | 18:2–4 | 68 |
| 34:4 | 64, 74 | 47:24 | 66, 67 | 21:2–11 | 129, 130 |
| 34:13–31 | 50 | 48:14 | 52 | 21:2–6 | 129 |
| 34:14–24 | 41 | 50:8 | 67 | 21:2–4 | 132 |
| 34:19 | 62 | 50:21 | 67 | 21:2–3 | 171 |
| 34:29 | 66 | | | 21:2 | 129, 130, 171 |
| 35:8 | 68 | Exodus | | | |
| 35:11–12 | 41 | 1:8–2:10 | 184 | 21:3–6 | 134 |
| 35:16–26 | 150 | 1:15–2:10 | 189 | 21:4–5 | 132 |
| 35:16–19 | 42 | 1:15–20 | 188 | 21:5 | 46 |
| 35:18 | 42 | 1:16 | 46, 65 | 21:7–11 | 129, 130, 132 |
| 37 | 10, 15 | 1:22–2:10 | 155 | 21:7 | 130, 133, 185 |
| 37:1–27 | 49 | 1:22 | 173 | 21:8 | 131 |
| 37:1–11 | 50 | 2:1–10 | 10, 35, 50, 151, 153 | 21:9 | 131 |
| 37:2 | 62, 63, 64 | | | 21:10–11 | 129 |
| 37:30 | 64 | 2:1–9 | 15 | 21:10 | 131 |
| 37:34 | 179 | 2:3–10 | 64 | 21:11 | 131 |
| 38:2 | 46 | 2:3 | 43 | 21:21 | 171 |
| 38:6–26 | 121, 122 | 2:4–9 | 173 | 21:22 | 64 |
| 38:27–30 | 68 | 2:5 | 172 | 22:20–21 | 121 |
| 39:1–20 | 140 | 2:6–9 | 43 | 22:21–22 | 53, 121 |
| 41:45–46 | 55 | 2:6 | 61, 63 | 22:23 | 54, 121 |
| 42:1–5 | 185 | 2:7–10 | 46 | 22:24 | 123 |
| 42:13 | 49 | 2:7–9 | 68 | 22:28 | 51, 117 |
| 42:15 | 49 | 2:7 | 173 | 23:1–11 | 54 |
| 42:20 | 49 | 2:8 | 14, 56 | 23:19 | 186 |
| 42:22 | 64 | 2:9 | 69 | 23:26 | 42 |
| 42:32 | 49 | 3:21–22 | 125 | 32:2 | 47 |
| 42:34 | 49 | 4:22 | 52 | 34:20 | 51, 117 |
| 43:8 | 49, 66 | 4:23–26 | 151, 152, 155 | 34:26 | 186 |

# Index of Biblical Passages

| Leviticus | |
|---|---|
| 6:21 | 186 |
| 10:14 | 47 |
| 12 | 7 |
| 12:3 | 41 |
| 12:6 | 46 |
| 13–14 | 159 |
| 18 | 5 |
| 18:21–24 | 112 |
| 18:21 | 117 |
| 20 | 112 |
| 20:2–4 | 117 |
| 20:20–21 | 42 |
| 22:4–6 | 159 |
| 22:13 | 73 |
| 25:1–7 | 54 |
| 25:35–37 | 54 |
| 25:36–37 | 123 |
| 25:39–46 | 129, 131 |
| 25:39–44 | 129 |
| 25:39–43 | 131 |
| 25:39–41 | 132 |
| 25:39 | 131, 133, 185 |
| 25:41 | 132, 134 |
| 25:44–46 | 129, 131 |
| 25:44 | 131 |
| 25:45–46 | 171 |
| 25:45 | 131, 132 |
| 25:46 | 129, 132, 171 |
| 26:9 | 42 |
| 26:22 | 100 |
| 26:29 | 48, 186, 187, 188 |
| 27:1–7 | 25 |
| 27:5–6 | 161 |

| Numbers | |
|---|---|
| 3:12–13 | 51 |
| 3:13 | 51 |
| 3:15 | 47 |
| 3:39–45 | 51 |
| 3:40–41 | 117 |
| 3:46–51 | 51 |
| 5:1–4 | 159 |
| 5:22 | 51 |
| 6:19 | 186 |
| 8:15–18 | 51 |
| 8:17 | 51 |
| 11:8 | 186 |
| 11:12 | 70 |
| 11:28 | 11, 73 |
| 12 | 183 |

| | |
|---|---|
| 12:1–15 | 159 |
| 14:3 | 66 |
| 14:28–31 | 44 |
| 14:31 | 44, 66, 67 |
| 16:27–33 | 66 |
| 16:27 | 66 |
| 17:23 | 69 |
| 18:9–10 | 47 |
| 18:11 | 47 |
| 18:15 | 51, 117 |
| 18:19 | 47 |
| 18:27 | 181 |
| 20:1 | 183 |
| 21:29 | 48 |
| 22:21–33 | 98 |
| 22:41 | 95 |
| 23:13 | 95 |
| 24:2 | 95 |
| 24:20 | 95 |
| 24:21 | 95 |
| 26:33 | 46 |
| 26:59 | 43, 50, 68, 183 |
| 27:1–11 | 47 |
| 30:4 | 73 |
| 30:17 | 73 |
| 31:9 | 66 |
| 31:17–18 | 66 |
| 31:17 | 66 |
| 32:16 | 67 |
| 32:17 | 67 |
| 32:24 | 67 |
| 32:26 | 67 |
| 36:1–12 | 47 |

| Deuteronomy | |
|---|---|
| 1:31 | 10 |
| 1:39 | 67 |
| 2:34 | 66 |
| 3:6 | 66 |
| 3:19 | 66 |
| 7:4 | 109 |
| 7:14 | 42 |
| 10:17–18 | 121 |
| 10:18 | 133 |
| 11:17 | 109 |
| 12–26 | 54 |
| 12:12 | 46 |
| 12:13–14 | 92 |
| 12:31 | 48, 110, 115, 117 |
| 13:14 | 46 |
| 14:21 | 186 |

| | |
|---|---|
| 15:12–18 | 129, 130 |
| 15:12–15 | 171 |
| 15:12–14 | 132 |
| 15:12 | 129, 130, 133, 171 |
| 15:14 | 181 |
| 15:16–17 | 130 |
| 16:7 | 186 |
| 16:13 | 181 |
| 16:16 | 92 |
| 17:10 | 92 |
| 18:9–12 | 112 |
| 18:10–12 | 117 |
| 18:10 | 48, 110 |
| 18:15 | 49 |
| 20:4 | 110 |
| 20:14 | 66 |
| 21:15–17 | 50 |
| 21:16 | 52 |
| 22:13–21 | 59, 60 |
| 22:15–29 | 62, 172 |
| 22:23 | 59 |
| 22:28 | 59 |
| 23:5 | 95 |
| 23:7 | 49 |
| 23:21 | 123 |
| 24:9 | 183 |
| 24:17–21 | 54 |
| 24:17 | 121 |
| 24:19 21 | 121 |
| 25:11 | 140 |
| 26:12–13 | 133 |
| 27:19 | 121 |
| 28:32 | 48 |
| 28:41 | 48 |
| 28:50 | 61, 63 |
| 28:53–57 | 186, 187, 188 |
| 28:53 | 48, 186, 187 |
| 28:54–57 | 186 |
| 29:9–12 | 44, 67 |
| 31:11–13 | 44 |
| 31:12 | 66, 67 |
| 32:1–13 | 10 |
| 32:25 | 23, 57, 70 |
| 33:19 | 69 |

| Joshua | |
|---|---|
| 1:14 | 67 |
| 5:2–8 | 41 |
| 6:21 | 61, 63 |
| 6:26 | 52, 100 |
| 7 | 5 |

## 236  Index of Biblical Passages

| Joshua (continued) | | 15:18 | 168 | 3:1–19 | 15 |
|---|---|---|---|---|---|
| 8:35 | 44 | 15:19 | 154 | 3:1–18 | 10 |
| 19:18 | 137 | 18:21 | 67 | 3:7 | 63 |
| 24:9 | 95 | 19 | 189 | 4:19–22 | 140 |
| | | 19:3–9 | 62, 172 | 4:19–20 | 42 |
| Judges | | 19:3–8 | 60 | 4:21 | 61, 64 |
| 2:12–14 | 109 | 19:22–27 | 126 | 9:2 | 58 |
| 2:20–21 | 109 | 19:22–26 | 172 | 9:6–8 | 120 |
| 3:8 | 109 | 19:23 | 49, 148 | 9:7–8 | 166 |
| 4–5 | 183 | 19:24 | 60 | 9:11 | 172 |
| 5:1–31 | 165 | 19:29–30 | 189 | 10:5–13 | 106 |
| 8:13–21 | 114 | 21:7 | 47 | 12:2 | 63 |
| 8:18–21 | 114 | 21:10 | 66 | 14:49 | 51 |
| 8:20–21 | 117 | 21:12–23 | 60 | 15:3 | 23, 70, 71 |
| 8:21 | 115 | 21:12–14 | 172 | 15:8–9 | 110 |
| 10:7 | 109 | 21:12 | 58, 59 | 16–17 | 173 |
| 11:9 | 118 | 21:21 | 47 | 16:1–13 | 173 |
| 11:10 | 118 | | | 16:11 | 62, 93 |
| 11:11 | 118 | Ruth | | 16:14–23 | 173 |
| 11:21 | 118 | 1:1–5 | 121 | 17 | 10, 173 |
| 11:23 | 118 | 1:1 | 68, 185 | 17:12–29 | 50 |
| 11:24 | 118 | 1:5 | 64 | 17:13 | 52 |
| 11:27 | 118 | 1:11 | 47 | 17:26 | 142 |
| 11:29–40 | 48, 112, 118, | 2:5–9 | 172 | 17:33 | 63 |
| | 189 | 2:6–8 | 172 | 17:43 | 95 |
| 11:29 | 118 | 2:6 | 60 | 17:55 | 56 |
| 11:30–40 | 110, 115, 117 | 2:7 | 3 | 17:56 | 56 |
| 11:30 | 118 | 2:22 | 172 | 17:58 | 56 |
| 11:31 | 118 | 3 | 122 | 18:17–21 | 51 |
| 11:32 | 118 | 3:2 | 172 | 20:21 | 56 |
| 11:34 | 108 | 3:10 | 58 | 20:22 | 56 |
| 11:35 | 118 | 4 | 121 | 20:35 | 56, 63 |
| 11:36–40 | 121 | 4:16 | 43, 64 | 20:36 | 56 |
| 11:36–37 | 118 | | | 20:37 | 56 |
| 11:36 | 118 | 1 Samuel | | 20:38 | 56 |
| 11:39 | 58 | 1 | 149 | 20:39 | 56 |
| 11:40 | 46 | 1:1–20 | 42, 183 | 20:40 | 56 |
| 13 | 42, 149 | 1:2–4 | 64 | 22:19 | 23, 70, 71 |
| 13:1–24 | 140 | 1:4 | 47 | 25:2–3 | 139 |
| 13:2 | 150 | 1:11 | 152 | 25:39–42 | 121 |
| 13:3–24 | 151 | 1:17 | 155 | 25:42 | 172 |
| 13:3–5 | 152 | 1:20 | 151 | 28:4 | 137 |
| 13:3 | 150 | 1:22–24 | 69 | 30:1–3 | 160 |
| 13:5–24 | 62 | 1:22 | 61, 62, 64, 152 | 30:3 | 47, 48 |
| 13:5–7 | 64 | 1:23–24 | 69, 70 | 30:12 | 154 |
| 13:5 | 61 | 1:23 | 68, 69 | | |
| 13:6–7 | 155 | 1:24 | 61, 68 | 2 Samuel | |
| 13:7 | 61 | 2:1–10 | 165 | 2:10 | 25 |
| 13:8 | 61 | 2:13 | 186 | 3:2–5 | 52 |
| 13:12 | 61, 63 | 2:15 | 186 | 3:22 | 160 |
| 13:21–23 | 155 | 2:18–21 | 15 | 3:26–29 | 159 |
| 14:10 | 58 | 2:21 | 46 | 3:38 | 139 |

# Index of Biblical Passages 237

| | | | | | |
|---|---|---|---|---|---|
| 5:4 | 25 | 4:15 | 47 | 20:30–34 | 158 |
| 5:13 | 47 | 9:13 | 49 | 20:31–34 | 158 |
| 6:23 | 42 | 10:5 | 154 | 20:39 | 181 |
| 9 | 60 | 11:7 | 109 | 21:27 | 179, 182 |
| 9:9–10 | 46 | 11:14–17 | 93 | 22:1–28 | 168 |
| 9:9 | 61 | 11:17 | 52 | 22:1–4 | 158 |
| 9:10 | 60 | 11:20 | 69, 70 | 22:1 | 158 |
| 9:12 | 52 | 11:23–25 | 158 | 22:7 | 105 |
| 11–12 | 85 | 11:33 | 109 | 22:29–36 | 158 |
| 11:27 | 151 | 12 | 93 | 22:39 | 175 |
| 12:15 | 43, 64, 65 | 12:8–14 | 64 | | |
| 12:18–22 | 65 | 12:26–33 | 92 | 2 Kings | |
| 13:1–29 | 50 | 12:28–30 | 92 | 1:8 | 94 |
| 13:1–20 | 50 | 13:20–28 | 98 | 1:9–14 | 100 |
| 13:2 | 59 | 14:1–18 | 117 | 1:9 | 100 |
| 13:4–20 | 49 | 14:1–3 | 62, 120 | 1:10 | 100 |
| 13:8 | 186 | 14:2–3 | 166 | 1:11 | 100 |
| 13:12 | 148 | 14:12 | 43 | 1:12 | 100 |
| 13:17–18 | 126 | 14:17 | 117 | 1:13 | 100 |
| 14:4–11 | 181 | 15:18–22 | 158 | 1:14 | 100 |
| 15:22 | 67 | 16:23–24 | 175 | 2–8 | 13 |
| 17:8 | 101 | 16:31 | 47 | 2 | 93 |
| 17:15 | 166 | 16:34 | 52, 100, 115 | 2:1–10 | 164 |
| 18–22 | 43 | 17:1 | 80 | 2:1–7 | 164 |
| 18:22 | 46 | 17:8–24 | 138, 153 | 2:1–3 | 92 |
| 19:5 | 145 | 17:8–16 | 80, 154 | 2:1 | 138 |
| 19:6 | 47 | 17:8–15 | 134, 135 | 2:2–3 | 92, 98, 138 |
| 19:8 | 63 | 17:8–12 | 154 | 2:2 | 94, 142 |
| 19:24 | 46 | 17:10–24 | 80 | 2:3 | 92, 120 |
| 19:33 | 139 | 17:12–13 | 80 | 2:4–5 | 138 |
| 23:36–39 | 117 | 17:12 | 134 | 2:5 | 92, 120 |
| | | 17:13 | 134 | 2:6–7 | 138 |
| 1 Kings | | 17:15 | 134 | 2:12 | 80, 181, 192 |
| 1:1–15 | 138 | 17:17–24 | 43, 80, 149, 151, 152, 154 | 2:13–14 | 83, 159 |
| 1:2–4 | 62, 172 | | | 2:14 | 163 |
| 1:2 | 59 | 17:17 | 154, 155 | 2:15–18 | 164 |
| 1:3 | 172 | 17:18 | 155 | 2:15 | 120 |
| 2:13–25 | 138 | 17:19 | 155 | 2:16–17 | 106 |
| 3:16–28 | 178, 181, 187, 188 | 17:20 | 154, 155 | 2:16 | 46 |
| | | 17:21 | 154 | 2:19–22 | 83, 91, 97, 101 |
| 3:16 | 187 | 17:22 | 154 | | |
| 3:17–21 | 187 | 17:24 | 154 | 2:23–25 | 15, 81, 82, 84, 89, **91–101**, 122, 124, 142, 192 |
| 3:17–18 | 187 | 18:1–16 | 120 | | |
| 3:19 | 187 | 18:3 | 120 | | |
| 3:21 | 68, 69 | 18:12 | 63, 73, 120 | 2:23–24 | 122, 197 |
| 3:23–27 | 187 | 18:19 | 105 | 2:23 | 52, 61, 92, 138, 160, 192, 197 |
| 3:24–25 | 187 | 19:15–21 | 13 | | |
| 3:25 | 64 | 19:21 | 186 | 2:24–31 | 186 |
| 3:27 | 43 | 20:1–30 | 158 | 2:24 | 65, 83, 116, 163, 179, 192 |
| 3:28 | 179 | 20:1–29 | 158 | | |
| 3:7 | 62, 92, 93 | 20:1–4 | 117 | 2:25 | 138, 192 |
| 4:11 | 47 | 20:5–7 | 117 | 2:39–41 | 83 |

## Index of Biblical Passages

**2 Kings** (*continued*)

| Ref | Pages |
|---|---|
| 3 | 103, 104, 111, 118 |
| 3:1–8:15 | 177 |
| 3:1–3 | 103 |
| 3:1–2 | 177 |
| 3:2 | 104, 118 |
| 3:4–27 | 81 |
| 3:4–5 | 103 |
| 3:4 | 105 |
| 3:6 | 103 |
| 3:7 | 103, 105 |
| 3:8–20 | 138 |
| 3:8 | 103 |
| 3:9–27 | 104 |
| 3:9–15 | 193 |
| 3:9 | 105 |
| 3:10–18 | 104 |
| 3:10 | 105, 111, 118 |
| 3:11–20 | 122 |
| 3:11 | 105, 118, 142 |
| 3:12 | 118 |
| 3:13–15 | 106, 122, 142 |
| 3:13 | 105, 111, 118, 122, 163 |
| 3:14–27 | 142 |
| 3:14–19 | 106 |
| 3:14–15 | 163 |
| 3:14 | 118 |
| 3:15–19 | 122 |
| 3:15 | 118, 122 |
| 3:16–19 | 122, 179, 193 |
| 3:16–17 | 106 |
| 3:16 | 118 |
| 3:17–20 | 79 |
| 3:17 | 118 |
| 3:18–19 | 110, 111, 122 |
| 3:18 | 106, 116, 118, 122 |
| 3:19 | 106, 111 |
| 3:20–26 | 193 |
| 3:20 | 106 |
| 3:21–24 | 107 |
| 3:21 | 106, 107, 114 |
| 3:24 | 80 |
| 3:25 | 111, 122 |
| 3:26–27 | 15, 48, 81, **103–18**, 117, 122, 193, 197 |
| 3:27 | 79, 107, 108, 119, 122, 123, 133, 160, 193 |
| 4:1–7 | 15, 43, 48, 80, 81, 83, 84, 97, **119–35**, 179, 181, 185, 193–94, 197 |
| 4:1 | 46, 47, 54, 65, 68, 181, 185, 193 |
| 4:2 | 193 |
| 4:3–6 | 163 |
| 4:3–5 | 193 |
| 4:3 | 163, 194 |
| 4:5 | 194, 197 |
| 4:6 | 160, 194 |
| 4:7 | 163, 193 |
| 4:8 | 159, 195 |
| 4:8–37 | 15, 80, 81, 128, **137–55**, 191, 194–95 |
| 4:8–13 | 194 |
| 4:8–10 | 80, 194 |
| 4:9–10 | 194 |
| 4:11–17 | 167 |
| 4:11–13 | 195 |
| 4:12–17 | 191 |
| 4:12–15 | 163, 164 |
| 4:12–13 | 164 |
| 4:12 | 163, 164, 192, 194 |
| 4:13–17 | 194 |
| 4:13–16 | 42 |
| 4:13 | 194, 195 |
| 4:14–17 | 194, 195 |
| 4:16–17 | 163 |
| 4:16 | 82, 194 |
| 4:17–35 | 43 |
| 4:18–37 | 197 |
| 4:19 | 160, 194 |
| 4:21 | 126 |
| 4:22–30 | 194 |
| 4:22–24 | 194 |
| 4:25–32 | 164 |
| 4:25–26 | 163, 164, 194 |
| 4:25 | 164, 192, 194 |
| 4:26–28 | 194 |
| 4:27–37 | 80 |
| 4:27 | 194 |
| 4:28 | 194 |
| 4:29–37 | 194 |
| 4:29–35 | 62, 64 |
| 4:29–31 | 163 |
| 4:30 | 194 |
| 4:31 | 194 |
| 4:32–37 | 191 |
| 4:32–35 | 83, 163, 179 |
| 4:33 | 126 |
| 4:35 | 167 |
| 4:36–37 | 43 |
| 4:36 | 163, 164, 192, 194 |
| 4:38–41 | 97, 120, 185 |
| 4:38 | 120, 186 |
| 4:40 | 181 |
| 4:42–44 | 84, 97 |
| 4:42 | 166 |
| 5 | 82 |
| 5:1–27 | 81 |
| 5:1–24 | 81 |
| 5:1–14 | 15, 81, 82, **157–74**, 195–96 |
| 5:1–6 | 197 |
| 5:1 | 80, 82, 84, 139 |
| 5:2 | 52, 63, 84, 93, 196 |
| 5:3 | 82, 105, 196, 197 |
| 5:4–9 | 82 |
| 5:4 | 196 |
| 5:5–6 | 196 |
| 5:8–14 | 179 |
| 5:8–10 | 142 |
| 5:9–10 | 82 |
| 5:13 | 82, 142 |
| 5:14 | 56, 74, 82, 84, 93, 196 |
| 5:17–18 | 82 |
| 5:19–24 | 143 |
| 5:20–27 | 164 |
| 5:20–24 | 164 |
| 5:20 | 164 |
| 5:22 | 120 |
| 5:25–27 | 84 |
| 5:25–26 | 80, 143 |
| 5:25 | 164 |
| 5:27 | 80, 143 |
| 6–7 | 177 |
| 6 | 183 |
| 6:1–7 | 97 |
| 6:1–4 | 120 |
| 6:1–2 | 120 |
| 6:5–7 | 84 |
| 6:5 | 181 |
| 6:6:24 | 158 |
| 6:8–24 | 82 |

Index of Biblical Passages   239

| | | | | | |
|---|---|---|---|---|---|
| 6:8–19 | 158 | 13:14–19 | 158 | 22:1 | 160 |
| 6:8 | 80 | 13:14–18 | 192 | 22:9 | 46 |
| 6:15–23 | 158 | 13:14 | 80 | 22:10–12 | 188 |
| 6:18–20 | 84 | 13:17 | 158 | 22:11 | 68 |
| 6:20–23 | 158 | 13:19 | 192 | 22:23–24 | 188 |
| 6:23 | 160 | 13:20–21 | 83, 84, 155, | 26:19–23 | 159 |
| 6:24–7:20 | 81, 82, 180, 182 | | 192 | 28:3 | 48 |
| 6:24–31 | 15, 81, 84, | 13:20 | 160 | 28:8 | 48 |
| | **175–89**, 196–97 | 13:21 | 149 | 29:9 | 47 |
| 6:24–25 | 158 | 13:22–23 | 158 | 31:15 | 52 |
| 6:26 | 133, 193 | 14:1–18 | 117 | 31:16 | 47 |
| 6:28–29 | 65, 160, 197 | 15:5 | 159 | 31:18 | 44, 47, 67 |
| 6:29 | 197 | 15:16 | 96 | 32:9–11 | 176 |
| 6:31 | 196, 197 | 16:2–4 | 112 | 33:6 | 110, 117 |
| 6:32 | 126, 179 | 16:2–3 | 117 | 34:22–28 | 183 |
| 7:16 | 183 | 16:3 | 110, 115, 117 | 34:30 | 52 |
| 8:1–7 | 194 | 16:11 | 118 | 35:13 | 186 |
| 8:1–6 | 15, 81, 143, 151, | 17:13–17 | 112 | 36:17 | 57 |
| | 155, **191–97** | 17:17–24 | 80 | | |
| 8:1–3 | 82 | 17:17 | 48, 110, 115, | Ezra | |
| 8:1–2 | 185 | | 117 | 2:61 | 46 |
| 8:1 | 180 | 17:31 | 48, 110, 117 | 8:21 | 66, 67 |
| 8:3 | 133 | 18:9–11 | 176 | 10:1 | 44, 65 |
| 8:4–6 | 83 | 19:1–2 | 179 | | |
| 8:4–5 | 80 | 19:6 | 61 | Nehemiah | |
| 8:4 | 164 | 19:21 | 59 | 3:12 | 133 |
| 8:5–6 | 181 | 20:19–20 | 106 | 4:8 | 47 |
| 8:7–15 | 158, 192, 195 | 21:1–9 | 112 | 5:1–13 | 132 |
| 8:12 | 15, 58, 60, 71, | 21:6 | 110, 115, 117 | 5:1–5 | 123, 133 |
| | 96 | 22:14–20 | 183 | 5:1 | 133 |
| 8:18 | 47 | 23:3–25 | 112 | 5:3–5 | 134 |
| 8:26 | 47 | 23:10 | 46, 48, 117 | 5:3 | 185 |
| 9:1–13 | 100 | 23:13 | 109 | 5:5 | 48, 128, 132, |
| 9:1–10 | 195 | 23:15–19 | 92 | | 134, 173, 185 |
| 9:1–3 | 192 | 24:2 | 160 | 5:8 | 49 |
| 9:12 | 166 | 25:1–3 | 176 | 10:29 | 47 |
| 9:14–15 | 158 | | | 10:36–38 | 51 |
| 10:13–14 | 100 | 1 Chronicles | | 12:43 | 44 |
| 10:14 | 100 | 2:13–15 | 52 | 12:43 | 65 |
| 10:29 | 92 | 3:1–3 | 52 | | |
| 11:1–4 | 184, 188 | 3:15 | 52 | Esther | |
| 11:1–3 | 188 | 5:29 | 183 | 1:5, 20 | 52 |
| 11:2 | 68, 188 | 8:1–2 | 52 | 2:2–4 | 172 |
| 11:4–21 | 188 | 12:10–14 | 52 | 2:2 | 61 |
| 11:21–12:2 | 188 | 15:20 | 57 | 2:3 | 59 |
| 12:1–22 | 188 | 28:8 | 41 | 2:4 | 63 |
| 12:1 | 188 | | | 2:7 | 49, 63 |
| 12:18–19 | 158 | 2 Chronicles | | 2:9–13 | 172 |
| 13:3–7 | 158 | 10:8–14 | 64 | 3:13 | 61, 63, 66 |
| 13:3 | 158 | 11:18–21 | 68 | 4:4 | 172 |
| 13:4–5 | 158 | 13:21 | 68 | 4:16 | 172 |
| 13:14–21 | 13, 192, 195 | 21:3 | 50 | 6:3 | 61 |

## Index of Biblical Passages

**Esther** (*continued*)
- 7:8 — 134
- 8:3–5 — 159
- 8:11 — 66

**Job**
- 3:10 — 51
- 3:12 — 69
- 10:11–12 — 152
- 13:26 — 73
- 16:11 — 72
- 19:18 — 72
- 20:11 — 11, 56, 73
- 20:16 — 69
- 21:7 — 65
- 21:8 — 72
- 21:11 — 72
- 21:19 — 72
- 22:8 — 159
- 24:3 — 121
- 24:9 — 53, 54, 72, 73
- 24:21 — 121
- 29:5 — 62
- 29:13 — 133
- 31:16–22 — 121
- 31:18 — 63, 73
- 33:25 — 11, 56, 73, 74
- 36:14 — 11, 73
- 40:29 — 172

**Psalms**
- 8:2 — 23
- 8:3 — 70, 71
- 9:1 — 57
- 14:4 — 187
- 22 — 7
- 25:7 — 73
- 29:31–30:24 — 42
- 46:1 — 57
- 68:6 — 133
- 68:25 — 57
- 68:26 — 56, 57
- 71:5 — 63
- 71:17 — 63, 73
- 78:31 — 58
- 78:51 — 51
- 78:63 — 57
- 88:15 — 73
- 88:16 — 11
- 89:46 — 11, 56, 73
- 94:6 — 53, 121
- 103:5 — 63
- 105:36 — 51
- 106:37–38 — 48, 117
- 106:37 — 115
- 109:9 — 54
- 110:3 — 73
- 113:9 — 42
- 114:4 — 46
- 115:13 — 52
- 119:5 — 165
- 119:9 — 165
- 119:19 — 165
- 119:23 — 165
- 119:110 — 165
- 119:141 — 165
- 123:2 — 162
- 127:3–5 — 42, 43
- 128:3–4 — 42
- 128:3 — 46
- 129:1 — 63
- 131:2 — 69
- 135:8 — 51
- 136:10 — 51
- 137:8 — 46
- 137:9 — 71
- 144:10 — 168
- 146:9 — 121, 133
- 147:9 — 46
- 148:12 — 57, 61, 63

**Proverbs**
- 2:1 — 46
- 7:7 — 74
- 7:13 — 140
- 9:3 — 172
- 15:25 — 121
- 17:12 — 101
- 22:15 — 74
- 27:27 — 172
- 29:15 — 74
- 29:21 — 11, 73
- 30:19 — 56
- 30:23 — 162
- 31 — 140
- 31:2 — 51
- 31:10–31 — 140, 144
- 31:11 — 141
- 31:15 — 162, 172
- 31:23 — 141
- 31:28 — 141

**Ecclesiastes**
- 11:9–10 — 10, 73
- 11:9 — 11, 73
- 12:1 — 11, 73
- 12:12 — 46

**Song of Solomon**
- 1:3 — 56
- 6:8 — 56
- 7:1 — 138
- 8:1 — 70
- 8:8 — 50

**Isaiah**
- 1:16–17 — 121
- 1:17 — 54, 133
- 1:23 — 54, 121, 133
- 3:3 — 159
- 3:5 — 61, 63
- 3:14–15 — 134
- 5:8 — 134
- 7:14 — 14, 56, 58
- 7:16 — 62, 67
- 8:4 — 61
- 9:5 — 64
- 9:14 — 159
- 9:16 — 53, 54, 58
- 10:2 — 53, 54, 133
- 11:8 — 69, 70
- 13:16 — 71
- 14:22 — 42
- 18:5 — 69
- 19:11 — 46
- 20:4 — 61, 63
- 22:4 — 46
- 23:4 — 57
- 23:10 — 46
- 23:12 — 59
- 28:9 — 69
- 30:33 — 117
- 31:8 — 58, 60
- 37:22 — 59
- 40:30 — 58
- 46:3–4 — 152
- 46:13 — 168
- 47:1 — 59
- 47:12 — 63, 73
- 47:15 — 63
- 49:15 — 51, 72, 73
- 49:22 — 10
- 49:23 — 70
- 49:26 — 186, 187
- 50:1 — 133
- 53:2 — 70

## Index of Biblical Passages 241

| | | | | | |
|---|---|---|---|---|---|
| 54:4 | 11, 56, 73 | 22:21 | 63 | Ezekiel | |
| 56:5 | 47 | 30:6 | 7 | 4:14 | 63 |
| 57:3–10 | 112 | 31:4 | 59 | 5:10 | 186, 187, 188 |
| 57:5 | 65, 117 | 31:19 | 63 | 5:17 | 100 |
| 60:4 | 47 | 31:20 | 10, 43 | 9:6 | 57, 66 |
| 60:16 | 70 | 31:21 | 59 | 16:1–14 | 7 |
| 62:5 | 57, 58 | 31:34 | 52 | 16:4 | 42 |
| 63:16 | 10 | 32:8 | 49 | 16:5–6 | 153 |
| 64:8–9 | 10 | 32:9 | 49 | 16:7–8 | 55 |
| 65:20 | 72, 73 | 32:24 | 176 | 16:15–26 | 112 |
| 66:11–12 | 70 | 32:29–35 | 112 | 16:20–21 | 117 |
| 66:11 | 69 | 32:30 | 11, 63, 73 | 16:20 | 48, 115 |
| 66:12–13 | 152 | 32:35 | 117 | 16:21 | 48 |
| 66:12 | 69 | 34:8–16 | 132, 171 | 20:25–31 | 117 |
| | | 34:8–11 | 134 | 20:31 | 110 |
| Jeremiah | | 34:14 | 133 | 22:5 | 94 |
| 1:4–10 | 10 | 40:7 | 66 | 22:7 | 53, 54 |
| 1:6 | 61, 63 | 41:16 | 66 | 23:15 | 46 |
| 3:4 | 10, 73 | 43:6–7 | 66 | 23:25 | 48 |
| 3:8 | 49 | 44:7 | 23, 70, 71 | 23:36–49 | 112 |
| 3:24–25 | 63 | 46:11 | 59 | 23:37 | 48, 115 |
| 4:11 | 46 | 48:4 | 53 | 23:47 | 48 |
| 4:19 | 145 | 48:7 | 109 | 24:21 | 48 |
| 5:17 | 48 | 48:13 | 109 | 24:25 | 49 |
| 5:28 | 54 | 48:15 | 58 | 46:20 | 186 |
| 6:11 | 71 | 48:46 | 48, 109 | 46:24 | 186 |
| 6:13 | 52 | 49:11 | 53, 54 | | |
| 6:26 | 108 | 49:26 | 58 | Daniel | |
| 7:5–7 | 121 | 51:3 | 58, 60 | 1:4 | 64 |
| 7:6 | 53, 54 | 51:22 | 57, 58, 61, 63 | 10:17 | 154 |
| 7:17–32 | 112 | 52:5–6 | 176 | | |
| 7:31–32 | 117 | | | Hosea | |
| 7:31 | 48, 110, 115, 117 | Lamentations | | 1:2–6 | 64 |
| | | 1:5 | 59, 71 | 1:8 | 68, 69 |
| 9:20 | 58, 71 | 1:6 | 46 | 6:9 | 160 |
| 11:22 | 58 | 1:15 | 58 | 7:1 | 160 |
| 14:3 | 53 | 1:16 | 145 | 9:11–16 | 42 |
| 14:17 | 59 | 1:18 | 57, 58 | 11:3–4 | 152 |
| 16:3–4 | 48 | 2:11 | 23, 70, 71 | 13:8 | 101 |
| 16:6 | 52 | 2:12 | 70 | 14:1 | 71 |
| 18:13 | 59 | 2:19 | 71 | | |
| 18:21 | 58, 60 | 2:20 | 65, 71, 186, 187, 188 | Joel | |
| 18:22 | 160 | | | 1:8 | 55, 58 |
| 19:1–5 | 117 | 2:21 | 57, 58, 61, 63 | 2:16 | 44, 70, 71 |
| 19:3–6 | 112 | 2:23 | 59 | 3:1 | 47 |
| 19:5 | 48, 110, 115, 117 | 4:4 | 70. 71 | 4:3 | 64, 65, 74, 134 |
| | | 4:10 | 65, 186, 187, 188 | 4:8 | 48 |
| 19:9 | 48, 186, 187, 188 | | | | |
| | | 4:21 | 46 | Amos | |
| 20:14–18 | 7 | 5:3 | 54 | 2:6 | 134 |
| 20:15 | 42 | 5:11 | 59 | 2:7 | 172 |
| 22:3 | 54, 121 | 5:13 | 58 | 2:11 | 58 |

## Amos (continued)

| | |
|---|---|
| 4:10 | 58 |
| 5:2 | 59 |
| 7:10–13 | 120 |
| 7:17 | 48 |
| 8:10 | 108 |
| 8:13 | 57 |

## Obadiah

| | |
|---|---|
| 10 | 49 |
| 12 | 49 |

## Jonah

| | |
|---|---|
| 2:1–11 | 98 |
| 3:5–8 | 182 |
| 3:5 | 52 |

## Micah

| | |
|---|---|
| 3:3 | 187 |
| 5:2 | 49 |
| 6:4 | 183 |
| 6:6–7 | 51, 112, 117 |
| 7:1–7 | 5 |

## Nahum

| | |
|---|---|
| 3:10 | 71 |

## Habakkuk

| | |
|---|---|
| 1:10 | 94 |

## Zechariah

| | |
|---|---|
| 7:9–10 | 121 |
| 7:10 | 53, 54 |
| 8:5 | 64, 65, 74, 93 |
| 9:17 | 57 |
| 11:9 | 187 |
| 13:4 | 94 |
| 13:5 | 63, 73 |
| 14:21 | 186 |

## Malachi

| | |
|---|---|
| 1:2 | 49 |
| 2:14 | 55 |
| 3:5 | 54, 121, 133 |

## Apocrypha/Deuterocanonicals

### Judith

| | |
|---|---|
| 10:1–19 | 122 |
| 11 | 122 |
| 14:1–9 | 122 |
| 16:1–17 | 165 |

### 2 Maccabees

| | |
|---|---|
| 7:27 | 67 |

## New Testament

### Matthew

| | |
|---|---|
| 9:23–26 | 155 |
| 21:16 | 23 |

### Mark

| | |
|---|---|
| 5:22–23 | 155 |
| 5:35–43 | 155 |

### Luke

| | |
|---|---|
| 1:7–25 | 149 |
| 1:26–56 | 149 |
| 1:39–45 | 149 |
| 1:46–55 | 165 |
| 1:57–80 | 149 |
| 2:1–20 | 149 |
| 7:11–15 | 155 |
| 8:41–42 | 155 |
| 8:49–56 | 155 |

# Index of Authors

Aasgaard, Reidar, 2, 3, 15, 16
Ackerman, Susan, 4, 49, 112, 115
Aichele, George, 88
Akoto, Dorothy, 128
Albertz, Rainer, 4, 48, 49, 115
Albright, W. F., 116
Alexandre-Bidon, Danièle, 33
Alter, Robert, 86, 139, 151, 152
Amit, Yairah, 86
Archard, David, 23, 24
Ariès, Philippe, 11, 12, 31, 32, 33, 34, 35, 36, 43
Arnold, Daniel, 92, 141
Aucker, W. Brian, 184
Auerbach, Erich, 84
Auld, A. Graeme, 97
Avioz, Michael, 78, 80
Axskjöld, Carl-Johan, 158
Axtell, James L., 29

Badinter, Elisabeth, 35, 36, 37
Baker, Jane, 25
Baker, Mary, 21
Bakke, Mary, 2
Balch, David L., 2
Barclay, John M. G., 5, 112
Bar-Efrat, Shimon, 85, 87
Barlow, Michael, 45
Barr, James, 45
Bartlett, John, 104
Barton, John, 5, 88
Baxter, Jane Eva, 7
Beedham, Christopher, 44
Bendor, Shunya, 5
Benjamin, Don C., 108
Bennett, Harold V., 54
Bergen, Wesley J., 92, 96, 138, 139, 143, 167, 177, 179

Berlin, Adele, 84, 85
Bernstein, Robin, 27
Berquist, Jon L., 10
Bird, Phyllis, 4, 48
Blenkinsopp, Joseph, 5, 11, 14, 67
Block, Daniel I., 5, 14, 67
Bodel, John, 4
Bohmbach, Karla G., 87, 118
Borowski, Oded, 3
Boswell, John, 30, 35
Branch, Robin Gallaher, 117
Brennan, Patrick McKinley, 2
Brenner, Athalya, 5, 118, 138, 188
Bretell, Caroline, 79
Brettler, Marc Zvi, 165
Brichto, Herbert Chanan, 92, 95, 104, 111
Brinkerhoff, David B., 25
Brodie, Thomas L., 155
Bronner, Leila Leah, 43, 82, 147, 153, 180, 183
Brown, Raymond E., 84, 155
Browning, Don S., 2
Brueggemann, Walter, 54
Buckingham, David, 38
Bühler-Niederberger, Doris, 22
Bunge, Marcia J., 2, 7, 16, 54, 67, 173
Burke, Catherine, 22, 28
Burnett, Joel, 93
Burney, C. F., 125, 140, 147, 162, 181
Burns, John Barclay, 112, 113

Cahan, Emily, 22
Callaway, Mary, 42, 150
Callender, Dexter E., Jr., 170
Camp, Claudia, 140
Campbell, Duncan B., 5, 176
Carasik, Michael, 3

Carr, David McLain, 4, 13
Carroll, John T., 2
Carroll, R. P., 80
Chamberlain, Andrew T., 9
Chaney, Marvin L., 132
Childs, Peter, 15, 183
Chirichigno, Gregory C., 48, 129, 130, 132
Chudacoff, Howard P., 25
Clarke, John, 34
Classen, Albrecht, 33
Cleverley, John, 28
Cluysenaar, Anne, 15
Cogan, Morcechai, 96, 97, 105, 112, 120, 125, 141, 147, 166, 171, 176, 181
Cohen, Shaye J. D., 1, 2, 170
Cohn, Robert L., 94, 142, 167, 192
Collins, John J., 5, 11
Conroy, Charles, 100
Cooper, John, 6, 9, 10
Coote, Robert B., 43, 167
Cornill, Carl Heinrich, 3
Corsaro, William A., 1
Coveney, Peter, 30
Cross, Frank Moore, 78
Crouwel, J. H., 170
Cunningham, 21, 26, 33
Cutler, B., 60

Dahood, Mitchell, 165
Dandamayev, Muhammad A., 123, 133
Davis, Paul K., 176
Day, John, 115
Day, Peggy L., 58, 59, 70, 115, 132
Dearman, J. Andrew, 5, 11, 103, 104, 109, 116, 129, 134
DeMause, Lloyd, 34, 35
de Moor, Johannes C., 165
Derchain, Philippe, 113
Derevenski, Johanna Sofaer, 7, 9
de Vaux, Roland, 3, 115, 171
Dever, William G., 4, 79, 117
Dieckmann, Detlef, 7
Diehl, Daniel, 186
Dijk-Hemmes, Fokkelien van, 48, 138
Dijkstra, Meindert, 48, 138, 165
Donnelly, Mark P., 186
Doody, Margaret Anne, 6

Drury, Helen, 15
Dutcher-Walls, Patricia, 5, 6, 7

Ebeling, Jennie R., 3, 4, 5
Economou, Dorothy, 15
Eissfeldt, Otto, 77, 115
Elkind, David, 37
Ellul, Jacques, 159
Emerton, J. A., 104
Eng, Milton, 9, 14, 45, 46, 55, 56, 60, 62, 63, 65, 66, 71, 74
Ennew, Judith, 24, 26
Erbele-Küster, Dorothea, 7
Esser, Annette, 2
Exum, J. Cheryl, 118

Farrar, Frederic William, 105, 114, 181, 195
Fass, Paula S., 1, 10, 22, 26, 28, 35
Fechter, Friedrich, 5
Fensham, F. Charles, 54, 121, 182
Feucht, Erika, 8
Fewell, Danna Nolan, 6, 39, 85, 138, 141
Finkelstein, Israel, 79
Finlay, Timothy D., 138, 147, 151
Finsterbusch, Karin, 115
Fischer, Irmtraud, 8, 14
Fleishman, Joseph, 7, 48, 59, 130, 132
Fokkelman, Jan, 120, 125
Forna, Aminatta, 184
Fortes, Meyer, 25
Fowler, Roger, 15, 183
French, Valerie, 33
Fretheim, Terence E., 67, 95, 110, 111, 163, 169
Fritz, Volkmar, 146, 175
Frymer-Kensky, Tikva, 4, 42, 48, 58, 59, 147, 165
Fuchs, Esther, 151, 153
Furniss, Tom, 29

Garroway, Kristine Sue Henriksen, 6, 16
Gertz, Jan Christian, 78
Gies, Kathrin, 7
Gillis, John R., 26
Giroux, Henry A., 27

Gittins, Diana, 24
Goldberg, P. J. P., 33
Golden, Mark, 33, 37
Gollin, Sandra, 15
Gowan, Donald E., 54
Grabbe, Lester L., 148, 175, 177
Graham, M. Patrick, xi, xii, 77, 104
Gray, George B., 115
Gray, John, 96, 97, 107, 155, 159, 166, 176, 177, 181, 195
Green, Albert, 115
Greenfield, J. C., 177
Greenspahn, Frederick E., 52
Greenstein, Edward, 159
Gressmann, Hugo, 195
Grossman, Jonathan, 3
Gruber, Mayer I., 68
Guest, Kristen, 186
Guillaume, Philippe, 155
Gundry-Volf, Judith M., 2
Gunkel, Hermann, 142
Günter, Andrea, 2

Haas, Louis, 35
Hafþórsson, Sigurður, 157, 158, 177
Harrison, Eveleen, 6
Hasan, Raqaiya, 15, 45
Hawes, Joseph M., 9, 33, 35
Hays, Sharon, 184
Heider, George C., 115
Hens-Piazza, Gina, 86, 112, 128, 163, 176, 178, 180, 182, 184
Henten, Jan Willem van, 5
Hentschel, Georg, 163
Herzog, Kristin, 2
Hiner, N. Ray, 9, 33, 35
Hobbs, T. R., 92, 97, 100, 104, 127, 143, 146, 147, 163, 166, 177, 179, 180, 188, 195
Hochman, Baruch, 83, 86
Holladay, John W., 79
Hölscher, Gustav, 77, 80
Honig, Michael-Sebastian, 1
Hoof, Dieter, 8
Hübner, Ulrich, 6
Hutton, Patrick H., 34
Huwiler, Elizabeth F., 137
Hymowitz, Kay S., 37

Jackson, Kent P., 104, 109, 110, 116
James, Adrian, 16
James, Allison, 1, 16, 25, 26
Janata, Jaromír, 30
Jensen, David H., 2
Jones, Gwilym, 91, 166, 176, 181, 195
Jones, Janet, 15
Jones, Russell, 27

Kaiser, Otto, 8
Kalmanofsky, Amy, 148, 153
Kamp, Kathryn A., 7
Kaplan, Yehuda, 171
Kehily, Mary Jane, 1, 24, 38
Kemmer, Suzanne, 45
Kilgour, Maggie, 186
King, Philip J., 3, 11, 12, 14, 41, 50, 67, 107, 108, 115, 133
Kirk-Duggan, Cheryl A., 43
Kissling, Paul J., 94
Kitzinger, Jenny, 27
Knoppers, Gary N., 77
Koepf, Laurel W., 7, 16, 26, 133
Komensky, John Amos, 28
Konner, Melvin, 68
Korbin, Jill E., 38
Kottsieper, Ingo, 177
Kraemer, David, 5
Kraemer, Ross S., 2, 3, 87
Kratz, Reinhard, 78
Kunz-Lübcke, Andreas, 8, 10, 12, 55, 65, 69, 71, 170, 172

LaBarbera, Robert, 82, 182
Lange, Armin, 115
Lareau, Annette, 27
Lasine, Stuart, 177, 182, 183, 186, 187
Leeb, Carolyn S., 61, 62, 114, 146, 172
Leithart, Peter J., 92, 112, 180
Lemaire, André, 78, 104
Lett, Didier, 33
Levenson, Jon D., 108, 109, 110
LeVine, Robert A., 9
Levinson, Bernard M., 48, 129, 131, 165
Littauer, M. A., 170
Liverani, Mario, 185
Logan, Alice, 3

## Index of Authors

Long, Burke O., 81, 82, 113, 127, 150, 181, 194
Long, Jesse C., 111, 112,
Lux, Rüdiger, 8, 12, 65, 71, 170

MacDonald, John, 60, 61, 62
Maier, Christl, xi, 60
Maloney, Robert P., 123
Mandelbaum, David G., 14
Marcus, David, 91, 98, 99
Marcus, Ivan G., 23, 33
Maretzki, Hatsumi, 68
Maretzki, Thomas, 68
Margalit, Baruch, 113
Marsman, Hennie, 3, 4, 42, 67, 129, 140
Martin, Dale B., 2, 170, 195
Martin, J. R., 15, 45
Martingale, Moira, 186
Marty, Martin, 2
Matthews, Victor H., 48, 58, 108, 165
Mattingly, Gerald L., 103, 104, 110
Mayall, Berry, 21, 38
McConnell, Douglas, 2
McConville, J. Gordon, 78
McKenzie, Steven L., 77, 78
Mechling, Jay, 22
Medforth, Nicholas, 26
Mendelsohn, Isaac, 129, 153, 170, 171, 172
Menn, Esther M., 173, 174
Mercer, Mark, 93, 95, 99
Meyers, Carol, 3, 4, 5, 11, 60, 67, 87, 118, 133
Michel, Andreas, 7, 8, 12, 14, 47, 55, 58, 59, 65, 66, 67, 71, 73, 75, 118, 131, 170, 186, 187
Milgrom, Jacob, 159
Miller-McLemore, Bonnie J., 2
Mintz, Steven, 22
Miscall, Peter, 88
Mitchell, T. C., 155, 165
Montgomery, James A., 138, 147, 166
Moore, Jenny, 7, 9, 21, 78, 82, 113, 158, 169, 176
Müller, Reinhard, 78

Neils, Jenifer, 33

Nelson, Richard D., 78, 97, 140
Neumann, Josef N., 8
Ngan, Lai Ling Elizabeth, 169
Nicholas, David, xiii, 26, 33, 35
Niditch, Susan, 13, 171
Niemann, Hermann Michael, 175
Noth, Martin, 77, 78
Nydegger, William F., 68

Oakley, Ann, 21, 33
O'Connor, M., 127, 150
Oded, Bustenay, 3, 170
Olyan, Saul M., 4, 78, 94
Orona, Jennifer, 2
Osgood, S. Joy, 195
Osiek, Carolyn, 2
Otto, Susanne, 78
Overholt, Thomas, 149

Parker, Simon B., 149, 159
Patterson, Cynthia, 152, 153
Payne, George Henry, 34, 35
Perdue, Leo G., 5, 11
Petersen, David L., 12, 79, 92, 106
Phillips, D. C., 28
Piaget, Jean, 29
Pippin, Tina, 43
Pitard, Wayne T., 177
Plotz, Judith, 30
Pollock, Linda A., 33, 36
Postman, Neil, 28, 31, 37, 38
Powell, Mark Allan, 85
Pressler, Carolyn, 48, 130, 132
Pritchard, James B., xiii
Provan, Iain, 97, 112, 159
Purvis, James D., 175
Pyper, Hugh S., 178, 187

Qvortrup, Jens, 1, 16, 24

Rad, Gerhard von, 169
Rehm, Martin, 195
Reinhartz, Adele, 2, 188
Renkema, Johann, 54, 188
Revell, E. J., 49, 63, 64
Richards, Kent Harold, 12, 79
Richardson, Alan, 31
Richardson, Laurel, 24

Riddy, Felicity, 33
Ringgren, Helmer, 46, 71, 123
Roberts, Benjamin B., 35
Robinson, J., 30, 97, 176, 195
Rofé, Alexander, 80, 81, 97, 122, 143, 147, 154, 182
Rogerson, John, 5
Römer, Thomas C., 78
Römheld, K. F. Diethard, 115
Roncace, Mark, 143, 150, 193
Rosenberg, A. J., 97, 138, 152, 180
Roth, Martha, 132, 171
Roth, Ray Lee, 158
Rousseau, Jean-Jacques, 28, 29, 30
Rundin, John S., 3

Sabol, William J., 27
Sadler, John E., 28
Šanda, Albert, 142
Sanday, Peggy Reeves, 185
Sapir, Edward, 14, 44, 45
Satterthwaite, Philip E., 168
Saussure, Ferdinand de, 14
Scheepers, Rajah, 2
Schmid, Konrad, 78
Schmitz, Philip C., 117
Schwartz, Daniel R., 153
Schweizer, Harald, 183
Scott, Eleanor, 7, 9, 21
Seow, Choon-Leong, 98, 106, 177
Shahar, Shulamith, 33, 36
Sharp, Carolyn J., 167, 168
Shemesh, Yael, 81, 82, 83, 94, 98, 101, 125, 126, 128, 134, 142, 153
Shields, Mary E., 142, 148, 150, 151
Shilling, Chris, 21
Shorter, Chris, 36
Siebert-Hommes, Jopie, 138
Siegel, David, 23
Simon, Uriel, 85, 104, 142, 143, 145, 146, 149, 150, 151, 152, 154
Skinner, J., 147, 180
Smoak, Jeremy D., 176
Sneed, Mark, 54, 112, 132
Spinka, Matthew, 29
Sprinkle, Joe M., 104, 106
Silberman, Neil Asher, 79
Stager, Lawrence E., 3, 9, 11, 12, 14, 41, 50, 61, 62, 67, 68, 93, 107, 108, 115, 133, 138, 176
Stähli, Hans-Peter, 60, 61, 62, 63
Stavrakopoulou, Francesca, 49, 110, 115
Stein, Siegfried, 123
Steinberg, Naomi, 12, 54, 55
Stephens, Sharon, 37
Sternberg, Meir, 85, 86
Stone, Lawrence, 26, 36
Strawn, Brent A., 61, 63
Sweeney, Marvin A., 120, 132, 137, 154, 155, 177, 182
Stockley, Paul, 2
Sutton-Smith, Brian, 22
Syrén, Roger, 51

Tadmor, Hayim, 96, 97, 105, 112, 120, 125, 141, 147, 166, 176, 181
Taylor, Mike, 33
Theis, Joachim, 24
Thompson, E. P., 26
Thompson, Geoff, 45
Thuesen Peter J., 58
Tolmie, D. F., 84
Toorn, Karel van der, 3, 4, 13, 53, 58, 121, 177
Trible, Phyllis, 118, 187, 189
Tropper, Amram, 5, 139

Uffenheimer, Benjamin, 80, 103, 177
Ussishkin, David, 170

Van Seters, John, 129, 130
Vann, Richard T., 32
Volk, Konrad, 8
Vos, Clarence, 42

Wall, John, 2, 16, 17
Walls, Neal H., 58, 70
Walsh, Richard, 88
Waltke, Bruce K., 127, 150
Wargo, Eric, 110
Watson, W. G. E., 70
Weinfeld, Moshe, 48, 79, 115
Wenham, Gordon J., 58, 59
West, Heather C., 27
Westbrook, Raymond, 110, 111, 129

White, Lynn K., 25
White, Marsha C., 80, 138, 152, 192
Whiting, Beatrice B., 68, 184
Wierzbicka, Anna, 44
Williams, James G., 150
Williams, Margaret, 5
Williams, Ronald J., 106, 127
Wilson, Robert R., 78, 79, 92, 106, 120, 149
Witte, Marcus, 78
Wolff, Hans Walter, 115, 171

Wright, Jacob L., 176
Würthwein, Ernst, 120, 138, 182
Wyse, Dominic, 1, 25, 26, 28, 34

Yarbrough, O. Larry, 10

Zelizer, Viviana, 26
Zevit, Ziony, 12, 79, 111, 181
Ziolkowski, Eric J., 96
Zuck, Roy B., 6, 14
Zwilling, Anne-Laure, 50

# Index of Subjects

adults, children distinguished from, 22–24
animals, doing harm to children, 100, 101
annunciation story, 150, 151
Ariès, Philippe, on children and childhood, 11–12, 31–34

babies, words designating, 67–73
birth, miraculous, 147, 148, 150, 151, 154
breastfeeding, in ancient Israel, 67–68

cannibalism, 177, 178, 182, 183, 184, 185, 186, 187, 188, 189
cannibals, mothers as, 177, 178, 182, 183, 184
*Centuries of Childhood* (Ariès), 31–34
child
    identification of, 21–24
    resuscitation of, 148, 149, 150, 151, 154, 155, 192, 195, 196, 197
    *See also* children
child characters, in Elisha cycle, 84, 85, 86
child sacrifice, 48, 109–17
childhood
    abstract Hebrew words for, 73
    concept and conception of, 23
    concepts of, in Hebrew Bible, 74–76
    disappearance of, 37, 38
    divisions within, 23, 74
    formal study of, 28–39
    historians' views of, after Ariès, 35, 36, 37
    modern theories of, 11–13
    Western assumptions about, 24–28

childhood studies
    in ancient Israelite society, 3, 4
    and ancient Near East, 8
    in biblical field, 1, 2, 3, 6, 7, 8, 9, 10, 11, 12, 13
childism, 16–18
childist interpretation, 16–18
    and Elisha stories, 83–88, 96–98, 109–16, 124–28, 146–52, 164–70, 180–85, 197
    methodology of, 86–88
children
    in age of technology, 38
    as agents of restoration, 195, 196
    biblical Hebrew vocabulary for, 46–73, 199. *See also* Hebrew words, used to designate children in the Hebrew Bible
    birth of, in Hebrew Bible, 42, 43
    bodies of, 25
    of color, 27
    cultural context of, 22, 24–28
    and debt slavery, 128–35
    as defenseless, 185–87
    dependence on adults, 185
    distinguished from adults, 22–24
    in Elisha cycle, 200–201
    emotional value of, 26
    in families, words designating, 46–53
    without families, words designating, 53–55
    as food, 177, 178, 182, 183, 186, 187, 188, 189
    influence of, 193, 196
    language used for, in Hebrew Bible, 41–76
    as markers of ideal society, 26

childred (*continued*)
  nursing, 67–68
  and power, 98, 99, 193
  presence and value of, in Bible, 41–44
  role in society, in Bible, 43, 44
  sexual abuse of, 27
  and slavery, 160, 161, 162, 165, 166, 170–72
  as slaves, 123, 124
  as soldiers, 106, 107
  as testimony to prophetic power, 195, 196
  theological role in Jewish tradition, 10
  unwanted, exposure of, 152, 153
  value of, 26, 48, 49, 52, 53, 59, 65, 124, 130, 133, 134, 152-53, 155, 199, 200, 201
  as victims of violence, 116, 117
  vulnerability of, 8, 24, 27, 48, 50, 66, 107, 122, 134, 185, 187, 200, 201
  and warfare, 114, 115, 116
  work of, 24, 25, 26, 133, 144, 145, 200
Comenius, Johann Amos, on children and childhood, 28, 29

danger, and Hebrew words for children, 75, 76
Debt-Collateral Children, narrative of, 119–35, 193, 194
debt collectors, 123
debt slavery, and children, 128–35
deMause, Lloyd
  on children and childhood, 34, 35
  reactions to, 35, 36

Elijah and Elisha narratives, 80
Elisha
  and children, 192, 193
  cursing of children by, 94, 95, 96
  and Deuteronomistic History, 77–80
  in narrative of the Israelite slave girl, 163–64
  in narrative of the Shunammite's son, 141, 142, 148, 154
  and narrative of Sons of Starving Mothers, 179, 180
  as shaman, 148, 149
  and story of debt-collateral children, 122, 124, 125, 126, 127, 128
  and story of Moabite Prince, 105, 106
Elisha cycle
  and childist interpretation, 83–88
  genre of, 80, 81, 82, 83
  and literary approach to children and childhood, 77–88
Enlightenment thinkers, on children, 28–31

family
  and childhood studies, 5, 6
  and destiny of children, 200
firstborn, 108, 109, 115, 116
foreigners, as slaves, 130, 131, 167, 170, 171

Gehazi, in narrative of Shunammite's son, 142, 143, 144

Hebrew words, used to designate children in Hebrew Bible
  אח *ʾḥ* (brother) 49–50
  אחות *ʾḥwt* (sisters), 49–50
  בן *bn* (son), 46–49, 145, 146
  בת *bt* (daughter), 46–49
  בחור *bḥwr* (young adult [m.]), 57, 58
  בכור *bkwr* (firstborn male), 50–52
  בכירה *bkyrh* (firstborn female), 50–52
  בתולה *btwlh* (young adult [f.]), 57, 58
  גמל *gml* (small child), 69
  גמול *gmwl* (small child), 69
  טף *ṭp* (infant), 66–67
  יונק *ywnq* (small child), 69, 70
  ילד *yld* (child [m.]), 64–65, 92, 93, 145, 146
  ילדה *yldh* (child [f.]), 64–65, 160
  יתום *ytwm* (orphan), 53–55
  נער *nʿr* (young man), 60–64, 92, 93, 114, 145, 146

נערה *nʿrh* (young woman), 60–64, 160, 172
עלם *ʿlm* (young man), 56
עולל *ʿwll* (small child), 71
עול *ʿwl* (small child), 71, 72, 73
עויל *ʿwyl* (small child), 71, 72, 73
עלמה *ʿlmh* (young woman), 56, 57
צעיר *ṣʿyr* (little one), 52, 53
קטן *qṭn* (little one), 52, 53

innocent, children as, 25, 26, 27, 29, 30, 32, 38, 67

Jephthah's daughter, 117, 118
Jewish family, in antiquity, 1, 3, 4

kidnapping, 157, 160, 162, 170, 171
kinship, and Hebrew words for children, 75
legenda, 81
legends of saints, 82, 83
life expectancy, and childhood studies, 9
Locke, John, on children, 28, 29

marriage, as dividing line between youth and adulthood, 55
Moabite Prince, narrative of, 103–18, 193
Mockers of Bethel, narrative of, 91–101, 192
mothers
  as advocates for children, 193, 194
  as cannibals, 177, 178, 182, 183, 184
  status of, 183, 184

Naaman, leprous condition of, 159, 160

poor, as slaves, 133, 134, 135

Rousseau, Jean-Jacques, on children and childhood, 29, 30, 31

sacrificial victims, sons and daughters as, 48, 109, 110, 111, 112, 113, 114, 115

safety, and Hebrew words for children, 75, 76
sexual abuse
  of children, 27
  of girl slaves, 131, 134, 172

Shunammite woman, 139, 140
  husband of, 140, 141
  son of, 144–55
Shunammite's son, narrative of, 137–55, 194–95
slave girl
  as deliverer of Naaman, 167–69
  Israelite, narrative of, 157–74, 195, 196
slavery
  biblical laws regarding, 129, 130, 171
  and children, 123, 124
slaves
  Hebrew and foreigners as, 131, 132, 170, 171
  women and girls as, 130, 131
social standing, and Hebrew words for children, 75
soldiers, children as, 106, 107, 114
Sons of Starving Mothers, narrative of, 175–89, 196, 197

value, of children, 26, 48, 49, 52, 53, 59, 65, 124, 130, 133, 134, 152-53, 155, 199, 200, 201
virgin, 58, 59
vulnerable, children as, 8, 24, 27, 48, 50, 66, 107, 122, 134, 185, 187, 200, 201

war, and children, 114, 115, 116
widows, in Israelite society, 121, 122
women and girls
  and children, 42
  scholarship on, and childhood studies, 4
  as slaves, 130, 131, 160, 161, 165, 166

youth
  abstract Hebrew words for, 73
  Hebrew words designating, 55–64

www.ingramcontent.com/pod-product-compliance
Lightning Source LLC
Chambersburg PA
CBHW030616230426
43661CB00053B/2016